C000302018

The Deil's ...

Roy J M Pugh

To Sheron McVitie with best wishes
RJMPugh

Foreword by

K. Robin Murdoch F.S.A.(Scot)

HARLAW HERITAGE

First published in 2001 by
Harlaw Heritage
21 Marchbank Gardens
Balerno, Midlothian
EH14 7ET
Scotland

ISBN 0 9540465 0 1

Origination by Harlaw Heritage and Transcolour (Scotland) Ltd

Printed and bound by
Belfast University Press

Dunbar Tolbooth or Town House c1900

Witchcraft. The epidemic demonopathy which raged in the fifteenth, sixteenth and seventeenth centuries.

Brewer, *The Dictionary of Phrase and Fable*

You shall not permit a sorceress to live.

Exodus, ch. 22, v. 18

...............for beauty is a witch
Against whose charms faith melteth into blood.

Shakespeare, *Much Ado About Nothing*

By drawing the blood of a witch, you deprive her of her power of sorcery.

Brewer, *The Dictionary of Phrase and Fable*

Whether the persons accused of this offence [witchcraft] really did imagine that they were possessed of unusual powers of any kind; or whether they had the will at least, if not the power, of doing mischief to their neighbours; or whether all the confessions, of which there were so many, when extracted by the mere cruelty of the witchfinders - these are questions which are not, I fancy, yet solved.

M R James, *The Ash Tree*

Contents

Illustrations   vii

Foreword   viii

Acknowledgements   xi

Introduction   xii

1   Witchcraft in Scotland from Early Times to 1603   1

2   'Wicked Consultationis and Divilische Charmes'   25

3   'Witchcraft Daylie Increaseth in This Land'   48

4   A Dunbar trial   66

5   Cromwell and the Witches   101

6   'Punished With the Paines of Death'   119

7   'Terrifeing and Abuseing the People'   139

8   Embers   154

9   Witch Festivals, Rites and Spells   169

10   Conclusion   181

Appendices

1   Statistics   199

2   Chronological table   203

3   Diagrams 1-3, flowchart   206-8

4   Ritual marks   209

5   Witch name index   211

Glossary   252

Bibliography   257

List of Illustrations

Dunbar Tolbooth or Town House c1900	Frontis
John Knox	6
The North Berwick Witches (woodcut)	13
Handbill advertising Dr Fian's execution	14
The ruins of St Andrew's church, North Berwick	15
Fast Castle, Berwickshire c1850	19
Shipwreck off the Bass Rock	24
Edinburgh castle in 1647	38
Greyfriars church, Edinburgh	49
Handbill advertising confessions of Helen Taylor Eyemouth and Menie Halyburton, Dirleton	62
The Tolbooth of Edinburgh c1790	64
Map of Dunbar and environs	68
Witch Bridle	73
Pilniewinks or thumbscrew	73
Oliver Cromwell	101
The burning of witches in Dumfries, 1659	120
Major Weir's land in the West Bow, Edinburgh	135
Neck jougs at Spott Kirk, East Lothian	157
Culross Tolbooth or Town House c1900	160
Witch alphabet	171
Ritual marks at Culross Palace, Fife	209
Diagram 1: illustrating process of accusation and counter-accusation in Tranent, East Lothian, in 1659	206
Diagram 2: similar to above	207
Diagram 3: Flowchart illustrating process from accusation to trial	208

Foreword

It hardly seems credible that the factual accounts which unfold in this book could have happened in Scotland. Most of us who live in a modern, comfortable, technological environment will scarcely credit what was happening here not many generations ago. The events varied from the chillingly sadistic to the absolutely ridiculous.

To understand how a belief in something like witchcraft could become almost a national trait, it is worth considering the nature of human thought. It could be argued that most of what we are is what we have learned. Knowledge is cumulative, with each generation learning the great majority of what it is about from the previous one. There is probably only a small percentage of original thought injected into the corpus by each generation The human race is a gregarious species, generally living in groups. These groups can vary from a few individuals in a family up to many millions in a nation and even to groups of nations. In order to maintain stability and even to operate at all, any group needs two things, leadership and a set of rules to operate by. This, of course, is generally where the problems begin because the rules tend to be made by the leadership, frequently with scant regard for the collective aspirations of the rest of the population.

What it all boils down to is control of the majority by the minority; once established, control can be very difficult to wrest from those who have it. One has only to access the media to find many examples in the world today. Control can manifest itself in a number of different ways of which the most common and effective are religious, military (to include all forms of physical force or intimidation), economic and political. It is reasonable to say that religion has been the prime mover in systems of control because it is mainly from religion that 'morality' sprang. The rest were merely means of facilitating or enforcing that 'morality'. There is little doubt that 'religion' has been a major factor in human conflict since man first developed 'creative' thought. Perceived differences between one creed and another, developed and refined over many generations, led to apparently insoluble conflict. Christian v. Muslim or Protestant v. Catholic spring readily to mind. I am not religious myself but would hope I am open minded enough to listen to the arguments for and, importantly, also against religious belief. Certainly, the fact that almost every primitive society ended up believing in some supernatural scenario is interesting, since many did it in total isolation. Does this mean that there is something to it or, is there something inherent in us which requires belief in the supernatural, perhaps it is a human way of explaining things we do not understand?

Religion is invariably accompanied by ritual and, in many cases, rules which pervade everyday life, frequently related to elements as trivial as dress code or types of food. The fact that the rest of the world's population who do not follow these 'laws' does not drop dead instantly for trangressing them appears to have no effect on the faithful who blindly follow. This, of course, is the object of the exercise. These 'laws' are all about conditioning, to accept whatever religious code it is, without question. A major step on the way to total control. Indeed, many of the world's religions will not tolerate criticism, decrying anyone who does so a heretic. Of course it is much easier to retain control if opposition is banned.This brings us back conveniently to late sixteenth century Scotland. The Reformation of the church in Scotland was all but complete and the 'high heid yins' of that organisation had a stranglehold on virtually every aspect of life. The population was virtually static, people could spend their entire lives within a few short miles of where they were born. In a claustrophobic environment such as that it is no surprise that extremely petty occurrences could loom large; this played no small part in the whole witch saga, as Roy Pugh will demonstrate.

Although the last execution for witchcraft took place in Scotland in 1727, some sixty years later, Robert Burns would pen probably the finest work on the subject ever to be produced in Scotland, the incredible *Tam o' Shanter,* purportedly written in one night. Burns' graphic description of the goings on at Alloway Kirk remains a highlight for 'cronies' on the 25th of January every year.

Proof that the subject was far from consigned to history was graphically illustrated in 1805 by the trial of Jean Maxwell in Kirkcudbright. Jean was in fact arraigned under the act which repealed the witchcraft statutes and she wasn't tried for being a witch, but simply for pretending to be one. A clear indication that superstitious prejudice was still alive and kicking. She was found guilty but fortunately(!) the punishment was one year in prison interspersed by regular appearances in the stocks.

Gullibilty appears to be a major human failing and, needless to say, there will always be those who will seek to exploit it. Without doubt there are people who can, and do, exercise power over others. How often do we meet with the expression 'frightened to death'? Unfortunately this can literally be true, where a victim believing in the power of the 'assailant' actually suffers stress levels sufficiently severe to affect their physiology, the most acute cases resulting in death. So it was with witchcraft. There was undoubtedly a belief, particularly among the poorer and less well educated classes, that such a thing existed. An attack on the person was not the only manifestation of witchcraft. All sorts of problems, large and small, were attributed to witches, as will become evident in the course of this book. Whether or not the authorities actually believed in witchcraft themselves is a debatable point. Some almost certainly did but, in my cynical view, many more used the superstitious beliefs of the chattering classes to further their own ends. The accounts which follow, were they not true, would surely tax the ability of the most fanciful of fiction writers.

Acknowledgements

Producing a book of this kind requires research. Initially, my interest in the witch hunt in Scotland was confined to a small area of East Lothian. I investigated some local witchcraft cases for my forthcoming book *Swords, Loaves and Fishes*, a history of Dunbar, East Lothian, birthplace of John Muir. My researches into the local witches convinced me a more extensive study covering the whole of Scotland was long overdue. It is true that a few books have appeared over the last thirty years but the subject has largely been addressed by the amateur historian interested in local history; some have treated it as a quaint, if regrettable feature of the Scottish scene. However, the witch hunt is increasingly attracting the attention of modern historians and academics who are keen to rescue the subject from the realms of folklore and local history.

Preparing this book required assistance from others. Accordingly, I wish to express my appreciation of the help I have received from the staff at the Scottish Record Office, The National Library of Scotland and the Scottish Room, George IV Bridge Library– all in Edinburgh. Their assistance in patiently answering my many questions is inestimable. I also wish to express my appreciationn of the co-operation of Clare White, Property Manager and her staff at Culross Palace, Fife. Particular thanks go to Catherine Bradley and Stephen Valelly, who provided information about Fife and Stirling witches. The illustration of the ritual marks on page 209 was drawn by Robin Murdoch and is reproduced by kind permission of the National Trust for Scotland.

The Frontispiece, Dunbar Tolbooth or Town House c1900 is reproduced by kind permission of Dunbar and District History Society

Finally, I wish to thank Robin Murdoch for his enthusiastic support and advice; for his foreword; and last but not least, for publishing this book.

Introduction

The witch hunt in sixteenth and seventeenth century Scotland was a phenomenon, a dark chapter in the annals of Scottish history. The persecution of alleged witches was by no means unique to Scotland, nor was it prosecuted to quite the same extent as in other European countries; for example, in the Protestant German States, it is believed that more than 100,000 witches and wizards were burnt at the stake. Even so, the hysteria generated by the belief in the existence of witches in Scotland led to executions which from time to time reached epidemic proportions. That the phobia continued in Scotland long after other countries had outlawed the persecution of witches is shameful. It may not be considered remarkable, given the political, religious and socio-economic climate which prevailed at the time. Nevertheless, the witch hunt in Scotland is a disturbing episode, an example of the effects of mass hysteria, bigotry, superstition and ignorance, fuelled by religious zeal, self-righteousness and a misplaced trust in those who were educated by those who were not.

The witch hunt was pursued more vigorously in Scotland than in England. Although surviving records fail to confirm the precise number of executions which resulted from the witch trials, there is no doubt that the figure was considerably higher than in England. This was partly due to differences in the law on both sides of the Border, Scots law being more draconian. Also, the Presbyterian church was far more repressive than the Anglican church; it had more say in the running of the country than perhaps was desirable. That the last witch burning in Scotland occurred in 1727 compared with 1685 in England perhaps underlines the difference in attitudes between the countries. It is also a comment on the stronger influence of religion in Scotland during the seventeenth and early eighteenth centuries. The reasons for the periodic epidemics which swept the length and breadth of Scotland between 1560 and 1662 are difficult to identify. It is relatively easy to explain the initial outbreak which began in 1560 and lasted until the late 1580s. The Reformation had been a long time in coming; by the time it arrived in Scotland, it was heavily larded with a dour, dreary Calvinism and a morbid obsession with sin- especially that believed to be inherent in or caused by women. There was scant mention of love in John Calvin's Bible. His crude and literal translation of the Hebrew texts made few concessions to poetic imagery; Calvin simply discarded or prosaically translated the parts whose meaning escaped him.

Where women were concerned, Calvin eagerly embraced the tenets of the Hebrew religion as enshrined in the *Old Testament.* Woman was inferior to man, not just because she was formed from his rib. It was Eve who persuaded Adam to succumb to temptation which led to their expulsion from the Garden of Eden, thus visiting Original Sin on all mankind. Hebrew culture was unashamedly misogynist in outlook and this suited Calvin. Women were untrustworthy, subject to uncontrollable and irrational moods; they were temptresses, liars, low in intellect and thereby low in status. They had to be kept in their place and watched carefully; their bodies were expected to be temples of purity and goodness. It was Paul of Tarsus who bridged the gap between the *Old* and *New Testaments* in his *Letters to the Corinthians.* He reminded them of the doctrine of Original Sin; and reinforced the Jewish tenet that man was not made from woman but woman from man, that she should be submissive and that she should not speak in church.

Calvin's Bible took the many references to witches and sorcerers out of context; the result was that witchcraft and sorcery became one of the primary fixations of the new Protestant faith. In Scotland, that faith was refined by Presbyterianism, the form of government of individual churches under a group of elders including the preaching elder or minister. Presbyterianism owed much to Calvin. The grim, cheerless men who were elected by their congregations ruled with an unforgiving hand; there was little of understanding or human pity in the approach to their god. Outwardly, the new religion appeared to sweep away the corruption and dogmatism of the Catholic Church but there was little light in it. And where no light shines, much that is reprehensible in the mind of man finds expression. Heretics and witches became the Protestant Church's particular nightmares which came from the darkness the Kirk created for itself and imposed on others. For the first thirty years of its existence, the reformed church identified its prime aim, which was to educate the illiterate, common people. It is perhaps ironic that initially at least, it signally failed to do so; worse still, it encouraged the spread of ignorance and superstition. The church turned the people into vigilantes, constantly urging them to inform on those it described as enemies of god.

As already mentioned, while few records have survived to confirm the number of witches and warlocks executed in Scotland, there is considerable anecdotal evidence which suggests the figure was high. Certainly, the records abound with details-albeit tantalisingly brief-of witch trials which took place in practically every shire in Scotland. Initially, the majority of victims were

Papists denounced as heretics. In a sense, this was poetic justice, for the Catholic Church had decreed that witches were heretics. After the Scottish Reformation in 1560, even if only fifty witches or heretics were tried each year until 1590, we arrive at the not unreasonable figure of 1500 probable executions. Add to these the 1,891 cases identified in a modern study (*A Source-Book of Scottish Witchcraft,* C J Larner) and we have some idea of the probable total. The late Dr Larner, a professional researcher, was careful not to make claims she could not prove; while her invaluable study gives details about every case she researched, she stopped short of speculation about the outcomes unless she identified corroboratory evidence as to sentences. Even so, in her later book, *Enemies of God,* there is much to suggest that the figure was higher than records would lead us to believe. Despite her scrupulous and unbiased approach, it is difficult to avoid the assumption that the majority of trials ended in death. The statistics are complicated because of poor or imprecise records and the fact that many communities ignored the need to obtain commissions from the central authorities to proceed with a trial. The editorial comments which appear in *Criminal Trials in Scotland* (contemporary cases between 1488 and 1662 edited in 1883 by a lawyer, Robert Pitcairn) come down strongly on presumption of death in most cases. Pitcairn may be accused of assuming the worst when he wrote that the majority who confessed they were witches were executed, but he wasn't far short of the truth. Death was by strangulation, the body then being consumed by fire. We know from contemporary accounts that some witches were acquitted; a few cheated the executioner by committing suicide or dying of injuries sustained in attempted escapes from prison-usually the local tolbooth or a kirk spire; and some of course died under torture. Given the pitiful few who could afford to defend themselves by challenging their accusers, it is unlikely that many survived. I believe the majority, particularly those who were tried by local commission, went to the stake.

Witchcraft and magic are as old as mankind itself. The history of man is one of survival through his attempts to control the environment in which he lives. In the beginning, survival depended on man's ability to obtain sufficient food by hunting or gathering; success was directly related to his skills and ingenuity in a hostile world. Throughout the ages, advances were made as man gradually overcame the problems he faced. However, when his intellect and tool-making skills failed to produce the desired results quickly enough, he sometimes resorted to magic, which is older than religion. It is thought by some that the prehistoric cave-paintings in the Dordogne area of France may be the earliest evidence of man's belief in and use of magic. The animals depicted on the cave walls are pierced with what appear to be spears; perhaps they represent the successful outcome of a hunt which man believed might influence future hunts. If that is the case, these cave paintings are probably among the earliest examples of imitative magic.

Throughout the centuries, imagery became an integral part of witchcraft and sorcery. A witch who wished to gain control or power over someone often fashioned an image of her victim in clay or wax, then pierced the effigy with pins or needles and cast it into fire or water. The object was to inflict pain through sickness or death from illness or by drowning. The desired result was usually coincidental although the authorities did not see it that way. In the centuries with which this book is concerned, life was precarious, medicine was in its infancy and sudden and mysterious deaths were common among the population. There had to be an explanation. Witchcraft came easily to the lips of a largely uneducated and superstitious population.

Prosecution of witches occurred relatively late in history. The mania began to gather momentum at the time of the Crusades at the end of the eleventh century. It reached new heights during the prosecution of the Knights Templar by the Church of Rome which was convinced the order practised the black arts to extend their power and influence and increase their wealth. The Spanish Inquisition established by Pope Innocent IV in 1248 for the suppression of heresy included witches. They also received particular attention. Witches were the subject of an hysterical treatise called *Malleus Maleficarum* (The Hammer of Witches) which was compiled in 1489 by two fanatical Dominican friars, Jacob Sprenger and Heinrich Kramer. Sprenger indulged in abusive tirades against women in general and witches in particular. The Hammer of Witches may be described as a blueprint for witch hunters. Women were liars, untrustworthy, temptresses and carnal creatures. They were more susceptible to control by the forces of evil since they had already proven themselves guilty of Original Sin. As disciples of the devil, they were heretical and anti-Christ.

When Germany converted to the Protestantism of Martin Luther, other European countries followed suit. Catholicism was declared anti-Christ and heretical. With the unerring logic of the bigoted, the Reforming fathers held that as Catholicism was heresy, its adherents were heretics; those who persisted in practising the proscribed religion were therefore labelled witches and sorcerers. As already mentioned, about 100,000 were burnt in Protestant Germany. Hitherto, witches had been burnt singly or in pairs; by 1560, the German churches organised executions of scores or even hundreds at a time.

In 1560, the fledgling Scottish Kirk felt insecure and vulnerable. Many influential people clung to the old faith; some openly flaunted their preference and used it to further their political ambitions. This probably accounted for the first outbreak in Scotland, although there are few records to support this view. It does not require much imagination to understand how witches were discovered during the early years of the Reformation. The Catholic service relies heavily on prayer and chanting and witches were known to incant their spells using rhymes. Thus the incantations of the Papists were regarded as spells, proving they were in league with or possessed by the devil. The transition from one form of religious dogma to another took many years to accomplish. There were many casualties along the way.

We will never know for certain how many Catholic women and men were slaughtered in Scotland for their faith between 1560 and 1590. The number must be significant. By the start of the seventeenth century, the new church was more secure and as a consequence, ought to have become more enlightened towards those whom it had formerly considered a threat to its survival. Exactly the opposite happened. How much this was due to excessive religious zeal or national misogyny cannot be said with accuracy. The periodic epidemics which erupted usually coincided with political or religious unrest (see Appendix 2); this is supported to a certain extent by historical events, although the precise reasons are difficult to unravel from records which verge on the hysterical. The Scottish Church saw witches everywhere. It also insisted on its right to try suspects as it had done 'in tyme of Papistrie'which gives credence to the belief that the witch hunts prior to 1590 were largely motivated by religious intolerance. This does not explain what happened after 1590; the reasons are more sinister, difficult to identify and are manifold.

At what point the established Scottish Church turned from religious intolerance to an unreasonable fear of women is difficult to determine. Perhaps that fear had always been there. Witches were discovered everywhere; few parishes escaped the mania. The collective frenzy which gripped some communities and localities was carried along on its own momentum; in some ways, it reflected the pogroms against the Jews in Russia and elsewhere. The hellish flames were certainly fanned by ignorance, superstition, bigotry, fear, greed and jealousy. Lust and sexual harassment also played a considerable part in the madness. When a witch was apprehended in a community, further discoveries followed. This explains why even very small rural communities burnt numbers of witches out of all proportion to their populations.

While power to try witches rested with the central authorities and circuit courts, that power was delegated by central government to local commissions. The scope for abuse was considerable and sentences were rarely challenged. The Privy Council in Edinburgh which judged such matters was content-perhaps in view of the numbers forced-to delegate its powers to local commissions. Members of these commissions were local dignitaries and officials—lairds who were invariably church heritors, burgh provosts and bailies-and of course the church was almost always represented by one or more ministers. Juries were seldom present. The local laird or landowning church heritor presided over the proceedings. A typical commission consisted of five members who were given wide powers. They could apprehend anyone suspected of witchcraft, try and sentence them and any others named as witches during the proceedings. Local commissions were also authorised to impound the possessions of suspects to meet the cost of their trials. The men who sat on the magistrates' bench could and did literally get away with murder. Those who served on these commissions usually knew the accused and may have harboured grudges against them. In the absence of an impartial jury, justice was the first casualty.

Once the Privy Council issued a warrant to try suspected witches locally, it usually expressed no further interest in the matter. There was usually no requirement on the part of the local commissioners to report the outcome of a trial to Edinburgh except in the few cases where the Privy Council ordered it. There was also no financial incentive for local communities to do so; it cost money to send an official on horseback to Edinburgh to request a warrant and with no prospect of payment of expenses incurred in reporting the outcome, most communities rarely did so. Even if a witch's 'guidis and geiris' were impounded, her scant possessions probably covered only the cost of the coals and faggots used to burn her. Many so-called witches were vagrants and beggars who being penniless, were a financial burden on, as well as a nuisance to small communities. Some parishes were obliged to meet these costs from meagre resources such as the church poor-box, which did not endear the victim to the local population, even if a public witch-burning offered something of a spectacle.

That the witch hunt went on longer in Scotland than in England and elsewhere is part of the phenomenon. The last Scottish witch was burnt in 1727, only nine years before the *Witchcraft Acts* on either side of the Border were repealed. England executed its last witch in 1685 but trials continued until 1712. Yet even after the law was repealed in both countries, persecution did not end. When a woman was found guilty of witchcraft, she was 'scored'. Her forehead was cut by a knife, sometimes in the shape of the Cross; blood drawn from her forehead was said to deny a witch the use of her power. This inhuman practice continued until well into the nineteenth century; there is a case recorded as late as 1831.

As already indicated, it is impossible to determine how many women and much less often men, were executed in Scotland between 1560 and 1727. Estimates vary from an unlikely 21,000 (mentioned in the appropriately titled *Memoirs of Extraordinary Popular Delusions,* C Mackay); 7,500 (*Scotland Social and Domestic,* C Rogers); 4,400 (*A Calendar of Cases of Witchcraft in Scotland,* G F Black). In his article *Witchcraft in Scotland,* which appeared in *The Scottish Review* of 1891, F Legge offers a cautious 3,400 executions between 1590 and 1680, although he admits the figure could be much higher. Surviving records are frustratingly vague. For example, some state that 'several persons were indicted' or ' many women were accused' and even 'many witches were executed'. Larner identifies 1,891 cases in her study; but of these, she was able to confirm only around 600 executions. Despite her professional impartiality, I am willing to hazard a guess that she privately believed that fewer than 10% escaped death. After reading extensively on the subject, I am willing to venture the true figure was probably in excess of 3,500

Witchcraft and magic are still practised today. Adherents are more inclined to practise 'white' magic, or homeopathic medicine using herbs and plants. Many of their antecedents in the seventeenth century had much in common with them. There are also those who simply prefer to worship the old gods, finding spiritual comfort in colourful ancient pagan beliefs and rituals which the modern Christian Church, for all its attempts to 'modernise ', fails to provide. But witchcraft is still preached against in the Bible Belt in America; the Christian Church in Arizona recently warned its adherents to be on their guard against witches. Like religion and legend, old habits persist.

February 2001
Castle Street
Dunbar
East Lothian

Witchcraft in Scotland
From Early Times to 1603

What was witchcraft? We know who or what was behind it, but why were people so eager to believe in its powers? Why were whole communities in sixteenth, seventeenth and early eighteenth century Scotland gripped by a craze for executing witches? This book will attempt to explain the phenomenon. Witchcraft and witches are terms rarely used in every day conversation today; they are part of folklore, featuring largely in the cartoon culture of television. However, there was much more to it than simple folklore, as will be seen. In the pre-Christian era, witchcraft was the term applied to the supernatural power which certain people were said to possess by entering into compacts with the devil. Belief in witchcraft was prevalent in all primitive societies. References to witches and their craft are to be found in Babylonian and Egyptian texts. Witches and wizards feature prominently in old pagan religions such as Druidism, then in the *Old Testament.*

With the advent of Christianity, the nature of witchcraft underwent a significant change. Among the early Christians, the doctrine of interference of evil in human affairs became more developed than previously. The early church believed that Satan, the Devil, was in league with the discredited gods of paganism; witches and wizards - warlocks in Scotland - were supposedly in contract with the dethroned gods and especially Satan. They were, in effect, the devil's servants on earth. Witchcraft, once considered a mild form of meddling in human activities grew out of proportion as early as the thirteenth century. Like a nightmare come true, the church transformed witchcraft and its practitioners into an oppressive force seeking to undermine and ultimately destroy God's kingdom by attacking His creation, the earth. Between the thirteenth and fifteenth centuries, the Catholic Church associated witchcraft with heresy, punishing its practitioners accordingly through the Inquisition, a court or tribunal expressly established for the examination and punishment of heretics. When the corrupt Roman Church failed to reform itself in time to countermand the impact of the Reformation, the stage was set for a re-appraisal of religious values, practices and attitudes. In the new Reformed church, one major consequence was the dramatic change in attitude towards witches and wizards; almost overnight, they became public enemy No I and were considered as dangerous as the discredited and heretical Church of Rome.

A general description of the various stages of the Scottish witch hunt appears in chronological order in subsequent chapters, together with specific cases which illustrate the extent and nature of the hunt and how it affected the country as a whole. It is perhaps appropriate here to place the cult of witchcraft in its historical context and describe the measures taken to contain it.

As mentioned briefly in the Introduction, magic and witchcraft are as old as mankind itself. By mankind, we mean man at the stage of development where he had acquired deductive powers and tool-making and tool-using skills. At this early stage, man's prime objective was to survive in a hostile environment. He had little to comfort him except food, fire and primitive shelter from the elements. Food was his first priority, got by hunting and gathering. In time, man developed skills to improve his success in food-gathering but sometimes his resourcefulness failed him or he made slow progress in overcoming his difficulties. In his frustration, he occasionally turned to an early form of magic, a practice common to many primitive societies, Africa being a classic example. Even today, some African tribes consult the local witch-doctor for advice and expertise. Among the earliest examples of possible imitative magic are the cave paintings discovered in the Dordogne district in France. Some archaeologists have ventured the theory that primitive hunters, depicting the outcome of a successful hunt, were attempting to predict or influence future hunts, as many of the animals shown are pierced with spears. On the other hand, perhaps the paintings are no more than the celebratory images of a skilful huntsman wishing to demonstrate his prowess. However, if the artist or artists were expressing a form of wish fulfilment, it is not unreasonable to suggest they were invoking magic to ensure future success.

Although the term witch derives from the Anglo-Saxon word *wicce,* practitioners of the craft of sorcery existed in the earliest times. References to soothsayers, sorcerers and witches are scattered throughout the *Old Testament* in which Hebrew tradition is enshrined; it leaves us in no doubt that witches were evil and that they were severely punished. The prophets fulminated about the evil inherent in woman; she was the weaker vessel because Eve had succumbed to temptation and polluted Adam with the forbidden fruit, thus visiting Original Sin on mankind and expulsion from the Garden of Eden. In the Hebrew culture of the time, women were sinful, untrustworthy creatures who were spiteful and prone to unreasonable and irrational moods. They were known to resort to guile in their dealings with men, whom they bewitched through carnal desire. The *Old Testament* gives unequivocal advice on how to deal with witches in *Exodus*, chapter 22, verse 18:

'Thou shalt not suffer a witch to live.'

The Scottish Kirk of the sixteenth and seventeenth centuries took particular heed of that advice.

As early as 1056 BC, despite his persecution of witches and wizards, Saul, king of Judea, turned to the *Witch of Endor,* a medium, for help in his struggle with the Philistines. Because of his reputation for dealing harshly with witches, Saul went in disguise to ask the witch to conjure up the spirit of the dead prophet Samuel. Although she recognised Saul, she agreed to help him if he would promise to spare her life. Samuel's spirit duly appeared and told the king he was beyond help because of his evil ways and that his god had turned his face from him. Samuel's ghost foretold Saul's death which occurred shortly afterwards. On that occasion, the witch's life was spared (see *1 Samuel*, chapter 28, verses 7-25).

In Hebrew culture women had low status. They were expected to be pure in mind and body and faithful to their husbands. Along with other *New Testament* prophets, Paul of Tarsus bridged the gap between the *Old and New Testaments* by reinforcing the Judaic attitude to women in his *Letters to the Corinthians*. In 190 AD, the year of his conversion to Christianity, Quintus Septimus Florens Tertullian, one of the earliest Roman theologians, wrote:

> 'Woman ! You are the gateway of the Devil. You persuaded him who the Devil dared not attack directly. Because of you, the Son of God had to die. You should always go about dressed in mourning and in rags.'

Tertullian's warning was taken to heart in the centuries that followed; as woman was often regarded as the devil's agent on earth, she was expected to lead a humble and obedient existence. Tertullian's dogma was embraced by the early Christian Church; it would persist until the turn of the eighteenth century. In Britain, when Christianity came to Scotland and England, the Judaic view of woman was reinforced by the early missionaries who were at pains to remind their converts that woman was the prime cause of Original Sin.

In Scotland, the earliest measure against witches appears to have been a law passed by Kenneth I in the ninth century which outlawed wizardry, juggling and necromancy, all punishable with death by burning. The precedent was set. One of the first known executions for witchcraft in Scotland occurred in the reign of Duffus in the tenth century, when a group of witches were discovered casting a spell on the king. They were caught in the act of anointing a wax image of Duffus with poison and roasting it over a fire while they recited a spell designed to bring about the death of the king who had recently fallen ill. When the witches were taken, the spell was broken and the king recovered. The women were burnt at Forres in Morayshire; the Forres Witches were possibly the first victims of the Scottish witch hunt.

Man is a creature motivated by ambitions and desires. That is part of human nature. Some will stop at nothing to fulfil these ambitions. In the early Middle Ages, many were prepared to seek the advice of witches and warlocks in Scotland when orthodox Christianity failed them. As Western society became more acquisitive, men were driven by greed or sought to curb their rivals' power; when the usual attempts to achieve their ambitions failed, some were prepared to consult witches. Witchcraft had its attractions; for one thing, it was clandestine and offered the chance of success by stealth which meant the perpetrator could escape justice. People often resorted to witchcraft in times of danger. This certainly holds true in primitive and unsophisticated societies. In the period with which this book is concerned, medicine was crude, often no better than the remedies offered by witches. Also, in times of political or religious unrest, the use of sorcery and magic often manifested itself when personal or national security were threatened. In the Scotland of the sixteenth and seventeenth centuries, national crises weakened the country's political and social stability whose fabric was underpinned by the policies and propaganda of the newly reformed church. Few voices were raised against its repressive regime; those who spoke out against the persecution of witches were denounced from the pulpits and sometimes even the courthouse. It is a paradox that superstition and bigotry - they go hand in hand - were spread by those who espoused the cause of a religion whose cornerstones were mercy and forgiveness. There was little of either shown to those suspected of witchcraft and supposedly enslaved by the devil. Was it not Jesus of Nazareth himself who said that those possessed by demons should be brought before him so that he might comfort them ?

That witchcraft survived well into the Second Millennium comes as no surprise. However, the nature of witchcraft changed radically during the fifteenth century, as will be seen. Belief in supernatural beings goes back into the mists of time. 'Dark Age' man, then Medieval man, acknowledged there were witches and warlocks in their midst in the same way as they accepted the existence of other supernatural beings like elves, fairies, goblins, brownies and sprites - the little people. These supernatural creatures were not considered a threat because religious belief was strong. The early medieval church offered protection against their unwelcome attentions; the effects of evil could usually be neutralised by the sign of the cross, holy water and prayer. But in point of fact, the little people held no fear for Medieval man; he even considered them friendly creatures who sometimes helped him, provided he respected and rewarded them.

The hunting of witches - or more precisely, heretics - occurred relatively late in the Christian church's history. The Catholic Church certainly punished heretics for their un-Christian beliefs but the ecclesiastical courts rarely inflicted the death penalty. Confessions were extracted under torture; when the erring faithful repented, they might suffer some punishment such as branding or banishment. Emphasis shifted from the correction of heretics when the church was faced with an even greater danger - the spread of Islam. In the eleventh century, Saracens and Turks desecrated the holy places significant in Christian mythology, pilgrims were denied access to sacred shrines in Jerusalem and some were slaughtered. The conflict between Cross and Crescent came to a head in 1096, when Pope Urban II appealed for a crusade against

4

the infidels. Suddenly, the devil and his servants were relegated. The Saracen was the new anti-Christ, posing a threat to the Christian, Western world. Several popes called for crusading armies to stem the tide of the evil that threatened to engulf the Christian world. The First Crusade ended in abject failure. The six which followed fared no better, achieving little in return for a waste of life, money and resources. Apart from satisfying the egos of the chivalrous and the godly, the crusades did bring a few useful benefits. New plants were introduced into Europe by crusaders who were interested in horticulture and medical knowledge was advanced slightly; most important of all however, East and West became aware of their profound differences.

When the last crusading pope died in 1484, Rome again turned her attention to heretics and their master, the devil. As the practice of witchcraft was heresy, it was condemned in papal bulls issued between 1484 and 1523 by Popes Innocent VIII, Julius II and Adrian IV. Innocent VIII was particularly alarmed by the increasing drift from the faith and a supposed preference for the devil. The Spanish Inquisition, set up three centuries before to correct the wayward proclivities of Christians, restricted its punishments to torture. Few heretics actually went to the stake, a misconception which has been proven in modern times. The Inquisition had a bad press. In terms of brutality, it came nowhere near the excesses of the Protestant German states which, in the early years of the Reformation, burnt 100,000 witches - and that is considered a conservative estimate. By way of illustration, the Bishop of Treves (modern day Trier) in the Rhine Palatinate ordered the mass execution of women in his diocese. Trier became a charnel-house; when the purge ended, there were scarcely any women left alive in the district.

On the heels of the first papal bull came *Malleus Maleficarum - The Hammer of Witches* - best described as a textbook for the detection of witches. The work of two fanatical and bigoted Dominican friars, Jacob Sprenger and Heinrich Kramer, the book was published in 1489. It is a monument to superstition, injustice, bigotry, hypocrisy and hysteria. It became the blueprint for ecclesiastical courts and led to the deaths of countless so-called witches.

In 1560, the Reformed Protestant religion was adopted by the state in Scotland; Papistry was denounced as heresy, the worship of saints was declared blasphemous, praying to images and relics was idolatrous. Those who clung to the old faith were hunted down and branded as heretics. Heresy was declared a major crime, punishable by death. In England, the Protestant religion had been re-instated in 1558. After the death of Henry VIII, his daughter Mary I re-introduced Catholicism as the state religion; her reign is remembered chiefly for the burning of Protestant martyrs. An English Act of 1401 entitled *On the Desirability of Burning Heretics* had inflicted the punishment of public execution by burning 'so that such punishment may strike fear to the minds of others.' The act was repealed during the reign of Henry VII (1485-1509); in re-enacting it, one of Mary's aims was to discourage Protestant attempts on her life. Thankfully, Mary ruled for only five years; even in that short time, she burnt nearly three hundred Protestants, including Thomas Cranmer, Archbishop of Canterbury and Hugh Latimer, an influential prelate and martyr. When 'Bloody' Mary died in 1558, her half-sister Elizabeth came to the throne. One of Elizabeth's first acts was to settle the question of religious belief and worship. England wanted to return to the reformed faith and Elizabeth concurred, despite constant threats on her life by Catholic plotters. When Elizabeth was secure on her throne, she repealed her half-sister's law against Protestant heretics, replacing it with her *Witchcraft Act, 1563*. The main effect of the Elizabethan measure was to introduce the death penalty for witchcraft but only where its use resulted in the death of a victim. This was a significant departure from the equivalent Scottish Act passed in the same year. In England, execution was by hanging, thus implying that witches were regarded as little more than common murderers.

John Knox

In Scotland, Mary, Queen of Scots continued to practise Catholicism, resisting John Knox's attempts to convert her. Under pressure from her Protestant Lords, Mary gave royal assent to a witchcraft act which was more draconian than its English counterpart. This probably resulted from the young queen's stubborn refusal to embrace the reformed faith. The Scottish measure of 1563 differed from the English act in two ways that proved disastrous for Scottish witches. The first was that witches were considered heretics, ironically attracting the death penalty imposed by the proscribed Catholic faith - death at the stake. The second was more significant and sinister. The Scottish reformers went a step further by declaring that those who refused to accept that witches and witchcraft existed and those who consulted, aided or abetted a person suspected of witchcraft were equally guilty of the crime.

The act specifically stated that 'nae person seek ony help, response, or consultation at ony users or abusers of witchcrafts....on pain of death.' This technicality denied the Scottish legal profession any chance of success in the defence of a witch, although in the latter half of the seventeenth century, cases of witchcraft brought before the High Court of Justiciary or the circuit courts had more chance of securing a verdict of not proven. This was not so in the majority of cases tried by local presbyteries and under commissions authorised by the Lords of the Privy Council in Edinburgh.

Trial by local commission was by far the most common practice in Scotland. It had several advantages. Local commissions freed the central and justice-ayres, or circuit courts, from an unmanageable caseload. They also offered a convenient solution to the problem of dealing with groups of witches, since inevitably, when a witch was apprehended, she informed on others in the district. The propaganda value of these local trials was more direct since the local magistrates and the kirk worked closely together and the common people were left in no doubt as to the fate of those convicted of witchcraft. And finally, trial and execution within the community encouraged local people to inform on others whom they suspected were witches. These local trials usually secured convictions and the death penalty. As Larner's 1977 study confirms, about 56% of her sample of 1,891 cases were handled either by local commissions or by other means: many of the latter were unauthorised and therefore illegal. This means that something in the region of 1,000 witches tried under these conditions probably met their deaths during the period 1560 to 1727. To this figure must be added convictions secured in the central and circuit courts; and those which authorised commissions without naming the individuals and which resulted in the execution of 'many witches' or 'several witches.' A further difficulty in assessing the true figure of prosecutions and executions is that before 1591, in which year central government began to record cases, witches were almost exclusively tried locally; records of these trials are invariably found - where they exist - in kirk session minute books which are often brief and incomplete. Most of the secular records have either been destroyed, or never existed.

The curious fact is that cases of witchcraft increased as persecution reached epidemic proportions; it is perhaps easy to explain this as zeal on the part of the witch-finders and the willingness of local people and apprehended witches alike to inform on others. That may be so, but it also suggests the death penalty did not act as a deterrent. The prime instigator, the Kirk, was often at odds with the secular and judicial powers in Edinburgh. The General Assembly robustly argued that the church and only the church could determine whether a person was guilty of the crime of witchcraft since witches acted contrary to divine laws, exclusively the prerogative of the ecclesiastical courts. For its part, the Privy Council argued equally forcibly that while it accepted the church's role in such matters, only the judiciary could conduct trials and sentence the guilty. This led to conflict which the Privy Council effectively resolved by devolving its powers to local commissions appointed to try witches in its name. Presbyteries were, however, free to appoint their own courts. Membership of the local commissions invariably included the local minister and others from neighbouring parishes within the presbytery. These kangaroo courts - there is no better way to describe them - were weighted against suspects from the outset. There was often no jury, no legal defence and the magistrates - seldom men of even average intelligence - selected and called witnesses from the local population, usually alleged victims or those who sympathised with them. The scope for injustice was limitless.

When a presbytery applied for a commission from the Privy Council through the local magistrates, it usually informed the Lords in Council that an accused witch had already confessed her crime or was known to be suspect 'by habit and repute a witch' or 'long suspectit' of witchcraft. The fate of an accused witch was often sealed before the formal trial began. In the words of an hereditary sheriff in seventeenth century Galloway, a person accused of witchcraft had about as much chance of acquittal as had a Jew appearing before the fifteenth century Spanish Inquisition. The Church of Scotland has always had its apologists where the witch hunt is concerned. Those with a mild interest in the subject argue that it was the local lairds rather than the ministers who were primarily responsible. Some have suggested that as it was the kirk elders, elected by the congregation - the people - thus by logical extension of the argument, the witch hunt was spearheaded by the people themselves. The fact is that even if the lairds were not responsible, they were church heritors with a vested interest in maintaining church and therefore their own discipline, so the clergy had a major influence on the proceedings. As already noted, it was presbyteries which made the initial accusations and called for commissions to try suspects. The Kirk also encouraged its congregations to act as informers; every church had a wooden box which was put there so that people could 'give up' a witch by name, allowing the informant to remain anonymous. A certain twentieth century German Chancellor would have found such a method quite acceptable. How can the church credibly defend its professed minor role in this shameful business?

The Kirk exhorted the people to be vigilant - perhaps the word should be vigilante. When one witch was 'discovered,' the ministers argued there must be others, since witches operated in covens of thirteen, the devil's dozen. Discovery of a witch was the talk of the parish. People suspected others, especially those closely connected with the accused. To be seen with a person rumoured to be a witch was dangerous. We know from the records that the initial examination of suspected witches took place at the *sederunt,* or periodic 'doon-sitting' of the kirk session. Evidence survives which shows that a witch's 'confession' was rarely the uninhibited response of the accused. Answers were given in response to questions which were carefully framed beforehand to trap the unwary. Thus by subtle manipulation, 'examinations' usually produced the desired result. Of course there is nothing unusual in this; modern lawyers follow the same approach. The difference in practice between then and now is that now, professional defence is available to the accused. And, more important, for the present and hopefully distant future, an impartial jury provides the verdict.

The methods used to try witches were simple. Before a secular trial took place, the kirk session - minister and elders - examined the suspect. Usually, they called in a witch-pricker - sometimes the local minister - who searched the victim's body for the devil's mark. These humiliating body searches were but a foretaste of the torture to come. Ministers who witnessed and even participated in these degrading examinations were as stone walls. Or so they seemed. In reality, they no doubt obtained a measure of sexual pleasure from the sorry business, as in many cases, women were stripped naked to allow a thorough investigation which would reveal the tell-tale sign. This often meant probing her private parts. The commonest marks were warts or moles which, when pricked with a long, thin brass needle or 'preen,' the pricker's trademark implement, either failed to produce blood or the victim felt no pain. These brass pins were pushed often to a depth of three inches into the flesh; the test was positive if the victim either failed to react or could not say which part of the body had been 'pricked'. Other areas were patches of rough skin, teat-like protuberances which were sometimes present in the vulva. The third 'teat' - usually a wart - was proof positive of guilt, being used to suckle the witch's familiar - dog, cat or toad. The prickers were clever, searching unlikely places like the eyebrows, in the hair under the armpits, the pubic hair and of course the head, which was often shaved. To give credence to their trade, the prickers and ministers often included in the witch's confession her pact with the devil, formally written in Latin, which the witch signed - if she could write. If not, she made her mark or her supposed signature was forged. The inquisitors forced the victim to read out the litany - it was in imitation of the Romish form of prayer for particular effect since Papistry was denounced as heresy for many years after the Reformation. The pact went something like the following:

> 'My lord and master Lucifer, I acknowledge thee as my God and
> prince, and promise to serve and obey thee as long as I shall live.
> And I renounce the other God as well as Jesus Christ, all the saints,
> the Scottish church; all the sacraments, and all the prayers and peti-

tions by which the faithful might intercede for me. And I promise thee that I will do as much evil as I can, and that I will draw every one else to evil. I renounce chrism, baptism, all the merits of Jesus Christ and his saints. And I shall serve and adore thee, and if I do not pay thee homage thrice a day, I give you my life as thine own.'

The second sentence in this statement is particularly significant; the kirk was at great pains to stress how once in the devil's power, a witch could not withdraw - and did not want to withdraw - her oath to him. The pact rejoiced in the lurid title of *Extractum Ex Infernis* - Extracted from Hell.

That many Scottish women were burnt as witches between 1560 and 1590 is not in doubt, even if few records survive to confirm it. The fledgling Presbyterian church was insecure for the first thirty years of its existence. There were several Catholic plots directed against Protestant James VI; witches - Papists - were everywhere. By the Kirk's own admission in a petition to the Privy Council in the 1640s, it reserved the right to take witches into custody as had occurred 'in the tyme of Papistrie.' We will never know how many closet Catholics were executed between 1560 and 1590 but it is certain the number discovered was significant, perhaps as many as two thousand.

Thus the attitude to witches altered dramatically from the outset of the Reformation. Hitherto, they had been part of rural folklore, tolerated at best and at worst considered no more than a nuisance. They were responsible for fairly innocuous mischief. They stopped mills, placed large stones in the path of the plough, cast spells on animals that made them fall sick - flesh shrank from the bones of oxen, milking cows dried up and hens ceased laying - all usually directed at the farmers who displeased them by refusing them food or, in the case of millers - an unscrupulous lot at the best of times - by short-measuring them. But sometimes, witches were accused of bringing about the deaths of men and women; they supposedly conjured up storms which sank small fishing boats, laid sickness on people, particularly that known as 'the sweating seikness' induced by making a waxen effigy of the victim and holding it over a fire. To the modern mind, these calamities are easily explained. Most of the victims were providers of food - millers, farmers, fishermen - against whom a poverty-stricken old woman would vent her spleen when they refused her something to eat. More alarming were the instances of death attributable to witchcraft. In that society, where illness could strike suddenly, there were few medicines to treat minor ailments, let alone serious illness. The onset of pain and fever which brought sudden death to apparently healthy people, the loss of life by shipwreck and drowning - common enough occurrences - were put down to witches who made effigies of their victims and cast them into the fire or the sea and thereby sealed their fate.

Worse than that to some, witches were intimate with the devil. They indulged in obscene carnal congress with him, kissing his buttocks and fornicating with him; they performed black masses in deserted churches, mocked the Sacraments and dug up the bodies of unchristened children to use in the preparation of their hellish spells. The authorities were running scared. They were afraid that witches might topple the shaky state religion and the monarchy with it. So the purging of witches began. Initially, the victims were Catholics who refused to embrace the new faith. Before long, however, witches were found everywhere, even in Protestant congregations.

As far as can be established, one of the first instances of witch execution occurred at the very outset of the Reformation in 1560, three years before the *Witchcraft Act* was passed in Scotland. A local history, *Elgin Past and Present* states that several witches were burnt in the town that year. The first case to be tried by the High Court of Justiciary was that of Agnes Mullikine, in 1563. She was banished from Scotland for witchcraft. The Regent Moray, reigning after Mary, Queen of Scots was deposed in 1567, is credited with several witch-burnings in Dundee and St Andrews in 1569. The first reference to a witch in the *Registers* of the Privy Council occurs in February, 1587, when Helen Ellott was 'callit the Witche, in Jedburgh.' A proclamation at the High Court of Justiciary held in the presence of James VI in Holyroodhouse mentions several cases involving witchcraft in Selkirk. An early case is that of Elizabeth or Bessie Dunlop of Lyne, Ayrshire in 1576. A married woman, her only offence seems to have been using supernatural means to locate stolen goods and cure diseases. When apprehended - probably on the information of one of the thieves - she said she had been taught her skills by Tom Reid, a warlock who had been killed at the battle of Pinkie in 1547. She solemnly informed her judges that Tom's apparition appeared before her on several occasions; she described him as honest, elderly, grey-bearded and that he carried a white wand. He gave her advice about how to cure illness by taking a root of beet, drying and making a powder of it. This harmless and pharmaceutically worthless concoction reputedly cured two children and a cow. Another remedy was concocted from ginger, cloves, aniseed, liquorice and strong ale, boiled and sweetened with sugar. Bessie made this for Lady Johnston's daughter whom Tom had said was suffering from cold blood round her heart which caused the fainting fits to which she was prone - Victorian society would have described this affliction as the vapours. The patient was instructed to take this concoction every morning before food. When asked about the payment she received for her 'cure,' Bessie said she got some meal and cheese. Perhaps she was a lonely woman seeking some excitement in her life. She said she'd never known Tom Reid in his lifetime but saw his apparition twice, in the kirkyard of Dalry, Ayrshire and in Edinburgh's High Street, where he'd laughed to her. Clearly the victim of hallucination, poor Bessie was executed.

One the first 'casualties' of witchcraft to be mentioned in the Privy Council *Register* is the Earl of Angus, who died in 1588. Angus is described as the victim of 'sorcerie and incantatioun'; his body 'pynned and melted away with sweates, and in the mean tyme the witches wer turning his picture in waxe befoir a fire.' Records confirm that at least sixteen formal trials were held in Scotland between 1563 and 1589, listed in Pitcairn's *Criminal Trials*. Of these, four were executed, one was acquitted, another received non-capital punishment and three probably committed suicide, died in prison or escaped. The fate of the remaining seven is unknown. As indicated earlier, the majority of trials held during this period were heard by church courts and often went unrecorded. By 1563, witchcraft was one of the four major crimes which attracted the death penalty. The witch hunt was gathering momentum.

In 1576, Katherene Roiss [Ross], Lady Fowlis [Foulis], the wife of Lord Monro of Foulis and daughter of Lord Ross of Balnagowan, was accused of attempting to murder her eldest stepson, Robert Monro, so that her brother George Ross might marry her stepson's widow and thus become heir to the Foulis estate. This also meant murdering George Ross's wife to allow the marriage to take place. The motive was clearly to increase the lands and finances of the Rosses. To help her with the double murder, Lady Foulis engaged a group of witches whose notoriety was well-known. As subsequent events proved, they were certainly notorious, not for their success but their ineptitude. The chief witch was Marioune McAlester, colloquially known as Losky Loncart. Under her direction, the witches made images of their victims from 'butter' and shot at them with elf-arrows, in reality Neolithic flint arrowheads. The witches missed their targets no fewer than twenty times! They next brewed a pail of poison; the pail leaked, the poison ran out and they were left with dregs; Lady Foulis obtained a second brew from Losky Loncart but the pipkin of poison broke and the servant carrying it drank some and obligingly died. Lady Foulis then took matters into her own hands. She fed her sister-in-law food laced with rat poison; the young girl didn't die but she was extremely ill for a long time. At least two of the unknown total number of witches involved, Christian Ross and Thomas McKendrick, were convicted of witchcraft and burned in 1577. By 1589, Lady Foulis was widowed and her second stepson, Hector Monro, had succeeded his brother Robert on his death. Hector Monro brought an action against his stepmother and several people including Losky Loncart, William McGillivray, Agnes Roy and John McNillan. There is no record of the outcome as far as the witches are concerned. At her trial, Lady Foulis was acquitted, not surprisingly since the jury was made up from her estate servants and dependents. In his turn, Hector Monro was arrested on suspicion of causimg the death of George Ross but he too was acquitted by a similarly sympathetic jury. As for the witches, it is probable that they were strangled and burnt at the stake.

Then the unthinkable happened. Witches made an attempt on the king's life. James VI had officially embraced the Calvinist faith although he continued to court Papist nobles for purely political reasons. He made it clear that he fervently believed in the evil inherent in man, and man - or more accurately, woman - did not disappoint him. In 1589, he married Anne of Denmark; severe storms delayed his bride's voyage from Norway, so James set out to escort her to Scotland. On the return journey, an even wilder storm scattered the royal fleet and the couple reached Scotland with difficulty, having been blown off course. It was said that the storms had been caused by a coven in East Lothian, later known as the North Berwick Witches.

A woodcut of the North Berwick Witches showing the Reader with a group of witches listening to the devil preaching; others are boiling a cauldron to make a storm in the background while still more are drinking in a cellar

All was revealed by a humble girl, Geilie Duncan, servant to David Seton, a magistrate in Tranent. Geilie was reputedly skilful at curing sick people by dubious means. She was often absent late at night from her master's house, behaviour which raised Presbyterian eyebrows in Tranent. When questioned

𝔑ews from 𝔖cotland :

DECLARING THE

DAMNABLE LIFE OF DOCTOR FIAN

A

NOTABLE SORCERER

WHO WAS

Burned at Edenbrough in Januarie last, 1591

WHICH DOCTOR WAS REGISTER TO THE DEVILL THAT

SUNDRIE TIMES PREACHED AT NORTH BARRICKE

KIRKE TO A NUMBER OF NOTORI OUS WITCHES,

WITH THE

TRUE EXAMINATIONS OF THE SAID DOCTOR

AND WITCHES, AS THEY UTTERED THEM

IN THE PRESENCE OF THE SCOTTISH KING,

DISCOVERING

HOW THEY PRETENDED TO BEWITCH AND DROWNE

HIS MAJESTIE IN THE SEA COMING FROM DEN-

MARKE; WITH SUCH OTHER WONDERFULL

MATTERS AS THE LIKE HATH NOT BEIN

HEARD AT ANIE TIME

The ruins of St Andrew's (old) Parish Church, North Berwick

about her nocturnal activities, she broke down and under torture, confessed she had joined a plot to kill the king. She named her co-conspirators as Dr John Fiene [Fian] or Cunningham, a Prestonpans schoolmaster, Ewfame McCalzean and Barbara Napier (both of Edinburgh) and Agnes Sampsoune [Sampson] of Nether Keith, described as a 'grace wyff' or wise-wife. Later, similar charges were brought against a well-known warlock, Richard Graham. Brought to justice, the four were tried for treason rather than witchcraft - despite the fact that during the trial it emerged that they'd thrown a dead cat, with the organs of a corpse attached, into the sea. They had chanted incantations and cast spells to raise the storm that almost drowned the king.

James VI attended the trial and interrogated the suspects personally. Fian somehow managed to escape from prison but was recaptured immediately. At first, he said he had renounced the devil but in his cell one night, the devil appeared in a vision and told him that 'Once ere thou die thou shalt be mine.' Fian was severely tortured. His fingernails were torn from his hands with pincers, needles were thrust up to the head into his fingers, his legs were encased in the boot (an instrument of torture) till 'the blood and marrow spouted forth.' At first, Fian stood up well to torture, then when he was more brutally abused, he confessed he was acting in conjunction with Francis Stewart, 5th Earl of Bothwell, whose secretary he was. Fian went on to say the coven - some accounts say there were thirty-nine witches in all, three covens - was working under Bothwell's instructions. He further alleged that Bothwell had met them and asked Agnes Sampson to make a wax image of the king and chant over it 'this is Jamie the Saxth, orderit tae be consumed be a noble man.' Bothwell was James' cousin; the family had been potential contenders for the Scottish throne for three generations.

The only humorous aspect in this sad tale was when Fian admitted he had once tried to bewitch a young girl to make her fall in love with him; the charm involved using the girl's hair but her mother, aware of Fian's intentions, substituted cow's hairs with the result that the cow, not the girl, fell for him; apparently, the animal followed him everywhere, showing all the signs of a love-sick girl, much to the amusement of his pupils at the local school.

The North Berwick Witches were supposed to have put to sea in sieves, no doubt a colourful addition to the story. At first, James was convinced the plot had more to do with treason than the black arts although he fervently believed these were practised in his kingdom. Agnes Sampson's trial began on 27th January 1591. She was charged with no fewer than fifty-three offences, most of which concerned the curing of sick people and animals. One of her cures was effected on Lady Kilbaberton of Baberton estate, near present day Juniper Green, an Edinburgh suburb. Apparently, Agnes was accused of 'hailling [healing] the Lady of Kilbaberton be hir devilishe prayeris, [who] wes diseasit [by] ane heavie diseis.' Another cure was that given to Robert Kerse of Dalkeith, whom Agnes claimed had been tormented by witchcraft and disease by a Dumfries warlock. She took his sickness on herself and cast it away in the close next to her house. Her judges said the sickness was thus transmitted to Alexander Douglas in Dalkeith by a passing cat or dog as Douglas died of the same disease. Agnes corroborated most of Fian's story, although there were some discrepancies in the two versions. However, they agreed that ninety-four women and six men - all witches - met the devil in North Berwick Kirk. Geile

Duncan played the trump, or jew's harp, to which the witches danced. James VI had Geilie brought into court to play the tune. In Agnes' story, the devil appeared as a black man and stood in the pulpit, calling out the names of those present. He asked if they'd been good servants and what they'd been doing in his name. Then he bade them open up four graves and remove toe, finger and knee joints from the corpses. He told them to dry the bones, then make a powder of them to use in their spells. Agnes said she had asked the devil why he hated the king so much; he reputedly said 'Because he is the greatest enemy I have and I have no real power against him.' No doubt this was an attempt to flatter the king but unfortunately it made no difference to the outcome of her trial.

All of this fantastic confession was extracted under torture. Agnes was examined for her witch-mark, then various instruments were used on her, including the sadistic witch's bridle - an iron hoop that fitted on the head like a helmet; part of the construction was a metal cross with four sharp points which was forced into the mouth and held in place by a padlock so that the victim could neither speak nor receive food or water. This hideous instrument, with its cruciform mouthpiece, meant that two horizontal prongs pressed into the inside of both cheeks and two vertical ones the palate and tongue. During the course of his personal examination of Agnes Sampson, the king changed his mind about treason when she astonished him by quoting almost verbatim certain details of a conversation he'd had with his bride in the royal bedchamber on their wedding night. From the details which have come down to us, Agnes seems to have been matron-like, grave and calm in her responses to James VI's questions. She was not hysterical, nor did she make wild statements except in one respect. James asked her if she possessed a familiar; she said she did and that she summoned it by calling out *Holla Master!* She also summoned the devil by calling out *Elva*, the devil appearing instantly in the shape of a dog.

The next witch to be interrogated was Ewfame McCalzean, the wife of Patrick Moscrop, a well-to-do Edinburgh advocate related to David Seton in Tranent; Ewfame was the daughter and sole heiress of the late Thomas McCalzean, Lord Cliftonhall, Lord Provost of Edinburgh in 1561 and one of the senators of the College of Justice. As Cliftonhall is situated in the parish of Ratho, Ewfame perhaps met Agnes Sampson in the vicinity when the latter was prescribing a cure for Lady Kilbaberton of Currie. Ewfame McCalzean was an unlikely suspect. That a woman with such an impeccable pedigree should be cited as a witch was rare, but not unusual. Like her father, Ewfame was a practising Roman Catholic and a zealous partisan for Bothwell's cause. She was charged with the usual crimes of witchcraft and one or two which were decidedly unusual - casting her child-birth pains on a dog and a cat for example. She was also charged with consulting an elderly crone in Edinburgh's Canongate, one Jonet Cwnnghame [Cunningham], who in 1572 was nick-named Lady Bothwell!! Money may also have been involved as Seton of Tranent and Moscrop were related. She was also charged with the more credible offence of attempting to poison her husband to end their unhappy marriage. Ewfame McCalzean went to the stake on Edinburgh's Castlehill protesting her innocence. In her case, a more cruel death sentence was imposed; she was burnt alive on 25th June 1591. Fian shared her fate. Barbara Napier was tried on 8th May 1591 on less serious charges; she was found guilty of several minor offences but acquitted of being at the North Berwick Kirk convention to plot the king's death and other more serious crimes. She was released at the eleventh hour, en route to the stake. She pleaded she was with child which was found to be the case. Her judges set her free. An incensed James VI stormed into Edinburgh's Tolbooth to lecture the judges on what he saw was dereliction of their duty. James prided himself on his knowledge of witchcraft; in 1597, he published *Daemonologie*, a short treatise on the subject.

The last member of the coven to be executed was Richard Graham, the arch-sorcerer; finally caught, he was executed in Edinburgh on 29th February 1592. Another suspect, Margaret Thomson, died in prison. As to the fate of young Geilie Duncan, the servant girl from Tranent, the records are silent.

Dr Fian had acted as Bothwell's secretary; so too did Niniane Chirnesyde, another of Bothwell's retainers, indicted in 1592 for conspiring to end the king's life 'be witchecraft, sorcerie and utheris traitorous and diabolicall meanes.' It is probable that he was one of the North Berwick Witches, but he appears to have died in prison before trial. Bothwell was becoming an embarrassment; the repeated failure of James VI's government to capture him contained an element of farce, particularly when Bothwell, who mounted several successful raids on royal residences, trapped James in Holyrood Palace in 1593. The king was effectively his prisoner, but Bothwell went on his knees and begged James' mercy. He was subsequently pardoned and his lands and titles were restored. A year later, Bothwell was again conspiring against the king, this time with Catholic nobles; the charge of witchcraft was re-instated and Bothwell was declared the king's rebel.

Then a somewhat bizarre incident occurred in 1594. Bothwell, son of John Stewart, Commendator of Coldingham and one of James V's several illegitimate offspring, was a frequent visitor to Coldingham and Fast Castle, the small but virtually impregnable stronghold near St Abbs occupied by Robert Logan, 7th Baron of Restalrig. In July that year, Logan and John Napier of Merchiston - was he related to Barbara Napier, one of the North Berwick Witches? - met at Fast Castle to discuss Logan's plan to discover treasure reputedly hidden in the castle. Logan, a burglar and robber, shared Bothwell's interest in black magic. The mathematician Napier, inventor of logarithms, was also interested in the supernatural, alchemy and astrology. It was at this meeting that Logan proposed a treasure hunt. The gold was reputedly stolen from a royal emissary on Coldingham Moor in 1429 by William Drax, a former Commendator of the priory and one of the Homes of Wedderburn. The legend persists to this day. Napier was fascinated by Logan's proposal since he wanted to demonstrate his powers of magic in the search. The scheme was more in keeping with Logan's character but the two men drew up a contract which would give Napier one-third of the loot. More important was the clause which guaranteed Napier's safe conduct to Edinburgh after the money was shared. Clearly, Napier did not trust the wily Logan. Whether or not any treasure was found, the contract was never destroyed as was intended after the money had been divided. There was animosity between Napier and Logan afterwards, suggesting that gold had been discovered and Napier was denied his share. Years later, selling some property, Napier insisted that it was not to be sold to anyone of the name Logan. Whether Bothwell was a party to the scheme is not known. He may well have been since he was a frequent guest at Fast Castle. He certainly needed the money, as his lands and titles were forfeit. Bothwell, a quixotic figure, was forced to escape to France, then Italy, where he died in Naples, still declared the king's rebel and guilty of witchcraft.

Fast Castle, Berwickshire c.1850

Cases of witchcraft feature regularly after the Bothwell fiasco. The period 1590 to 1597 witnessed the first 'epidemic' in the witch hunt. Several cases occurred in Aberdeen in 1596-97. The outbreak in Aberdeen in 1597 is thought to be directly attributable to James VI's *Daemonologie,* his treatise on witchcraft published that year. James fervently believed there was a link between treason, heresy and witchcraft and what he decreed few, if any, presbyterian leaders would deny. The Aberdeen Witches were tried by the provost and bailies. The first was Jonnet Wischert [Janet Wishart], wife of John Leyis [Lees], a stableman. Her main crime appears to have been petty revenge on her neighbours over a period of thirty years. Most of her victims accused her of putting a spell on them which caused changes in body temperature - extremes of heat and cold - accompanied by an insatiable thirst. They probably had the flu. Some of her so-called victims died; one was described as 'melting away like ane burning candle.' Janet also reputedly caused twelve fowls

to die at the feet of one neighbour. She bewitched a cow so that it gave venom instead of milk - clearly, the animal was afflicted by mastitis. She made a neighbour accompany her to the gallows one night where she removed parts of a hanged man for her spells. Janet was executed immediately after her trial. Her son Thomas Lees was accused of assisting his mother and described as a common witch and sorcerer. He confessed that he went to the mercat and fish crosses at Aberdeen at midnight on Halloween, 1596, there to take part in a meeting with the devil, who changed him and others into cats and hares; he said they danced round the mercat cross. Thomas admitted he had been intimate with one of the witches and he promised to marry her, telling her that they would find all they needed for life's necessities at the foot of a nearby mountain. He was executed; his father John and three sisters Elspet, Jonet and Violat were banished from Aberdeen.

Another in this trial was Helene Frasser [Fraser], accused of many common and not so common spells. She was said to have bewitched Andrew Tullideff so that he transferred his love from his wife to a common harlot, Margaret Neilson; so badly was he affected that he was never reconciled with his wife, nor could he leave the harlot. Helen Fraser seemed to specialise in breaking up marriages. She next bewitched Robert Merchant, happily married for two years; he went to sow corn seed for a widow, Isobel Bruce, then fell madly in love with her because Helen had put a spell on him. Helen Fraser was executed.

Next to be tried was Isobel Cockie, who killed horses by touching them. She had been named by Thomas Lees as one of those who danced at the mercat cross in Aberdeen. She was executed, as was Meriore Mutche, who destroyed many cattle, made people sick and attended all the witch conventions in the district. Another member of the coven was Andro Man who was clearly deranged. He claimed to have met the Queen of Elfland as a boy -really the devil in disguise - when he was carrying water to his mother's house. The strange visitor told him he would have knowledge of all things and that he would have the power to cure all kinds of illness but not prevent death. He said he had cured many people simply by baptising them anew, striking them in the face with one hand and holding a fowl in the other and calling out:

'If thee will live, live! If thee will die, die!'

Andro Man saw the devil that year; he appeared in the likeness of a young male horse, accompanied by the Elfish queen and her retinue. He called the devil Christsonday and said he had seen Thomas the Rhymer - the famous thirteenth century poet and mystic who'd lived in Elfland for seven years in order to learn the secret of writing poetry - and James IV who was killed at Flodden. Although Andro denied all the charges made against him, he was executed.

In all, twenty-three women and two men were executed in Aberdeen that year. An example of the cost of burning witches at this time survives in the Aberdeen Dean of Guild's account book:

			£	s	d
1595	Item	For four tar barrels, pine peat, tow and stakes used in burning witches	3	0	0
1596	Item	IV tar barrels	1	6	0
	Item	For trailing Menteith [accused witch] through the streets in a cart, she having hanged herself in prison	0	10	0
	Item	Katharine Gerard, Christian Reid, Janet Gerard, For coals, peats and similar articles	8	2	0
	Item	For hire of horse to carry John Crichton, who is apprehended as a witch, to Dunnottar	0	3	4
	Item	To Alex Reid, smith, for two pairs of shackles to the witches in the steeple	1	12	0
	Item	To Thomas Dickson for halbert broken at their execution	1	10	0
	Item	To John Justice for burning on the cheek four persons suspected of witchcraft	1	6	0
1597	Item	To Alexander Home for making Joggis and Stepillis to the witches	0	16	8

The Dean of Guild, William Dun, keeper of the records, received a bonus of £47:3:4 from Aberdeen Burgh Council for his diligence in burning a great number of witches in Aberdeen in 1596. So altogether, something in the region of £67 Scots (about £11 sterling) had been spent in controlling the spread of witchcraft in the granite city. In contemporary terms, the bill would have required a contribution of one shilling from every adult in the town (modern day equivalent about £20 per household).

The Privy Council agreed that small communities should be spared such expense. Perhaps the Lords in Council had a more sinister motive. If townships and small communities were having to meet the expense of trying and executing witches, it might dampen their enthusiasm for hunting them down. The solution was simple, if macabre; witches themselves or their surviving relatives would, in future, contribute to the cost of their trial, maintenance while in prison and the cost of the materials used in their execution! A very practical solution to a financial dilemma!. Why, it was argued, should good, honest, god-fearing people have to pay hard-earned money to rid them of the evil in their midst? The records abound with examples of what might be called the witch tax. For example in 1643, in Pittenweem, Fife, John Dawson had to pay the authorities a sum equivalent to a year's free grazing for a cow and £40 Scots to met the costs associated with his wife's trial and execution. Two other Pittenweem men, John Crombie and Thomas Cook paid £80 and £60 respectively for the trial and execution of Crombie's wife and Cook's mother, Margaret Horsburgh.

There was money to be made from witch-pricking. John Dickson, the Elgin witch-pricker, was paid six shillings a day in 1622, with a bonus of £6 Scots for every witch he discovered. The same rates were paid to the most infamous pricker of all, John Kincaid of Tranent. Money is a great motivator in any society which perhaps puts into perspective the zeal and success in searching for and finding witches in the territories these men covered. The authorities were content to allow these charlatans to carry out their evil trade until 1662 when the Privy Council ordered them to stop.

James VI's enthusiasm for suppressing witchcraft encouraged communities in their witch hunts. Despite considerable success in apprehending suspects, some women managed to clear themselves of the charges brought against them. In 1597, Jonett Finlasoun [Finlayson] complained to the Privy Council about the bailies in Burntisland, Fife for their persistent persecution of her as a witch although she had been declared not guilty by a secular court. The Privy Council upheld her plea. In Fife the same year, Margaret Atkin [Aitken], the so-called Great Witch of Balwearie, was considered an extremely dangerous witch. She was taken into custody, where she told her accusers that in exchange for her life, she would identify witches in other parts of Scotland. She knew many; she had attended a convention attended by 2,300 under the direction of the devil on a hill in Atholl. She claimed to possess special skills; she could detect a witch by a certain mark in the eye, possibly the likeness of a white horse as claimed in Scot's suppressed book *Discoverie of Witchcraft*. Aitken travelled to Glasgow and other places accompanied by her captors, eager to make further arrests. She in fact became the first official witch-finder, a 'profession' which was later proved fake. According to Archbishop Spottiswoode, 'Many were brought in question to her delations, especially at Glasgow, where divers innocent women, through the credulity of the minister, Mr John Cowper, were condemned and put to death.' Margaret Aitken was declared a fraud and taken back to Fife, where she stood trial, confessing her crimes on the day she was executed.

The case of Margaret Aitken was reported to James VI as an example of how easily injustice could occur during witch trials. James reacted predictably; while he said he appreciated the danger, it was his duty to rid Scotland of the filthy abomination of witchcraft. Perhaps he had a discreet word with the Lords in Council who, concerned about the growing number of trials, dismissed several local commissions in an attempt to halt the epidemic. Even so, trial by local commission would remain the most common method for dealing with suspected witches after 1597. Despite James VI's interest in and enthusiasm for ridding his kingdom of evil, there were some who resisted. In 1598, the Earl of Atholl and his countess were denounced for failing to hand over two women suspected of witchcraft. Marion Macause and Bessie Ireland managed to convince the Atholls they were innocent; the Atholls were declared rebels but appear to have escaped censure. As for poor Bessie and Marion, they were executed. One law etc!

As mentioned earlier, consulting a witch was as bad as the crime itself and punishable by death. In 1601, David Roy of Balhousie, an old castellated mansion in North Perthshire, had sexual designs on his employer's daughter. Roy was cook to the laird of Balhousie, Colin Eliot, until he raped Eliot's daughter. David Roy had first attempted to seduce the young woman using Spanish Fly, a well-known aphrodisiac. When it failed to produce the desired results, he next injected an apple with his 'nature' and gave it to the girl. That did not work either. Finally Roy consulted a witch and obtained a potion concocted from daffodils so that, in the words of the Privy Council *Register*, he might satisfy ' his filthie and beastlie appetyte'. At his preliminary trial for rape, Roy was surprisingly declared innocent by what seems suspiciously like a hung jury. However, when details of the witch involvement were reported to the Privy Council, Roy was cited for the far more serious crime of consulting a witch. In the meantime, Roy escaped from the district and as far as is known, no further proceedings were brought against him.

That James VI linked Catholicism with witchcraft was understandable and he made no secret of his views. The Reforming fathers in Scotland had constantly looked for support from their co-religionists in England. That support was strengthened in 1603, when James took the thrones of both countries.

One of his first acts as James I of England was to introduce additional legislation against witchcraft in 1604. The new law went further than the Elizabethan measure by bringing English law in line with that in Scotland. Previously, those convicted of witchcraft were sentenced to death if their magic had resulted in death. From 1604, the death penalty was given to anyone suspected of witchcraft or consulting those who practised it. In this respect, the Union of the Crowns of Scotland and England drew the two countries closer. However, the hell fires would burn brighter, fiercer and longer in Scotland than in England, as will be seen.

Shipwreck off the Bass Rock

2

'Wicked Consultationis and Devilische Charmes'

What did a witch look like? The answer is simple. Anyone. While there were undoubtedly some who conformed to the stereotype hook-nose-and-chin old crone disfigured by warts, living alone with her invariably black cat and broomstick, the reality is that many were young or middle-aged. A fair proportion were married to men with steady employment - farm workers, fishermen, tradesmen, burgesses, merchants and men of property. Although a few came from even higher strata of society - lawyers, doctors and the nobility, in the latter case, practically none was found guilty. In that largely illiterate and unsophisticated society, a significant number of those suspected of witchcraft were unmarried women with children, widows and beggars; the last were the most likely suspects. Regarded as public nuisances in the same way as 'Egyptians' or gypsies, they slept rough, roamed the countryside begging alms at lonely cottages and isolated farms, pestering travellers for money and food and threatening those who refused them. Beggars, or vagabonds as they were often known, were commonplace. Ragged, dirty and disease-ridden, they undoubtedly stank to high heaven. They were the uninvited guests at baptisms, weddings and funerals, standing in strategic places with open palms. Some were vicious and roundly cursed those who refused them; it was inevitable that one day, someone they abused would report them to the local magistrates, who were only too willing to remove them from the parish. Or worse.

Why did so many of those accused of witchcraft confess? Again, the answer is not difficult. Confessions were extracted under torture. And yet there were some who freely admitted they were witches without the need for torture. In such cases, the reason was simply that they wanted people to believe they had supernatural powers; worse still, many deluded themselves they actually did possess such powers. It was a form of protection against interference from those they wanted to avoid. Some accused of witchcraft are described in the records as being of 'ill fame,' 'a rank witch,' 'by habit and repute a witch,' 'long suspectit of witchcraft' and 'of evil repute'. With such reputations, it is a wonder so many survived for so long without being called to account by the civil authorities.

We know that superstition and ignorance were rife in Scotland in the seventeenth century. People saw evil everywhere because the church said it existed; the devil was constantly active, seeking human souls with which to populate his dark kingdom. The Kirk, feeding on the fears of the ignorant and superstitious, urged congregations to be vigilant and to report any suspicious behaviour in their neighbours. In that nightmare society, it was dangerous to be different, eccentric or to curse anyone in the heat of an argument. Natural disasters, sudden and inexplicable death, sickness in animals, shipwreck, failure of harvests - all were attributed to witches. Like the government, the Scottish church needed scapegoats; witchcraft could account for unexpected occurrences. People fell sick without warning, animals died under mysterious circumstances, crops failed and capricious herring shoals didn't appear where and when they should. It was all down to witches, whom an austere and unforgiving church hunted ruthlessly.

With the reformed church established in Scotland and the thrones of Scotland and England secure, the persecution of heretics (Catholics and witches) should have ended a dark chapter in Scottish history. Not so. There were four major epidemics of witch hunting in the space of about seventy years from the late sixteenth to mid-seventeenth centuries. The horror that began in 1590 reached new heights in the late 1620s, then during the period of the Covenanting church from 1638 until 1650 and finally in 1660-62, after the Restoration of the monarchy in the person of Charles II. It is perhaps not coincidental that the craze was most virulent during periods of national crises, as will be seen.

From about 1597, the witch hunters were local lairds, ministers and kirk elders, aided and abetted by a largely passive population which needed reassuring. If, as has been suggested earlier, the common people were the real culprits in the witch hunt, they were acting on the prejudices and counsel of those who governed them at local level. And if the witch hunt was sparked off by national crises, it was usually only those in authority in the small rural communities who knew of such crises - the same people who controlled the local population. Before proceeding to examine some of the cases which occurred after 1603, when James VI became James I of England, it is perhaps useful to consider certain aspects of the Scottish trials. It has been shown that, by and large, the majority were heard by local commissions, a convenient arrangement. Some districts were so enthusiastic about hunting witches that they petitioned the Privy Council for powers to escheat (impound) the goods and assets of women and men executed for witchcraft in order to avoid imposing unwelcome taxes on local people to meet the expenses of trial and execution. The first presbytery to do so was Dalkeith, particularly active - and successful - in apprehending and executing witches.

In 1605, the year of the Gunpowder Plot against James VI, Scotland no doubt received the news with grave concern. The plot to kill the king and blow up the English parliament was masterminded by a group of Roman Catholics seeking revenge against James for his persecution of their religion. The most famous of the plotters, Guido, or Guy Fawkes, was executed with the real ringleaders. Here was evidence that despite the founding of the Reformation nearly forty-five years earlier, the authorities could not afford to be complacent about the 'evils' in their midst. The witch hunt gathered momentum. In the year of the plot, at least two witches were executed in Scotland. In Ayrshire, on the night of All Hallows, the devil gave Patrick Lowrie - indicted for consulting a local witch, Jonet Hunter, who had recently been executed - a hair belt, the end of which was fashioned in the shape of a claw-like hand. Lowrie later admitted he frequented deserted kirks and dug up corpses for use in spells. He was executed. Two years later, Issobell Greirsoune [Grierson], wife of John Bull in Prestonpans, apparently had a grudge against a neighbour, Adam Clark. Isobel was charged with witchcraft; it was claimed she changed herself into a cat and, along with other cats, invaded Clark's house making 'ane grit and fearfull noyse'. so that Clark's wife and servant nearly went mad. Clark then claimed that the devil appeared in the form of a black man who dragged his servant up and down the room by her hair so that she was ill for nearly six weeks afterwards - doubtless suffering from shock. Isobel was also accused of laying sickness and subsequent death on William Burnet; she threw a piece of raw 'inchanted' meat at the door of his house. Her spell must have been weak as it took eight months for Burnet to expire. Another of her victims, Robert Peddie, was said to be swooning and fading away on account of a spell she'd put on him for refusing to pay the nine shillings and four pence he owed her. His illness lasted over a year and went away as soon as he paid his debt. Another charge was that Isobel could 'turn' ale much in the same way as milk turns in the heat of the sun - a common enough occurrence in those days. She was declared a witch; her accusers left her in no doubt as to how they felt about her, nor how they would deal with her:

> 'The faggot of Hell lycht on thee, and Hellis cauldrone may thow seith in !'

It needs no translation.

In 1607, Bartie Patersoun [Paterson] of Newbattle, near Dalkeith, was arrested for administering poison she claimed was medicine to a sick man and woman who subsequently died. She also reputedly cured James Brown of an unknown disease by giving him potions and massaging him with salve. She supposedly cured his son who was sick by washing the boy's shirt in a nearby loch, leaving the shirt there with the disease on it, as she later confessed. She used the same loch for water which she gave to Alexander Clark in Crichton, also near Dalkeith. Paterson told Clark to raise his cup and repeat the following words before he drank:

> 'I loft this water in the name of the Father, Son, Holy Ghost, to the good for the health for whom it is lifted.'

Bartie Paterson was executed.

The penalty for witchcraft was to be 'werrit '- strangled - to death, followed by burning. Sometimes it was worse. In 1608, the Earl of Mar complained to the Privy Council about several witches executed in Brechin - Pitcairn's *Criminal Trials* gives Broichtoun, or Broughton, Edinburgh, a misreading of the Earl of Haddington's notes; Haddington, a Privy Councillor, identified the place as Brechin - who 'wer brunt quick [alive] despite thair denial of the crime'; a few of these doomed women even 'brak out of the fyre and wes cast in quick in it agane quhilk thay wer brunt to the deid.' Whether this taxed the consciences of the Lords in Council unduly is not recorded; there is no reference to the incident in the *Register* for 1608. However, in the following year, their Lordships were considerably alarmed by the increase in the number of local trials, so much so that they were at pains to define the extent of the respective jurisdictions of the ecclesiastical and secular courts. The Kirk argued its case robustly; it insisted on retaining the right to try witches, the same right as had existed 'in tyme of Papistrie'. While the Privy Council concurred, it also upheld the right of the secular courts to conduct trials, hear evidence and pass sentences.

As mentioned earlier, Dalkeith was a dangerous place for witches. In 1609, a woman in Crichton, near Dalkeith, Jonet Drysdaill [Drysdale] was arrested on suspicion of witchcraft and the alleged murder of Andrew Michelson of Currie, Midlothian. The Dalkeith Presbytery secured a commission for trial by Sir William Hare of Preston, the king's depute and several Musselburgh bailies. Jonet's employer, Sir James Newton of Crichton and several of his retainers attacked the king's officer escorting Jonet to the Musselburgh Tolbooth. Freeing her, Newton took her back to Crichton; clearly, she was more to him than just a common servant. After this, Newton's manservant -

also called Newton - appeared at the Crichton minister's manse and threatened him with a sword and expulsion from the manse if he tried to arrest Janet again. No less a person than Sir George Home, Earl of Dunbar, the king's chief representative in Scotland, ordered the Newtons to appear in Musselburgh to answer for their 'insolence'. What transpired next is not known; however, Jonet appears to have escaped her accusers as there is a reference to her being bailed for 500 merks in the Privy Council *Register* for 1607-10. The case is interesting because it illustrates how determined some parishes were in seeking out and trying witches. Dalkeith figures again in the same year when Geilis Johnstoun [Johnston] complained to the Privy Council that she was being held in custody by the Presbytery on suspicion of witchcraft. It is not surprising to find that among her accusers was the Crichton minister, William Penman, whom Sir James Newton's manservant had threatened. Geilis Johnston supported her plea to the Privy Council with a character reference. She said she was of good behaviour, had lived in Musselburgh for thirty years and had never been accused of any crime, let alone witchcraft. The Privy Council ordered the Dalkeith Presbytery to drop all proceedings against her. It almost seemed that a more enlightened attitude to witchcraft was emerging. Sadly, it was to be short-lived.

In 1610, the Earl Marischal petitioned the Privy Council about what he described as the inconvenience and scandal caused by the church courts; he recommended that these courts should try only special cases, although he failed to define such cases. There was dissension in the subsequent Privy Council debate on the matter; at least one voice - a bishop's - was raised against this interference. The Lords pondered the question and came up with a compromise. The majority view was for trial by secular courts; it was decided however that church courts could try those caught performing an act of witchcraft. The Lords took the trouble to give an example; the kirks might try anyone apprehended in the act of making a spell or found in 'any kirkyard raising deid bodies and cutting off thair joyntes or dansing in any desert[ed] kirk at midnight.' Church courts were expressly forbidden to try cases based on hearsay, rumour or gossip; these were to be investigated by secular courts.

In 1611, two women suspected of witchcraft in Morayshire, Marioun Tailyeour [Taylor] and Marjory Mongomerie, were tried by the Bishop of Moray and the Presbytery of Elgin who pronounced them guilty of giving

> 'wicked consultationis and divilische charmes to the poore ignorant people'.

A local commission was granted for the trial in 1612. We do not know the outcome but it is more than likely that the women were executed. Trials were on the increase yet again; between 1612 and 1617, more than a score took place up and down the country, twelve of them occurring in Dunbar, East Lothian, in 1612-13.

A classic and particularly tragic case of cruelty masquerading as justice took place in 1618 at Irvine, in Renfrewshire. Margaret Barclay was accused of witchcraft which had caused the loss of a ship and practically all its crew and passengers. The case is extraordinary in the annals of the witchcraft trials, so much so that it moved Sir Walter Scott to record it in his book *Letters on Demonology and Witchcraft*. The circumstances are particularly poignant as well as confusing. Apparently, Margaret Barclay, the young, respectable wife of Archibald Dean, a local burgess, had quarrelled with her sister-in-law, Janet Dean, who was married to Margaret's brother-in-law John, her husband's brother. The reason for the quarrel is not entirely clear; one account attributes it to theft, John Dean having allegedly stolen money from Margaret. More convincingly, a second account states that Margaret and Janet Dean quarrelled about petty theft on Margaret's part, a crime of which she was totally innocent. Whatever the reason, Maragret Barclay cursed her sister-in-law Janet in the heat of the moment. She also raised an action for slander in the local church court; the kirk session declared the whole matter a minor domestic affair and bade the two women shake hands and resume their friendship. They did so publicly but later, Margaret said she was only acting in obedience to the kirk and that she would settle the score herself. Her brother-in-law John Dean was the skipper of a merchant ship, ironically named *The Gift of God*. Owned by Provost Andrew Tran or Train of Irvine, the ship was laden - possibly overladen - with a full cargo in which several local people had invested their savings. The ship set sail with a full crew and several passengers including Train. It was wrecked off the coast of Cornwall near Padstow a few weeks later and all but two of those on board perished. Tongues began to wag, principally that of Janet Dean who had lost her husband as well as her source of income. Margaret's overbearing sister-in-law reminded several people that she had cursed her. She had also been heard to curse *The Gift of God* as it left its home port. Margaret was arrested on suspicion of witchcraft.

The trial involved four people. The real villain of the piece was John Stewart, an itinerant vagabond posing as a clairvoyant or fortune-teller. He visited Provost Train's wife, telling her she was a widow as the ship had been lost. Rather than receive a reward for his clairvoyance, Stewart was arrested on suspicion of complicity with Margaret. Initially, he told his accusers that Margaret Barclay had pleaded with him to teach her the magical arts so that she might get 'gear, kye's milk, love of man, her heart's desire on persons who had done her wrong and that she might obtain the fruit of sea and land.' There is a false ring about this, given the young woman's hitherto unblemished character. Stewart said he had told her he couldn't teach her such things as he had no powers of sorcery. His tale sounds somewhat glib. After he was tortured, he confessed that he had visited Margaret's house to find her and two other women making clay images of people and a model of *The Gift of God*. He implicated Isobel Insh, saying she and her eight year-old daughter Margaret could corroborate his story and that Insh and another woman, Isobel Crawford, were Margaret's accomplices. It is thought that Stewart had frightened Isobel Insh and her daughter to confess. Two ministers interviewed the young and probably terrified child to obtain evidence against her mother. The child waxed poetic, adding to the story by claiming that the devil had appeared in the house that night in the shape of a black lap-dog which had flashed fire from its mouth and nostrils; she also said a black man had helped to make the effigies. One of the three confessed that Margaret Barclay had expressed the wish that salt water 'might never bear the ship' and that partans [crabs] might feast on the crew 'at the bottom of the sea.' It later emerged that Margaret and the two others had gone to the seashore one night to throw into the sea the clay images of *The Gift of God* and several people on board including Provost Train and John Dean. Stewart said when the images were cast into the waves, 'the sea raged, roared and became red like the juice of madder in a dyer's cauldron.'

Margaret Barclay, John Stewart and Isobel Crawford were tortured at the instigation of the Earl of Eglinton, a local magnate; he described Margaret's and Isobel's torture as 'gentle'. Isobel Crawford admitted she was an accessory to what had happened. Margaret confessed to the ridiculous charges against her; no doubt her thinking was confused by fear and pain. The only suspicious evidence her judges had against her was that she was often seen holding a sprig of rowan and a piece of red thread; when asked why she did so, she said it was to make her cow give milk. It seems to have escaped the notice of her accusers - perhaps this was deliberate - that in Scotland, rowan sprigs and red thread were considered effective protection against witches; none could have failed to know the supposed efficacy of the rowan tree in Scotland in this respect. Not one of the four involved in the trial escaped death. In his prison cell, John Stewart somehow managed to slip his fetters and hanged himself with the ribbons of his bonnet; Isobel Insh, attempting to escape from the kirk spire in which she was warded, fell from a great height and died of her injuries a few days later. On the very last day of the trial, Margaret had a glimmer of hope when her husband appeared in court, apparently with a lawyer. Archibald Dean, a respectable burgess who had no doubt lost money and friends as well as his brother in the shipwreck, had attended none of the court hearings either because he was afraid he would put at risk his reputation among the Irvine people or he believed his wife to be guilty of witchcraft and the crimes of which she was accused. There was no saving Margaret. She spoke for herself, retracting her confession and admitting she had falsely accused Isobel Crawford:

"All that I have confessed was in an agony of torture. And before
God all that I have spoken is false and untrue."
Then, turning to her husband, she said bitterly:
" Ye have been too long in coming."
Margaret Barclay and Isobel Crawford, the Irvine Witches, were strangled and burnt at the stake.

In 1621, the authorities in Inverkeithing, Fife, discovered six witches in their midst. The magistrates applied for a Privy Council commission to try Bessie Harlaw, Bessie Chalmers, Beatrix Mudie, Christian Hammyltoun, Margaret Kent and Margaret Chatto. The six women were accused of

'witchcraft, sorcerie, and useing of charmes and utheris divilishe
practizes offensive to God, sclanderous to the trew religion, and
hurtfull to our good subjects.'
The women were examined by the minister and magistrates of Inverkeithing; the first five named confessed their guilt, accusing Margaret Chatto as the chief witch with most dealings with the devil. Margaret was examined a second time and a report of the proceedings was sent to the Privy Council. With her accomplices arranged against her and no doubt after further torture, events proved too much for her. She broke down and confessed everything. In all probability, the six women were executed; Stephen's *History of Inverkeithing and Rosyth* identifies the place of execution as the Witch Knowe or Witch Hill to the east of the Forth Railway Bridge and south of the road passing under it towards the cemetery.

In 1622 occurred the curious case of Margaret Wallace, wife of John Dinning, a Glasgow tailor; she was tried by the High Court of Justiciary for several acts of witchcraft under the influence of Christian Graham, a notorious witch burnt earlier in the year. The two women seemed to have been close friends; Margaret clearly worshipped her mentor who loved her in return. At her trial, Margaret admitted she had been a witch for eight or nine years. About four years earlier, she had been visiting neighbours and having fallen sick, she asked Christian Graham to visit her. Removing the sickness, Christian Graham reputedly said "Nothing shall aill my dear bird." Coming out of a neighbour's house, the two women passed a small child sitting on the stone stair outside the house. Margaret said that Christian put her sickness on the child. The child cried all night in pain; the following day, Margaret advised her neighbours to send for Graham. The mother refused, saying she'd have nothing to do with the devil or any of his servants. Unbeknownst to the mother, Margaret summoned her friend who came to the house, lifted the child, said some words over it and cured it. Margaret and Christian may be described as white witches. Even so, Margaret's adulation for her mentor did not deter her from at least one vindictive act. She hated Cuthbert Greig, a local cooper, for making insulting remarks about her friend; she put a spell on him, saying he would be unable to work in a few days. Greig fell sick and in despair, he asked Margaret to fetch Christian Graham to help him. She did so and he was cured. Margaret was executed.

Inverkeithing figured again in trials in 1623, when thirteen women and two men were accused of witchcraft. The first trial, that of Bessie Anderson and Marjorie Aitkyne [Aitken] appears to have been swift and resulted in execution. Another, that of Thomas Greave, is interesting in that he appears to have carried on a medical practice using witchcraft. At his trial, he confessed that to get rid of a disease, he ordered a large fire to be lit, took a live hen and put it in a hole in the north side of the house, then carried it inside and held it under the patient's armpit, then cast it into the fire alive. The objective was of course to transfer the sickness from the person to the hen. He also cured people by washing their shirts in south-running water; he could also effect a cure by passing his patient through a hasp of yarn or wool three times, then throwing the yarn on the fire where it reputedly turned blue. Thomas was examined by an assize which heard the depositions of several parish ministers; he was pronounced guilty of witchcraft and burnt to death.

Next in that year, Inverkeithing was granted a commission to try Beatrix Thomsone, Christiane Balfour, Jonnet Robesoun [Robson], Bessie Logie,

Margaret Bull, Jonat Keirie, Margaret Merschell [Marshall], John Young, Margaret Kynnell, Christian Harlaw, Marjory Gibson, Marion Henderson and Elizabeth Broun - the last six are not named in the Privy Council commission but are referred to in the history mentioned above. Balfour, Bull, Logie, Marshall, Young, Kynnell, Harlaw, Gibson and Brown all fled 'thus taking the guilt upon them.' Margaret Kynnell and Marjory Gibson were caught and tried along with Marion Henderson; the first two confessed to their crimes but Marion Henderson proved more stubborn, even offering herself for trial. In all probability, the three women received the death penalty, bringing the total to six executions in Inverkeithing in less than two years. Fife, virulently anti-Popish and later a hotbed of extreme Covenanting views, was not a good place to be accused of witchcraft at any time; Inverkeithing and Culross, where seven women were brought to trial and probably executed, were described as 'nests of the epidemic,' borne out by the fact that at this time, nearly half of the commissions issued by the Privy Council were requested by these burghs. Was this in part due to the famine which visited Scotland that year? Perhaps that may have accounted for the rising number of witches caught between 1622 and 1623.

In 1624 occurred the convoluted case of Issobell Falconner [Falconer] of Eyemouth, Berwickshire. Isobel was accused of witchcraft on at least two occasions and probably a third which is not recorded. The first occasion was in 1606, when she outwitted her accusers by petitioning the Privy Council about the competency of the sheriff-depute in Berwick. Isobel argued her case well; she said he wasn't a fit person to try her for such a serious crime as witchcraft. The Privy Council concurred, dismissed the sheriff-depute and the case was dropped on 29th August, 1606. Curiously, Larner's *A Source-Book of Scottish Witchcraft* erroneously states that Isobel was executed on that date. Witches can cause trouble even today!

There must have been a second attempt to try her in the intervening years between 1606 and 1624, the latter being the year when a further commission to try her was granted by the Privy Council. In the words of the commission, Isobel had

> '....most subtilie and faislie alledgeit [on a previous occasion] she wes with chyld.'

Referring to that unspecified occasion, the commission stated that she had been released from custody on condition that she present herself for trial after the baby was born which:

34

'....after mony yeirs is not done.'

It is likely that in the third attempt to try her, Isobel's resourcefulness failed; while there is no record of the outcome of the final trial, she was probably executed for contempt if not for witchcraft.

Between 1618 and 1625, over sixty cases were reported in the Privy Council *Registers*; of these, twenty-one occurred in Inverkeithing. From 1625 to 1627, the witch hunt was concentrated in Fife and Aberdeenshire; Wemyss, Dysart and Kirkcaldy between them tried sixteen women and one man for witchcraft. Five of the women arrested in Dysart in 1626-27 were named in the depositions of several witches who 'worthelie sufferit death for witchecraft in our burgh of Dysart and deit penitentlie' - probably three who had been executed the year before. One of the women, Elspet Ross from either Wemyss or Dysart, managed to escape to England but she was later brought back to face her tormentors. Like Isobel Falconer of Eyemouth, Elspet said she was pregnant; the records are silent on the outcome of her trial, although it is more than probable that Elspet Ross was executed since she had compounded her guilt by running away.

About this time, the Privy Council was having further thoughts about granting commissions for local trials. The Lords in Council were growing alarmed by the 'obscure and dark' information coming to them from those who wished to try witches. It seemed for a moment that light was about to shine in those dark days. But yet again, the Privy Council did not feel strong enough to take a firm stance against the Kirk. Once more they compromised. Perhaps more anxious than the Kirk to protect the innocent and punish the guilty, the Council decreed that all indictments should be referred to the diocesan bishop for his consideration before requests were submitted for warrants to hold secular trials at local level. In this decision can be seen two things. The chief administrative body in the country was aware that something was seriously amiss; the second was that devolving power to the bishops - already unpopular among radical presbyterians since their restoration to the church by James VI in 1609 - on whether local witch trials should proceed, the Council was, in effect, making them scapegoats. What did it matter if they came to arbitrary decisions? They were disliked in any case. In doing so, perhaps the Lords in Council were mindful of the bishop who in 1610 had complained about secular interference in what the Kirk considered its divine-given right to try witches first and institute legal proceedings afterwards.

In Aberdeenshire in 1626, twenty women and three men were arrested under a single commission issued by the Privy Council. In 1628, it was un-healthy to curse anyone in anger or even in jest anywhere in Scotland. By 1629, the epidemic seemed unstoppable; it would not end until 1633, by which year more than two hundred and fifty people had been tried, the majority almost certainly going to the stake.

In 1628, Dalkeith yet again figured in the witch hunt when Margaret Unes of Borthwick and Janet Schitlington of Newbattle were arrested. Margaret Unes was indicted with using alchemy to bring about the death of Lord Borthwick and the wife and children of James Borthwick of Newbyres. She and Janet Schitlington were also accused of murdering the Earl of Lothian; clearly, the women had a grudge against those men who were probably their landlords. Whether they were executed is not known but given the rank and status of their alleged victims, it is more than likely. It was at this time that the Presbytery of Dalkeith petitioned the Privy Council to allow it to impound the assets of witches to meet the costs of their trial and execution. The Presbytery argued its case well; it had been so

> 'troubled with the discoverie, apprehending, examination, entear-taining [sic] and execution of nombers of wretched and miserable personis guiltie of witchecraft'

that churches had been obliged to use money from the poor box to meet the costs. The Privy Council did not hesitate to concede to the demand.

In seventeenth century Scotland, the law on witchcraft often discriminated in favour of the well-to-do at the expense of those less so. A classic example of this occurred at the end of 1628 involving an East Lothian woman and the 'Lee Penny'. Isobel Young, the widow of George Smith, a portioner or tenant farmer in East Barns, near Dunbar, successfully cured some cattle of a disease known as the 'Routting evil' - excessive roaring and bellowing among cattle, probably caused by drought - which had broken out all over the county that year. Somehow, Isobel had learnt of the Lee Penny, a semi-precious stone owned by the Lockharts of Lee in Ayrshire. The origins of the Lee Penny and how it came into the possession of the family is recounted in S M Lockhart's genealogy of the family *A History of the Lockharts of Lee and Carnwath: Seven Centuries*. A colourful fourteenth century tale, it is historical fact for all that. After the death of Robert the Bruce in 1328, the 'Good' Sir James Douglas - the Black Douglas, Bruce's brilliant guerrilla leader during the Wars of Independence - went on pilgrimage with the king's heart, intending to lay it to rest in Jerusalem. As is known, Douglas had the king's heart embalmed and

36

placed in a locked casket; what is perhaps less well-known is that the key to the casket was entrusted to a knight, Sir Simon of Lee whose family later adopted the surname Lockhart for obvious reasons. On route to the Holy Land, the Black Douglas and Sir Simon got no further than Spain, large areas of which were then occupied by the Moors. Sir James Douglas went into battle against the Moors, throwing the casket containing Bruce's heart before him, rallying his men with the war-cry that Bruce was once again leading them to victory. Douglas was killed in the fight but somehow the casket was retrieved and brought back to be buried in the grounds of Melrose Abbey, where it now rests. In the course of the campaign, Sir Simon took prisoner a wealthy young emir whom he put to ransom. The emir's mother subsequently came to Lee's tent to negotiate the sum, during the course of which she let fall from her purse a semi-precious stone, which Lee claimed as part of the ransom. At first, the woman was reluctant to part with the jewel but Lee insisted she hand it over. Knowing her son might be put to death, she did so. She also told Lee that the jewel had magical properties; it could stop bleeding, cure fevers and hydrophobia contracted from the bite of a rabid dog and sickness in horses and cattle. Years later, one of Sir Simon's descendants mounted the stone on a silver groat (a four penny piece) and thus the Lee Penny acquired its name. Yet another descendant, Sir James Lockhart of Lee used the Lee Penny to cure some illness or other around the beginning of the seventeenth century. Learning of this, the Synod of the Church of Glasgow accused him of sorcery and brought him to account; however, being a wealthy landowner, he was able to argue his way out of the charge and received only a rebuke from the Kirk.

As for Isobel Young, she was neither influential or lucky in her dealings with the Laird of Lee. She travelled to Ayrshire to beg the loan of the Lee Penny to cure the sick cattle at East Barns. Lee told her that wasn't necessary since if the Penny were dipped in a flagon of water, it would be sufficient to effect a cure. Isobel gave the water to the cattle of several people in her home district and they were cured instantly. The Presbytery of Dunbar got wind of this and acted against her. Isobel Young found herself on trial for the crime of witchcraft and sorcery. Her name was also linked with two women from nearby Pinkerton, Margaret Melross or Mewross [Melrose] and Janet Achesoun [Aitchison] who had been tried for witchcraft four years earlier but acquitted on lack of evidence against them. The two women were arrested a second time and taken to Edinburgh for trial. There they confessed that along with Isobel Young, they had met with the devil to plan the murder of George Clarkson of Dunbar. This time, the pair were unlucky; they were found guilty of witch-craft by the High Court of Justiciary and executed on Edinburgh's Castlehill early in 1629. During her trial, Isobel Young, already accused by these women, was found to have had associations with a third local witch, Christian Grintoun, executed several years earlier for witchcraft. It transpired that Isobel's husband, George Smith, had once seen Christian Grintoun emerge from his barn in the shape of a cat and transform herself into human form. When he told Isobel about this, she'd warned him it would go ill with him if he told anyone about the incident. Whether he kept silent or not is not known but the following day, he dropped dead while ploughing, a common enough occurrence in those days. The case was proven. Even although Isobel had not gone alone to fetch the Lee Penny potion, none of her companions was tried for witchcraft; they were simply rebuked by the Dunbar Presbytery. No action was brought against James, Laird of Lee. Isobel Young was found guilty of the crime of sorcery and executed on Castlehill, Edinburgh on 4th February 1629.

Edinburgh Castle in 1647 (note the gallows in right foreground)

On 3rd November 1629, Katharine Oswald, wife of Robert Acheson in Niddrie, Edinburgh was 'deponed' by Elizabeth Steven, a confessed witch who, before her execution, said that Katharine was a witch by habit and repute. She admitted that Katharine had been with her and other witches at Prestonpans using charms the night of a great storm in 1625. Katharine was also named as a witch by Alexander Hamilton, himself prosecuted for witchcraft. He said they were with many witches and warlocks between Niddrie and Edmonston, near Musselburgh, where they met the devil. Katharine and the devil copulated that night. Katharine's judges were no doubt shocked by this revelation although it was quite common in trials. Katharine Oswald was accused of using evil charms and incantations for taking off and laying on diseases on both human beings and animals. By way of example, she had bewitched a cow so that it gave blood instead of milk; she laid spells on the cows of people who had displeased her so that the beasts went mad; she cured a young boy of the 'trembling fever'(ague) by pulling up a nettle by its roots on three successive mornings, casting the roots over his gate and returning home before sunrise. The boy soon recovered. Katharine was executed.

As for Alexander Hamilton, her accuser, he was tried for his crimes as a warlock. He confessed he had met the devil in the form of a black man in the Kingston Hills in East Lothian. At that meeting, he agreed to be the devil's servant. The second meeting took place in the Garleton Hills, near Haddington, where the devil appeared on a black horse at midnight. Hamilton said he renounced his baptism and accepted four shillings from his new master. The devil told him he would never want for anything. He was shown how to summon his master by striking the ground three times with a stick, calling out "Rise up, foul thief!" Hamilton said they met on several occasions thereafter, when the devil appeared as a dog, a cat and a crow. He confessed that he had destroyed Provost Cockburn's mill by pulling out three corn stalks from the provost's stacks and burning them. He was executed in January 1630.

Another case of shipwreck occurred that year, this time in Aberdeen. Marion Hardie of Fraserburgh was accused of wrecking a ship owned by Richard Cadenhead of Futtie. During her trial, Marion named her accomplices - Margaret Lumsden, Mallie Cowper and Marion Rodgie. The four women were seen together at the mouth of the river Dee, throwing stones into the sea as Cadenhead's boat was coming in to dock. The ship sank and all but one of the crew lost their lives. Marion Hardie went on to name another ten accomplices, eight of whom had the forename Margaret - a nightmare for the clerk of court. We know that Marion Hardie was executed; it is more than likely that her three accomplices met the same fate but we have no indication of the fate of the other ten women.

Several trials which took place between 1631 and 1634 are of particular interest because they are well-documented and show disparity in treatment by the latter year. The first concerns John Philp or Philip, a vagabond who roamed through Banffshire. On 8th September 1630, the Privy Council granted a commission to James, Lord Deskford and the sheriff of Aberdeen and his deputies to try 'Johne Philpe, vagabond, for witchcraft.' The report of the subsequent trial is extensively covered in the Privy Council *Register* dated 22nd February 1631. Philp was tried in the Banff courthouse by Deskford and Robert Wilson, the sheriff-depute; William Sharp, notary public, was appointed clerk of court and James Winchester, a Banff burgess, was appointed procurator fiscal. The doomster was Alexander Mure. That he was appointed before the trial seems significant and perhaps indicates that Philp was presumed guilty before the trial began. James Winchester was assisted by the entire ministry of the Presbytery of Fordyce along with Thomas Mitchell, minister at Turriff, William Steinson, minister at Fintry and James Melville, minister at Alva. At the outset, Philp was described as a vagabond who

'this lang tyme bygone suspect and delate guiltie of the detestable cryme of witchecraft, sorcerie, inchauntment, useing of charmes and utheris devilish practises offensive to God, scandalous to the true religion, and offensive to dyverse his Heines subjectes; togidder with the dittay indyteing the said Johne Philpe of the poyntes under writin, deny it and confessit as followes.....'

Philp was accused of charming Gilbert Leslie in the parish of Fintry by putting him through 'a hesp of yairne' - probably a skein of unwashed wool - which he of course denied. He put a spell on Alexander Clark, also of Fintry, by taking away his illness and putting it on an ox valued at 40 merks (£40 Scots), the ox dying afterwards. After 'lang dealing' - in witch terms, torture - Philp confessed that he had put spells on many Fintry parishioners suffering from fever; he also said he had had to leave Fintry 'for feare of Mr William Steinson, minister thaire.' Charge after charge followed. He had 'washed' several people; washing was akin to baptism except that the water had to come from a southward running stream. Philp had washed Alexander Gifford in Alva and charmed James Mathieson's son in Banff to free him from a fever; in this he said he was assisted by the queen of the fairies, which Mathieson senior confirmed. He washed George Fraser of Oathlaw, Banff, by using water from a south facing well, there being no stream conveniently near; he washed the man thrice and he recovered. A lighter touch to this was that Fraser's cat jumped over the water which had been thrown to the ground; it went berserk and leapt on the church officer, Walter Fraser of Alva, almost strangling him. Philp washed Janet Alexander, wife of George Wallace in Insch-there are gaps in the records at this point - then John Ferguson in Forefaulds. In his testimony, Ferguson said Philp nearly set the house on fire during his ministrations.

It gets worse. Philp charmed a cow belonging to the wife of Thomas Glen by using a belt which he had tied round the body of a dead child. He charmed Margaret Eyott, wife of Thomas Weddell in Banff, James Cumming's wife in Seatown of Banff and John Pittendreich's wife Janet, also in Banff. He cured Robert Smyth's mare by putting a piece of leather over the horse's womb and her back; charmed the oxen of Thomas Byithe with hasps of wool; washed Helen Turner, wife of Robert Wight at the Miln of Alva; charmed Andrew Gilbert and Alexander Gates in Whitehill against fever; washed Margaret Gellie in Davry, Elspet Thomson in Berrihillok, Gilbert Symes' wife in Badinspink, George Raeburn's wife in Toristown and Agnes Milne in Milntown of Deskford. He cured John Donald of Strathblay by potions and an 'ourison' – incantation - and George Braibner in Cullen, this last incident verified by George Douglas, minister at Cullen Kirk who had mentioned it to a friend in Fordyce. He said that it was made clear to Philp that his spells were not welcome; when Philp left the house - no doubt without receiving either alms or payment - Braibner's condition worsened.

The case against Philp was not in any doubt. Having already appeared before Fintry Kirk Session and warned about his behaviour, he had been banished from Fintry and several other parishes in the locality. A jury of fifteen was appointed to hear the evidence and testimony of witnesses; the foreman of the jury, John Abernethy of Tobax delivered the unanimous verdict of guilty of sorcery, charming and imposture and that Philp was 'worthie of deith.' Furthermore, John Philp had himself confessed his guilt and agreed that he deserved to be executed. He admitted he was aware that his washings and other devilish practices had brought harm to people. The sentence read by Doomster Mure was that Philp be bound to a stake and strangled and burnt at the common place of execution. Sentence was carried out immediately.

The next case is that of Christian Paterson who lived in Hermiston, Haddingtonshire [East Lothian]. In 1631, she was indicted on the following seven counts:

'The laying on of ane heavie disease upon Jonnett Forrester, spouse to Baillie of Templefield; laying on ane madnesse and phrensie upon Katherine Allane, her servant;

For the cruell murdering be witchecraft of umquhill Elizabeth Caldecleuche, spouse to Archibald Maissoun in Samwelstoun and Bessie Maissoun, his daughter;

The cruel murdering be witchecraft of James Knight of Hirdmistoun;

For laying on be witchecraft of ane heavy sicknesse upon Elizabeth Anderson;

For the death taike [mischief] and decay of thair goods;

For wracking and undoing of James Wadie in Saltoun be witchecraft.'

Christian Paterson was executed by order of the Privy Council, which is unusual.

Another case is a classic example of the self-confessed witch. Some women suspected of witchcraft appear to have been eager to confess and were even boastful about their knowledge and use of the black arts; a few even gave themselves up to the authorities, which suggests they were either suffering from a mental disorder, hallucinations or downright egotism. The case of Marion Mure of Leith is a typical example of self-delusion and mental illness. In 1632, Marion went to the bailies in Leith and freely volunteered the fact that she had renounced her baptism and been given the name Katharine by the devil himself. The Privy Council directed she be examined by a physician - an unusual reaction to suspected witchcraft. The physician examined the poor woman and diagnosed her complaint as hypochondria; he prescribed medicine for her at the local apothecary which Marion disdained to take, insisting she was a witch. Before she was executed, she named Helen Hamilton and Marion Lumsden of Leith as witches. Helen Hamilton, a widow, complained to the Privy Council about the torture inflicted on her; the local magistrates put her in the stocks, laid heavy iron bars on her legs so that her flesh was cut to the bone. At first she confessed she was a witch, then retracted. Perhaps she was acquitted but this is unlikely; the other woman, Marion Lumsden was not considered a witch. The damage a demented old woman could do simply by naming other people was incalculable; occurring all over Scotland.

The next case concerns Alison Nisbet of Hilton, Berwickshire, in 1632. She was indicted for witchcraft by curing a woman of illness by bathing her and uttering words in a strange language, then running thrice round the woman's bed *widdershins* - contrary to the sun's path - repeating this chant:

"The bones to the fire and the soul to the devil."

She played out this charade with other people; she caused the death of a serving girl by putting enchanted water on the threshold of the house where she worked. But perhaps most significantly, she gave birth to an illegitimate child by a married man, She was executed.

In 1633, the unfortunately named William Coke and his wife Alison Dick were found guilty of witchcraft in Kirkcaldy. The kirk and the burgh council agreed to share the expense of their execution which took place on the seashore; the costs are recorded in the session records as follows:

Item	In purchasing the commission	9	3	0
Item	For one to go to Finmouth for the laird to sit upon their assize as judge	0	6	0
Item	For harden to be jumps for them [hempen coats]	3	10	0
Item	For making of them	0	8	0
	Summe for the Kirk's part Scots	17	10	0
	The Town's part of the Expences Debursed xtraordinarliy upon William Coke and Alison Dick			
Imprimis	For ten loads of coal to burn them, 5 merks	3	6	8
Item	For a tar barrel, 14s	0	14	0
Item	For towes [the hangmans rope]	0	6	0
Item	To him that brought the executioner	2	18	0
Item	To the executioner for his pains	8	14	0
Item	For his expences here	0	16	4
Item	For one to go to Finmouth for the laird	0	6	0
	Summe Town part Scots	17	1	0
	Both Scots	34	11	0
	Or Sterling	2	17	7

Perhaps this document illustrates the extraordinary and shameful part played by the church in witchcraft trials.

The absurd credulity of those appointed to hear the evidence in local trials is unbelievable, even for the time. How could men sit complacently and take seriously the nonsense in indictments brought against supposed witches? A graphic illustration of this is found in the account of the trial of Marion Layland, a beggar woman in Orkney. On 29th May 1633, Marion was brought before a local court on suspicion of witchcraft. The indictment begins rather grandly by accusing her of contravening the *Witchcraft Act* of Mary, Queen of Scots; was this to lend some learned and academic credibility to the fatuity of the charges which followed? One suspects so. The first charge was that six or seven years earlier, she and a friend, Katherine Grieve, were discovered in an old house with the devil in the shape of a black man. The pair were discovered by Marion's grandson, tending his master's pigs. Katherine cried out:

"Take him for he will tell upon us !"

Marion replied that no one would believe the boy. Someone did, for the lad told his master and by evening the two women were in the stocks on Stronsay. The next charge was one of curing illness in Elspeth Sandeson who had been 'bereft of her sences' for some time. Marion's cure was a bowl of water into which she emptied something resembling salt from her purse; she then spat in it thrice and blew on it. She gave the potion to the serving woman, telling her to rub it on her mistress' hands and feet and she would be well again. She also warned the servant not to tell anyone about the charm or else she would never thrive. The woman disregarded this and died shortly afterwards. Marion confessed this to the Stronsay kirk session. She also cured the whole household of Helen Hamilton, wife to James Keith, of an insatiable thirst they had known for many days simply by giving them some small beer to drink - was the thirst caused by an excessive intake of whisky in that inhospitable climate? Another incident concerned several cows belonging to Margaret Thomson who complained to Marion that they refused to mate; she solved this simply by asking for and obtaining some alms. Next came an incident where a neighbour lost her supply of milk; she came to Marion for help and was told to go to the seashore and count nine waves breaking on the beach, then take some water from the tenth one and put it in her milk churn, which would and did restore her milk. Worse follows. Marion washed the feet of the cats of two fishermen, John Davidson and David Jokis in their bait-water so that they would catch more fish when she threw the water into the sea after their boats left shore.

She was refused alms by William Fotheringham's wife and put a curse on his best cow, which died. Perhaps even more absurd was the spell she reputedly put on Andrew Couper, skipper of a Stronsay barque two or three years earlier. Marion had been begging alms from him and he dismissed her thus:

"Awa wich carling, devil a farthing ye will fa [get]."

Marion went away grumbling, but there is no mention in the account that she put a spell on the skipper. Shortly afterwards, the boat put to sea and Andrew Couper was described as going mad, running about the deck and wanting to jump overboard; he was restrained by his son who, in doing so, took the madness from his father and he too began to race about the boat until one of the more perceptive crew members hit on a remedy. He took the ship's dog, placed it on the son's shoulders to remove the madness, then threw the poor creature into the sea! Every single charge made ends with the legend 'quhilk ye, rank wich, cannot deny.' Marion was cleared of the charges concerning the thirsty Keith family, causing the death of William Fotheringham's cow and using John Davidson's cat in a spell to increase his catch of fish; it does not seem to have taxed the court's conscience that illogically, she was found guilty of using David Jokis' cat for the same purpose! Marion's accomplice, Katherine Grieve was found guilty and branded on the cheek; she was also warned that if she appeared before the court again, she would be executed. As for Marion Layland, the verdict of the court was as follows:

'The Judges ordains the pannell [prisoner] to be carryit be the lock-man [executioner] to the Gallowhill, worryit to death and brunt to asches.'

The graveness of Alison Nisbet's and Marion Layland's crimes seem paltry in comparison with that of Elizabeth Bathgate, spouse of Alexander Pae, a maltman in Eyemouth in 1634. Despite eighteen charges being raised against her, she was acquitted. One of these involved the death of a child. She reputedly gave the child's mother an enchanted egg which produced a lump the size of a goose's egg in the child's body; the lump continued to grow until the child died. Apparently she had fallen out with the child's father, George Sprot, a clothmaker who had kept cloth belonging to her longer than she thought necessary; perhaps she thought Sprot had sold it. This was the reason given for the spell she put on the child. Another charge was that of causing lameness. A local man had called her a witch; she ran after him but unable to catch him, she shouted:

"Well, Sir, the devil be in your feet"

whereupon he became an impotent cripple. Elizabeth had been seen dancing *widdershins* in the mill at Eyemouth; in court, she said she had been simply amusing herself while she ground barley for malt. A witness said she had been dancing in this fashion because it was customary for witches to do so, especially in mills; the same witness said as soon as the miller appeared, she stood still, afraid that he would detect her true intention. Perhaps she got her revenge on the miller, as she was accused along with other witches of burning down the mill . She was supposed to have killed David Hynd watching the boats from the shore at Eyemouth during the herring drave. She was also accused of boarding a local boat with other witches, then causing it to sink with the loss of some lives. She reputedly made people sick, caused illness and death in animals; perhaps worst of all her 'crimes' was that she was seen by two young men in her Eyemouth backyard at midnight, bare-legged and talking to a man wearing green clothes. Such scandalous behaviour would have been particularly noted. Elizabeth Bathgate was named as a witch by Margaret Ballamie or Bellamie, an Ayton witch and by William Mearns, a local warlock who, when taken into custody, committed suicide before his trial. Elizabeth Bathgate was taken to Duns Tolbooth by Sir Patrick Home of Ayton and the local minister, John Home. She was subsequently removed to Edinburgh's Tolbooth to await trial. Her dozen prosecutors failed to turn up in Edinburgh, complaining to the Privy Council that the inclement February weather had prevented them from travelling from Duns. They further requested that the prisoner be returned to Duns and tried there. Elizabeth Bathgate complained to the Privy Council she could not possibly expect a fair trial in Duns; some time after June 1634, she was released from prison, possibly after having been tortured. Perhaps in Elizabeth Bathgate's case we may detect a mood of enlightenment in the Privy Council. In the same year as her trial, another Eyemouth woman, Isobel Sinclair, was freed on caution. Two years earlier, the Lords in Council had ordered John Balfour, a self-appointed witch-pricker from Corhouse to appear before them to explain his knowledge of witches and his powers of examination of them. He was declared a charlatan and ordered to cease his evil practices but not before he had pricked several women in Tranent who were subsequently burnt at the stake.

In the period 1625 to 1634, between three hundred and fifty and four hundred persons were tried for witchcraft in Scotland; not all of them received the death penalty but the figure underlines the strength of feeling against witches up and down the country. Particular black spots were Wemyss, Dysart and

Kirkcaldy in Fife and Aberdeenshire. In Peeblesshire, no fewer than twenty-six people were named in a local commission of 1629 and described as 'vehementlie suspect of witchcraft.' East Lothian and Berwickshire, always particular black spots, accounted for a considerable number of cases. By 1635, the second epidemic in the witch-hunt had run its course. Even so, the kirks continued to exhort their congregations to be vigilant and a scattering of cases were tried during the remainder of the third decade of the century. Perhaps the sinking of Charles I's treasure ship between Burntisland and Leith in a storm in 1633, supposedly caused by the Lancashire Witches lent credibility to the kirk's continuing stance. The king managed to escape drowning but his treasure ship was lost with its valuable cargo. (As this book is being prepared, attempts to locate the ship are in progress.) The Lancashire Witches were taken to London and hanged. Two of the last witches to be tried in Scotland at the end of this period were Helen Isbuster and Margaret Sandieson in Orkney.

Perhaps some communities were sickened by their excesses. The witch craze would lie dormant until the third major epidemic broke out in 1643 and grew to a crescendo during the English Civil War until the Cromwellian campaign in 1650-51 brought Scotland to its knees and ended the burning of witches for a time.

3

'Witchcraft Daylie Increaseth in This Land '

After 1634, there is a marked drop in the intensity of the witch hunt and consequently, the number of suspects brought to trial. But by 1643, the obsession with witches had begun again. We have already seen that some trials were not primarily about what we understand as witchcraft; politics, greed and envy were often the underlying motives. Kirk politics played an even greater part in the hunt after 1633, when Charles I came to Scotland. On 13th June that year, Charles I celebrated his coronation in Edinburgh after succeeding to the throne in 1625. He had come north in response to repeated Scottish invitations; his long-promised visit had taken eight years to materialise, which surely told the Scots something. At his coronation ceremony in the Abbey Kirk of Holyrood, Charles insisted on an Anglican service, which alienated many of his Scottish subjects; it was the first of several disputes he would have with the Established Church of Scotland.

It is at this time that the Covenanting spirit was born, or perhaps more accurately, came to the fore. Among other things, it would bring about the third major epidemic in the witch hunt. To understand the effects of the National Covenant on the subject in hand, it is necessary to revisit the events which led to its signing in 1638. The Scottish Reformation had established a Kirk whose religious tenets were soundly based, not on Lutheranism but Calvinism, with its bitter hatred and intolerance. The Calvinistic Presbyterians saw themselves as the Elect of God and damned the rest of the world for wickedness. In 1560, the Reformation in effect established a theocracy which would continue for the next four hundred years; in the mid-seventeenth century, the Kirk became the effective government of Scotland, supreme in matters secular as well as spiritual. Despite James VI's considerable achievement in restoring Episcopalianism in 1609 - the bishops presiding over secular as well as spiritual questions in every diocese were considered Papists - the Scots rejected what to the Kirk was the equally Popish English Common Prayer Book. The reformed Kirk ministers did as they pleased, answerable to none but kirk sessions and local presbyteries. The parish minister was not only leader of his flock, praying extempore and thundering sermons from the pulpit; he was also the local newsmonger. It was little wonder that the people filled the churches every Sunday; they were in fear and awe of their ministers, enduring their overlong sermons in order to learn what was happening in the wider world. The people enjoyed the antics of the hell-fire preacher, with his colourful tales about the wickedness of Papistry and the titbits of gossip about the great and the good. They also listened avidly to his exhortations to identify and denounce any of their neighbours whom they suspected of witchcraft.

Greyfriars Church around 1880; it was restored after a disastrous fire in 1845

In 1637, matters came to a head when Charles attempted to introduce the Church of England's Book of Common Prayer in Scotland.   On 23rd July 1637, members of the Scottish Privy Council, two archbishops and eight bishops solemnly filed into the Kirk of St Giles in Edinburgh to hear the first service conducted in accordance with the liturgy of the English Prayer Book. As the Dean began to read from the new prayer book, a riot broke out, involving as legend has it, Jenny Geddes, an Edinburgh housewife who reputedly threw her creepie-stool at the Dean, shouting that he had had the audacity to say Mass in her 'lug' or ear.   The unruly rabble was quickly ejected by the church officers and the Kirk's doors locked against them.   The disaffected spread the news throughout the High Street, Edinburgh's main seat of government, law-enforcement and business.   What was not known at the time was that the riot had been organised well in advance by others; the rioters became political insurgents in the ensuing six months. The Presbyterians finally lost patience with a king who had arrogantly brushed aside their form of religious worship and they took decisive action. In 1638, the National Covenant was drawn up and signed in Greyfriars Churchyard. The Covenanters swore to oppose any attempts to interfere further with their version of the Presbyterian form of worship as they believed it to be more pure than that practised in England. The document was sent to every parish in Scotland with the order that everyone must sign it or if they could not write, that their signatures be notarised. It is said that children as young as ten years were made to sign. In certain areas like the South-West and Fife - both virulently anti-Episcopalian - some signed in their own blood. Ominously, those who refused to put their hand to the Covenant were identified by name; perhaps those who were black-listed would later be accused of something much worse.

The Covenant was the inspiration of two men, Alexander Henderson, a Fife minister and Archibald Johnston of Wariston, a young Edinburgh lawyer. The idealistic Johnston rather grandly described the signing of the Covenant as 'the glorious marriage day of the Kingdom with God.' A year later, the stage was set for revolution. The Covenanters and the king were openly preparing for armed conflict. In somewhat crude and fumbling attempts to impose his royal will, Charles had managed to alienate the three kingdoms of England, Scotland and Ireland in just over a decade. What had begun as a religious quarrel in the north was nothing compared with the full scale civil war in the south; because of their violent opposition to Charles' religious policies, the Scots threw in their lot with the English parliamentary forces. It is at this time that the spectre of witches again grew large, although at first, Kirk and government were preoccupied with more pressing matters.

The history of the English Civil War is well-documented and needs only brief mention. In turn, Charles and the English parliament approached the Scots, seeking their help in the conflict. Reluctant at first to be drawn into what they saw as a purely English affair - lack of finance being a major factor - the country's leaders finally agreed to support the parliamentary cause but at a price; they insisted their English allies become party to the Solemn League and Covenant in 1643, a contract which would guarantee the 'firm peace and union' of Scotland and England, the rooting out of Popery, Prelacy, superstition (!), heresy, schism and profaneness, preservation of the Scottish form of religious worship and – significantly - the reformation of the religions in England and Ireland 'according to the Word of God and the example of the best Reformed Churches' - the Covenanters' own. The last clause in the Covenant was deliberately vague; implicit in it was the Covenanters' determination that this would result in the union of two separate Calvinist traditions with the Scottish form of Presbyterianism uppermost. The English went along with the undertaking out of necessity rather than enthusiasm. The Army of the Covenant under the command of Alexander Leslie crossed the Border in January 1644 to take up arms against the king.

The war went badly for Charles from the outset; desperately short of men and material by the end of 1647, he attempted to enlist Scottish support to continue the war. The moderate wing of the Covenanters entered into negotiations with Charles, naming the price for their support - nothing less than a three-year experimental period of Scottish Presbyterianism in England and the ultimate union of the three kingdoms as envisaged by his father, James VI and I. However, this time the king did not feel obliged to accept the Covenant and the Scots negotiators conceded this point. The whole cornerstone of the Covenanting policy was thus rescinded at a stroke, an act considered by many historians as the biggest u-turn of that century and certainly abhorred by the 'pure' Covenanters of the Kirk. There were consequences for the country as a whole and for witches in particular, as will be seen. The Covenanters who signed the treaty, or Engagement, were subsequently known as Engagers and reviled by elements in the Scottish Kirk for having sold out the Covenant. Within a year, the Engagers were completely discredited after their defeat by Cromwell at Preston.

By 1649, the Kirk Party had become the predominant political force in Scotland. They reached the pinnacle of their power in 1650. During the period between 1640 and 1649, the General Assembly of the Church of Scotland was able to pass acts for the suppression of witches in 1640, 1643, 1647 and 1649. The last of these authorised the establishing of a Commission of ministers, lawyers and physicians to consider the trial and punishment of witches, or those who consulted known witches. Of its thirty-three members, twenty-one were ministers, nine were lawyers and three were doctors - not surprisingly, we find the name of Sir Archibald Johnston of Wariston among the lawyers. Not content with purging the Scottish army of Engagers and Malignants in 1649-50, the fanatical and cruel Wariston was also determined to rid the nation of witches. There was little humanity in the pitiless creed of the Covenanters. The Kirk party was clear about its prime objective - the suppression of sin. Some of these dour men believed God was punishing the Covenanter-dominated church for failing in its duty to root out sin and evil. Although the Kirk was enjoying a measure of political power it had never known before and would never enjoy again after the defeat of the Army of the Covenant at Dunbar in September 1650, the Committee of Estates of the Scottish parliament was anxious to demonstrate its independence from ecclesiastical authority. In 1649, during the summer recess of parliament, the Committee issued no fewer than one hundred and seventy commissions to try witches, once again seen as the greatest threat to the country and certainly more so than the so-called Papist threat of 1637-38. In 1649, the Kirk strengthened the laws against witchcraft in a way which would preoccupy the superstitious imagination of church and state for the next twenty years.

So, against a background of religious fervour and national insecurity caused by the execution of Charles I in January 1649, the threat of witchcraft was again undermining the authority of the church and the mores of the land. The fires began to burn again. In that unsettled year of 1649, the witch hunt did not happen overnight. The mania had began much earlier, imperceptibly at first in 1641, when the Kirk exerted pressure on parliament to renew the acts against witchcraft, sorcery and consulting with witches. Spalding's *History of the Troubles in Scotland and in England 1624-45* registered the prevailing mood:

> '1643 - About this time many witches are taken in Anstruther, Dysart, Culross, Sanctandrois [St Andrews], and sindrie uther pairtis of the cost [coast] of Fyf. They maid strange confessionis and war brynt to the death.'

Between 1641 and 1649, there were more than sixty trials; many simply record that several witches were indicted at such-and-such a place. In Fife in 1643, thirty women were tried; one of them was accused of offending against *Deuteronomy*, chapter 18 - verses 10 to 11, which state that no one shall be a sorcerer, a charmer, a medium, a wizard, a necromancer - all of which were abominable to the Lord. At Queensferry in 1644, thirteen women were accused of witchcraft; eight of them went to the stake. Witches were burnt from Orkney to the Borders. For some in the Kirk, it was not happening quickly enough.

During the period of the witch hunt, Orkney enjoyed devolved administrative powers, which meant it was almost a separate state. This explains why no applications were needed for commissions to try witches and probably why so many there were executed. By 1643, the authorities in Orkney had brought to trial several witches; the records confirm at least ten executions, although it is likely this does not reflect the true figure. In that year, William Scottie, a vagabond, Jonet Thomesone, Helen Hunter, Cirstain Marwick and Thomas Cors were tried. Although the outcome of their trials is not recorded, they were probably executed. Where witchcraft was concerned, Orcadian justice was decisive. By comparison, nearby Shetland had also tried a few witches, although only two of them were confirmed executions.

In Orkney, Katherine Craigie was tried in 1640 and 1643. Among her 'crimes' were her attempts to cure Robert Robson or Costar, the terminally-ill husband of Janet Craigie, probably a relative. Before casting her spell, she swore Janet to secrecy. Her charm involved the use of three stones three times over three successive nights. The stones were put in the fire until sunset, when they were placed on the threshold until just before sunrise, then immersed in a bucket of water so that one of them would 'chirne and churle'. Katharine Craigie claimed the purpose of the spell was to discover whether

Robert's illness had been caused by a hill-sprite, a kirk-sprite or a water-sprite; perhaps not surprisingly, it turned out to be a kirk-sprite. Whatever the cure was, it failed and the poor man died. Janet Robson could not keep her promise to remain silent; she told her child about the incident. An enraged Katherine told Janet she would suffer for her indiscretion and caused a 'buckie' or large boil to sprout on her cheek. When the boil burst, it left the poor woman's face permanently disfigured; the flesh was drawn up to her right ear. Katherine Craigie was executed for witchcraft.

An English traveller in Scotland in 1643 commented that the deprivation of sleep was the favoured method of discovering witches. The kirk session in Dunfermline certainly took that view in the same year:

> '...the watchers to begin at sex houris at even[ing] and to byd and continue all the nyt and the day followeing till 6 at evin[ing] againe.'

In Fife, the authorities believed that sleep deprivation after capture was crucial in case the witches' old master might exercise power over them again. In 1644, Margret Thomsone, wife of Alexander Gray in Midcalder complained to the Privy Council that the minister of the parish had kept her awake for twenty days, naked except for sackcloth; he put her in the stocks and kept her apart

> 'from all company and wordly comfort'.

What, one wonders, was the minister's true motive? At least the Privy Council was sympathetic; Margaret was released on bail.

Between 1643 and 1644, forty-nine women were indicted for witchcraft, including six woman burnt at the Witch Knowe, Dunfermline. As mentioned earlier, of thirteen women arrested in Queensferry under the same commission, eight were executed. In April 1644, the Synod of Moray expressed grave concern about its witchcraft problem to the Privy Council; in the Synod's view

> '...the great increase of witchcraft, for the better repressing and more easy trial of the same, it is thought fit be Act of the General Assembly [of the Church of Scotland] there be commissions in every Presbytery for apprehending, trying and executing witches.'

The Kirk was clearly criticising what it believed to be a *laissez faire* attitude on the part of the central authorities.

In the same year, the burgh of Peebles was unable to dispose of its guilty witches and was obliged to send a local official, Alexander Lauder, to Edinburgh or Musselburgh for an executioner to 'deal with the impannelit [imprisoned] witches.' There is no record of the trials there, nor is it possible to determine how many witches were put to death - yet another example of a small community acting on its own initiative without reference to the Privy Council.

What was uppermost in the Kirk's mind in 1644 is apparent from the session records of the Presbytery of Strathbogie; rigid observation of the Sabbath, the suppression of witchcraft, the maintenance of a serious style of manners and the extirpation of Popery. Discipline was more austere than ever and punishment for breaking the rules was harsh. Penitents were obliged to wear sackcloth and sit on the penitential stool before the congregation. There was a rising scale of punishment; three Sundays for a first offence, a second offence attracted public humiliation for six successive Sundays and a third meant sackcloth and the stool for six months' of Sundays. Most punishments were usually for minor transgressions, certainly not in the same league as witchcraft.

By 1644, the witch hunt was slowly but steadily cranking into gear. Occasionally, some of the cases contain elements of grim if unintended humour, like that of Agnes Finnie in 1644. Agnes sold small goods at the Potterrow Port in Edinburgh. One day, she threatened William Fairlie's son with lameness because the boy had shouted a nickname at her, calling her Annie Winnie. The following day, the boy lost the power in his left side. Doctors who examined him said it was a clear case of witchcraft; when he subsequently died, the report of his death said his whole substance 'ran out of his ankle' which is obviously nonsense. Agnes next caused Beatrice Nisbet to lose the power of speech because she refused to pay interest on a small sum of money she'd owed Agnes for some time. Then she sold Jonet Grinton herrings that weren't fresh; when Jonet came to ask for her money back, Agnes lost her temper and cursed her, saying she'd never eat again. Jonet died shortly afterwards. Agnes tried to treat palsy in the child of John Buchanan and Bessie Currie; when she was brought into the house to attend to the child, Agnes asked the parents to sit in the next room and pray for it. Whatever she did made no difference; in fact the child grew worse and died eight days later. Perhaps the next incident is not unconnected with her attempts at faith-healing. Agnes fell out with the same Bessie Currie over a counterfeit sixpence she'd given her. In the course of the quarrel, she said the devil would bite Bessie; then for good measure, she 'laid' the sweating sickness on her husband, John Buchanan. In a quarrel with Euphame Kincaid, Agnes said she was a drunkard; Euphame Kincaid retaliated by calling Agnes a witch, to which she replied:

'If I was a witch, you and yours should have better cause to call me so.'

Shortly afterwards, a heavy wooden beam fell on Euphame Kincaid's daughter, crushing her leg. Agnes next fell out with Isobel Acheson over some matter; she said the devil would ride about Edinburgh with her and hers - a vague enough curse. However, the following day, Isobel fell off her horse and broke her leg. Agnes heard of the accident and made a point of visiting her,

saying
> 'See that ye say not that I have bewitched you, as other neighbours
> say.'

Agnes, growing alarmed by her 'power', was nonetheless unable to resist using it. Further charges were brought against her, one being that she made a woman blind. It is clear that Agnes Finnie was simple-minded, a lonely woman who lashed out at her neighbours when they displeased her. It was imagination working to excess in a period when the unexpected could happen at any moment. Agnes Finnie was executed.

In 1644, at least one sceptical voice was raised against the farce of trying witches. According to McCall's *History of the Parish of Midcalder*, Sir George Mackenzie, the future Lord Advocate, privately examined a few witches. In his own words:

> 'One of them who was a silly creature, told me under secrecy she
> had not confessed [she was a witch] because she was guilty.... [but
> because] ....she desired to be out of the world.'

It transpired that the poor woman, a beggar, preferred death to being thought of as a witch; she said she would be denied food and lodgings, beaten and have dogs set on her.

Like many Scottish communities in the 1640s, Dalgety in Fife was first visited by famine in 1644, then pestilence in 1644-45. In the latter years, people were forced to leave their homes and live in huts and no services were held in St Bridgid's, the local church, until it was fumigated. No doubt both disasters were blamed on the witches in Dalgety and nearby Aberdour. Dalgety kirk session minute-book records the examination of Robert Maxwell, described as a warlock living close by in Little Fordell. The Dalgety minister, Andrew Donaldson and four elders examined Maxwell and reported that he had confessed to 'witchcraft and paction with the devill'. Maxwell was subsequently tried by the local magistrates; despite evidence that he was simple, possibly feeble-minded - he had been '..... put from the communione for ignorance....' - he was found guilty of witchcraft. In his confession, Maxwell named several witches in the district, including Issobell Kelloch of Dalgety. The session clerk recorded the 'late ' Robert Maxwell's testimony which confirmed that Issobell had meetings with the devil.

Issobell Kelloch had long been suspected of witchcraft and recently denounced by several Aberdour witches prior to their execution. She was brought before the kirk session, which attempted to recover their expenses in bringing her to trial from Issobell's landlord, Lady Callender. Lady Callender bravely refused to pay a penny. The kirk session was thus obliged to find funds from another source; they decided to raid the poor box, confirmed by an entry in the session records for 1st July 1649:.

'Given off the [poor] boxe for Issobell Kelloch's charges in procuring ane commissione for her tryall, and in things that concerned her burning, 24 lib. 4. 4d.'

No doubt Robert Maxwell and Issobell Kelloch met their deaths on the Witches' Knowe, Aberdour at the hands of Pat Main, local witch burner and hangman

As mentioned above, Scotland was visited by a plague of great virulence in 1645. The Scottish parliament was forced to leave Edinburgh, moving first to Stirling, then Perth as the contagion swept northwards. Consequently, there were practically no witch trials that year since public executions attracted crowds which spread infection. Church gatherings, local fairs and markets were suspended during the epidemic. Nonetheless, two women of Creiche in Fife were hunted down; a woman was held in prison in Dunfermline, several in Midcalder and one in St Andrews. The plague lingered on until 1646; in that year only two women were arrested for witchcraft, in Elgin. One of them, Janet Cuj or Cowie escaped from her captors; it is not known what became of her co-accused, Margaret Murray of Spynie. There appear to have been no trials held in 1647, the first 'witch-free' year since 1600.

As already indicated, those of more moderate Covenanting opinion made a treaty in 1647 with an embattled Charles I, offering the king military support against the English parliamentary forces in exchange for certain promises concerning the future of the church in Scotland. As previously stated, the Engagers diluted the pure spirit of the Covenant by withdrawing the condition - or hope - that Charles I would embrace it. The Engagers would rue the day. After their defeat at Preston in September 1648, power passed to the Kirk Party. In a brief period of supremacy, the Kirk Party punished the Engagers for selling the Covenant short. In January 1649, parliament passed the *Act of Classes* which banned Engagers and Royalists alike from public office, which led to the purging of many from the army as well as central and local government. However, the purging did not divert attention from witches; in fact, the hunt intensified. In his contemporary account, *Historical Works,* Sir James Balfour states that between July and December 1649, many witches were executed in Fife, Perth, Stirling, Linlithgow, Edinburgh, Haddington and in the Merse [Berwickshire]. On 20th July that year, he witnessed the execution of twenty-seven women and three men and boys who had been tried under Privy Council commissions. He also cites the case of one witch who, in her deposition, said she had recently attended a meeting with the devil and about 500 witches. The propaganda value to the Kirk was inestimable.

At a small village two miles outside Berwick, two men and three women were burnt for witchcraft on 15th April 1649; a further nine followed them. The village contained only fourteen families - perhaps less than one hundred souls - and twenty of them ultimately went to the stake (Whitelock, *Memorialls*)

In the early part of 1649 occurred the trial of Robert, or Hob Grieve, in Lauder. Hob Grieve 'trafficked' or made false deals, deceiving the simple people in that part of the country. Imprisoned in Lauder Tolbooth, he confessed he was the devil's chief agent in the area, assembling his servants for meetings. He also said his wife, who had been burnt for witchcraft in Lauder twenty years before, had led him into a pact with the devil as they were both poor and the devil promised to make them rich if they served him. At his trial, Hob Grieve named many witches; however, the local magistrates concealed the name of one of them for a time for reasons best known to themselves. The devil apparently appeared before the woman and told her that although Hob had named her as a witch she should challenge him. Whatever the truth of the matter, the woman went to Lauder Tolbooth, called Grieve a warlock and a slave to the devil; she was told to go home as no one had accused her of anything. She refused to go away, vehemently denying she was a witch before the magistrates and town guard, who tried to get her to leave the place. Hob Grieve was not put off by her protests of innocence; when they next confronted each other, he reminded her he had visited her house many times to inform her about forthcoming meetings with the devil. The woman lost heart when he described several places she'd visited where the devil had been present; she broke down and confessed everything, begging the minister to intercede with God to save her. She was executed. Many others named by Grieve were executed, including one woman who rather generously forgave the ministers and magistrates for pronouncing her guilty of witchcraft. She also made the remarkable statement that she had confessed on purpose as she was weary of her miserable existence.

Perhaps one of the women executed on the testimony of Hob Grieve was Margaret Dunham who kept an inn at the Lauder end of the old herring road through the Lammermuirs from Dunbar. A full account of the expenses of her imprisonment and trial are preserved in Arnot's *Criminal Trials*. The bill was compiled by the factor of the estate - presumably where the inn was situated - as the owner was under age. His account makes interesting reading, although the total does not add up.

		£	s	d
Item	Watching of accused by William Currie and Andrew Gray, 30 days	14	0	0
Item	John Kincaid for pricking	6	0	0
Item	Food and drink and wine to above and his assistant	4	0	0
Item	For cloth [probably sackcloth] for the prisoner	3	0	0
Item	For two trees to make the gallows	xcs		
Item	For making the above and to the workmen	3	0	0
Item	For the hangman in Haddington and fetching him	4	14	0
Item	For food and drink and wine for the hangman	3	0	0

Item	For one man and two horses to fetch him and take him back to Haddington	xls		
Item	For food and drink for the prisoner	6	0	0
Item	For two officials	10	0	0
	Summa	92	14	0

Note: xcs = ninety shillings or £4 10s, and xls = forty shillings or £2

The factor stated that the expense of keeping Margaret in prison came to £65:14:4; he proceeded to itemise the various expenses as above. He also stated that the prisoner contributed £27 of her own towards the cost, thus reducing the net cost to £65:14:0. The above total does not tally; perhaps that has something to do with the seventeenth century method of book-keeping as Margaret's contribution is not itemised.

About this time, the civil authorities in Inverkeithing were having problems in dealing with witches, unusual for a locality notorious for its executions because of the zeal of its minister, Walter Bruce. Bruce was no respecter of persons; he also rejoiced in the reputation of being a successful witch-pricker in the eyes of the seventeenth century Presbytery of Dunfermline, although he experienced some difficulty in bringing to trial several witches in 1649. On 13th April, the Presbytery appointed several of their number

'to labour with those incarcorat [imprisoned] women [in Inverkeithing] suspect of witchcraft for bringing of them to confession of that hynous [heinous] sinne.'

Perhaps the local bailies and the Kirk Session had a problem; their ardour for justice had mysteriously cooled by July due to the fact that among the suspects were the wives of some of the magistrates themselves! By August, matters had still not been resolved although accusations of witchcraft had been made against Beatrix Douglas, Margaret Durie and Katherine Smith. When attempts were made to apprehend Margaret Durie, her husband Robert Brown told the authorities she had left the country and was now in France; this was of course untrue, a fact which Brown acknowledged and made repentance for before the Presbytery of Dunfermline on 3rd September. By this time, Margaret Durie - the daughter of George Durie, Town Clerk of Inverkeithing - had been taken into custody.

On 19th July 1649, the Committee of Estates in parliament announced that as the

'sine of witchcraft daylie increaseth in this land Thair for they have givine and grantit full power and commissioun for trying and puting to execution certaine personis guiltie of the cryme of witchcraft.... subscribit be the ministers and elders within the parochin of north berwik [sic], Borroustounnes [Bo'Ness], Quenisferie [probably South Queensferry] and Haddingtoun.'

Authorisation for trials in these localities is enshrined in the Acts of Parliament for that year. On 7th August, the Committee of Estates ordered the local shire committees - established to raise troops for the expected conflict with England - to ascertain whether torture had been used on anyone suspected of witchcraft and to report all cases before sentences were carried out. This demonstrates the conflict between the Covenanting Kirk and the civil authorities in their struggle to dominate the moral high ground; their efforts to achieve supremacy in the increasingly volatile climate of impending war would undermine the country's ability to prosecute a successful campaign against the English the following year. Meanwhile, witches were the first priority.

Trials increased at an alarming rate; the witch hunt reached a new high in the summer of 1649, when the Committee of Estates issued 170 commissions involving 350 individuals for trials at local level. Even a conservative estimate of the number of witches brought before local courts is difficult to calculate but it is not unreasonable to suggest that between 700 and 1,000 people were taken into custody in the latter half of the year. One commission alone cited twenty-nine suspects in East Lothian. At the same time, nineteen people were accused of witchcraft in Inverkeithing. In the six months between September 1649 and April 1650, the Presbytery of Dunbar brought to trial upwards of twenty-five suspects; the figure is inconclusive because in addition to that number were 'several unnamed persons;' possibly these were the ten witches whose trials are dramatised in Chapter 4. Even if the true figure is only fifteen, it is still considerable for a small presbytery.

At the end of August 1649, a woman called Bessie Graham in Kilwinning was arrested for being drunk and slandering the wife of John Rankin. Shortly after the brawl, Rankin's wife succumbed to some sickness or other and died. Bessie was put in the Kilwinning kirk steeple for thirteen weeks. John Fergusson, the local minister, admitted that in all that time, she remained obdurate and occasionally led him to believe she was completely innocent of the crime of witchcraft. In fact, he went as far to say that he sympathised with her and wished she had never been taken into custody, which is unusual not only for the time but also in the entire climate of the witch persecution. He even hoped she would escape from her prison. She was pricked by the local witchfinder, Alexander Bogs; he found the mark on

'her ridge-back, wherein he thrust a great Brass Pin, of which she was not sensible; neither did any blood follow, when the Pin was drawn out.'

The provost of Kilwinning decided to send a man to Edinburgh for a Privy Council commission to try her. The minister was still unconvinced of Bessie's guilt; but the warrant for her trial was obtained, albeit with difficulty and the trial went ahead. The minister continued to wrestle with his conscience:

> 'This put me to manie thoughts and Prayers, wherein I did engadge myself to God, that if he should find out a way for giving me, and the Assize full clearness, either by her own Confession or otherwise, I should remarke it as a singular Favour and special Mercy. This resolution I did often reiterate, Lord make me mindful of it. After a short time, Providence brought to light the unexpected Presumption of her guiltiness, which did convince me more, than any of the rest.'

The minister went with his servant and a kirk officer to ascertain whether Bessie would at last confess. She maintained a stubborn defence. Then, as he was leaving, he paused on the stair of the Tolbooth, hearing her speak a single sentence. He listened intently and maintained that another voice he heard whispering in the darkness was that of the devil. He stayed awhile in the dark silence, then heard Bessie speak again after a while. He described the voice which answered her as

> 'low and ghoustie, that I was certainly perswaded that it was another voice than hers.'

His servant, Alexander Simpson, was afraid for he too had heard the low, eerie voice. The two men went back to the steeple and took Bessie to the schoolhouse where she was guarded by no fewer than six men. By 13th November, the minister appears to have been convinced that Bessie was about to confess, promising William Wat - no doubt one of those who watched her - that she would admit everything the following day, a Sunday. When the minister interviewed her, she said she was heartily sorry for misspending her time and displaying malice towards him, giving the reason as temptation by the devil. She said this in a barely audible voice; when the minister asked her to speak up, she said she dared not or else the devil would give her the strength to shout as she was accustomed to do. He also commented that she stared to her left and right, which he put down to the invisible - to him - presence of the devil. The next day, Bessie spoke strongly and bitterly; she told the minister she'd been a wicked woman and had never repented but she hoped she'd be forgiven in heaven. That same day, her keepers reported that she had fallen on her knees to pray for forgiveness for her vile life and that she wanted to die. Bessie Graham went to the stake, confessed of all her 'crimes' except witchcraft, which she denied up to the very moment of her death.

There were so many cases that year that the courts were unable to cope with the workload - hence the reason for local commissions. One of those concerned, Elspet Seith or Seath of Balmerino, Fife and two other women who were accused of 'rydeing' - one can but speculate on the meaning - a man to death. Elspet managed to defend herself successfully, much to the annoyance of the ministers who were intent on executing her.

By 1649, the Kirk Party's power was at its zenith; perhaps this is best illustrated by the fact that the year was one of the few occasions in Scottish history when the nobles were called to public account for crimes of adultery. Against the background of impending war and national crisis, small communities re-doubled their efforts to detect the witches the church insisted were everywhere. Looked at from another perspective, the witch hunt was one way of taking the people's minds off the greater problems of state, especially those consequent on the execution of Charles I at the start of that unsettled and unsettling year. At the year's end, the persecution and burning of witches had become so commonplace that it was taken for granted. On 15th November 1649, the Commission of the General Assembly decreed that

> 'advertisement be sent to the Presbyteries of some fugitive witches that they may be searched for according to the desire of the Synod of Lothian.'

About a week later, the Commission further strengthened their decree by asking local presbyteries seeking Privy Council warrants for commissions to try witches locally to be sure to choose the ablest men for the task. The actual letter issued to the presbyteries states the following:

> 'Being informed of the great number of poore people whom the Divell hes deluded and drawen away to that sin of witchcraft, we must desire yow that when yow send for any commissions for their tryell and punishment, that yow withall send informatioun of the most conscientious and vnderstanding men to be vpon the Commission.'

Because the witch hunt was now a part of daily life, some communities seemed to dispense with the need to send a man on horseback all the way to Edinburgh to obtain a commission from the Privy Council. As mentioned earlier, one such community was Dunbar, East Lothian, where in the autumn of 1649, ten witches were put on trial. Even respect for the laws of the land seemed to be crumbling. In that terrible year, the Privy Council issued a warrant to try twenty-three witches and six warlocks awaiting trial in East Lothian. There is no clear indication that any were executed but it is likely that the majority were found guilty, some of them suffering branding or banishment from their parishes.

In 1649 occurred a case which demonstrates how heavily the dice were loaded against women accused of witchcraft. James Henrison and his wife Marion in Stow were taken into custody for the crime. James admitted that he had used a charm he had learnt from Isabel Thomson, recently burnt as a witch. On 3rd September, man and wife were pricked by John Kincaid of Tranent; Kincaid gave his oath before the kirk that the pair were 'great witches.' There are no details given of the charges against Marion Henrison. Despite the fact that Kincaid claimed to have found the devil's mark on husband and wife, we know that only Marion was executed; what happened to James is not recorded.

THE

CONFESSIONS

OF

HELEN TAYLOR IN EYEMOUTH

AND

MENIE HALYBURTON IN DIRLTON,

ACCUSED OF WITCHCRAFT, 1649

WITH THE

DECLARATION

OF

JOHN KINCAID, PRICKER

The Kirk continued to ruthlessly pursue its God-given right or God-driven fight to exterminate what it believed the most pernicious and insidious evil in the land. It carried this crusade to absurd conclusions when at the end of 1649, a suspected witch died before being brought to trial. On 2nd January 1650, the General Assembly wrote to the Presbytery of Dunfermline conveying their displeasure regarding the burial of Margaret Henderson, Lady Pittadro or Pitathrie, who had committed suicide in the Edinburgh Tolbooth while awaiting trial for witchcraft. Lady Pitathrie had been accused of the crime in

62

Inverkeithing by several witches, subsequently executed. At the beginning of July 1649, she escaped to Edinburgh, no doubt in fear of the aforementioned Walter Bruce who not only had a keen nose for sniffing out witches in his parish but was also something of a maverick in the eyes of the church. (He was suspended by the presbytery at one point, suspected of swearing and giving sermons which verged on the profane. Despite his suspension from clerical duties, Bruce insisted on attending at least one witch trial in his capacity as minister which, of course, he had no right to do). Lady Pitathrie was soon apprehended and taken into custody in Edinburgh's Tolbooth.

Lady Pitathrie's case came before the General Assembly which on 19th July petitioned parliament to arrange her trial so that 'this land and city may [be] free of her and justice done upon her.' She was accused by several persons of having caused the death of some of their acquaintance and that she had kept company with the devil as was clear from the depositions of many other witches. For one reason or another, Lady Pitathrie's trial was delayed until December. One morning, during the course of her trial, she was found dead in her cell; as the account goes, she was thought to have committed suicide:

> 'It was thought and spoken by many, that she wronged her selfe, ei-
> ther by strangling or by poyson; but we leave that to the judgement
> of the great day.'

There is a bizarre sequel to this case. Lady Pitathrie's remains were removed from the Tolbooth and taken to Fife for burial. The benighted General Assembly expressed

> 'their dislike of the fact of the buriall of the Lady Pittadro, in respect
> of the maner and place, and that the said Presbyterie [of Dunferm-
> line] may labour to make the persons who hes buried her sensible of
> their offence in so doeing; and some of the persons who buried hir,
> being personallie present, are desired by the Commission to shew
> themselvis to the Presbyterie sensible of thir misscarriage therein.'

The Presbytery records take up the story. On 30th January, William Blackburn, Alexander Henderson, Andrew Dickson, James Wilson, David Bull and John Brown were

> 'made sensible off thair fault for countenancing the buriall of Margt
> Henderson, sometyme Lady Pittadro, under the scandal of witch-
> craft.'

We do not know where she was buried although in addition to having been accused of witchcraft, she had committed suicide and would for that alone be denied burial in consecrated ground. If as is likely, her remains were removed from the cemetery and interred in similar manner to Isobel Marr of Inverkeithing, an accused witch and suicide who six years previously was buried, without a kist, in the local Witches' Knowe. Presumably Alex Henderson, one of the repentant gravediggers and possibly a relative of Lady Pitathrie, had organised the removal of her corpse from Edinburgh and buried it in some kirkyard, then after rebuke by the General Assembly, was obliged to remove it. It is incredible that even although she had not been found guilty of witch-craft, Lady Pitathrie's remains were considered tainted, not fit for Christian burial.

The Tolbooth of Edinburgh c1790; the west door of St Giles Cathedral is on its immediate right.

Yet again, the witch hunt was driven along on its own momentum. All through spring and the unusually wet summer of 1650, the trials and burnings contin-ued. The motivating force behind the mania was the Kirk's alone. While Archibald Johnston of Wariston devoted his efforts to a vigorous purging of the army of the Malignants and Engagers, the General Assembly matched his efforts in ridding the nation of its sins and the wicked crimes committed by the devil and his servants. The purging of Royalist supporter and witch alike continued until the very eve of Cromwell's invasion. For those awaiting trial on suspicion of witchcraft, only the subsequent appointment of English commissioners to administer justice backed by Cromwell's Ironsides would bring to a halt - albeit temporary - the Scottish Kirk's cruel and relentless obsession. Perhaps that terrible decade of witch burning from 1640 to 1650 is best summed-up in Chambers' *Domestic Annals*:

> '[witches were] tortured to confession, savagely burnt, in vast numbers, the clergy not merely concurring but taking a lead in the proceedings....'

The Kirk would continue to play a leading role in the witch hunt for a further fifty years.

A Dunbar Trial

It is early autumn. In Dunbar, East Lothian, the herring-drave is almost over. It has been a good season for the fishermen. Only one boat has been lost at sea, not without suspicion of witchcraft. David Robertson, minister of the Collegiate Church at Dunbar locks the kirk gate behind him. That October morning, he is making his way to the Tolbooth or, to be more precise, the burgh chambers. There is a seasonal mist. It is a gloomy day for the fishing, indeed for any outdoor work, let alone the work of God. It is the year of Our Lord 1649. Almost a century has passed since the Reformation in Scotland. For many on both sides of the Border, the year began badly. On 29th January, the predominant political party in England ordered the unthinkable- the execution of Charles I at Whitehall. The news has brought confusion to Scotland, where the late king's son has been proclaimed Charles II of both countries without the consent of the English parliament. Scotland is riven by several political and religious factions. There are those who are for church and no king; others for church and king and yet more who favour king but no church. Foremost among these factions is the Kirk Party and its mouthpiece, the General Assembly, currently enjoying unprecedented power, if not popularity. The Kirk Party is about to come into what it sees as its true dominion. Since the defeat of the Royalist Scottish army at Preston the previous year, the Kirk has rapidly consolidated its position. It will exercise absolute power, exceeding even that of the Scottish parliament until Cromwell invades the country in 1650 and destroys the kirk-dominated Scottish army at Dunbar.

For the moment, the Kirk Party is in ascendancy. Its instincts are those of any revolutionary faction. It is purging the country of those it regards as politically impure, those who are tainted with discredited beliefs-the Malignants and the Royalists. All such persons are being removed from public office, whether in the state, local government or the army. In Edinburgh and elsewhere, particularly East Lothian, radical Kirk Party supporters are heard exclaiming that "The Lord hath shown what he can doe by a few." Even so, the Kirk Party is not entirely in complete agreement about all matters political, although it is unanimous about one issue. The seeking out and extermination of witches. The spectre of the Devil stalks the land. This time, it is not

Papism which threatens the country's stability. It is witchcraft, an abomination which, in the minds of those who govern the church, is growing. The Committee of Estates has pronounced several times that witchcraft 'daily increaseth in this land.' At least in this matter, church and state are reconciled.

During the parliamentary recess in the summer of 1649, the Committee of Estates has issued no fewer than 170 commissions to local authorities to apprehend and try persons suspected of witchcraft in their parishes. These commissions are almost exclusively for trials in East Lothian and Berwickshire. The power granted by these commissions is extensive; local courts are authorised to take into custody, using torture if need be and pass sentence on those found guilty of practising witchcraft or consulting with witches. Members of these small commissions are named and duly appointed in Edinburgh. They are usually local lairds and parish authorities such as the provost and two bailies. And of course, at least one minister of the church. There is no jury as in common law. The word of the local commissioners is usually final. This method of trial has the support of the General Assembly of the Church of Scotland, which has lately demanded and been granted jurisdiction in such matters. The Assembly has successfully argued that God's law takes precedence over secular law. There is no one strong enough to oppose this view.

In the small royal burgh of Dunbar, several witches have already been tried and executed in recent years. Today, on his way to the Tolbooth, the Reverend David Robertson expects more to be brought to justice. Master Robertson has good reason to indulge himself at the expense of others as he has himself suffered for sin he committed but two years ago. He remembers how he was made to repent for his fornication with a woman he subsequently married. It is possible that one of those suspected of witchcraft reported his sin to the Kirk session. He contemplates the morning's work as he walks along the High Street, rubbing his hands together. Whether he does this because of the chill air or the pleasure he feels at the prospect of accomplishing God's work is difficult for the occasional passer-by to decide. It is indeed a cold, inhospitable morning for the end of September. A sea-haar insinuates the side-streets and vennels. It is gloomy outside, and even darker indoors; the light is so poor that candles have been lit in shops and the burgh chambers.

There are no candles burning in the cell on the second floor of the Tolbooth, where a young female has languished for several days. Jonet Dalrymple, a washer-woman at the nearby coaching inn, which in time will be called the St.

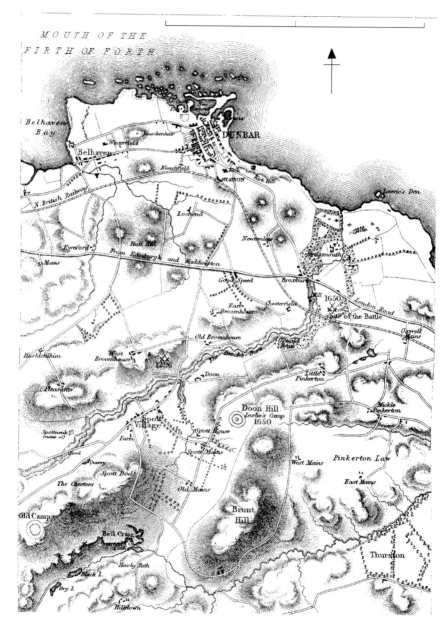

Dunbar and its immediate environs in 1857

George, lies on dirty straw that is scattered thinly over the wooden floor of a cell measuring six feet by ten. There is nowhere for her to sit. Jonet's raven black hair is spread out on the floor where she lies. It is so dark she cannot see her hand in front of her face. She is in pain, although that pain has dulled to a continuous throbbing in her back. What she longs for most is light. The darkness is as black as a cat.

Na, think nae on that, she whispers to herself.
. For she knows about black cats and what they mean. Black cats are considered unlucky by many, especially fishermen who refuse to put to sea if one crosses their paths. And many believe that a black cat is the Devil incarnate.

Far below, she hears the drawing back of a bolt, then muffled voices and the heavy tread of feet on the stone stairs. She knows it will be the jailer. And perhaps the minister, who has attended her before, urging her to confess her crimes and repent. Jonet has eaten nothing for three days. She has been denied sleep for several days and nights. This form of torture is known as 'waking.' One or two men have been constantly with her, even during calls of nature. The church has decreed that suspected witches must be kept awake because during the hours of sleep, the Devil may easily enter their bodies and exert his power. Lack of sleep has added to her confusion. She can hardly lift her head from the floor because of weakness and pain. All Jonet has had to sustain her is a pitcher of water to unclog her tongue. Her tormentors have left her alone for a day but she knows they have not finished with her yet. She hears the key in the lock. The cell door swings open, protesting on rusty hinges. A thin shaft of light falls on her face. She feels rather than sees it. Now that light has been restored, she cannot bear it; it is harsh on eyes swollen by lack of sleep. The jailer bends down on one knee beside her and shakes her roughly.

"On yer feet, witch. Up, up, ye hag. The maisters await ye. It'll gang ill wi' ye tae keep them. Now ye go tae meet yer betters."
Jonet tries to stand. Her legs will not support even her slight weight for they are bruised and burnt by the cashielaws - the iron frame which is used to encase a prisoner's leg and then held over a small brazier till the metal grows hot and singes the flesh. At first she withstood the pain, then the minister instructed the jailer to use the contraption on her other leg but two days ago. It was then that she confessed. The jailer helps her to her feet, steadying her. As Jonet clings to him for support, she necessarily lets fall the meagre scraps of her bodice to reveal her small, white breasts. The jailer looks at her nakedness

69

briefly, then turns away quickly. She is a condemned witch; he believes she is deliberately using her charms on him. He pushes her against the wall of the cell.

"Yer black airts'll no' work on me, witch. Ye'll no deceive a God-fearin' man wi' yer devilish cantraips."

Jonet shakes her head, gathering her rags about her. With difficulty, she supports herself by the wall with her free hand. She cannot use her thumbs because they have been crushed by the pilniewinks, or thumbscrews. The jailer sets her straight, then pushes her ahead of him into the dark, narrow corridor. Her dress has been torn from her back revealing a criss-cross of weals made by the lash; they are suppurating with blood and pus. The jailer and lockman laid it on well a week ago but Jonet was stubborn. They wanted to put the lash to her cheeks but the masters expressly forbade them. Perhaps the men do not realise that it is Jonet's pretty face which is on trial so it must not be disfigured. As Jonet shuffles along the corridor which connects the cells with the burgh chambers, she can just make out the shape of a tall man in the gloom. As he comes closer, she recognises the lockman, or public executioner.

"Aye, man."

"Aye, jailer. Ah was comin' tae fetch ye. The maisters are ill-willed this mornin'."

"Be they ? They should ken the witch canna walk. Is yer rope ready? It'll nae be empty for lang."

The lockman laughs, hands on hips as he watches Jonet's unsteady gait.

"Aye, the witch is fair hauchlin' along. The maisters'll see we have done oor duty and earnit oor drink-siller. So they canna be ill at us for the waitin'. Weel, there's anither waits for me below, tho' Ah doubt she'll be pleased tae see me."

The lockman descends the spiral staircase. The jailer pushes Jonet ahead to the oak-panelled door which leads to the burgh chambers. He knocks three times, then enters. Jonet blinks in the light. The room is narrow and long. The oak table at the far end where the magistrates sit is lit by numerous candles. A few candles placed on the window ledges provide meagre light for the rest of the room. There is a small stool set before the table. Jonet is cold and shivers, trying to hold together the rags of her bodice for modesty's sake. One of the men at the table speaks.

"The panel may sit doon."

Jonet does not understand he is referring to her. The jailer steps forward and bids her sit. She stares in the general direction of the table. There are five men in all. The man who has spoken wears a long, curled wig. His face is lined, his eyes are hooded and puffy. His cheeks are bright red, his nose is bulbous and of similar colouring. He is a man whose fondness for the pleasures of life is written large in his face. She knows him as one of the local lairds and landowners who frequent the inn where she works.

"So, whit hae ye tae say for yersel' the day ? Speak, witch, speak. We hae nae time tae waste. Gie us the names o' the others. We ken others hae helped ye in yer black airts."

He then bids the clerk seated at a small trestle table nearby to read out the charges against her.

"Item. That ye did charm Thomas Craig, fisher and bachelor o' this parish by lewd flauntings.

Item. That ye did samewise tae Thomas Brunton, fisher and bachelor.

Item. That ye did lift up thy skirts above thy knees in Crow's Wynd tae the effrontery o' one John Home, gentleman.

Item. That ye did consult wi' ane Agnes Hardie, lang suspectit o' witchcraft and charming the people.

Item. That the aforenamed got ye a potion which she said would gie ye the power tae charm men.

Ye are a loathsome witch who did display thy thighs tae the aforenamed gentleman. Ye were seen and heard tae utter an incantation afore ye drawed the blood frae the gentleman's face. Hae ye onythin' tae say tae thy delators?"

Jonet lifts up her head.

"Aye. Ah have aye been clean. No' a wanton. Ah have never had any dealin's with any man. Ye maun get a physician."

The laird explodes in anger.

"Witch! Witch! Ye are impident! Ye wad mak us send for a physician when oot o' yer ain mooth ye hae confessed ye had congress wi' the deil ! Think ye we are sae addled ?"

Jonet shakes her head and tries to speak again. The laird holds up his hand.

"Stay! Wheesht ye! Ye have confessed ye are a witch. Gie us the names o' the others ye consort wi'. It'll gang easier wi' ye. Otherwise, ye waste oor time."

Jonet looks at him. She is not defiant. She knows better. But she is sincere.

"Maisters. By yer contraptions ye hae wrought frae me words under sic pain Ah hae never kent before. Ah'm nae witch. An' Ah ken nae others."

The laird's whole body is shaking with anger.

"Whit? Whit? Are ye retractin'? Ye telt us the name o' Agnes Hardie."

He turns to his colleagues.

"The damned witch is retractin'!"

The four men at the table hiss at her. The laird looks at her coldly now.

"Ye compeared at the last doon-sittin' o' the kirk, ye did confess oot o' yer mooth. We heard ye. Ye hae uttered lies tae us this day. Ye did tell the meenister ye are a witch. Master David, is that no' the way o't ?"

The minister nods. Then he speaks slowly to Jonet.

"Four days syne, ye was asked if ye were a witch. Ye answered me aye. Ye was asked if ye renunced yer baptism. Ye answered me aye. Ye was askit if ye wad bide by yer confession and ye answered me aye. For the good Lord kens a' things, for though he be on high, he looks low. Are they no' yer ain words ? Ye said them four days syne afore the jailer an' me."

Jonet nods in agreement.

"They are indeed words o' mine. But Ah spoke them tae mak ye stop. Ye will say ocht when ye are in pain. Ye maun ken that."

The laird beats so violently on the table his wig tilts askew.

"Wheesht! Ye hae been compeared as a witch. Ye hae confessed. Ye maun be sentenced. Afore the sentence is spoken over ye, ye can mak it gae easy. Name the others."

Jonet is trembling but she is adamant

"In the name o' Lord Jesus, Ah'm nae witch. Jesus is ma saviour."

Now it is the minister's turn to rage at her.

"Ye hae renunced the Lord ! Ye hae renunced yer baptism and thus yer protection frae the deil. Ye are a self-confessed witch an' there's

an end on't !"
Jonet stares at the minister in disbelief.
"Ah love only God. Only he is the master."
The laird completely loses his temper.

"Enough! Enough! Jailer, tak the witch awa'. She needs more work on her back, man'.

The following day, Jonet Dalrymple is taken from her cramped cell to a larger one on the first floor of the Tolbooth. She has been there before. The cell contains two stools and a small stocks or pillory. Chains and whips hang from hooks on the walls. She sees the witch's bridle; she is already familiar with the pilniewinks and the cashielaws. The jailer orders her to sit on the smaller three-legged stool which is set before the stocks. He pulls her arms and legs through the apertures, bidding her to stretch out her legs so that her heels rest on the second, slightly higher stool. Presently, he is joined by the lockman. Jonet looks up at the two men; she cannot hide her fear. The jailer has a sharp sleekit face. She knows that to the people of Dunbar, he is known as the Whittrick on account of his weasel-like features. But never to his face. The lockman, lately come to the burgh, is unknown to her. He looks down at her. And he smiles. But there is no gentleness or kindness in that smile.

The Whittrick speaks.

"Man, ye'll have tae gie me a

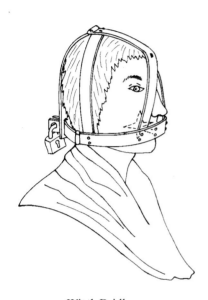

Witch Bridle

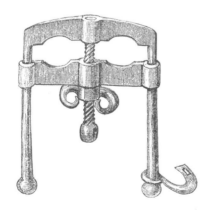

Pilniewinks or thumbscrews

73

hand wi' the iron."

Stacked against the cell wall are several long iron bars. The two men lift one and lay it on Jonet's outstretched legs. They lay another beside it, then another and another. Slowly the weight begins to take its toll. She cannot stop her legs from involuntary shaking and ultimately her whole body trembles. The iron bites deep into her skin, chafing with every movement. Then the lockman takes a good handful of her long black hair and pulls her head violently forward so that her face is thrust against the rim of the stocks.

"Right, man. Lay on."

Behind her, the jailer takes up the lash. At each stroke on her back, she jerks. This makes her legs move so that the iron bars grind on the front of her legs where the skin is easily broken. After twenty strokes have been laid on her back, the blood flows freely. The iron bars have chafed her legs so badly that the bone shows through. She screams again and again as the iron bites deeper into the bone. Jonet's mouth is now also bleeding as she has bitten into the stocks to try to stifle the pain. She screams at her tormentors, begging them to stop.

"Tak aff ! Tak aff ! Oh, mercy, tak aff !"

The lockman stays the jailer's hand.

"Gie us the names. Wi' each name, ane bar will come aff. Gie us the names."

Jonet's head is swimming. She is blinded by sweat and tears. The mucus dribbling from her nose becomes a long silver thread, thin as spider silk; it finally breaks and falls in her lap. The pain in her back and her legs is unbearable. Her screams are drowned by the roar of the sea that rushes through her head. Then it is dark.

"Ach, she's fainted. We'll hae tae revive her."

The jailer fetches a bucket of water and throws it in Jonet's face. She is abruptly brought back to consciousness and pain.

"The names o' the others. Are ye ready tae speak, witch ?"

She looks at them, her face twisted by pain and pale with exhaustion.

"Oh, sirs, Ah hae nae names."

The lockman raises his arm to bid the jailer continue. She breaks into uncontrollable sobbing.

"Nae mair ! Nae mair ! Ah'll name."

Shaking and sobbing, she hears herself give the name of Agnes Hardie.

"Ye hae named her afore. Nae bar comes aff."

She gives the name of Helen Ross, fishwife. A bar is removed. Then Isobel Peddie, a beggar. Another bar is taken away. She gives the name of Grissel Craw, an old woman who lives in Lochend Wood on the outskirts of Dunbar. As she speaks, the weight on her legs is more bearable. Only two bars remain.

"Ony mair ?"

Jonet is unsure whether he means more names or whether she wants him to take off the remaining bars. Perhaps he expects her to beg for mercy.

"Ah hae nae mair names tae gie ye. Oh, pity sirs, hae pity. For the Lord's sake !"

The lockman laughs in her face.

"Ye hae renunced the Lord, mistress witch. He canna hear ye."

But he nods over her head to the jailer.

"We might as weel tak aff the others. She's done."

When the last bars are removed, Jonet screams as feeling returns to her legs. She faints again for a moment, then as she comes round, she vomits. Out of her mouth comes a thin, watery dribble. In it, there is a small gout of blood from which pinkish tentacles trail. The jailer shouts to the lockman.

"See ! See ! The witch has spewed up the evil possessin' her. We maun tell the maisters the morn. Aye, man. We hae earned drink-siller this time."

At last, Jonet is taken from the stocks. Her body is arched and rigid with shock until the pain dulls to a throb. The two men support her. Her lifeless legs drag behind her. As the men half-carry, half-drag her back to her cell, her limp feet burst into explosions of new pain as they strike every stone step. She sweats profusely. Her eyes are closed. She cannot see the bloody trail she leaves behind her, like a snail. After what seems an age, she is back in her cell, lying on the dirty straw. The jailer throws water on her torn back and the ugly fresh wounds. Then he splashes water on her legs which makes her faint again.

"Weel done, weel done. We maun be sure o' the siller."

"Aye, but it was twice. The maisters'll no' tak kindly tae that. They'll gie less. They werena' gude-tempered yestreen. Hoo much dae ye think they'll gie us? "

It is as if Jonet does not exist. They leave her lying on the bloody straw, her body trembling. She hears them arguing about the money as they go down the stairs. Once more, she is left in darkness.

On her next appearance before the magistrates, Jonet repeats the four names she gave to the jailer and lockman. Agnes Hardie and Grissel Craw are local, the fisherwife Helen Ross is from Eyemouth, a fishing village further south and the fourth, Isobel Peddie is a beggar with no fixed abode. As Jonet intones the names, there is a buzz of satisfaction from the magistrates. The laird is clearly pleased and informs her that since her last appearance, the court has heard depositions from two material witnesses.

> "After ye were compeared, we examined Thomas Brunton, fisherman and John Home, gentleman. They were telt the dittay on ye. We heard their delations against ye. The forenamed Brunton telt the assize ye did bewitch him and the lately dead Thomas Craig. But Brunton spoke for ye. He forespoke ony airt and pairt by ye in the death o' the man Craig, that yer cantraips were lewd and ye did cast a spell on his heart and the said Thomas Craig but nae other hurt did ye dae tae him. John Home also spoke o' his bewitchment by ye. Dae ye confess that ye did charm thae three men ? "

Jonet denies the accusation vigorously.

> "They attemptit tae force lewdness on me, forbye, the man Home did touch me the day Ah was washin' the claes at the inn wynd. Ah cast nae spells on ony o' them."

The laird is unimpressed.

> "This assize will hae nane o' yer contempt, witch. Forbye, the gentleman Master Home bears the mark o' yer teeth in his face. Ye maun no' forsay ye did him nae harm."

Jonet protests that she was defending herself. Her pleas are to no avail. The laird orders the jailer to take her back to her cell. Chairs scrape on the floor as three of her judges rise to leave. The minister is seated beside the clerk to make sure he has entered the correct names in the magistrates' book. As Jonet is leaving, she hears the laird direct the jailer to give her some broth. She turns to look back, meaning to thank him, then thinks the better of it. After all, she knows she is innocent of any crimes.

The laird goes to the clerk's desk.

> "Hae ye no' done the scribin' yet ? Ye maun order oot the toon guard tae apprehend the three women afore the causey-clash starts. They'll hae their work cut oot tae fetch in Peddie, the rovin' beggar-wife."

The clerk hurriedly sprinkles the ledger with sand to dry the ink. He tucks the book under his arm and scurries into the Tolbooth to raise the alarm.

In her cell, Jonet sees the jailer remove the stout wooden board from the small barred window. It was deliberately placed there to keep out the light. Now she has confessed, things appear to be going easier for her. Later, the jailer returns with fresh, clean straw he has begged from the abattoir to the rear of the Tolbooth. His wife carries a wooden bowl from which steam rises.

"A coggie o' broth for ye. An' some breid. "

Jonet thanks her. No other words pass between them although Jonet is sure she sees sadness in the woman's eyes. Later, lying alone, Jonet hears the lowing of a stirk. It is probably tethered to the iron ring set in the wall at the top of Silver Street, next to the abattoir. She guesses it is there to be slaughtered. The lowing grows louder. Tears are running down Jonet's cheeks. She whispers aloud.

"Poor beastie, poor beastie. "

Over the next few weeks, Jonet is left alone. Food is given to her daily. Even a candle-end at night. She knows that one by one, those she has named will be brought to the Tolbooth to be examined. She prays they will not be put in the cell with her. One morning, the jailer brings news which raises her spirits.

"Weel, witch. Ye're tae be moved to anither howff. On account o'
the other prisoners. Wir up tae oor oxters in witches. Ye're tae go
tae the kirk spire, where ane or twa elders will watch over ye."

After he leaves, Jonet weeps with relief. That afternoon, she is led out into the weak autumn sunshine by two men of the town guard. They take her along the back streets to avoid drawing attention. The townspeople of Dunbar know there are witches on trial and the guards are too few to deal with a mob in the High Street. In the kirk steeple, there is fresh air, a plentiful supply of clean straw and even a bench to sit on. The elders who watch over her remain outside the door. That night, she sleeps sounder than she has for weeks.

The court is now sitting several days each week. Next to be examined after Jonet Dalrymple is Isobel Peddie, the beggar woman who surprisingly was taken without difficulty. Her trial is lengthy, for her story is as convoluted as her endless wanderings. She roams the countryside as far south as Coldingham, near Eyemouth and westwards to Haddington, seeking her alms. The magistrates have decided to hear her confession before any others since they rightly surmise she will have more information to give. They believe she will name other witches she has met on her travels. And they know she is certain to have accomplices in the parish.

The laird has played little part in the proceedings since Jonet Dalrymple's second appearance. The provost has had to deputise for him as he has been sick. As he enters the chambers that morning, the minister David Robertson, enquiring after his health, expresses the fear that perhaps he has been bewitched by some evil spirit. The laird makes light of it.

> "If Ah hae been afflicted in the wame be evil spirits, Ah'll hae
> words wi' the innkeeper wha providit them."

Privately, the laird dislikes David Robertson. He considers him more mealy-mouthed than is usual in a cleric. The brief banter over, the laird calls for order. The prisoner Isobel Peddie is summoned. The beggar woman is brought into the chambers. She is filthy. Her hair is matted and tousled. Her thumbs are bloody from the pilniewinks. Like Jonet Dalrymple, she has been whipped. She is ordered to sit on the stool before the magistrates' table. The stink of her forces the laird and his colleagues to draw kerchiefs from their sleeves to cover their faces.

> "Isobel Peddie. Ye hae been accused o' consultin' wi' witches, the
> making o' charms, the casting o' spells and of repeatedly abusing the
> people. How d'ye answer the charges ? "

Isobel keeps her head bowed as she mumbles.

> "Bid the panel speak up jailer."

The laird repeats the question. She answers aye. Then she begs the court's mercy and asks them to hear her tale.

> "Maisters. Ah wish tae tell ye a'thing."

The laird nods and bids her continue.

> "Maisters, ye a' ken me. For many's the bit lock o' meal and coggie
> o' brose yer servants hae pleasured me wi'. Ye are a' Christian gen-
> tlemen. Ah hae much tae thank ye fur the good selves ye are. Ye
> hae been mercifu' lang syne. Tis a hard life without a mannie tae
> look after ye. Sae good hae ye been-"

The laird is impatient.

> "Stay thy spleiter! Ye maun tell the assize what ye ken. Nae mair o'
> yer tongue o' butter. Get on wi' it."
> "Weel then. Ye ken Ah shift for myself by beggin'. Ah depend
> on the goodness o' folk. But ye wish me tae tell ye o' witches
> and 'tis of them Ah shall speak. "

The laird sits back wearily in his chair, pressing his kerchief even closer to his nose.

> "Ah hae met many witches in this parish. Ah'll gie the first name.

Helen Ross, fisherwife. Next is Agnes Hardie, inn servant."

Isobel embarks on her story, several stories in fact. She first tells the court she is accustomed to sleeping where she can find shelter from the weather.

"Aftwhiles, Ah hae tae sleep in the auld ruined castle. In ane o' the auld cellars that gie shelter frae the cold wind frae the east. Nae-body bothers me there. Nae fisherman of this toon will go there in the mirk, for ye ken the castle is thocht tae be haunted by the spectre o' Lady Agnes, her they cried Black Agnes. She lived there hunners o' years syne"

The laird interrupts her, bids her not to lecture the court about things that have nothing to do with the matter in hand.

"Unless ye are gaun tae tell us ye hae brocht Lady Agnes Dunbar back frae the deid."

Isobel tells the court she sought shelter in the castle cellars on a night in July last. How she was almost asleep when she was wakened by strange noises.

"They were footsteps but they were unco in that place. Ah lay still as a stook in a harvest field. Ah saw the twa o' them. Helen Ross and Agnes Hardie. They'd a wee caunle-dowp that showed their faces. They were whisperin' an' jeerin' then ane went wheesht ! and another came by. Noo maisters, 'twas a mannie that spoke but in a tongue that was unco tae me. For whiles they spoke in whisperins, till syne it was gettin' light, the mannie telt the twa they'd to go. But afore he dismissed them, his tongue was mair familiar. He bade the women gie him their spirits and he would reward them wi' siller and bonnie gowns. He said ye maun dae as Ah bid ye and ye will aye hae clean linen. But ye maun be obedient tae me, yer new mais-ter. He asked if they were frightened and Agnes Hardie said to him she was nae cried Agnes for nothin' for she was possessed o' the same spirit as Black Agnes an' nae feart o' aucht."

Isobel Peddie tells the court that when the three were leaving the ruins, she followed them at a discreet distance. She is asked to describe the man.

"Weel, sirs, he was humpy-backit. He had a muckle heid wi' twa horns like a goat. An' 'twas not the only time Ah saw him."

The magistrates whisper among themselves. Then the laird asks her whether he is her master. She shakes her head but says he has come to her in her dreams at night.

"When did ye next see him ?"

79

Isobel Peddie tells them it was not long afterwards, when she was begging in Cockburnspath, a few miles south of Dunbar. She was looking for work at the harvest and she said she had planned to sleep in the ruined kirk of St Helen's, near Cockburnspath.

"It was nicht when Ah got there. A black nicht wi' nae moon. As Ah drew nigh the kirk, Ah saw wee movin' lights. Like glimmer-worms ye ken. Then as Ah creeped up close to the wall, Ah saw four shapes, unco shapes jowkin' aboot in the eldritch light. Candles was next lighted on a gravestane and lo! the humpy-backit was there. Wi' three women Mayse Ridpath, Bessie McKenzie and Christian Boyd frae Doonhill o' Pinkerton. The wee mannie wi' the horns on his heid bade them dance as he played a wee bit pipe, an unco thing, no' like the Scottish pipes."

By now, the magistrates are showing keen interest in her tale. The minister whispers to the laird, who nods.

"The panel may continue."

"Weel, sirs, there was Ah, fear'd fur ma life, yet Ah couldna leave. Ma legs wouldna move. Ah hid in the ruin as best's Ah was able. The pipin' and the jowkin' went on whiles, then the man clapped his hands for silence. He spoke unto the three. Ah swear he spoke thus;

"O spirits above and spirits below and spirits here wi' me

Ye hae a hame in St Helen's on the Lee."

The laird bids her stop.

"No' lang syne, ye telt us the man's tongue was strange tae ye. Noo ye speak o' it readily. How so ?"

The beggar-woman looks slyly at him.

"Sir, the deil has mony tongues, mony voices. Ye maun ken that."

The laird confers with his colleagues, then speaks to her sharply.

"Ye are a delated witch. Hoo did ye no' join in the jowkin'. Ye hae confessit the deil is yer master. So ye maun have nae fear o' him."

The woman looks at him askance.

"Oh, sirs, it was for ma contumacy. Ah was feared. Ye see, just then, Ah'd renunced the deil and his works. Ah fought agin him lang syne, tae get back tae the true Lord and master, but sirs, the deil had a hold o' ma soul. Ah was fightin' him a' the whiles at St Helen's that night an' in the auld castle."

There is some further discussion among the magistrates, then the laird bids her continue.

"Weel, sirs, efter that unco night in the deserted kirk, Ah was bidin'
at Doonhill o' Pinkerton fur the harvest. That 'twas the wey o't. Ah'd
gone tae Cockburnspath for the same work but wi' the deil there,
Ah couldna thole it. But the harvest was nae started an' the
herrin-drave was on so Ah went tae the harbour tae beg a wheen o'
Dunbar-wedder for myself. Helen Ross that guts the fishes kens
me weel. The herrin' wis plentifu' so Ah begged a wheen o' the
wedder frae her. She telt me tae be aff, then she said Ah could have
a puckle fish presently. Ah waited an' waited but never a fish did
she gie me."

"Syne a big black cat cam by an' Helen Ross was familiar wi' it,
cryin' Hola Sathan ye scamp! and fed it some fish heids. The cat
was girnin' and growsin' about her. Ah threw a stane at it, for Ah
saw it was gettin' ma bit promised herrin'. Helen Ross, the dirten-
gab, cried me beggar-witch, then she lifted the cat in her arms and
said somethin' into its ear. She telt me Ah'd rue that day's work and
cursed me tae the deil. Ah canna mind her hell-words but she was
ill-temper'd."

"The cat was at ma heels a' that day. Ah went beggin' tae Eweford
ferm for a lock o' meal for the servant lassie there has oft been kind.
But no' that day. She cried me tae be off wi' the deil o' a cat. Next
Ah went tae Doonhill o' Pinkerton tae beg some meal an' Ah threw
stanes at the cat but still it cam after me. Never the meal Ah got that
day."

"But next day, the black cat was no' tae be seen, so Ah tried at the
fermhouse. Christian Boyd came to the door and telt me she'd fetch
a lock o' meal frae the barn and looked at me sleekit-like. She said
never the herrin' would Ah get at the harbour like afore. Noo sirs,
she was no' at the harbour that day Ah was beggin'. Hoo did she
ken Ah was there? Ah followed her tae the barn where Ah seen the
black cat wi' a fine rid ribbon roon its thraipple. The great beastie went
in the cat-hole then lo! oot cam Mayse Ridpath wi' a rid ribbon roon her
neck. Ah asked her if Christian was fetchin' ma lock o' meal but she
telt me tae be gone fur the meal kist was locked and the maister had the
key. Ah waited till she went up tae the hoose an' Ah went into the barn
but never a sight o' Christian Boyd nor black cat did Ah see. "

Isobel Peddie pauses to catch her breath. All that is heard is the furious scratching of the clerk's quill and the shuffling of feet under the magistrates' table.

"Ah got some work at the harvest in Doonhill o' Pinkerton. But Ah kept awa' frae the three that had been tae St Helen's kirk. Efter the hay was ingathered, ane efternoon Ah espied the three women oot walkin'. Ah followed them tae see what they etled. Ah keeked oot o' the wee barn nearby an' Ah spied them standin' afore three hay ricks wi' their arms ootstretched so their shades fell on the ricks. The three o' they stood an' chanted some cantraip thrice. Their shadows wis cast lang ower the ricks. As they came awa' along the path, Ah heared Mayse Ridpath speak tae Bessie McKenzie that deil the mannie she'd seen an' the work was wasted. An' Bessie did say that the day was no' over, no more the night. Master, ye maun ken yersel the thing that passed three nights on. Ye ken the ricks were burnt tae the ground. But by then Ah'd gone tae Haddinton tae beg. Next time Ah went beggin' tae Pinkerton, the maister telt me Ah was a vagabond witch for the hay that was lost in the fire an' Ah was ne'er tae come back to the ferm. Ah telt him the way o't but he set the dugs efter me. Maisters, 'twere never this auld sowl that burnt doon the hay."

By the end of the day, Isobel Peddie has confessed she has used potions got from Grissel Craw to make the three women tell the truth about the rick burning. She has admitted she made wax images of them which she'd put in a fire. She has also confessed that she sold potions made by Grissel to others to obtain money. The laird enquires why she saw the need to administer potions to the three women to make them detract that she had had anything to do with the rick burning when she had a sound alibi, having been seen in Haddington the night they were fired. Isobel Peddie pleads that she wanted to be sure.

"Na, na, witch. Ye did attempt the deed for ye are a witch an ye hae nae control ower that. Tak' her awa' jailer."

Next to be interrogated is Alesoun or Elie Knox whose name has been mentioned in the course of Isobel Peddie's testimony. Elie Knox is accused of several crimes including consulting with Grissel Craw, long suspected of being a witch. Elie Knox is a woman of some means. She is a widow whose husband was a baker and from who she inherited money. She also keeps chickens and sells eggs at the town's mercat cross. She is slatternly and has too much to say for herself. She has made many enemies in the parish, often selling eggs she knows to be bad. She is an idle gossip who holds court at the mercat cross every day, maligning her neighbours and anyone she dislikes. At her first court appearance, she is defiant, denying any knowledge of witchcraft, let alone practising it. This is her second appearance; it is clear she has been tortured and denied sleep for several days and nights, for on this occasion, she is quiet, even submissive. The laird instructs the clerk of court to read out the charges.

"Item. That ye did aftwhiles consult with ane Grissel Craw, lang suspectit of witchcraft. That ye did severally obtain from the forenamed potions which ye gave tae yer lately dead spouse, Robert Douglas, baxter and burgess of this parish. Ye said the potion was for the sweatin' sickness that took him to the deid."

"Item. That the forenamed spouse was no deid but ye did entertain a sojer in the Earl of Leven's regiment, lately come back frae the wars in England and whae served in this parish for some time afore he was sent tae Perth."

"Item. That ye did hae unclean fornication wi' said sojer and ye did bear a chance-bairn but said it was a bairn of the late Robert Douglas. That ye later compeared at the kirk and named the sojer as faither when it was found he was to disband frae the army and he refusit tae return tae Dunbar tae compear for his filthy sin o' fornication for he did say ye had bewitched him and he never would come in yer hoose again."

"Item. That ye did etle tae take the bairn's life by another potion ye got from the aforenamed Grissel Craw for the bairn was disformed and was aye sick. "

"Item. That ye did lay a curse on the good-wife that delivered ye in bairn-bed for ye said she had cursed ye for bringin' forth the deil's bairn oot o' evil an' unlawfu' fornication."

The final charge may seem trivial and is obviously a comment on Elie Knox's morals by the local midwife, Elspet Thomson. However, sadly, deformed children are commonplace and some midwives often deliberately allow such children to die at birth. They have to be careful not to attract suspicion for midwifery is crude and the death of a child before it can be baptised has sinister undertones. What is far from trivial is that Elie Knox had, before witnesses at the birth, cursed Elspet Thomson to Hell. In the eyes of the church, that is witchcraft, proof of practice. Under subsequent examination and after hearing the depositions of several witnesses, the court finds Elie Knox guilty of practising witchcraft and consulting a witch. They reserve final judgement on the alleged murder of her husband and the attempted murder of her illegitimate child, which it must be supposed is an inconvenience to her in her business. The court expresses the urgent need to interrogate Grissel Craw, whom it is already known prepares potions. Clearly, the magistrates wish to establish whether there has been collusion between Grissel Craw and Elie Knox in the death of Robert Douglas.

Grissel Craw is brought before the court. She is old and confused. Her mind wanders easily and she does not understand where she is or why she has been brought there. During her interrogation, her vacant eyes stare into space; she seems to see things that are not there. She frequently laughs out loud and points into the air at nothing. At least she has not suffered torture, for when she was taken into custody, she readily volunteered the information about making potions to help the sick, thus admitting she is a witch. All the court seeks to prove is that she has administered poisons or put evil charms or spells on people for the likes of Elie Knox to use. She tells the court she is no witch, only a wise-woman. She admits she learnt her skills as a young girl and that she was taught how to prepare certain herbs and plants by a wise-woman who came from the Highlands.

"Ah'm no but an auld yirb-wife. Ah make medicine tae help the sick and the deein'."

When she is asked about the contents of her potions, she admonishes the laird, wagging a bony finger in his face.

"Na, na, maister. Ah'm no' tellin' ye ma secrets. If Ah tell ye, the pow'r will be taken frae me."

The laird confers hastily with his colleagues. He suggests torture; the provost ventures that the local physician be brought to the court since he may know about such potions and how they are made. The physician appears before the magistrates the following day. He agrees to question Grissel but insists it is done in her cell. The magistrates concede he may gain more information that way; for his part, the doctor perhaps sees a way to increase his knowledge of herbs and their effects and therefore his income. As he says;

" We maun learn more by wiles than by torture. "

At her next appearance, Grissel smiles and waves to her accusers from the stool on which she prefers to stand rather than sit. The doctor is asked to report his findings.

" Sirs, the panel had no' much tae say. She telt me she gathers the field flower ladies' mantle that the folk call hive gress and is thought tae mak evacuations in young bairns wi' the bowel-hive. It is a weel kent remedy and harmless. She also gathers dentelions for the milk. Ye maun ken the dentelion is also cried witch-gowan an' the milk is kent as deil's milk. But the potion she used for the sweatin' sickness in Robert Douglas gives me concern. "

The laird bids him proceed.

"The panel tell me it was made frae a plant she calls witches' thimmles or dugs' lugs. It is kent among proper folk as the foxglove, a flower from which poison can be distilled. She says she has aye mixed it wi' drops o' the nightshade, a weel kent poison. "

There is a definite reaction to this from the court.

"So, are ye sayin' Robert Douglas was given physic that was poisoned?

He nods. The court dismisses him. Grissel is summarily declared guilty of complicity with Elie Knox in the murder of Robert Douglas by means of witch-craft. The laird asks her if she has any names to give them, names of other witches or others who have consulted her. Grissel is dancing and humming to herself. She is brought back to the stool. The jailer is ordered to restrain her. The laird repeats the question. Suddenly, she smiles at him.

"Aye maister. Ah ken lots o' names. The beggar-wife Isobel Peddie who sells ma potions for pennies. An' the fowl-wife Elie Knox hae gotten many potions fur the sickness in her spouse and her bairn. Aye an' her hens as weel."

The laird looks at his colleagues, then asks her for more names.

"Och, Ah canna mind them a'. Mayhap the fishie-wife an' her friend Agnes can. Ah canna think o' others."

"Ye maun tell the court aboot yer familiar. "

Grissel looks confused.

"Yon bird, the magpie ye keep in a cage."

She smiles.

"Och, 'tis only for company. The poor thing hurt its wing and

85

couldna fly ony mair. Ah was trying tae get it tae speak."
The laird nods.

"Aye, and 'tis weel kenned the magpie is the deil's bird."
The laird rubs his hands and bids the clerk enter Grissel's final words in his ledger. He then asks the other members of the court whether they wish to interrogate Grissel further. The minister indicates he has a few questions.

> "Ye hae not been to the kirk for mony a year. Can ye say the reason? "

> "For ma lameness. Ah canna mak the road any more."

> "Hae ye renunced yer baptism ? "

Grissel astounds the court by admitting she has never been christened because her mother was too poor. She does not realise she has just signed her death warrant. An unbaptised child is known to be the devil's own. The minister shakes his head and returns to the bench. The laird pronounces sentence

> "Ye hae been found guilty o' the crime o' witchcraft, sorcery and makin' charms tae the abuse o' the people. Jailer, tak the panel awa' and see she be warded i' the kirk steeple wi' the young ain."

As she is led away, Grissel smiles and waves to the court.

At her third appearance, Elie Knox has no choice but to confess she administered poison to her husband and a concoction to her child which he did not need. To give an emetic to a child not suffering from bowel-hive, an inflammation of the intestines, would have brought on dysentery, or as it is more commonly known, the bloody flux. The flux kills many strong adults, let alone sickly children.   Though she has confessed to the charges against her, Elie Knox does not go gracefully. She indicts Elspet Thomson, the midwife who attended the birth of her child, as a witch.

> "The hag-wife did lay a spell on me at the mercat cross afore the bairn was birthed. Ah hae witnesses. She foretold ma bairn tae be was cursed for Ah'd entertained the deil and she kent his works. As she said the words, she placed her hands on her wame and pressed them hard. She spoke a few words to hersel'. Ye maun seek the truth o't frae others by the mercat cross. She also telt me the hens would stop layin' an' they did soon efter."

> "At the birthin-time, Ah telt them a' that the howdie-wife Elspet Thomson was nae tae come tae the birth-bed but she did come for Ah was in sic pain. The bairn was disformed in his foot. It was club-toed, wi' nocht but a muckle toe an' nae others. The howdie-wife

said it was the deil's bairn for it was cloven an' that is was goin' tae hell wi' nae baptism. Ah was feared for the bairn and telt her tae leave ma hoose an' deil the howdie-fee she'd get frae me. She turned on me and swore she'd see me in Hell afore ane year was oot. They were the last words she spoke afore witnesses."

Elspet Thomson is next to appear before the court. Calmly and clearly, she answers the questions put to her . She admits to all Elie Knox has said. She is an intelligent woman.

"Sirs, it is weel kent that bairns born oot o' wedlock are aft sickly. Ah did nae harm tae the bairn. Its mother did that by hersel'. That was the meanin' o' the words."

The laird asks if the child was born sickly as well as deformed.

"Aye sir. Better the poor wee soul had been taken."

"Did ye wish it so ? "

"Aye. Wi' Elie Knox as its mother, whit life would it hae ? "

The laird whispers to the other magistrates. He suggests that the midwife may have allowed other sickly children to die. One or two of the judges recall other births Elspet has attended in recent years, some of which have resulted in death. Unbaptised. And an unbaptised child goes straight to hell, as the minister reminds the court. A soul for the devil. The laird nods.

"The panel will answer the next question in truth. Have ye let bairns die afore ? "

"Ah hae aye thought life is holy but some young souls are nae meant tae live."

"So ye admit ye have let some die ? That ye have the pow'r o' life and the deid ? Only the Lord haes that."

"Na, maister. Ah ken that the sick bairns that die hae been given the Lord's blessin'. Ah ken His work an' hae seen His mercy."

The laird bangs on the desk with a gavel.

"Wheesht, ye ! We maun hear mair o' yer thoughts on the work o' the Lord presently. Tak her away jailer. Anither tae be warded in the kirk steeple."

Helen Ross and Agnes Hardie are next to be examined. Helen Ross is taken first. She is accused of making waxen images of the fishermen Thomas Brunton and Thomas Craig. She protests her innocence, then after torture, confesses that she and Agnes Hardie conspired together to make mischief for the men who had slighted them for Jonet Dalrymple.

"But ye ken maisters, Jonet Dalrymple is the witch an' she laid
a spell on them baith. We never meant ony harm to the men, only
that their boat would coup and the fish would be lost. We choosed the
day weel. The sea was quiet and calm. 'Twere no' oor blame that
Thomas Craig was lost. He was promised tae me."

She breaks down and weeps. The laird ignores her tears despite the fact that
witches are supposed to be unable to shed them. He asks about her consulta-
tions with the devil in the ruins of Dunbar Castle. She protests violently about
that.

"He's nae deil. Nothin' but a pedlar-man frae England wha is-"

She stops abruptly. She remembers what the pedlar said he would do if she or
Agnes informed on him. She remembers his words.

Speak o' me an Ah'll gut ye like yer herrin.

The laird drums on the desk with his fingers, telling her to proceed and not
waste the court's time. Helen Ross decides to tell all since she realises she
may be facing the stake.

"It was a pedlar that promised a new gown if we telt him about the
gaugers. "

The laird leans back in his chair. He is smiling.

"So ye are contrabands noo. Ah see. Whit butter is in yer mooth.
Ye are a confessed witch and damned for't."

Agnes Hardie repeats the story. The laird enquires whether the jailer has kept
the pair apart so that the magistrates can compare the two women's accounts.
The jailer nods.

"Ye see, the charge is proven. They baith be witches. But we maun
hae the delations o' the fisherman that was saved frae the sea."

The court interviews Thomas Brunton and several others who witnessed the
capsize of the fishing cobble at the herring-drave. All say the same. The
weather was calm, the sea was quiet on the fateful day. And one important
revelation. The two accused women were seen in daylight, in the ruins of the
old castle shortly before the drowning of Thomas Craig. They were observed
casting something into the sea. Thomas Brunton completes the story.

"Maisters, the corpse cam tae rest below the part o' the castle they
stood on tae pitch their spells into the sea. The corpse was fankled in
the net, confounded by witchcraft."

The tortuous events unfold, the minister remarks to the court that abomina-
tions and evil are abroad in the parish, something he has suspected for a long

time. The laird agrees. The court decide to examine the three women from Doonhill of Pinkerton farm who are accused of consorting with the devil, desecrating the ruined kirk of St Helen's and for setting alight three haystacks by magic.

" We might as weel make an end o't this day."

The first to be examined is Mayse Redpath. She is rosy-cheeked, a comely, buxom girl, but after the torturers have finished with her, her grey eyes are sad like those of a seal. She confesses that she, Bessie McKenzie and Christian Boyd met with a pedlar who had a cart and promised to take them to Cockburnspath one afternoon so that Mayse could visit a sick relative there. They had stayed longer than intended and had to spend the night in the old ruined kirk, where the pedlar gave them meat and drink. She said he had promised them new gowns in exchange for their help.

"An' how were ye tae help him ?"

"By tellin' him aboot the gaugers, sir. The times they cam tae Dunbar and the Cove at Cockburnspath."

The laird smiles to his colleagues.

"Better tae consort wi' a smuggler than the deil eh? Na, na, lassie,
it'll no dae. For ye are the deil's servants and ye hae proved it by
the burnin' o' the ricks in the field next tae yer master's, belongin' tae
the farmer who cried ye a witch some time ago. Confess! We hae
a witness that saw ye and yer hellish accomplices.

The girl sobs and shakes her head.

"Nay sir, it was nae charm like ye speak o'. It was just an idle ploy."

The court buzzes with whispering. She is asked to explain. Mayse Redpath tells the court of the innocent game which is known as fathoming - measuring a haystack thrice with outstretched arms to obtain a glimpse of a future spouse.

"It was Bessie McKenzie showed us the ploy. Ye stand afore a hay-
rick in good sunlight so that yer shade is cast on it. Ye then
speak the words that will gie ye a look at yer spouse wha's tae be.
Ah swear 'tis whit we did that day."

"So, ye admit it is a cantraip?"

"Aye, but nae a spell, sir."

It is all the same to the court.

"Noo, tell the court about yer shape-shiftin' into a black cat that had
a rid ribbon that belonged tae ye."

The young girl is frightened but is able to speak.

"Oh, maister! It was also a ploy tae frighten Isabel Peddie the beggar-wife. She aye wheedles and whines at ma maister's kitchen tae get meal. 'Twas tae frighten her."

"The prisoner Peddie has also been convicted o' witchcraft but in her defence she did say the black cat disappeared in the barn along wi' Christian Boyd but ye cam oot wi' the rid ribbon the cat was wearin'. What say ye tae that?"

Mayse manages to smile.

"Aye sir, nocht but a ploy. Christian hid the cat in her apron and crawled under the straw tae bamboozle the beggar-wife."

The laird waves her away and calls for the next suspect, Bessie McKenzie. She confirms Mayse's story, as subsequently does Christian Boyd. The laird sums up the three women's tale briefly.

"Gentlemen. Ye have heard the dittays. A witch will say anythin' tae escape the gallows. The women have been seen jowkin' wi the horned deil in a deserted kirk, desecratin' the place. No doubt they were diggin' up corpses and usin' the joints for their spells. It is weel kenned they dae that at midnight. And ye hae heard them speak o' a spell they laid on three hay ricks. They be guilty o' witchcraft. 'Tis certain."

The trials are all but over, although the magistrates continue to interview witnesses. The court sits through Yuletide, then rises in the New Year, especially to observe Handsel Monday. The minister is despatched to consult with his colleague at Cockburnspath to determine whether there is evidence of desecration at St Helen's Kirk on the Lee. The minister confirms this and that strange lights have been seen in the ruins from time to time and recently during the harvest. The two men visit the kirk and find candle-grease on a gravestone; several of the old tombstones have been lifted and a fire has been lit. The church has clearly been desecrated, although the Cockburnspath minister does not care to admit to his colleague David Robertson that casks of brandy are hidden there. He has heard Robertson preaching against strong drink from the pulpit. But he enjoys his brandy, especially when the weather is inclement as it frequently is by the east coast. A small drop of brandy does wonders for the chill in old bones that have been jogging about on a horse in the hills.

The magistrates are growing alarmed at the mounting costs of the trials. They express their fear to the laird. The laird reminds them that the law allows a commission the right to impound money and movables possessed by a witch to pay for her trial and execution. He is told that nothing can be expected from Peddie the beggar or Craw the herb-woman, nor any of the servant girls. However, they learn that Helen Ross' father is skipper of a boat out of Eyemouth and of course, Elie Knox has considerable means.

"So gentlemen, Ah believe ye have nae fear o' the money. These twa will meet a' the costs."

The laird tells them it will not look good in Edinburgh if the parish of Dunbar fails in its duty to apprehend known witches. However, he wants no argument which might come to the attention of the Privy Council in the capital as he knows that no commission to try the ten women has been obtained from the powers that be. The trial is, in effect, illegal.

January proves to be a bitter month of snow and high winds which prevents some witnesses in outlying districts from answering summons. However, all depositions have been heard by the final week and the court is ready to pronounce formal sentences on the ten women. In the kirk spire, Jonet Dalrymple has languished for many weeks. She has been glad to have the company of Elspet Thomson during that time, for the beggar Isobel Peddie has made life difficult, cursing and spitting on her for giving her name to the court. As for Grissel Craw, she is enjoying her new surroundings and the chance to have some company for a change. She still has no idea of what is happening to her and she sits humming to herself and occasionally going to the small slit window in the spire to gaze in wonderment at the town spread out below her. It is a totally new experience for her and she is preoccupied with watching the boats entering and leaving the harbour each day. She points out the old castle to the others and tells them the spirit of Black Agnes, the Countess of Dunbar, walks nightly in the ruins. Her companions do not wish to hear of such things.

On the last night of January, it is pitch black in the kirk spire. The prisoners have been told they will appear in the burgh chambers for sentencing the following day. As Jonet Dalrymple hears the Tolbooth clock strike twelve, she knows that time is running out. She weeps on her bed of straw. Elspet Thomson crawls over to her on hands and knees. She touches the young woman's hand and puts her arm round her shoulders.

"Wheesht, lass, wheesht ! Ah, ye are nocht but a bairn. Ah mind the day ye lost yer mither, then yer father. ye have seen sae little o' the world, yet sae muckle o' it has entered ye."

Jonet weeps even more.

"Ah didnae gie the maisters yer name Mistress Thamson."

91

The older woman strokes her forehead gently. She tells her she knows it was Elie Knox. She asks the young girl what it was she has done to be branded a witch.

"They said Ah'd laid a spell on the fishermen Brunton and Craig. That Ah bewitched them tho' they was promised tae Helen and Agnes. Then it was the gentleman Home who telt them Ah'd bewitched him tae. He did press himsel' on me in the inn whiles he was there. On the day he was leavin' Ah was tramplin' the claes in the wynd wi' ma skirts breeched as aye. Master Home chanced by. Looked at me in an unco way. He did place his hand on ma thigh. Ah begged he tak it off. He pit his twa fingers in ma forkin' an pressed his mooth on mine. So Ah bit his cheek till the blood ran oot."

Elspet shakes her head.

"Bad enough lass. Home's kin o' the laird who's tryin' ye. But did they accuse ye o' murderin' Thomas Craig?"

She shakes her head.

"Mayhap ye'll escape with a touch o' the burnin' iron on yer cheek."

That night, Jonet manages to sleep. Elspet sits beside her, thinking of the sermon the minister preached the previous Sabbath. The words reached the kirk spire, so loud was his voice. He urged the congregation to be more vigilant for witches were stalking the land. That evening, he visits them in the spire to inform them the trial is nearly over.

The next morning is the first day of February. Candlemas Eve, a festival witches are known to celebrate, for their powers are great that night. Elspet Thomson smiles to herself when she thinks of this. Early that morning of mist and chill, the four women are taken to the Tolbooth to join the others. Nearly all the women are weeping. The time for recriminations is over. They have been told that the sentences will be announced by the court at ten o' clock. Promptly on the stroke of ten, the jailer and the town guard arrive to escort them into the burgh chambers. They are allowed to stand where they will. The magistrates confer amongst themselves. Helen Ross and Agnes Hardie stand together. Jonet and Elspet hold each other. The three farm servants are weeping profusely. Elie Knox and Isobel Peddie keep to themselves, away from the others. Grissel Craw is dancing a lop-sided jig in a corner, smiling to herself as she hums a tune.

The laird makes loud hemming noises and orders the ten women to stand in a line. The jailer has to coax Grissel out of her corner. He places her at the end of the line the better to hold her. She cannot stand still and wafts her skirts about her as she moves from one foot to the other. The laird motions for David Robertson to address the women.

"Do ye here renunce the Deil an' a' his works ? Are ye ready tae mak yer peace wi' the Lord thy God?"

Most but not all mutter their ayes. The minister looks at Elspet Thomson and Jonet Dalrymple who have said nothing.

"Be reminded. A' who remain silent will be damned."

Still the two women say nothing, then Jonet whispers she accepts the Lord as her only master.

"May the Lord hae mercy on ye."

The minister returns to his seat as the laird calls forth a small man from the gloomy interior. He is known to the women. He is the court dempster, the official who will read out the sentences. He takes an uncommonly long time to prepare his documents. The suspense is too much for Mayse Redpath, who is sobbing loudly. She falls to the floor. A bubble of voices bursts in the chambers, the weeping grows louder. The laird bangs on the table with his gavel.

"Wheesht ! Wheesht ye a'! The dempster is ready tae read. Get the witch tae her feet!"

Christian Boyd and Bessie McKenzie lift their friend from the floor and support her between them. There is silence once more. Except for the scratching of the clerk's quill. The dempster speaks. His voice is cold, his words colder.

"Hear ye. These be the crimes o' which ye hae been declared guilty."

"Jonet Dalrymple. Guilty o' bewitchin' three men be charms and be witchcraft."

"Isobel Peddie. Guilty o' consultin' wi' a known witch, sellin' charms and potions made be a known witch. Guilty o' abusing the people and cursin' same."

"Alesoun Knox. Guilty o' murder o' Robert Douglas, her spouse, be poison. Guilty o' attemptit murder o' her bairn. Guilty o' wicked fornication wi' a sojer. Guilty o' consultin' a known witch. Guilty o' layin' a heavy curse on Elspet Thomson, canny-wife."

Elie Knox tries to speak but is ordered to be silent.

"Elspet Thomson. Guilty o' layin' a curse on the forenamed Alesoun Knox tae the ill o' her chance-bairn. Guilty o' layin' a curse on her hens that they laid nae mair. Guilty o' wicked acts as a canny-wife in that she did let bairns dee unbaptised and be sent tae the Deil, her master, unbaptised. Guilty o' cursin' the forenamed Elie Knox's bairn that he was born wi' a cloven hoof."

"Mayse Ridpath. Guilty o' shape-shiftin' as a black cat. Guilty o' consortin' lewdly wi' the Deil in St Helen's Kirk on the Lee near Cockburnspath and desecratin' same. Guilty o' wilfu' evil acts, layin' a spell an' causin' a hay stack tae be burnt tae the ground."

"Bessie McKenzie. The same. No' guilty o' shape-shiftin'."

"Christian Boyd. The same. No' guilty o' shape-shiftin'."

"Helen Ross. Guilty o' consortin' wi' the deil i' the Castle o' Dunbar an' enterin' into a covenant wi' him there. Guilty o' fashionin' waxen images tae obtain the murder of Thomas Craig, thereby guilty o' witchcraft an' sorcery"

"Agnes Hardie. Guilty o' the same. Also guilty o' summonin' up the spirit o' the long deid Lady Agnes, Countess o' Dunbar, commonly kent as Black Agnes, the said spirit summoned in her aid."

"Grissel Craw. Lang suspected o' witchcraft and sorcery. Guilty o' preparin' spells an' potions that brought tae the deid the forenamed Robert Douglas, in complicity wi' the forenamed Alesoun Knox. Guilty o' possession by the deil."

The dempster pauses for breath. Some of the women are whimpering and whispering to each other. When she hears her name, Grissel Craw waves her apron at the dempster and smiles. The laird calls for silence.
"Ye here gathered. A' has been written in the magistrate book. Ye are guilty o' witchcraft, sorcery, makin' spells, layin' seikness, makin' curses an' consortin' wi' the deil. The magistrates accept the pannell's guilt and declare sentence be that ordained by the law

made be Queen Mary o' blessed memorie and be His Majesty's
Privy Council an' the Lords thairof in Edinburgh toon. The magistrates ordains that the panel be carried by the lockman tae the Gallows
Green furth o' the toon, thair tae be worryit to the deid and burnt
tae ashes. Thy goods and thy gear shall be escheat tae the toon o'
Dunbar for tae meet the costs o' yer trial and execution. This sentence tae be execute by the lockman on the next day of Februar."

There is widespread wailing and clamour as the women realise they are to
be executed the following day. The laird dismisses the dempster and orders
the town guards to hold the women in check with their lochaber axes. He
attempts to speak but the women are tearing at their clothes and hair, scream-
ing in their anguish. He beats impotently again and again on the table with his
gavel and shouts at them.

"Ye witches! Ye loathsome creatures! Ye maun ask the Lord's forgiveness for thy crimes. He maun forgive ye. But the law maun
never forgive ye for whit ye hae done. We hae sat lang. We hae
heard ye compear ye are witches. Whit we dae here we dae in the
name o' the Lord. Some among ye hae long been suspectit o'
witchcraft' But the law hae brought ye tae account, as hae the Lord
who ye maun answer for yer crimes, noo and in time comin. May
the Lord hae mercy on ye."

He orders the guards to remove the prisoners. As they are herded away, Jonet
Dalrymple approaches the bench. She stands before the laird.

"Beggin' yer pardon, maister. But ye did say it would gae weel wi'
me if Ah named others.   How will it gae sir?"

The laird turns purple, disbelief evident in his face.

"Whit? Whit? Are ye sae bold even noo?"

He leans over the table, thrusting his face into hers.

"Ah'll tell ye whit Ah will dae. Ah will see to't ye gang first so ye
will be spared the wait. Awa wi' the witch! Get her oot o' ma
sicht!"

Jonet, Elspet, Isobel and Grissel are led back to the kirk. News of the
sentences has already reached the street. As they walk the High Street, they
are pelted with rubbish and jeered.

"Whaur's yer freend the deil the day? Burn in hell-fire ye witches!
Burn! Burn!"

At last they reach the safety of the church. That night, they are given a meal

95

and a small candle to see by. Elspet Thomson is quiet for a while, then she speaks softly to Jonet.

> "So, 'tis the morn. They hae chosen the right time, the right day. This be Candlemas Eve. They'll hae double the guard on us lest we brak oot. An' the morn is Candlemas Day, when a' rents hae tae be settled and bills met. Aye, they hae chosen the right day."

She remembers the sermon the minister preached the past Sunday.

> "Ye maun be vigilant against witches. For if ye be not vigilant, ye are as guilty as they whae are in the Tolbooth and in the spire o' this kirk. Ye ken whit the Holy Book bids ye tae dae. 'Thou shalt not suffer a witch to live.' It is there in Scriptures for ye a' tae see. Exodus, chapter 22, verse 18. Amen."

That night sleep escapes all but Grissel Craw. As the clock in the Tolbooth chimes twelve, Elspet Thomson sighs.

> "We maun wait the daylight. But the day has come."

On the morning of the execution, the guards arrive before first light to escort the four from the kirk to the Tolbooth. That morning, the burgh chambers are buzzing with the excitement and chatter that fear generates. The laird calls for order and bids all who have no business there to leave the chambers.

> "Weel done, weel done ! We hae dinged doon Tantalloun. It micht hae been a lang sitting-doon but we hae broken the powers o' evil. Thanks be tae ye a'."

It is a chill February morning. A sea-haar drifts up the High Street. As the clock in the Tolbooth strikes ten, the women are shackled together and led out of the holding cell down the spiral staircase to the exit. At the foot of the stair, Jonet Dalrymple, first of the chained women, is spat upon through the bars of the iron gate. Faces press against the bars, hands reach out to claw at Jonet. Hate is in the faces of one or two she knows, twisting their features out of all recognition. Jonet stares at them, numb with fear. Behind her, there is commotion. The dempster struggles to the front of the prisoners.

> "Wait, lockman ! Ye maun ken the prisoner Dalrymple is tae be first so ye maun pit her on the cairt last."

The lockman tells the jailer to sort it out. The jailer is not in any mood for this, having spent a considerable part of his drink money the night before. But after some jostling and pushing, the order is settled.

> "It's beyond me we hae tae dae this. Efter a', whit does it matter? 'Twould best be done at t'ither end."

The lockman ignores the jailer. He is about to open the Tolbooth gate and bids the town guard hold back the crowds. The High Street is thronged with people. Shops are closed. As the prisoners are led out of the Tolbooth, the cry goes up.

"They come oot o' the Towbooth! Burn the witches! Burn them in hell-fire! Intae the flames wi' them!"

The sergeant of the town guard orders his men to hold back the crowds with their lochaber axes, the six-foot long wooden spears tipped with a blade and a hook for dismounting horsemen.

"Mind oot ye clamjamfray! Mak way, mak way! Let the lockman dae his work!"

The foul smelling burgh midden-cart is standing close by at the mouth of the Tolbooth. The pitiful line of women are ushered towards it. Afraid of the ugly mood of the crowd, the sergeant of the guard bids the town drummer beat a tattoo to drown out the noise. It is pointless. He shouts to the lockman to get the women into the cart, but little seems to be happening..

"'Tis the shackles! They cannae get into the cairt on acoont o' the shackles!"

But at last, the cart is loaded with its sad cargo. The carter whips the horses into life. As the cart moves off, the crowd surges into the space it leaves like water rushing to fill a hole. Although the crowd has to part to let the horses through, they surround the cart, pelting the women with stones, refuse, rotten vegetables, even dung. The mercat cross is festooned with small boys who have climbed the stone pillar to see better. One has even managed to reach the top, from where he casts herring-heads and stones with the unerring aim of a school boy.

At the Gallows Green well beyond the town wall, the field is already thronged with people, gathered there early to get a good view. Some sit on the grass, eating bannocks and bread, watching their children at play. A pieman is doing a brisk trade, as is the gingerbread seller. A chapman moves through the crowd, trying to sell pins and ribbons. He is the chapman who sold Mayse Redpath her red ribbon the previous summer.

The cart proceeds down the West Port, followed by the lockman and two ministers on foot; some of the magistrates come behind in a coach. As the procession reaches the Gallows Green, a cry goes up from the crowd assembled there.

"Here they come, Burn them! Burn the witches!"

The women are led from the cart. Before them, they see Doon Hill. A weak watery sunshine falls on its earth which is the colour of blood. The gorse has not yet come to flower. It is a bleak hill today. The magistrates have a physician with them to make sure the women are dead before they are cast into the fire, a luxury not always afforded in such circumstances. Near the gallows is a large heap of faggots and coals. The minister David Robertson confers with his colleague, Mr John Lauder, minister of Tyninghame Kirk who has been ordered by the Dunbar Presbytery to attend the execution. Mr John, as he likes to be called, is telling David Robertson about two witches recently apprehended in his parish.

First to ascend the ladder to the gallows is Jonet Dalrymple. Her head is bowed, her once beautiful black hair matted and uncombed. Her face is chalk-white, her lips move slightly as though she is saying a prayer. A man in the crowd shouts out.

"See! The witch speaks tae her maister! He'll no' aid ye noo, witch!"
The lockman slips the noose over Jonet's head with some difficulty because of her long, unbound hair. She continues to pray as the stool is kicked from under her. The crowd jeer and whistle in approval.

"Aye, she's dancin' tae the deil's sang noo!"
Jonet's slight body hangs limply, her head lolls to one side, her tongue protrudes from the side of her mouth. Slowly, her slack body turns in a half-circle to the right like a weather-vane in a soft breeze. North, north-east, east, a pause, then east, north-east, north. She is taken down from the gallows, examined by the doctor and pronounced dead. Two town guards carry her remains to the pyre. The next to be hanged is Grissel Craw. She has to be helped up the ladder. It is a slow process. When she reaches the platform, she waves to the crowd. Below her, most of the other prisoners are weeping. They can see nothing but the gallows. The wail goes up.

"Oh Lord God, oh Jesus hae mercy on us!"
The crowd responds with jeers.

"Where's Auld Clootie noo?"
One by one, the women are executed. When it is Elie Knox's time, she does not go quietly. She curses the crowds, spits on the lockman. He silences her with his fist. The last to be hanged is the midwife, Elspet Thomson. As she climbs the ladder, the lockman stares down at her. He is playing with a piece of rope in his hands. Like a child, he twists it through his fingers. He asks her if she has anything to say. He remembers how she assisted his wife in her

difficult birth a year ago. She speaks to him briefly, hangs her head, then she lifts it high. She stares at the crowd and begins to speak. Her words are drowned out by their shouts and jeers. As she is hanged, her feet kick and jerk. Again the crowd jeers, especially some of the women who have had difficult births in their time.

"Tae be worryit is quick. Tae birth a bairn is a lang time in purgatory." As Elspet's body is removed from the gallows, a strange thing occurs. Out of a clump of nearby trees flies a magpie. It lands on the crosspiece of the gallows, utters its dry, throaty rattle three times, then flies off. A man in the front of the crowd calls out.

"See! See! The Deil's come for his ain!" By now the pyre is burning briskly. The flames leap up. Some stand as near as the heat will allow. They watch the hair catch alight, the flesh blacken, the eyes sizzle and pop in the flames. There is a hissing sound, like bacon frying on a griddle. There is the unmistakable sweet cloying stench of burning human flesh.

"How weel they are noo! A' ableeze!" A great pall of smoke hangs over the Gallows Green. It drifts towards Doon Hill in the breeze that comes from the sea. By nightfall, all that will be left is a pile of ash.

The crowd begins to disperse. Among the first to leave is a pedlar lately come out of England. During the executions, he has covered his face with his hands, Those near him think he is just a weak-stomached Englishman. He prefers them to think thus. As he turns to go, he hitches up his bulky pack, adjusts his outsize bonnet which has two long pheasant feathers on either side. The pack on his back makes him look like a hunchback. The feathers could be mistaken for the horns of a goat. He disappears among the knots of people making their way back to Dunbar. Later, David Robertson and Mr John speak to the lockman. They ask what it was the woman Elspet Thomson said. Perhaps they are hoping she begged forgiveness for her crimes.

"Na, maister. She said there was nae innocent folk present on Gallows Green this day." That evening, the magistrates meet in the coaching inn for the customary meal after a funeral or execution. They are joined by the two ministers. The next evening, John Lauder of Tyninghame will make the following entry in his kirk session minute-book:

'I went to Dunbar, being ordairit to go, quher ten witches were execute.'

99

It will be the sole account which tells of these proceedings for, later that year, when Oliver Cromwell invades Scotland by way of Dunbar, the local records will be placed in barrels where they will be lost in a storm that will sink the boat taking them to the Bass Rock.

In the warmth of the coaching inn, the claret is flowing. The laird stands before the fire. He is in convivial mood and calls for more wine. Then he asks for silence.

"Gentlemen, we be here for the deid-chack an' never was meat mair earnit. We be pleased also tae welcome Mr John frae Tyninghame Kirk. Mr John, will ye say words ower this meat ?"

Grace over, they sit down to a rich meal of broth and rump steak. The claret bottle goes round many times, then there is whisky and brandy. The laird asks Mr John how things fare in his parish.

"Have ye apprehended mony witches ?"

The minister shakes his head, although he remarks that every pulpit in the land is being asked to urge its congregation to be vigilant.

"We hae to be watchfu'. They have apprehended and burnt witches near Dunbar. Nae parish is safe. Root them oot, sir! Root them oot!"

The laird upsets his glass, such is the violence of his fist on the dinner table. It is Candlemas Day, 2 February 1650. In exactly seven months to the day, the Covenanting army, in yet another act of folly in Scottish military history, will descend from its position of strategic strength on Doon Hill to meet Oliver Cromwell who, the following morning, will destroy it in less than an hour. Cromwell's presence in Scotland will suppress the witch hunt for some years to come but the perpetrators themselves will escape justice. David Robertson will continue to occupy the incumbency at Dunbar. For those accused of witch-craft, Oliver Cromwell will be their saviour for a few years.

Footnote: This trial of ten women took place as confirmed by the Tyninghame kirk session minute book entry for February 1650. It is the sole record of the trial and execution of these women, whose names are however manufactured, as is the evidence against them. Both are however typical for the time. David Robertson and John Lauder, ministers at Dunbar and Tyningehame respectively are historical persons.

5

Cromwell and the Witches

Oliver Cromwell's name does not readily spring to mind as the saviour of witches. Popular history would have us believe he was a staunch Puritan who invoked the name of his god before, during and after many of his battles, which of course is true; however, Cromwell was something of an enigma. More of a soldier-statesman than a religious zealot, his enemies attributed his military victories to his supposed covenant with the devil. As the propaganda of the times put it, Cromwell was said to have sold his soul to the devil. Writing shortly after Cromwell's death in 1658, the Royalist physician and poet Abraham Cowley maintained that his meteoric rise from obscurity to that of virtual king was due to a pact with the devil:

Oliver Cromwell

' What can be more extraordinary than that a person of mean birth, no fortune, no eminent qualities of body....should have the courage to attempt, and in happiness to succeed in, so improbable a design as the destruction of one of the most ancient and most solid-founded monarchies upon the earth ? That he should have the power and boldness to put his prince and master to an open and infamous death ?....To oppress all his enemies by arms, and afterwards his friends by artifice ? ....To be feared and courted by all foreign princes and adopted as brother to the gods of the earth ? To call to- gether Parliament with a word of his pen and scatter them with a breath of his mouth ? ....'

Cromwell was unquestionably a great man who wielded extraordinary power over the people by sheer force of personality, directing the key events of his time. Perhaps it is possible that his soldiers believed that Noll, as they called him, was indeed in league with the devil. Cromwell was no stranger to witch-craft, as will be seen. His master at Huntingdon Grammar School, Thomas Beard, published a volume of sermons on witchcraft; it is without doubt that he lectured his young charges on the subject, filling their minds with fear, terror and fascination. In later life, Cromwell wrote to a cousin about his wickedness; whether this was a reference to his dabbling in the black arts or simply a confession about his dissolute youth before he got religion is not clear. Dated 1638, his letter is ambiguous and hints of dark things in his past:

'You know what my manner of life has been. Oh, I have lived in and loved darkness, and hated the light. I was a chief, the chief of sinners.'

A logical interpretation of his admission is that Cromwell, a recent convert to the Puritan faith, was expressing regret for the wildness of his youth - except that at the time of writing he was aged thirty-nine and had been married for ten years. Did he have witchcraft in mind? We will never know. He was never heard to make any public pronouncements on the subject. Nor can we detect any views in Cromwell's official or private papers. His contemporary, Lord Denzil Holles, who publicly shared Cromwell's political sentiments, pri-vately detested him. Holles, an MP in the Long Parliament, was moved to attack Cromwell in 1648; he believed that Cromwell had indeed dealt in witch-craft, expressing his scathing view before a portrait of the great man:

'.... only [those] whose eyes and hand have been with you at your meetings, your Sabbaths, when you have laid by your assumed shapes (with which you have cozened the world) and resumed your own; imparting to each other, and both of you to your Fellow- Witches, the bottom of your designs, the Policy of your Actings, the Turns of your Contrivances, all your Falsehoods, Cozenings, Vil-

-lainies and Cruelties, with your full intention to ruin the three kingdoms. All I will say to you is no more than what St Peter said to
Simon the Sorcerer, "Repent therefore this your wickedness."'

Cromwell made no attempt to deny this publicly-held view of him. Was
it because it contained a germ of truth? Was there more to Holles' attack than
personal animosity? Had Cromwell indeed consorted with witches or at least
practised the black arts? He had second-hand knowledge of witchcraft from
events involving his grandparents, Sir Henry and Lady Susan Cromwell. No
doubt his elder sisters enthralled him with the story of the Witches of Warboys,
whose reputed black arts caused the death of Lady Susan in the last decade of
the sixteenth century. The story is that Robert Throckmorton, a wealthy busi-
nessman in Warboys, had five daughters, all of whom suddenly began to suffer
from fits in 1591. The girls accused Alice Samuel, a local witch; they said
she had bewitched them through her familiar, a chicken. Doctors were called
in from nearby Cambridge who diagnosed the illness as the effects of witchcraft. Some time later, Lady Susan Cromwell visited the Throckmortons in
Warboys; while there, she confronted Alice Samuel and accused her of witchcraft, which the woman denied. Lady Cromwell suggested that Mrs
Throckmorton cut off a lock of Alice's hair and throw it into the fire to counteract the spell on her daughters. Alice protested to Lady Susan:

'Why do you treat me thus ? I never did you any harm, as yet.'

As yet? Lady Susan turned the words over in her mind; they preyed on her and
she got it into her head that sooner or later, she too would be bewitched. Such
is the power of auto-suggestion. Shortly after the incident at the
Throckmortons' house, Lady Susan contracted a wasting illness of which she
died just over a year later, in 1592. Her death was attributed to witchcraft.
About six months before, Alice Samuel and her daughter Agnes were examined by the Bishop of Lincoln and two Justices of the Peace, one of whom was
Francis Cromwell. Alice was made to stand before the Throckmorton children and say the following:

'Even as I am a witch and consented to the death of Lady Cromwell,
so I charge thee, spirit, to depart and let her be well.'

The children were cured but not poor Lady Cromwell. Unfortunately for him,
John Samuel, Alice's husband, arrived at the Throckmortons' house as this
charade was in progress and he was made to repeat Alice's words. Agnes
Samuel declined to declare she was pregnant which could have saved her life.
Before going to the gallows, she defiantly said

"Nay, that I will not do. It shall never be said that I was both a witch
and a whore."

Alice, John and Agnes - the Witches of Warboys - were hanged in 1591 and
their bodies put on display, doubtless to serve as a warning to others. The

Samuel estate, worth £40, legally passed to Sir Henry Cromwell; he was so moved by his wife's death that he gifted the money to Queen's College, Cambridge University for a sermon to be preached against witchcraft every Lady Day on 25th March - the first day of the New Year under the old Julian Calendar.   (Unlike Scotland, which adopted the modern Gregorian Calendar in 1600, England did not convert until 1752).   Cambridge preachers were paid a fee of £2; the Samuel estate was invested and the income ensured that sermons were funded until 1814, almost a century after the witchcraft laws had been repealed.

That Cromwell was a willing and repentant convert to Puritanism is not in any doubt but his was a strange approach; while it was not unusual for military commanders on both sides of the Civil Wars to call for divine aid before, during and after battle, Cromwell seemed to be possessed of divine - or dark - impulses as he went into the fight.   At Naseby in 1645 and again at Dunbar in 1650, eye-witnesses said he seemed to be drunk, laughing excessively, his eyes sparkling.   Little wonder the propagandists accused him of selling his soul to the devil.   But then propaganda came easily to the lips of his many enemies during the English Civil Wars, then in the brief war with Scotland in 1650-51.   That he had a darker side to his nature is evident.   In his compelling study *Witchcraft in British History*, Ronald Holmes relates a strange incident which took place after the battle of Naseby on 14th July 1645, yet another triumph for the Parliamentary army against Charles I.   Holmes tells us that a thousand women accompanying the Royalist baggage train were either killed or mutilated by the Ironsides and their bodies strewn across the field. There is little doubt that these defenceless women were the victims of sadistic and vengeful dealings by the Parliamentary army.   The incident is barely touched on in surviving state documents but it is unique for the time.   We cannot be sure whether this war crime was committed under orders but it seems likely.   A contemporary account describes the women as no better than Irish whores who had been ordered to creep among the Parliamentary wounded and slit their throats.   This is crude propaganda, since many of the women were wives of quality, married to serving Royalist officers. The account given by the Parliamentarian John Vicars is clearly an attempt to justify the actions of the Roundhead soldiers who in the blood-lust of battle, had slain or mutilated the women; they were

> 'marked in their faces or noses with slashes and cuts and some cut off; just rewards for such wicked Strumpets.'

It is not unreasonable to suggest that the women were considered witches, since the method of marking them was similar to that inflicted on those found guilty of witchcraft and sentenced to non-capital punishment.   A not dissimilar incident occurred after the defeat of the Royalist Marquis of Montrose by

David Leslie and the Army of the Covenant at Philiphaugh later the same year. In his *History of Selkirkshire,* T Craig-Brown tells us about twelve Scots males, sixteen Scots women, four Irish males and six Irish women held captive in the jail at Selkirk in December. The women were either camp followers or the wives of some of the officers and men in the Royalist army. At any rate, the Irishmen, being mercenaries and Catholics, were executed out of hand along with their women; contrary to orders from David Leslie that no rebels be killed, the local authorities shot the ten Irish in the market-place in March the following year. There was no trial. Could it be that they were considered no better than witches if not heretics? It is entirely possible, even if the records do not confirm it. A postscript to this story is the wickedness of one Highland woman whose husband had been slain in the battle; she begged a Covenanter trooper to take her on his horse, then, when seated behind him, she drew a dirk and stabbed the unsuspecting soldier, pushing him into the stream they were crossing and galloping off on his horse. There is perhaps more of witchery in that than in the countless bogus trials and the equally bogus charges brought against women suspected of witchcraft.

There is no doubt that the Puritan Roundheads were fanatics with a bitter and all-consuming hatred of Catholics and Anglicans, both being regarded as heretics. It is understandable that officers like Cromwell would have whipped up their troops' fervour for battle in what they saw as a crusade against the enemies of their religion. As for Cromwell's personal reaction to the atrocity at Naseby, both he and history are silent. Did it exercise his conscience unduly? He knew that the Puritan extremists in the army - Baptists and Separatists - shared an equally intense hatred of witches and heretics with their Scottish Presbyterian allies. He probably expected that Royalist women caught in or near any battlefield would be 'blooded' or scored to remove any witch powers they might use to influence the outcome of a battle. Whether Oliver Cromwell was guilty of dabbling in the black arts will never be known. At the end of the English Civil Wars, his character and determination were the driving forces behind the execution of Charles I. In January 1649, a nervous parliament instituted legal proceedings against the king; while content to try him, they lacked the resolve to kill him. It was Cromwell's strength of personality alone that sealed Charles' fate. Oliver personally guided the hands of the waverers, forcing them to sign the king's death warrant. It is said that he played the fool when the document was duly attested; he threw ink at one of the signatories, who replied in kind. This is hardly the behaviour of a dour Puritan.

In Scotland, news of Charles' execution was greeted with mixed feelings. Scottish commissioners were appointed to treat with the late king's son Charles, living in exile in Holland. After protracted negotiations, Charles came to

Scotland to be declared king in 1650. At first, Charles seemed to be the king the Scottish Covenanters had hoped for in 1638. Charles II was more politically astute, less obviously arrogant than his late father. He went along with the Covenanters' demands for purely political reasons. The price of Scottish support was that he uphold the Presbyterian form of religious worship; Charles did so but he hated Presbyterianism, so much so that while treating with the Covenanters, he was engaged in secret negotiations with the Marquis of Montrose, the brilliant Royalist general whom he hoped would bring about a successful rising in the north. Unfortunately, Montrose's phenomenal military success deserted him at Carbisdale, where he was defeated and taken prisoner with Charles' letters on his person. He was brought to Edinburgh and hanged as a traitor. In England, the republican Parliamentary Party, having disposed of Charles I and the concept of the divine right of kings, were incensed when the Scots proclaimed his son king In the first half of 1650, the English parliament, rather than the army, dictated events; it would not settle for anything less than the invasion of Scotland. Lord Fairfax refused to comply and resigned his command of the army, arguing that it would be more politically acceptable if the Scots invaded England. The command was offered to Cromwell who reluctantly accepted it. Riding out of London that July morning in 1650, Cromwell remarked to his aide, General Lamberton, that the crowds cheering them in the streets would as soon call for their heads. Cromwell was a good judge of character and nothing if not a realist.

The impending invasion of Scotland galvanised the Kirk Party, now at the zenith of its power, into greater activity; it called for national unity while continuing to purge the army of Malignants - persons loyal to Charles I but who refused to swear an oath to the Solemn League and Covenant - and the Engagers who had sided with Charles in 1647 and were defeated by Cromwell at the battle of Preston in 1648. Sir Archibald Johnston of Wariston headed the Committee of Purging all that summer. The Kirk had strengthened the laws against witchcraft over the decade, passing four acts against it between 1640 and 1649. As mentioned in the previous chapter, a Commission was established by the General Assembly in 1649 to consider the problem of witchcraft; its membership was, as one would expect, heavily weighted in the church's favour, two-thirds being ministers, the remainder representing the legal and medical professions. Among the nine lawyers was Johnston of Wariston. In tandem with this, there was no let-up in the trying of witches. It was said that when Cromwell entered Berwickshire that July, he was met by the devil and two thousand witches. The propaganda machine was operating at full blast from the pulpits; many in the Kirk conveniently forgot that Cromwell had subdued the Catholic Irish the year before and that he had more in common with Presbyterianism than with the devil. However, Cromwell was too late in crossing the Border to save some of the witches who were executed in those last months of freedom in 1650.

A somewhat colourful and bizarre case of unrequited love posing as moral outrage against witchcraft occurred around this time; the date is given as c.1650, such is the uncertainty. The details are not well recorded; there appears to be gaps in the local records, perhaps deliberate. However there is a strong tradition in the area that Maggie Osborne, a very attractive woman, kept an alehouse in Ayr. Apparently, she began her adult life as a barmaid and probably because of her sexual favours, soon found herself owner of the inn. Again, tradition has it that the local minister at Ayr, William Adair, fell under her spell and asked her to marry him. He was probably too dull for the winsome and extrovert Maggie. One can imagine his frustration. Broken-hearted at first, his lovesickness turned to anger as often happens in matters of the heart; Adair's hate was that of the slighted suitor and he was determined to have his revenge. Perhaps it was Adair who put it about Ayr that Maggie was a witch - or at least he was the instigator of the accusations made against her. At any rate, she was taken into custody, suspected of witchcraft; it comes as no surprise that Adair was appointed one of the judges at her trial.

The charges preferred against Maggie were the usual preposterous nonsense but with our knowledge of the emotional crisis which triggered them, they are all the more sad and tragic. One of the charges was that Maggie, having partaken of Holy Communion in church in the Moor Kirk of Luce, Wigtonshire, was observed to spit out the Holy Wafer at the kirk entrance and feed it to a toad - the devil in disguise. This ridiculous incident was recounted by one of the church officers some time after the event; possibly he was acting under Adair's direction. On another occasion, Maggie was walking from Barr to Glenluce when she met a funeral procession and wanted to pass it unseen for some reason. She did so by changing herself into a beetle. The story becomes ever more bizarre. Maggie in beetle form narrowly escaped being crushed unwittingly by one of the mourners, a shepherd; he stepped on the ground where she was crawling but she managed to hide in a rut in the road! Said to have been frightened and angry by her brush with near death, she resolved to get even with the unsuspecting shepherd by bewitching him. However, apparently being a very devout man, none of Maggie's spells had any effect . Finally, her chance came. One night, the shepherd forgot to say grace before his supper. Maggie pounced. A sudden snowstorm arose and after some time, she caused an avalanche to fall on the shepherd's cottage, smothering him, his wife and ten children to death.

The final charge was another instance of Maggie's shape-shifting which took place at her inn. Apparently one evening, a servant girl whom she'd asked to make a brew of ale was insolent to her mistress. A quarrel ensued, hot words were exchanged and no doubt Maggie, given her trade, cursed the girl roundly. The servant girl went off sullenly to the brewhouse to do her duties. At about midnight, the brewhouse was invaded by several cats, the largest of which leapt on the girl's neck and tried to force her into the vat of boiling liquid. The terrified but resourceful girl managed to draw off a ladleful of the bubbling brew and threw it over some of the cats including the one which had so violently attacked her. The next morning, her mistress appeared to have overslept, so she went to her bedroom, drew back the bedclothes and saw that Maggie's back was badly blistered. This was proof positive of her guilt as a witch. She was tried by the kirk, then by the civil authorities who sentenced her to death, no doubt to William Adair's intense satisfaction. What followed later is absurd in the extreme. Today, the events would not be out of place in the slapstick anarchy of a child's television cartoon; in that benighted time however, the outcome was fatal.

Even as she was being led to her place of execution, Maggie Osborne's resourcefulness did not desert her; perhaps it was drawn from the reserves of courage all female publicans must have since they lack the physical strength needed to deal with unruly male customers. At any rate, as the ministers gathered round the stake to which she was about to be bound and the faggots were stacked round her feet, Maggie offered to make startling revelations, provided the ministers agreed to give her two pewter plates which had never been wet. The ministers agreed and sent a man off to town to obtain the plates. On the way back, he dropped one in a puddle but thinking it of no consequence, he dried the plate on his coat and carried on his way. The story descends into utter absurdity. Given the plates, Maggie supposedly attached one to each shoulder where they expanded into wings! She rose from the ground but the pewter plate that had gotten wet flopped like a broken pinion, her deal with the devil having been compromised. A sergeant of the town guard reputedly hooked his Lochaber Axe into her dress and hauled her back to *terra firma* where she was duly strangled and burnt. How in any society - even that one - could ordinary people take the ministers present seriously ever again? That they continued to believe them sprang simply from an even greater fear of witchery.

A less attractive case at Ayr about the same time was that of Jonet Smellie, who appears to have been something of a virago and as a consequence, brought considerable trouble to herself over a period of thirty-seven years. In 1613, she was accused of making filthy and slanderous attacks on her neighbours; for that, she was gagged and bound to the Fish Cross at Ayr. Then in 1621 she was sentenced to a spell on the penitent's stool in the church for un-Christian behaviour. At that time, she apparently attempted to take her own life by poison. In 1628, Jonet was in trouble yet again for some undisclosed crimes; she was warded in the Black House for women, situated under the tolbooth stair. She was put on a diet of bread and water and her jailer was given strict orders not to allow her any 'stark drink'! Perhaps by then Jonet had become an alcoholic vagrant, which would explain her anti-social behaviour. It was also inevitable that she would be charged with witchcraft, which happened in 1629. Jonet barely escaped execution; she was banished from Ayr for life. However, twenty-one years on she returned, probably thinking that her past was forgotten. Not so. There must have been many still living who remembered her and were only to eager to inform the local minister, William Adair, about her activities. Adair had of course played a prominent part in bringing Maggie Osborne to justice and his enthusiasm had not lessened.. He was about to bring an action against Jonet when she died in prison. Not to be outdone, Adair insisted that her corpse be dragged through the streets of Ayr on a sled, then taken to the Gallows' foot to be burnt to ashes. The burgh records confirm this took place.

The tragic farces of Maggie Osborne and Jonet Smellie possibly occurred before the ministers' minds and those of the nation as a whole were transfixed by Oliver Cromwell's spectacular and crushing victory on the east coast of Scotland. The disastrous battle of Dunbar is well-documented and need not be repeated here. The ruthless purging of the Scottish army by men like Johnston of Wariston and the Committee of Purging undoubtedly contributed to the defeat; some eighty seasoned officers and three thousand battle-hardened troops were dismissed, some even on the day before the battle. As one disgruntled Malignant, lamenting the state of the army facing Cromwell on 2nd September put it, the army had been taken over by

> '...ministers' sons, clerks and other sanctified creatures who never
> saw or heard of any sword but that of the spirit.'

Suffice it to say that the first to leave the field were the ministers who had exhorted General David Leslie to leave his superior position on Doon Hill and lead the Army of the Covenant to its worst defeat. The ministers fled to Edinburgh to take shelter in Edinburgh Castle. Known from ancient times as Maiden's Castle because the Iron Age Votadini tribe protected their women there in times of war, the disaffected Edinburgh citizens hostile to the Kirk Party renamed it Prostitute Whore. Shortly after the defeat at Dunbar, one Scottish preacher, quoting from Scripture (*James*, chapter 4, verse 7) said of Cromwell:

'The English General is worse than the Devil; for the Scripture says 'Resist the devil and he will flie from you'; but resist Oliver and he will flie in your face.'

When Cromwell entered Edinburgh, one of his first acts was to dismiss the senior civil servants from key government positions, especially the judiciary. Writing to the English parliament, he requested that commissioners be sent to Scotland with all haste to administer the country. The English law-commissioners who replaced those in the Court of Session were George Smith, John Martin, Andrew Owen and Edward Mosley. These men found Edinburgh Tolbooth crammed with prisoners awaiting trial; among them were several women accused of witchcraft. The English commissioners examined the charges against them, declared the cases not proven and released the women, a decision which no doubt Cromwell endorsed. Presbyterian eyebrows were raised to the heavens. Was this not adequate proof of Cromwell's complicity with the devil? Did it not vindicate the belief that his successes in battle were down to assistance from the Prince of Darkness? Had he not desecrated the kirk at Dunbar, where he permitted his artillerymen to stable their horses inside it and use the kirkyard for grazing? This became common practice during the ensuing occupation, since the English army thought the Scottish Church inferior to their own. Incredibly, despite the enlightened attitude of the Cromwellian authorities, the burgh of Peebles arrested eleven witches, including Janet Coutts, 'a confessing witch'. There was a problem with the case however; the local magistrates refused to maintain so many prisoners in jail pending trial. Financial expediency brought about a solution; the women would be sent back to Crawford Douglas from whence they came, under guard, until the witch-pricker George Cathie could be brought from Lanark to test them. Cathie pricked all of them before witnesses and with their own consent; the account of this states that '....the said George did prick pins in every one of them, and in divers of them without pain the pin was put in, as the witnesses can testify.' As a result, the women were detained in jail, while the Presbytery appointed watchers from the parishes to which they belonged to guard them, their local minister also attending 'to take pains by prayer and exhortation, to bring them to a confession.' It is more than likely all eleven were executed (see p111). Money was a constant problem however; in 1650, the small Peeblesshire parish of Newlands resisted a request from the local magistrates to meet the cost of providing watchers to guard some witches held in Peebles Tolbooth; the kirk session refused to pay on the grounds that as there were only four witches in custody, little watching was necessary.

In 1651, the occupying forces were spread thinly throughout the country; a sizeable force was garrisoned in the Borders and the south-west, the stronghold of the remnants of the Covenanter army. The troopers settled down to their duties under the command of General George Monck who made his headquarters in Dalkeith, scene of many a witch burning in the past. Be that as it may, belief in witches among the English troopers had almost disappeared by 1651. Writing home that year, a trooper confirmed this view when he described some women in the area where he was stationed:

'....they doe look like witches (if there be any such creatures) where with their [the Scots] frequent burning of them, it seems this country abounds (14 and 16 being burned in a little village neere Wadington [probably Mordington in the Borders] about a yeere since.....'

In Chapter 3, reference is made to the execution of twenty people in 1649 in a small unidentified village two miles outside Berwick. Mordington, which apparently witnessed the burning of thirty witches, lies about 5 miles west of Berwick. This means that in the period 1649-50, in an area of a few square miles, no less than fifty people, including the Mordington Witches, were executed, perhaps 10% of the population of two small Berwickshire villages.

Propaganda against Cromwell persisted, as one might imagine. At some point during the English Occupation, an English soldier wrote of how Scottish ministers were:

'....excommunicated for not answering whether Cromwell is Antichrist or not.'

It did not escape the notice of those who hated Cromwell that 3rd September was a special date for him. On 3rd September 1649, he had mounted the successful siege of Drogheda, Ireland; on 3rd September 1650, he defeated a superior Scottish army at Dunbar; on 3rd September 1651, he defeated Charles II at Worcester, a battle Cromwell described as 'the crowning mercy.' Eerie as it undoubtedly is, Cromwell died on 3rd September 1658. On that day, his enemies said the devil had come to claim his soul in exchange for the victories he had given him. There is something decidedly uncanny in this.

Despite the power and authority of the newly-instated English law commissioners, witches were still being detained in prison and executed in out of the way corners of the country. On 28th July 1652, the Presbytery of Drummelzier in Peeblesshire paid £3 Scots to Andrew Watson, part of a bill of 100 merks due to him for executing witches, perhaps the eleven executed at the end of 1650 mentioned above. On 23rd October, prisoners accused of various crimes including witchcraft appeared before the English judges; the commissioners demanded to know the grounds on which the charges against the witches had been based. They were informed that two of them had made previous appearances before the Scottish courts immediately prior to the invasion in 1650 which had prevented their trial. Furthermore, those who stood at the bar had already confessed their crimes. When the commissioners probed deeper into the manner in which their confessions had been obtained, they were no doubt sickened by what they heard. Six women awaiting trial had been accused of practising witchcraft. Their confessions had been extracted under extreme torture. Only the two before the court had survived the ordeal. They said they had been bound and strung up from the ceiling of their cell by the thumbs and whipped by two Highlanders - the English considered Highlanders little more than barbarians - who had also applied lighted candles to the soles of their feet, between their toes, in their mouths and on their heads. One of the survivors recounted how she had existed on a bread-and-water diet for twenty-eight days, kept naked save for a hair shirt steeped in vinegar which stripped the skin off her back. The other woman said she too had been left naked but for a hair shirt and made to lie on the cold stone of her cell. The women were released on caution.

In the same month of 1652, Bulstrode Whitelock, an English administrator, commented that sixty witches had been brought before the circuit court

'but they found so much Malice and so little proof against them, that none were [sic] condemned.'

In the autumn of that year, the four English law-commissioners went on circuit throughout Scotland dealing with criminal cases in Edinburgh, Stirling, Glasgow and Aberdeen; they may also have held assizes in Inverness, Ayr, Dumfries and Jedburgh. They were impartial; while sentences were harsh, they were imposed only for the worst of crimes. Many cases involved murder, witchcraft, adultery and buggery - the last punishable by hanging and burning, usually reserved for witches. The English judges were rightly proud of their enlightened attitude to witches. The writer of the *Worcester MS* applauded their decision to release witches since it accorded with his own assertions that

'....there are verry few if any of those men usually call witches & that the torments they were put to by the witch finders & the Malice of their neighbours, together with the partiallytie or ignorance of the former Judges in Scotland (and I feare in England two [sic]), hath taken away the lives not onely of many even persons but Good & pretious Christians too, by condemning them to the severest punishmts [sic] of the fire.'

Cromwell did not remain long in Scotland. After his victory at Worcester in 1651, he retired from active service and devoted his energies to ruling England. In the past, he had close associations with Robert Rich, Earl of Warwick and Lord High Admiral of the Fleet whose grandson had married Cromwell's daughter. The Earl was well known for his robust pursuit of witches in England and while it is perhaps not strange that Cromwell continued his associations with those who were eager to try witches, he never voiced or wrote about his own opinions on the matter. However, he was personally involved in a case of witchcraft in 1655, the year of the Penruddock Rising.

In March, Colonel John Penruddock with over 150 men swept quixotically into Salisbury, proclaimed Charles Stuart as king and arrested two visiting judges before riding off to gather more supporters in Cornwall. The 'rising' was over within a few hours when the Roundheads scattered the rebels and took fifty prisoners. Among them was a woman, Margaret Gingell. She was accused of witchcraft, a convenient way of ridding the district of a nuisance. Cromwell pardoned her. Was his leniency due to sympathy for the woman, knowing as he did the unfair methods used to try suspected witches? Why did he personally intervene in this single case but apparently took little interest in hundreds of other trials? Perhaps he showed mercy because he sympathised with witches - his enemies certainly saw his actions in that light - but it may be that knowing the hysterical accusations of those who detected witches and brought them to trial and almost certain death, he was lenient.

In Scotland, few witches were brought before the courts between 1651 and 1660. Some were fortunate to escape execution by the intervention of the English commissioners; in 1652, all fifty-nine cases of witchcraft tried by the circuit courts resulted in aquittal. An English jury sitting at Stirling in September 1653 dismissed the cases of several suspects on caution of good behaviour until April 1654. It seemed as if at last, the witch hunt had run its course; in reality, the fires had only been dampened down, ready to be rekindled at the first suitable opportunity. That would not be long in coming. In 1654, four women in Fife were examined by the local witch-pricker and it appears that proceedings were raised against two, Margaret Cant and Janet Bell of Aberdour. The English commissioners released Cant. Despite the fact that Bell was a close friend of the 8th Earl of Morton, who petitioned for her release, she was executed in 1654. Cant was arrested a second time in 1661 along with others like Margaret Currie, also of Aberdour.

In 1655, William Barton and his wife in Kirkliston, West Lothian, about ten miles outside Edinburgh, were tried and executed for witchcraft. Barton's wife confessed she had taken part in a dance with a coven of witches in the Pentland Hills, where the devil appeared in the shape of a 'rough tanny dog'; he led the dance playing on a pair of pipes. There is a touch of grim humour about this case. As the Bartons were being led out of jail by the executioner, he dropped down dead at their feet! Standing nearby, the executioner's wife eagerly volunteered to take his place, no doubt to obtain the fee.

In 1654-56 there was a case of what today would be attributed to the action of a poltergeist (German for noisy spirit). What became known as the Glenluce Devil is extensively reported in Sinclair's *Satan's Invisible World Discovered*; it concerned a beggar, Andrew Agnew who was hanged at Dumfries for blasphemy but who had also cursed the family of one Gilbert Campbell, a weaver in Glenluce, near Newton Stewart in Galloway, for refusing him alms. There was much more to it than that. The curse was used by the son Thomas Campbell for his own ends, as will be seen. Young Thomas was a brilliant pupil at Glasgow Grammar School and fearing that a reverse in his father's fortunes would mean his removal from the school, he decided to punish him by trading on the old beggar's curse. The first manifestation of his scheme occurred one day when a strange whistling was heard by Thomas' sister Janet, on her way to draw water from the well. Janet related how she heard a voice say

"I'll cast thee Janet into the well."

A few months later, the 'devil' began to throw stones at the house doors, windows and down the chimney - usual ploys of the poltergeist. Inside the house, bedclothes were stripped from the sleepers, leaving them naked; clothing was removed from trunks and chests and scattered about the rooms. In desperation, Gilbert Campbell sent his children away to neighbouring houses for safety; the activities ceased, only to resume when the children returned. Thomas caused fires which nearly burnt down the house. The Campbell family called in the minister to exorcise the spirit troubling them. Thomas kept up his ventriloquism; so skilled was he that local people began to believe the Campbells were able to converse with the devil himself. Thomas was called home but the boy said he could not come inside the house because he heard a voice telling him not to, nor indeed any house where his father had worked. Thomas played the role of poltergeist for nearly two years, laying his mischief on the family all the while until a Synod of Presbyteries was set up to help the Campbells. Sooner or later, the ecclesiastical authorities would learn of the beggar Andrew Agnew and his curse, even although in his intonations, Thomas Campbell had never used his name in his disembodied speeches. He had however named several local witches as authors of the mischief at Glenluce. Because of Thomas' boyish pranks, poor Andrew Agnew - his surname means lamb - was apprehended and executed at Dumfries for blasphemy.

At this time, it was thought that several Fife witches created a storm which drowned John Cunningham of Barns, the architect of the first lighthouse on the May island. Whether or not the witches were taken to task is not known.

In August 1656, Culross kirk session experienced considerable frustration in their attempts to bring to justice one Elspeth or Eppie Craiche, held in the local tolbooth on suspicion of witchcraft. As mentioned earlier, Cromwell's government did not look favourably on religious persecution of any kind and it extended this policy to heresy and sorcery. Because of the mounting expense of keeping Eppie in prison, the local authorities were forced to let her go free; she was released on caution of 500 merks and told to appear before the court on some future occasion. She was arrested again in March 1662 and watched by two men while in prison so that

'day and night....she do no eville to herself.'

There is no record of the outcome of her trial but it almost certain she was executed, otherwise why did the authorities go to the trouble of re-arresting her?

In England, Cromwell urged the Long Parliament to pass the *Act of General Pardon and Oblivion* which gave amnesty to all who had opposed or taken up arms against the English parliament. Even so, there were exceptions; the act specifically excluded certain people guilty of

'All Offences of Invocations, Conjurations, Witchcrafts, Inchantments and Charms; and all persons now Attained or Convicted of the said offences.'

This underlines again Cromwell's ambivalent - but in reality enlightened - attitude towards witches. But his enlightenment failed to save a few witches and warlocks. In February 1656, John McWilliam, a slater in Dumbarton was arrested on suspicion of sorcery. He confessed he had made a pact with the devil, who appeared before him as a Highlander. McWilliam said he was given the power to cause and cure sickness in people. He also claimed to have been appointed official cloak-bearer to his Satanic Majesty, attending his person on ceremonial occasions. One of these took place in an old house near Castle Semple. The devil was so delighted with the arrangements for the feast that he thanked his hosts for their lavish hospitality, referring to them endearingly as 'my bairns.' John McWilliam was executed. A list of the expenses incurred in burning two witches in Dumfries in May 1657 is recorded in McDowall's *History of Dumfriesshire*; the bill of £4:18:0 was for 38 loads of peat, a tar barrel and a herring barrel. On 14th October, a Tranent woman was burnt for witchcraft on Castlehill, Edinburgh.

Perhaps the reason for the growing number of cases is not unconnected with a move by the English parliament to reinstate Scottish Justices of the Peace in 1657 in a gesture of reconciliation towards the country's nobility and local lairds. During the Cromwellian Interlude or Interregnum, the upper classes had been virtually excluded from public office; for example, of the thirty parliamentary seats allocated to Scotland, nearly half were occupied by English army officers. So in 1657, the newly-appointed JPs were anxious to re-establish themselves; what better and easier way to do so by apprehending and trying witches? By 1659, the hunt was in progress once more; the madness was about to begin all over again.

Writing from Ayr to an unidentified correspondent on 26th April 1658, Colonel Robert Sawrey commented on a recent witch trial:

'Upon Fryday the 23rd instant was one Janett Saers [Sayers] late an inhabitant of this towne, according to a sentence passed by the

Judges (the Assize having found her guilty of witchcraft), strangled at stake, and after that her whole body burnt to ashes......When the minister was urging her to confesse she had these words, "Sir, I am shortly to appear before the Judge of all this earth, and a lye may damne my soule to hell. I am cleare of witchcraft, for which I am presently to suffer......" The people of this country are more sett against witchcraft then any other wickedness, and if once a person hase that name and come upon an Assize it's hard to get of with lesse then this poore creature.'

After civil powers were restored to Scotland, forty-two women and men were tried by the High Court of Justiciary in April 1658 although there is no record of the outcome.   In the same year, eleven women and two men were accused of witchcraft in Alloa. One of the women, Margrat Tailzeor [Taylor], said the devil, in the likeness of a young man wearing grey clothes and a blue cap, gave her his mark in her 'secret member.' No doubt the witch-pricker enjoyed his task on that occasion, finding the *sigillum diaboli* - the Devil's Seal - in so intimate an area of the body.   It is almost certain that the majority of the women and men in Alloa went to their deaths.

Many witch-prickers were burgh employees, like John Kincaid in Tranent. As the historian Ralph Gardiner noted in 1655:

'....when the sergeants had brought [the pricker]....to the town, the magistrates sent their bellmen through the town....crying: All that would bring in any complaint against women for a witch, they should be sent for and tried by the person appointed....women were brought and stripped, and then had pins thrust into their bodies......'

The prickers were cruel men indeed but it must be remembered they were acting on behalf of the magistrates and the kirk ministers, who between them must bear the greater burden of guilt.

During the Cromwellian Interlude, the Privy Council was disbanded and the Scottish parliament suspended. In the period from 1653 to 1658, only a dozen cases of witchcraft are recorded but this in no way reflects the total tried and probably executed.   In 1658 and 1659, there can be detected an increase in the number of trials, thirty-eight occurring in 1659. Even so, the English judges were criticised for being too lenient by the clergyman, Robert Baillie:

'There is much witcherie up and downe our land, though the English be but too spareing to try it, yet some they execute.'

In 1658, Margaret Anderson was arrested in Haddington; she was accused of making a pact with the devil. She confessed, then recanted on the grounds that she was 'distracted' when she made her confession. The court disregarded her plea on the testimonies of the clergymen at her trial who said she was quite sound in mind when she was being questioned and admitted her guilt. Margaret was executed on 2nd February.

In 1659, eighteen of the thirty-eight witches executed in Scotland were from East Lothian; five unnamed women from Dunbar were executed in Edinburgh. In Tranent, East Lothian, thirty-three witches were named although only nine were executed (Two diagrams illustrating the convoluted process of 'discovery' of the Tranent Witches of 1659 appear on pp206-207). In the nearby small village of Stenton, eleven people were arrested that year; of these, seven were executed, two were acquitted and two either escaped from prison or died while in captivity. Perhaps the high number was due in no uncertain way to the fact that the county was home to John Kincaid, witch-pricker extraordinary who, like other prickers, operated for profit rather than out of religious principles. Dumfries managed to execute no fewer than ten witches on 13th April; Bessie Stevenson, Agnes Comenes, Janet McGowane, Jean Thomson, Margaret Clerk, Janet McKendrig, Agnes Clerk, Janet Corsane, Helen Moorhead and Janet Callon all went to the gallows on the Whitesands. Only one woman, Helen Tait, managed to escape death; her charges were not proven but she was obliged to pay the authorities £50 sterling - a staggering £300 Scots - for her good behaviour. She was also banished from her parish. Among the East Lothian cases were several in Tranent at the time of the spring flowers:

> 'At this tyme, great numbers of witches wer takin and brint, all of them admitting copulation, renunciation of thair baptisme, and tak-ing fra Satan new names and markis in thair flesche.'

Of those arrested that March, eight women and one man were strangled and burnt to death on 3rd May.

Oliver Cromwell, who died on 3rd September 1658, took to his grave whatever personal dealings he may have had with witches. His remains were not left undisturbed however. After the Restoration of the Monarchy in 1660, his body was disinterred, his head severed and stuck on a pike then put on public display - reminiscent of practices belonging to the Middle Ages - he being one of those who had signed Charles I's death-warrant. Cromwell was a man of vision. In the last seven years of his life, he was virtual dictator of England - he was even offered the crown - but he made Europe respect his government. To do so, he maintained a standing army of 50,000 and a navy of 200 ships. His far-seeing outlook envisaged great changes for England, or perhaps that should be Britain. He rid the country of the ancient right of kings, making them subservient to parliament and therefore the people instead of the other way round. He ended the atrophy of intellect which had existed for centuries. He founded the basis for modern government and introduced religious toleration. As to Oliver Cromwell's reputation for dealing with the devil and his servants, the witches and wizards of his day, the records remain silent. In his lifetime, belief in witches persisted but once the Civil Wars ended, the new government under his direction brought about a feeling of security. In England at least, subsequent trials were based on hard evidence rather than hearsay and even then, the death penalty was less frequently used. Not so in post-Cromwellian Scotland, where the hell-fires were to burn more fiercely than ever, even before Cromwell was cold in his grave.

6

'Punished with the Paines of Death'

After the death of Oliver Cromwell in 1658, his son Richard assumed the role of virtual king. Known as Tumbledown Dick, Richard Cromwell lacked his father's authority and vision. By the end of 1659, such was his ineffectiveness that he was reduced to the rank of humble commoner. In Scotland, General George Monck, commander of the occupying forces, decided to take matters into his own hands. Marching out of Dalkeith in January 1660, he arrived in London to restore order; he persuaded the Long Parliament to dissolve itself and a new parliament, known as the Convention, offered the throne to Charles II on certain conditions. In future, the king would be subservient to parliament's will, not the other way round. Charles would rule with the consent of parliament and therefore the people. More politically astute than his late father, Charles accepted the throne and his diminished role. One of his first measures was to pass an *Act of Indemnity and Oblivion* which gave amnesty to all who had opposed his father save those who had signed his death warrant in 1649. This time, witches were not excluded from the amnesty. Unfortunately however, Charles' *Act of Indemnity* was not applied to Scotland; if it had been, it might have prevented the last manic phase of the witch hunt. Although the rump of the Covenanter Kirk Party was aware of this measure in the south, it did not feel disposed to stretch the elasticity of conscience - even if it existed - where witches were concerned. Early on in his reign, Charles introduced tolerance for all forms of religious worship, irrespective of creed. Whatever else his enemies might accuse him of, Charles II was never vindictive; his main opponents in Scotland were the Marquis of Argyll, a treasonable and corrupt noble who, while espousing the Covenanters' cause, thought nothing of betraying them when it suited him. The other arch enemies of the restored king were James Guthrie, the Covenanter minister who bitterly opposed the king's proposal to reinstate Episcopacy and the bishops to the Scottish Kirk and the architect of the National Covenant, Sir Archibald Johnston of Wariston. But for these men, the new reign held out the promise of stability and peace in Scotland.

It was not to be. Although only a shadow of its former political self, the Kirk Party nonetheless maintained rigid discipline in Scotland. While grudgingly acknowledging the sovereignty of the new king, it continued to exert a grinding control over the lives of the people. As Charles' amnesty did not apply in Scotland, the Kirk did not feel obliged even to enter into the spirit of it. For Scottish witches, the transition from persecution to something approaching tolerance was neither immediate nor painless. It is perhaps paradoxical that on the eve of what was to become known as the Age of Enlightenment, the worst epidemic of all in the annals of the witch hunt took place. Contrary to T S Eliot's poetic prediction, the witch hunt ended with a bang rather than a whimper. The new craze began in 1660 and would run its course until 1662. The epidemic which occurred in that period has been attributed to the great number of untried witches which had accumulated during the Cromwellian occupation, festering away in the dark recesses in the minds of their pitiless persecutors. To some extent, this is true. When the brakes came off, retribution was swift and terrible. The mania returned with a vengeance; it would cost the lives of several hundred innocent people.

The Burning of 10 witches on the Whitesands, Dumfries, in 1659

So, with king, Privy Council, parliament and judiciary restored, Scotland might have expected to enjoy a period of relative calm. However, the nature of the religious settlement relating to Scotland did not become clear until 1661, when Charles II declared he would reinstate bishops and Episcopacy in the Scottish Kirk. In May 1662, parliament ratified the return of the bishops which led to a mass exodus of Covenanter ministers. Until then, the Kirk carried on much as it had done before the advent of the Commonwealth, which meant it was not constrained by any secular law that might safeguard people from accusations of witchcraft. When the bishops returned, many in the Kirk were resigned to the inevitable; not so the diehards, the 'purer' elements who clung to their oaths to the National Covenant of 1638 and the Solemn League and Covenant of 1643. When the religious settlement was brokered, many rebel Covenanter ministers led by James Guthrie - himself expelled for non-conformity - left the Kirk. Guthrie, one of the early Covenanter martyrs, led 200 ministers opposed to Episcopacy in rebellion, joined by a further 100 - in all, a third of the Scottish clergy - who were expelled from their churches. To contain the exodus of ministers, Charles subsequently passed an act which denounced the Covenant of 1643 and declared its oath seditious. Those like Guthrie who refused to rescind the oath were proscribed as traitors; adherence to or swearing the oath was declared a treasonable offence, punishable by death. By 1662, Argyll, Guthrie and Johnston of Wariston had been executed. Their removal had a fortuitous side-effect; after 1662, fewer witches were sent to the stake because, quite simply, the most active ministers in the witch hunt were those expelled from their parishes and forced to preach in fields, woods, barns and isolated communities. They held their illegal Conventicles in out of the way places to be safe from the dragoons scouring the countryside. However, before this occurred, Scotland witnessed an epidemic of witch-mania on a hitherto unprecedented scale.

For this, we need look no further than the embattled Kirk of 1660 which once again took the lead role in witch persecution. In the first year of Charles II's reign, trials were resumed. However, the Privy Council, perhaps with an eye on Charles' policy of appeasement, religious tolerance and the amnesty afforded by the *Act of Indemnity and Oblivion* in England was quick to disassociate itself from the more fanatical clergy who demanded that justice be meted out to the witches who had escaped justice during the Cromwellian Interlude. Where witches were concerned, the Privy Council expressed its view in unequivocal terms:

> '....a great many persons in severall parts of the kingdom have been apprehendit and hurried to prisons, pricked, tortured and abused, as being suspect guilty of the horrid cryme of witchcraft by such persons as have no warrant or authoritie soe to doe....'

The Council decreed that in future, no one would be allowed to arrest people suspected of witchcraft except by warrant issued in its name, or that of the Lord Justice General, local sheriffs and other like officials in authority; that the practice of witch-pricking would cease forthwith and that no torture or other illegal means would be applied to secure confessions. It was all very well on paper. Woefully lax in the past in their attitude towards witch-prickers in particular, the Privy Council at least felt strong enough to end the regime of men like John Kincaid of Tranent, John Ramsay and John Dick; even so, it took two years before these charlatans were safely behind bars. It was largely due to the efforts of a young advocate, Sir George Mackenzie, to discredit them; in 1662, Mackenzie denounced them as 'villainous cheats'. His observations made optimistic reading; his mocking tone must have caused considerable consternation in the minds of the clergy, especially those who clung to the old Covenanter principles. However, Mackenzie's overtures were deceptively reassuring; the men of blood in the Kirk ignored him. The same men would have great cause to heed him in the 1680s when, as Lord Advocate of Scotland, he was known as 'Bluidy Mackenzie' because of his lack of scruples in hunting down the fugitive Covenanters in what was known ironically as the 'Killing Time'. Men who shared Mackenzie's views on witchcraft and dismissed the fatuous evidence prepared against suspected witches brought hope that the nightmare was finally coming to an end. Their attitude and that of a less fanatical clergy seemed to promise an ebb in the hitherto inexorable tide of superstition and bigotry, taking with it the rubbish it had voided.

The dawning of enlightenment did not arrive in time to prevent the final persecution. Again, Scotland was convulsed by a witch hunt that reached its peak in 1662. Between 1660 and 1662, witches were brought to book in greater numbers than in the three previous epidemics; even after 1662, sporadic outbreaks in various localities would continue until the early eighteenth century. What hope was there for those labelled witches when in 1661, the scholarly Elias Ashmole, solicitor, antiquary and founder of the prestigious Ashmolean Museum in Oxford, could unselfconsciously confide to his diary:

'I took early this morning a good dose of elixir and hung three
    spiders round my neck; they drove my ague away.'

In Scotland, the churches were packed to the doors on the Sabbath as usual; the people seemed to hunger as never before for fiery sermons and fulminations from the pulpit against witches. Many preachers were thought to have a direct line to the Almighty. The clergy assured sinners and evil-doers that they could expect to reap the whirlwind of God's anger. According to the more fanatical ministers, witches were again stalking the land, believing themselves immune from the punishment they had escaped during the Cromwellian Interlude. As one preacher warned:

'....God shall smite them and all those who aid and abett them.'

With this continual barracking and barrage of propaganda shouted from pulpits up and down the country, it is small wonder the witch hunt thrived yet again; it was nigh impossible for Scottish churchgoers of even average intelligence not to believe in witchcraft, sorcery and evil.

Among the first trials were those which had been dismissed during the Cromwellian Interlude. In 1660, 'many witches' were executed in Dysart, Anstruther, Culross, St Andrews and other parts of the country. Lyon's *History of St Andrews* records the execution of forty people in the space of a few months in that year; there are no details of these cases because, as the author ruefully reflected:

'....so common had they [witch-trials and burnings] become....so commonplace in the opinion of the nation.'

In Edinburgh, the skyline over the Castle and its Castlehill gallows was marked by drifting smoke all that summer of 1660 and the two which followed. The good citizens of the town went about their daily business in the High Street, mindful of the reason for that midsummmer smoke but paying little heed to it. They no longer seemed to care. By 1661, the hunt was working at full capacity; witches were discovered everywhere, batches of them.

On 3rd August 1661, Elspet Graham and Christiane Wilson of Dalkeith, Christian Patersone of Newbattle and Issobell Fergusone and Marjory Wilson, also in the Dalkeith area were arrested; all but one, Christiane Wilson, nicknamed Lantern, confessed. The evidence against her was that she had cursed James Clerk and he had died the following day. She also told his widow that she would soon be childless and shortly afterwards, the woman's child died. Then Christian fell out with her brother Alexander Wilson over some domestic incident; he took his revenge by killing one of her hens and no doubt she cursed him. She was accused of murdering him by sorcery. Apparently in good health at 3pm one afternoon, Alexander Wilson was dead two hours later. His face was scratched and when Christian touched it, blood gushed from the wound - proof of her guilt. Before he died, Alexander Wilson had said there was a lantern - his sister's nickname - glowing in his face and a big rat jumped on him and would not leave him. Christian and the other women were executed. Only four days later, Margaret Bryson, Agnes Pogavie, Bessie Wilsone, Elspett Blackie, Thomas Black and Jonet Gibson, from Liberton and Gilmerton, were executed at Edinburgh. The hunt was back on course with a vengeance.

The Privy Council received petitions to try witches in Mid and East Lothian, Berwickshire, Fife and the north; these included familiar places like Musselburgh, Dalkeith, Newton, Newbattle and Duddingston. The church heritors - lairds and minor nobles - complained to the Privy Council that there were

'....a great many persons, both men and women....who are imprisoned as having confest or witnesses led against them for the abominable sin of witchcraft...'

In Newton, Midlothian, twenty-eight witches were named; East Lothian accounted for seventeen, nine of them from Dunbar; there were three in Peebles and two in Eyemouth. In the period April to December, over two hundred people were arrested; some were from Cromwell's time, like Margaret Cant and Margaret Currie of Aberdour, Fife, whose case had been dismissed in 1654 and was raised again in 1661 and Elspeth Craiche of Culross who was discharged in 1656 and tried again in 1662.   In Newburgh, near Cupar, two unnamed women were hanged for burning down the house of Laurence Oliphant, the local minister.   The women had also been accused of witchcraft as well as arson by several recently executed witches; they died protesting they were innocent of both charges.   In that same year, John, 4th Earl of Haddington, petitioned the Privy Council for a warrant to try several witches on his estate in Samuelston, near Haddington.   The embattled Earl said that if he didn't do something about the witches on that part of his estate, his tenants had threatened to leave.   Samuelston was little more than a farm town with a mill but it became very unhealthy for those suspected of witchcraft.   Response to the Earl of Haddington was swift, in no small part due to the fact that he was a Privy Councillor, even if not a particularly effective one like his grandfather Thomas, 1st Earl of Haddington who was Lord Privy Seal in 1633.   (The Haddingtons were staunch Royalists and Episcopalians).   Between 3rd April and 6th June 1661, no fewer than thirty witches in Samuelston were named and arrested; some were burnt at a local site known as Birlie Knowe, no longer in existence.   One of the accused, Agnes Williamson, was arrested and tried on 27th January; she was still in prison on 7th November, so the Earl of Haddington pressed the Privy Council to try her or set her free as she was costing him and his tenants money for her upkeep.   The last of the Samuelston Witches, Agnes was tried in 1662 and surprisingly acquitted of the charges against her, even though the magistrates found her a witch 'by habit and repute'; perhaps it was the cost of keeping her in prison which weighed the scales in her favour.

It is known that between 1661 and 1662, six hundred and sixty people were accused of practising the black arts.   At least three hundred met their deaths - a number greatly in excess of the Covenanters who were to be executed in the 1680s, known somewhat fatuously by comparison as the 'Killing Time'.   (Legend stubbornly persists that thousands of Covenanter martyrs were put to death; in reality, about a hundred were executed, a further eighty were cut down in the field and about three hundred were deported to the colonies).   On a single day, 23rd January 1662, the Privy Council's business was wholly devoted to the issuing of commissions to try witches - ironically, numbering thirteen, the traditional complement of a coven.   In that month, Marion Grinlaw and Jean Howison of Ormiston, the only survivors of a so-called coven of ten women and one man detained in the Musselburgh Tolbooth petitioned the Privy Council for their release.   They and their companions had languished in jail for a year, presumably while the Presbytery was gathering evidence against them.   The Council granted their release.   Not so fortunate was Janet Cock of Dalkeith who, despite having been acquitted of witchcraft in 1661, was kept in prison until the Dalkeith Presbytery could gather more information about her activities. At her second trial the same year, she was accused of prediction, bewitching and curing sickness in people; found guilty by a majority vote, she was strangled and burnt.

A brief, but sad, entry dated 7th May 1662 in the kirk session minute-book in the parish of Cortachy, Forfarshire puts the witch hunt in perspective:

'No service at Cortachy, the minister being away at Clova, at the execution of Margret Adamson, who was burned there as ane witch.'

In March 1662 occurred a remarkable case of self-condemnation for witch-craft at Inverkip, Renfrewshire. There, the eighteen year-old Marie or Mary Lamont offered herself for trial willingly because she said God had spoken to her, urging her to confess how she had long been in the service of the devil. Marie was tried along with six other witches - Kathrin Scott, Jonet Hynman, Margret Letch, Margret Rankin, Margaret Rankin *secundus* and Margret Duff. During her confession, Marie said that Kathrin Scott had taught her how to steal cows' milk by reciting the following charm:

'In God's name, God send us milk, God send it and meikle of it.'

So much milk did they obtain in this way, they were able to make butter and cheese. Marie also confessed that about two years earlier, she was in Kathrin's house along with two other witches, Margret McKenzie of Greenock and Janet Scott of Gourock when the devil appeared as a large black man who sang to them while they danced. The devil gave them wine and wheaten bread – luxuries for the lucky few in those days - and they were 'all very mirrie [merry].' Marie confessed she had renounced her baptism and gave herself to the devil by putting one hand on her head and the other on the sole of her foot, giving him everything in between. (Isobel Gowdie in Auldearn, of whom more fol-lows, described a similar ritual a month later at her trial). The devil gave Marie the new name of Clowts [Clothes] and said she was to call him Serpent when she wanted to speak with him. The young girl's imagination knew no bounds; she said the devil had made his mark on her by nipping her right side which caused her pain for a while until he stroked and healed her. More followed. Marie implicated Jean King, Jonet Holm and several others who raised a storm to prevent boats from fishing. Then she and others went to Allan Orr's house in the form of cats and stole a herring from a barrel. They took a bite out of it and left it behind; when Orr's wife ate it, she fell sick and died. This was by way of avenging Jonet Holm when Orr evicted her from the house where she'd lived, a fulfilment of her threat that he and his wife would not live long together. Next, the coven put to sea to do harm to local boats, raising a storm which ripped the sails of one to shreds; Marie said she had little to do with that as she was sick and lost a good deal of blood during this excursion. Perhaps the excitement caused her to menstruate prematurely; her mental state was probably affected by such biological episodes. We do not know the outcome of the trial but as one of their victims died, it is likely that the Inverkip Witches were executed.

In the same month in 1662, eight women in Eyemouth, two from nearby Coldingham and one from Foulden, near Berwick, were executed. In May, four witches were tried in Bute and named no fewer than sixteen women and two men. Two of them were described as 'maidens' - to his credit, the devil liked to have young attractive girls seated beside him at meals - one of them being Jonet, daughter of Alexander McIlmartin. The comely creature is described as

> 'a young lasse blake [black] haired broad faced mirriy [happy] disposed.'

Others favoured by the devil were Annie Heyman, Marie Stewart and another Stewart whose forename is missing from the records; she is described as the daughter of 'Black Heug.' All were said to be 'great witches' - perhaps their greatness had something to do with their physical appearance. Another of the accused, Margret McWilliam, was well-known as a witch; her reputation appears to have gone back as far as 1631; although charges had been brought against her in 1645 and 1649 she had eluded the authorities for nearly thirteen years.

On occasions, witchcraft was used for political ends as in the case of the North Berwick Witches in 1590-1; it was also useful for getting rid of undesirable beggars and even worse, unwanted tenants. In 1662, witchcraft was used to justify the eviction of tenants. In the summer of that year, having failed to eject several families from his lands by legal means, Alexander Chisholm of Comar resorted to accusations of witchcraft to remove them. He applied for a warrant to try seventeen people living on his estates at Conveth, Inverness-shire for witchcraft. The Privy Council *Register* names several of the suspects; the clerk must have baulked at recording Gaelic names like McFinlay (Nean Finlay) Vic Ean Vic Homas, Beak, and McEan (Ninian) Ean Vic Ean Culleam (Vic Connell, Vic William) Kathrin! Fortunately, these poor people - members of the Clan MacLean - had a friend who was prepared to take on Chisholm. On 2nd July, Sir Allan MacLean of Duart in Mull, Chief of Clan Maclean, petitioned the Privy Council for their release. He was successful, but not before the female prisoners had been pricked, severely tortured and denied sleep; they were suspended from their prison ceiling by the thumbs, had the soles of their feet burnt in a fire and were dragged through the streets of Conveth by horses. These MacLeans had farmed Chisholm lands for nearly three centuries, so they were entitled to some kind of consideration. Although the seventeen escaped the stake, one of them died in prison and another went mad. There is a postscript to this sad story. It seems that before the MacLeans were pricked, the witch-pricker, known as Mr Patterson, had not been in Inverness-shire by chance. He had been invited there to test several people for devil marks; in Elgin, he pricked two women who were subsequently executed; in Forres, another two women were pricked and in Inverness, Issobell or Margret Duff, described as 'ane rank witch' was pricked and executed. Patterson was next called to the church at Wardlaw to prick fourteen women and one man brought there by Alexander Chisholm - his MacLean tenants - and another four brought in from elsewhere, probably to add credulity to Chisholm's designs. As to the character of 'Mr Patterson', witch-pricker, James Fraser, in his *Chronicle of the Frasers* was moved to comment as follows:

'This villain [who] gained a great deal of money....at last was discovered to be a woman in mans cloathes.'

It is an unusually bizarre episode in the annals of the witch hunt.

No book on Scottish witches would be complete without mention of Isobel Gowdie of Auldearn, Nairnshire. Although she figures in practically every account on witchcraft, it is necessary to repeat her story as it has a bearing on other cases. Isobel Gowdie was known as the queen of the witches, a name she earned because of her graphic account of what she understood witches were all about and which happened to conform to popular conceptions of the time. Isobel was self-confessed; she was never pricked, tortured or coerced in any way. She made not one but three voluntary confessions to her judges. It is not beyond the realms of understanding to determine her motives; it is likely she was an exhibitionist who craved attention. Possessed of a vivid imagination and an excellent memory, she was eager to claim her fifteen minutes of fame - much longer in fact as it turned out - to which the twentieth century pop artist Andy Warhol believed we are all entitled. She set out to impress her judges, revelling in the attention they paid her. Her fanciful tale has style and panache; it contains all the popular conceptions of what witchcraft was all about, almost a blueprint, as will be seen.

Whether Isobel Gowdie was a practising witch or not is a still a matter of conjecture; her colourful account suggests she had certainly participated in some rituals. It is likely that she gained her knowledge of witches and their doings as a child at the winter fireside, then as a young woman consorting with other superstitious young girls who gathered round the village water-pump, a popular meeting-place for exchanging gossip. By the time she appeared before her judges under the commission granted to Sir Hew Campbell of Calder on 10th July 1662, she was married to John Gilbert of Lochloy. It was at Auldearn, a small village situated between the straths of the rivers Nairn and Findhorn on the Moray Firth - the scene of a spectacular victory of the Royalist general, John Graham, Marquis of Montrose, over a numerically superior force of Covenanter soldiers under General Hurry in May 1645 - that she recounted her fantastic story to the kirk session between 13th April and 27th May 1662. She began by saying she had encountered the devil fifteen years previously when travelling between two farms in the vicinity. The devil invited her to meet him that night in Auldearn Parish Church. She went there after dark to renounce her baptism. Because the devil was in the pulpit, she had to be held up to him by another witch, Margret Brodie; in her own words, the devil next sat at

> '....the Reader's desk and he had a black book in his hand. And he marked me on the shoulder and sucked my blood and spat it on his hand..... He said "I baptise thee Janet in my own name.......
> The next time I met him.....he copulated with me....and I found his nature [semen] in me cold as spring-well-water.'

The practice of receiving a baptismal name from the devil was in mockery of the medieval Catholic church's rituals when a young person attending his or her confirmation mass was christened anew. After the devil baptised her, he put one hand on the crown of her head and the other on the sole of her foot and she promised that all that lay between his hands was dedicated to his service. Had Isobel Gowdie learnt of this from the recent trial of Marie Lamont? Perhaps not, as it was common enough knowledge. At any rate, she described how the devil read a sermon from his black book; she said he was 'a mickle [great] black, hairy man.' She then went on to say that the witches who foregathered in Auldearn Church that night were organised in covens of thirteen, under a leader and that her leader was John Young.

Many of the spells she and he would perform together concerned agriculture, the major industry of the country at that time; for example, they attempted to gain for themselves the crops of a local farmer whom they disliked. To achieve their ends, they took parts from the corpse of an unbaptised child in its grave, parings from their nails, some ears of corn and cabbage leaves, then chopped and mixed the mess and put it in a bag which they buried in one of the fields. The result was that the crops failed although they were able to obtain some corn for themselves. Rising to the occasion, Isobel waxed poetic about the nicknames the devil gave to some of her co-witches and their familiars - Swein, Rorie, the Roaring Lion, Red Reiver and the more ridiculous Pickle-Nearest-the-Wind, Able-and-Stout, Throw-the-Cornyard and Over-the-Dyke-with-It. Clearly, there were many witches in the district. We know the names of several including Jonet Braidheid, the warlock John Young, Margaret Brodie and Keathren Sowtar, known as the Witch of Bandon, executed in September that year. In his contemporary *Diary*, Alexander Brodie of Brodie records that his son went to witness her execution. At Jonet Braidheid's trial, she named no fewer than thirty-eight witches, one of them being Agnes Grant who also went to the stake.

In another ritual, the devil and John Young ploughed a field, using an unconventional plough on that occasion. Again, in Isobel's own words:

'We went east of Kinloss and there we yoked a plough with frogs. Frogs pulled the plough like oxen; the traces were of dog-grass, the blade [of the plough] made from a half-castrated lamb......we went round in a circle twice and the coven prayed to the Devil that thistles and briars would grow there.'

On another occasion, Isobel described how she and others

'....went to Alexander Cummings dye-houses in Auldearne.
I went in the likenes of a jackdaw, Elsbet Chisholme was a cat,
Isobel More was a hare and Magie Brodie, a cat.'

(No doubt the clerk of court was busily scribbling down these names.)

She went on to say how meetings were held at the end of every quarter. There were again thirteen in each coven and every witch and warlock could summon a spirit or familiar to wait on them when they so required.

At some point in these fantastic proceedings, her judges asked how the witches were able to leave their beds at night without the knowledge of their husbands. That was easy. Isobel said they usually put a broom or a stool in the bed which then took on human form so that their spouses were none the wiser. She was also asked how witches travelled the distances to their meeting-places. That too was easy. Contrary to popular belief, they didn't use broomsticks. They put a straw between their feet, the straw was blown by the wind and they summoned the power to fly on it by calling out "Horse and Hattock in the Devil's name !" Thus mounted, covens of witches must have arrived at their destinations like clattering cavalry!

Isobel went on to reveal more and more of witchcraft activity in Auldearn. When asked how she and her accomplices managed to stop cows from producing milk, she said they twined and plaited a rope the wrong way round, invoking the devil's name as they did so. This tethering rope was led between the cow's hind legs and round between its forelegs so that no milk would come until the rope was cut. She described the spells used to raise and abate wind; each spell involved an incantation recited three times. To modern eyes, the verses are pure doggerel but to those of that time, they were frightening. To raise a wind, a witch needed a dampened cloth which was beaten on a stone with a flat piece of wood as she recited the following:

'I knock this rag upon this stone
To raise the wind in the Devil's name.
It shall not lie until I please again.'

When a witch wanted to calm the wind, the cloth was dried and she recited the following:

'We lay the wind in the Devil's name

It shall not rise until we raise it again.'
Isobel revealed her coven's connections with Fairyland. She said the fairies weren't gentle creatures but broad, short, strong beings who made elf-arrows for them and taught the witches how to shoot them by using their thumbnails; they were, in effect, poisoned darts. As they were fired, the witches chanted the following:

'I shoot yon man in the Devil's name
He shall not win whole hame
And this also shall be true
There shall not be a bit of him in lieu [alive].'

Terrible poets, witches! Isobel Gowdie was either clinically deranged, suffering from hallucinations or simply the victim of her outstandingly vivid imagination and her absurd fantasies. Despite our modern scepticism, her stories were treated with utmost gravity in 1662.

As might be expected, the minister of Auldearn Kirk, Harry Forbes, was the sworn enemy of the local witches and warlocks. On one occasion, Isobel's coven learned that Forbes was ill and it was decided to hasten his death by charms. They prepared a revolting concoction of the flesh, entrails and gall of a toad, a hare's liver, grains of barley, nail parings and bits of rags, probably once belonging to the minister. They placed the noisome mess in a bag, steeping it in water while the devil led them in the following chant:

'He's lying in his bed
And he is sick and sore
Let him lie in that bed
Two months and three days more.'

As the witches recited the devil's words, they knelt before him, their arms outstretched beseeching him to destroy Harry Forbes. Bessie Hay was chosen to carry the bag to the minister's house as she was on 'intimate' terms with him - what on earth did that mean ? At any rate, Bessie never laid the spell on him - she was meant to beat him with the obnoxious bag while he slept; when she arrived at the manse, several people had come to visit their ailing minister, thus preventing the spell from being carried out.

But the most serious 'crime' of all was the proposal to bring harm to all the male children of a local landowner, the Laird of Parks, who was probably a church heritor. One of the warlocks in Isobel's coven, John Taylor, took home some clay which his wife, Jonet Braidheid, crumbled up like meal, sifted it finely and added water, stirring it like porridge. The clay became workable and from it, John Taylor made an effigy of the laird's son. The effigy was placed in the fire till it shrivelled in the heat; this was repeated every day so that the children would suffer. It seems not to have worked. This and Isobel's wild stories were corroborated by other witches in the group after Jonet

Braidheid's subsequent trial. These other witches made it abundantly clear that their quarterly Sabbats were in fact occasions for sexual orgies, which perhaps Isobel felt shy of admitting. What is remarkable is that some of the district's most respectable people were named as active participants in these orgies. As all fornication was a sin in the church's eyes, the consternation and embarrassment caused by such revelations in that stiff, strait-laced and god-fearing community is unimaginable.

No fewer than forty-one arrests were made after Gowdie and Braidheid confessed. There is no record of what happened to Isobel Gowdie or Jonet Braidheid; nor indeed do we know the fate of the seductress Bessie Hay, Margret Brodie and the others. In all probability, Gowdie and Braidheid were executed along with Agnes Grant and Keathren Sowtar, mentioned earlier. They at least could not hope to escape the stake. As one commentator put it:

'They have confessed enough to burn half of Scotland.'

Isobel Gowdie had a remarkable and detailed knowledge of the arts and parts of witchcraft; her account conforms to the popular conception, then and now, of what witches got up to. She knew about renouncing baptism, re-baptism by the devil, spells, incantations, shape-shifting, flying through the air on straw and the deadly effects of elf-shots as well as stealing milk and corn. Was she possessed? Or mad? Perhaps she had listened too intently to tales told at the fireside and the village water-pump, stories intended to make the flesh creep. Was she the victim of an over-active imagination among those who, tormented by their superstitious fears and prejudices, broadcast them in that small community near Nairn to obtain relief from them? We will never know. However, at least two works of art derive from Isobel Gowdie's story. Drawing from her tale, Robert Burns wrote his song *Whistle Ower the Lave O't* and arguably his finest poem and masterpiece, *Tam o' Shanter.*

At about the same time as Isobel Gowdie was astonishing her judges in Auldearn, other more sinister - because they are credible - revelations were being predicted across the Moray Firth, on the Black Isle. It is a strange story, well-known in Scotland, so this account only briefly touches on it. It concerns one Coinneach Odhar - or Dun-coloured Kenneth, *the Brahan Seer.* Kenneth was born on the Isle of Lewis - an island which burnt not a single witch - as Kenneth McKenzie. He left home to work on his cousin's farm at Brahan, near Dingwall, Ross-shire. He appears to have antagonised his cousin's wife to such an extent she decided to murder him by poisoning his workman's 'piece' or sandwich. After a hard morning cutting peats, Kenneth lay down to rest; when he woke, he found a small round stone in his hand. Lifting it to his eye, he 'saw' what his cousin's wife had done to his food. He threw the piece away and watched a raven eat it, then die. This was the first occasion Kenneth discovered he possessed second sight; later he also found he could see into the future. His prophecies are still talked about in the Highlands today; they were collected and published in the nineteenth century, some two hundred years or so after his death. He is the most famous of all those who reputedly had the gift of seeing; some say certain of his predictions are yet to be fulfilled. For example, at Strathpeffer, near Dingwall, he predicted that if an old carved stone which stands outside the village fell on three occasions, ships would anchor at it with their cables attached to it. What he was in effect predicting was that Strathpeffer would be inundated. As the stone has fallen twice already, the villagers are taking no chances; they reinforced the area to prevent the stone falling a third time. Another of Kenneth's predictions for Strathpeffer concerned a local well; he foretold that one day, it would be kept under lock and key. In his words:

> 'Uninviting and disagreeable as it is now, with its thick crusted surface and unpleasant smell....crowds of pleasure and health-seekers shall be seen thronging its portals in their eagerness to get a draught of its waters.'

Strathpeffer later became a world-famous spa when mineral springs were discovered there. Kenneth also predicted that a mysterious black rain would fall in the Highlands with serious consequences for the north of Scotland. Today, the 'black rain' is accepted as North Sea Oil.

Because of his second sight, Kenneth was taken on as family adviser to the McKenzies of Seaforth. After the Restoration, the chief of Clan McKenzie had to go on state business to Paris; his wife Isabella, annoyed at the time he was taking in France, asked Kenneth to tell her what he was doing. All Kenneth would say was that her lord was in a great room in very fine company and far too agreeably occupied to think of leaving Paris. Kenneth was economical with the truth; his diplomacy only increased Isabella's suspicions. After a few weeks, she asked for more news of her husband. Kenneth finally admitted he could see the chief of the McKenzies on his knees before a fair lady, his arm about her waist and her hand pressed to his lips. The jealous Isabella had suspected as much and she took out her spleen on the poor seer. Isabella had Kenneth arrested and condemned to death for witchcraft. On the eve of his execution, Kenneth made his last prediction:

> 'I see far into the future and read there the doom of my oppression. I see a Chief, the last of his House, both deaf and dumb. He will be the father of four fair sons, all of whom he will follow to the grave, and his possessions shall be inherited by a white-coiffed lass from the east, and she is to kill her sister. And as a sign by which it may be known that these things are coming to pass, there shall be four great lairds in the days of the last deaf and dumb Seaforth. Gairloch, Chisholm, Grant and Raasay, of whom one shall be buck-

toothed, another hare-lipped, another half-witted and the fourth a stammerer. When Seaforth sees them he may know his sons are doomed to death and his broad lands shall pass to the stranger and that his name shall come to an end.'

Chilling stuff. And what is more eerie, it came true. In 1815, the Chief of the Seaforths died, his four sons having pre-deceased him. He was deaf and almost dumb. His estates passed to his eldest daughter, the widow (white-coiffed, as widows were in those days) of Admiral Hood. Some years later, she accidentally caused the death of her sister in a horse and trap. *The Brahan Seer* was burnt to death in a tar barrel at Fortrose in 1662.

By the end of 1662, the witch hunt was running out of steam, probably as a result of the expulsion of the Covenanter ministers who had taken a leading role in the trials up and down the country and especially in the south-west of Scotland. Even so, the trials continued. In 1662 John Ray, the English naturalist who had a somewhat jaundiced view of Scotland anyway, was at pains to point out that during his famous tour, one hundred and twenty witches were put to death. Only a handful of executions occurred in 1663; a few women went to the stake at Auchtertool, Fife, two in Forres, two in North Berwick and one at Eastwood, near Glasgow. It seemed that the hysteria had run its course, yet in 1664, 'sundry' witches were burnt at Culross, the only community to execute witches that year. At Inverkip, a woman accused of witchcraft died in prison; another who had been banished from other parishes was released in August and sentenced to banishment from Dumfries, where a public proclamation forbade the local people from offering her food and drink. One of the saddest cases of 1664 was that of Barbara Drummond who had been unjustly put in prison by the Laird of Kilbride. She was moved from Kilbride to Edinburgh, then Stirling when, in June, she petitioned the Privy Council for her release since she was lying

'in great misery, and no person appears to insist against her'.

Barbara Drummond remained a prisoner for two years, appealing every so often for her release; she was sent for re-trial in 1666 but no one would speak against her. Like another hapless victim, Jonet Howat of Forfar who languished in prison from 1662 until 1666, Barbara Drummond remained in jail until 1667 accused of - well, nothing!

The year 1666 ended with only one trial in Torryburn, Fife, where seven women were incarcerated in the tolbooth and in all probability were executed. This is to some extent suggested in *The History of Dunfermline* which includes an extract from the kirk session records; commenting on the hunting of witches in 1679, the session clerk wrote that for all the drowning and burning of witches which had taken place there

'they dinnae decrease, but are as common and horibly[sic] at their work as ever.'

In February 1666, William, Earl of Morton and his depute had sought permission to try 'a great number of persons' for witchcraft; Morton got his commission but there are no details of any proceedings. In 1667, witchcraft was yet again menacing the kirks in Dunfermline and nearby Torryburn, both places being particularly virulent in their part in the witch hunt. That year, a suspect died in prison in Paisley and one trial took place at St Andrews. There were no trials in 1668.

In Aberdeen, the year 1669 began with complaints from the magistrates and the kirk session in February and April that witchcraft was on the increase there. Some time after 8th April, a man was tried in Duns although we have no details of the outcome. In July, four witches were imprisoned in Aberdeen awaiting trial; they were probably among several witches executed in August, a month which the Privy Council *Register* states, brought

'....a great conflueance of people to the toune of Abirdein upon occasion of a publick execution, certain persones being convicted and condemned to be brunt for sorcery and wichcraft [sic].....'

These were probably the last witches executed in Aberdeen

In September, three people were imprisoned in the Castle of Tirram [Tioram], Inverness-shire, awaiting trial for witchcraft. On 11th November, Dundee executed Grissell Jaffray, thought to have been the last witch tried there. In 1670, three women were arrested in Bo'Ness; several were executed in Carron, near Falkirk and one in Montrose. In February that year, a somewhat nervous Presbytery of Inverkip, Renfrewshire had written to the Synod asking what course of action they should take against

'those who go under the name of witches.'

Clearly, attitudes were changing at last. However, between 1671 and 1687, forty-seven executions were confirmed with a possible further twelve about which the records are inconclusive. In 1676, Isobel Davidson of Belhelvie, Aberdeenshire, drowned herself while awaiting trial. In the following year, Margaret Kirkwood of Haddington took her life while in prison awaiting trial; the local people said she had been strangled by the devil and his witches which, in a sense, was true. Her servant Lizzie Mudie, also in prison as her accomplice was executed in April 1677. However, during the sixteen years from 1671, about twenty people were either acquitted or released under a verdict of not proven.

Although never convicted of witchcraft, the case of Major Thomas Weir deserves a mention in this account. His is indeed a bizarre story which skirts round the black arts and much of his so-called evil has been obscured by the inevitable legends. In 1670, he was living with his sister Jean at the foot of the West Bow, adjacent to Edinburgh's Grassmarket. The Weirs had an impeccable background; born to a good family in Lanarkshire, they seemed to be pillars of Edinburgh society. Weir was something of an enigma however; he lived a double life. In 1641, he was sent by the Covenanting Committee of Estates to quell Irish Papists and he was appointed captain of the city guard in 1649. But by 1670, when he was as old as the century itself, he somehow fell foul of the Edinburgh authorities. It is thought today that Major Weir suffered from a mental illness. His behaviour became so irrational that his neighbours in the Head of the Bow petitioned for him to be removed into custody. Weir and his sister Jean - sometimes known as Grizell (a witch baptismal name?) were put in the Tolbooth, where Weir voluntarily confessed to leading a life of fornication, incest, sodomy and bestiality; for good measure, he claimed he used witchcraft by means of his black walking stick. He denounced his sister Jean as a witch. It seemed an open and shut case.

Major Weir's land in the West Bow, Edinburgh

But the authorities and the Presbyterian kirk were faced with a dilemma. How in all conscience could they bring a charge of witchcraft on one of their most loyal supporters? The answer is - they didn't. Sidestepping the issue of witchcraft, Weir and his sister were declared guilty of incest with each other and foul fornication with others, including in Weir's case, men and animals. Weir was hanged and burnt at Edinburgh's Gallowlee on 14th April 1670; his thornwood stick, said to have been a gift from the devil, was burned with him.

His sister Jean was hanged in the Grassmarket the following day. Years after their execution, the Weirs' house at the Head of the Bow remained empty, the subject of street gossip. It was reputed to be haunted; lights were seen in the house at midnight and there were sounds of dancing and howling. Some of the good citizens of the West Bow and the Grassmarket claimed they saw Weir ride out the low close at midnight on a black horse which galloped off in a whirlwind of flame. His legend as a warlock persists to this day, as such legends will.

In 1671 occurred the trials of Janet McMuldritche and Elspeth Thomsone in Dumfries. The case against Janet McMuldritche consisted of eight charges, two of which were not proven. She was found guilty of using witchcraft to bring about the death of Robert Brown who, finding her grazing cattle on his pasture, had driven them off. When Janet confronted him, she lost her temper and in her anger, cursed him. She was also accused of stealing corn and hay from Robert Cairns' barn and she cursed him also. When Cairns fell sick, he asked Janet to visit him to remove her spell. She refused. Before he died, Robert Cairns made his friends promise him they would hunt her down and bring her to justice. At her trial, Janet was found guilty of causing the death of both Brown and Cairns and that of the child of John Morris for some unstated reason. So Janet was executed for petty theft and a loose tongue. Her associate, Elspeth Thomsone, was accused of causing illness in John Corsbie or Crosbie and his wife because the couple hadn't invited her to their child's christening. Elspeth's husband, William McGhie, defended his wife's reputation against an accusation of witchcraft by Donald McGhie, probably his relative and a friend of the Crosbies. William told Donald it would go ill with him for calling his wife a witch, whereupon Donald obligingly died. When his corpse was being laid in the coffin, Elspeth was standing nearby and came to pay her last respects, touching his body. Eyewitnesses swore that when she did so, blood

> 'rushed forth from his nose, navell and yeard [possibly his coffin although the word means 'grave'] and his corpes bleed all the way to the Buriall place.'

In Scotland, when a dead body bled at someone's touch, it was proof that the person was the murderer. Elspeth also reputedly put a spell on James McGhie because he refused to give her work. Clearly, she didn't get on well with her husband's relatives. That both she and Janet McMuldritche were executed is confirmed by an extract from the magistrates' minute book and quoted in McDowall's *History of Dumfriesshire*.

Among the other cases heard during the period between 1671 and 1687 are three worthy of interest. The first concerns Sir George Maxwell of Pollok and his family. At the end of 1676, Sir George was laid low with a fever said to have been caused by witchcraft. On 18th January 1677, Jonet Mathie, her son John and her daughter Annabell Stewart, Margret Jackson, Bessie Weir and Marjory Craig were indicted for bewitching Sir George Maxwell and causing his illness. All but one of the accused went to the stake; the youngest, Annabell Stewart was under age and so she was spared the death penalty. She was kept in prison however, first in Paisley, then in Glasgow. The second case concerns a challenge to the authority of the magistrates in Prestonpans, East Lothian against wrongful arrest. Perhaps the woman, Katharine Liddell was acutely aware that the witch hunt had not ended for good; in that year, five witches were executed at Edinburgh's Gallowlee, three each in Fala and Lasswade, Midlothian and four in Ormiston - the trial and execution of the Ormiston women cost £38:3:0 which shows that as far as combustibles were concerned, inflation had not affected prices in nearly a century. In Prestonpans itself, two women were executed which probably prompted Katharine Liddell to approach the Privy Council with her complaint which was duly heard with her accusers present. Their defence was that she had been searched by the pricker with her own consent; that the pricker had learnt his trade from John Kincaid so was lawful; that the pricker acted only when called upon by the clergy and the magistrates; that the trial was lawful; and finally came the usual citing of precedents where the devil's mark had been discovered and had led to conviction. The prosecution said that Katharine had denied giving her consent and that no one could validly consent to torture; for good measure, the pricker was declared a cheat. The Privy Council found in Katharine's favour, although she was released on 500 merks caution in the event of a further trial (Larner's *A Source-Book of Scottish Witchcraft* claims that she was executed, but the Privy Council *Register* for 1677 is clear on the matter). It was a victory for common sense.

In 1678 the Privy Council ordered the Sheriff of Edinburgh to arrest Gideon Penman, a former clergyman in the city. Penman was known to his coven as the devil's chaplain; he apparently enjoyed beating up those who danced too slowly at Sabbats!

In 1679, five witches and a warlock were taken into custody at Bo'ness. Bessie Vicker, Margaret Hamilton, Margaret Hamilton *secundus,* Annaple or Annabell Thompson, Margaret Pringle and William Craw were accused of giving their bodies and souls to the devil; they had also danced to tunes played by the devil on 13th October that year. Worst of all their crimes was to plot the destruction of Andrew Mitchell of Kinneil. On 19th December 1679, the six were formally tried by local commission; on that gloomy winter day, all were declared guilty and sentenced to be executed on 21st December. The clerk of court recorded that they were to be taken to the usual place of execution and 'wirred at a steack till they be dead and thereafter to have their bodies burnt to ashes' between the hours of 2 and 4pm. On 23rd December, the six 'Bo'ness Witches' were led out of the Bo'ness Tolbooth in South Street, taken along the Corbiehill to their place of execution on the shore of the Firth of Forth to the west of the town.

Between 1680 and 1684, three women were tried in Edinburgh, and one in Aberdeen; the Aberdeen case and two of the Edinburgh cases were dismissed although there is no record of the outcome of the third. The only casualty in 1684 was Marion Purdie, a 79 year-old former 'milk-wife' turned beggar in Edinburgh's West Bow who was taken into custody as a witch. She was accused of laying sickness and madness on her neighbours. In the shorthand of the day, she was quite simply a public nuisance. By 1684, the King's Advocate was virtually ignoring witchcraft trials so the old woman was left to languish in prison. She tried unsuccessfully to be released and died of cold and poverty in the Tolbooth that Christmas. Despite, or perhaps because of, the King's Advocate's lack of interest in witches, Sir Alexander Home of Reston was moved to write to Lord Polwarth, a Privy Councillor. Home complained that witchcraft was on the increase in his district, in places like Eyemouth; he reminded Polwarth that his (Home's) father had burnt seven or eight of the creatures while he was sheriff and that the increase was due to slackness on the part of the judges. Home proposed a solution:

'....if some [witches] were apprehended, others would come to light.'
Of course he was absolutely right. It was the tried and tested way, beloved by a church which interfered to an extent unprecedented in the lives of the people of Scotland, bullying them into submission and coercing them in the name of God to inform on those in their midst who were witches.

By the 1680s, the biters - ministers of the Covenant and their supporters - were not only being bitten but savaged by the government in the eyes of some of their sympathisers. The 'Killing Time' mentioned earlier was in full swing. The last act in the Covenanter saga was played in 1685 when Archibald Campbell, 1st Duke of Argyll, the last major magnate to support the cause was captured in Glasgow and brought to Edinburgh to be executed for treason. Perhaps it was poetic justice that those members of society who had wreaked such havoc on so many innocent women and men were themselves being de-stroyed by those who came after them. It is almost an example of Darwinism, where the weakest were sacrificed on the altar of evolution.

By 1685, the enthusiasm for hunting witches had all but evaporated. Per-haps at last, light was beginning to shine in the dark corners of the Kirk. The witch epidemic was finally over. Well, the hunt had run its course; belief in witchcraft however took much longer to erase from the collective memory of the Kirk and its congregations.

7

' Terrifeing and Abuseing the People'

One of the most bizarre and unusually well-documented cases in govern-ment records occurred in 1688, that of Catherine McTargett or McTaggart in Dunbar, East Lothian. A full account of the trial appears in the *Register of the Privy Council (Third Series, vol. xiii,* pp245-262). While the charges preferred against Catherine McTaggart are fairly typical of the kind, the de-tailed account of the trial is invaluable to the social historian and psychologist alike. The proceedings, the nature of the evidence, the way the law was ap-plied and the witnesses' testimonies between them illustrate graphically what a person accused of witchcraft endured. The case is remarkable in that no fewer than twenty-seven charges were brought against the accused, exceeded as far as can be established only in the case of Agnes Sampson, one of the North Berwick Witches who, in 1591, was accused of fifty-three offences.

Catherine McTaggart was the wife of a Dunbar weaver, William Brown, a shadowy character who is mentioned only twice in the entire proceedings. By the time of her trial, Brown may have been dead. On 10th May, a commission was granted by the Privy Council for her to be tried locally. Her judges were Sir John Sinclair of Lochend, Sir William Baird of Newbyth, Robert Hamil-ton, Andrew Moray of Spott, James Mare of Bourhouse, Robert Lauder, clerk to the Exchequer, James Forrest, lately bailie of Dunbar, William Kirkwood, James Smith, both merchants of Dunbar, George Purves, George Rutherford and George Sinclair, serving bailies of Dunbar; the burgh Clerk, William Kirkwood, was appointed clerk of court; Patrick Brown, a local lawyer, was appointed procurator fiscal, with two burgh officials, Robert Innes and Alex-ander Crombie acting as officers. An accusation of witchcraft was brought against Catherine McTaggart by Thomas Wood, minister of Dunbar Kirk who had previously reported to the court that she had confessed herself a witch to him. Catherine was brought before the court and confessed the same there. Her case was heard on 30th May. The commissioners took pains to instruct Thomas Wood and one or two of the commissioners and Clerk Kirkwood

'....if she be brought to furder confessione of her guilt [to note] the tymes and circumstances thereof.'

On 15th May, the Privy Council issued summons to witnesses to appear at the local hearing; these were named as follows:

John Home, postmaster at Cockburnspath

Margaret Vertrie, his spouse
John Kerr, their servant
Helen Patterson, lately their servant
James Simpson, mason at Cockburnspath
Thomas Lamb, chapman at Cockburnspath
John Hogg, mason at Dunglass
George Lyall, Saltpanhall
Isobel Reston, spouse to George Milne in East Barns
Janet Chisholm, widow of Thomas Ross, smith in East Barns
Margaret Ross, her daughter
George Wallace, baker and burgess of Dunbar
Alexander Affleck, burgess of Dunbar
James Forrester in Spott
Catherine Forrester, his spouse
Patrick Ferguson, mason and burgess of Dunbar
Marion Bairnsfather, widow of John Ferguson, mason in Dunbar
Richard Merstone, seaman, Dunbar
Sarah Aitchison, widow of John Laurie, Dunbar
John Smith, indweller, Dunbar
Janet Symonton, wife of John Affleck, shoemaker, Dunbar
Thomas Thomason, West Links, West Barns
Mary Johnstone, his spouse
Arthur Simpson, Easter Broomhouse
Janet Hamilton, his spouse
William Bryson, slater, burgess of Dunbar
Lucress Smith, his spouse
Agnes Colme, spouse to George Kemp, cooper and burgess, Dunbar
Margaret Jackson, their servant
Maurice Ferguson, mason, burgess of Dunbar
Jean Boig, servant to Patrick Brown (procurator fiscal)
Christian Dunbar, servant to Patrick Mathie, burgess of Dunbar
George Shirreff in Knowes (near East Linton)
Christian Orme, his spouse
Patrick Shirreff in Knowes
Helen Pringle, his spouse
Patrick Wood, maltman, burgess of Dunbar
Andrew Stevenson, Newtonlees
Margaret Aitken in Drem
James Congalton, burgess of Dunbar
Helen Milne, his spouse
George Walker, wheelwright, burgess of Dunbar

Jean Johnston, his spouse
George Reston } ordinary officers in the burgh
Patrick Kellie }
James Lauder
Catherine Sandilands, his spouse
William Smaill, indweller, Dunbar

The preamble to the indictments is as follows:

'Indytment. Mr Patrick Broun, procurator fiscall, against Catharin
Mactargett, for witchcraft.'

The formal charge was that she would be tried under the *Witchcraft Act* of
1563. In point of fact, Catherine was a beggar; it may be that she took to
begging after her husband died or left her, although this is not entirely clear;
the next part of the indictment suggests that William Brown was still alive:

'....haveing shaken of all fear of God and respect to the laues of this
natione, without any necessitie (you and your husband haveing ane
competent way of living), did take up ane trade of begging, quherin
you have used such uncouth and strange words, gestures and practises as convinced the people quher you went a begging that you
wer a witch; and you haveing contineued under that common fame
and reputte for a longe tyme without complaineing to any magistrat
that ye wer called ane witch, bot rather in a maner gloried in it, and
terrified the people soe as you became insolent and imperious in
your way of begging, in sua far quhen you gott such almes as the
people could lest spair, you not being satisfied therwith you used to
demand ane uther almes, quhich the people out of fear and terrour
wer constrained to satisfy you in, and if any refused you used to
threatne and predict damnage to them for refuseing, quhich accordinglie came to pass many tymes, and you came to that hight that
quhen youe wer any uther wayes displeased you threatned damnage
and hurte, quhich accordinglie came to pass, quherby you have soe
deluded the people by rendering them soe superstitious in distruste-
ing the Almightie God and being affraied of the evill and of you and
your witchcrafts, that quhenever they sau you they wer in use to
sean [protect] themselves, and your ordinar expressiones upon such
occasiones wer that they never prayed soe hard much befor they
saw you, and that they would never pray soe much untill they
should sie you againe. And to evince that you are guiltie of the said
blak art of witchcraft, sorcerie, committeing malefices hereby, useing
of charmes, terrifieing and abuseing the people in maner forsaid.'

Quite a mouthful, even for a professional lawyer. Clearly, Mr Patrick Brown,

141

the procurator fiscal, was in no mood to leave room for any doubt in Catherine's or anyone else's mind of the crime of which she was accused, she having been tried locally on an earlier occasion, which resulted in the remission of her case to the Privy Council for further consideration. The twenty-seven charges brought against her largely relate to incidents which occurred over thirty years; these appear in the Privy Council *Register* as numbered articles or indictments but for convenience, they are reproduced below in chronological order.

1658: Catherine quarrelled with a local man, John Milne and swore he would never thrive: 'his gear vanished away and he came to extreame povertie' despite being a sober, industrious man: one day, his horse strayed into her kail yard, trampling some plants. While coaxing the horse out of it, she said it would never get home because it would break its neck. The same night, the horse 'fell over the heughs and brak its neck.'

1671: James Congalton owed her money for some plants; she asked for it a month before it was due to be paid. Catherine went to his house and refused to leave; she 'satt all the nicht over in the stair with your hair about your eyes, that he was terrified and affraied till he payed you; bot efter that tyme he never threave [throve] not soe much as to gett meall to his bairnes.'

1672: In July or August, against her wishes, Catherine's husband William sold a cow to James Reid, a local butcher; it was said that she 'cryed up to your husband in a great Passion and anger and said if James Reid bought your cow he should never draw blood of her.' An apparently healthy man until then, Reid fell ill a few days later and died.

1673: Catherine was at the Knowes, a farm town near East Linton, lodging with Patrick Shirreff, whose wife Helen Pringle was pregnant and whom she was visiting in the hope of selling some onions; however 'haveing taken her paines of childbirth, you was put furth of your lodging.' Catherine had to sleep in the stable with the horses. Visiting George Shirreff's house nearby, she found his wife, Christian Orme 'lyeing seik [sick] at the poynt of death, and [you] spock to her in the bed and said "Take a good heart, for that quhich was etled [intended] for you shall light upon ane uther, and within four dayes ye shall be alse weill [well] as ever you was"; and soe it was against the fourt [fourth] day therefter she was so fullie recovered

that she not only arose from her bed bot went and visited her
nigbours [neighbours]; ....and the said Helen Pringle, her nigbour,
be came to be extramlie tortured and tormented, and conti newed
so for ane quarter of ane year soe it was a generall convictione upon
the haill [whole] countrie that the said Helen Pringle was wronged
by your sorcerie.'

1674: One day, Catherine approached Andrew Stevenson at Bourhouse
who was sowing oats; she said to him she "would have ane boll [an
old Scots dry measure not exceeding six bushels] of them". He said
that she "deserved rather ane boll of coalls to burne you with."
She straight away went to his house to ask his wife for a drink of
water.   A day or so later, Stevenson's wife was seen talking to
Catherine and shortly afterwards, she died.

1675: Janet Symington, wife of John Affleck, asked Catherine for some
barley but she scolded her. When Janet said she was "ane incarnate
devill, you immediatlie took off your head cloathes and cast
them at her, and therefter she haveing a steep of good and sufficient
malt lyeing besyde her quherof she was in use to brew good aill, bot
efter that outcast of all that malt she nor none in the toun could ever
make a drop of good aill of it.'

1676: In October, when calling in John Laurie's house one Sunday morning,
Catherine went into Laurie's bedroom where he was asleep; he
woke and saw her throw down a hair tether known to be used by
witches in their spells and he fell into 'ane most unnaturall deseas
[disease] and never closed his eyes till he died, quhich was upon the
Thursday imediatlie folloueing.'

1677: Catherine stole a piece of coal from John Ferguson's cart and he 'did
justlie stryke you'; she responded by saying they would be 'dear
coalls to him and he should never stryck more.' Ferguson went home,
fell ill and later died.

1677: In June or July that year, at 3am or 4am on a Sunday morning,
Catherine brought 'ane nolt best [an ox or steer] east throw
[through] the streat of Dumbar, and did sett it outsyde of ane byre of
William Brysones, sklaiter [slater]...in the same pouster [position]
as his cow stood within, and took up some dung [manure] from the
midding [midden or refuse heap] and held it to the mouth of that

beast and uttered some words and charmes, and immediatlie the said William Brysone his cow did decay and never threive [thrived] efterwards.'

1677: Catherine was at the Knowes farm, pestering the Shirreff family while they were making pottage. Shirreff's wife, whom Catherine had 'cured'of illness in 1673 gave her the pan to lick. Then Catherine asked for some milk - a more valuable commodity then than now - or some ale; she was given 'some small wort [brew] quhich was then boylling upon the fire, and ye said it would be good aill if it had salt; the said George Shirreffs wyf Christian Orme was angrie with you for soe saying, and said "Ye witch theeff, who uses to put salt amongst aill"; you said there was better drink in the hous, and the said Christian answered ther was some bot it had not got barme [yeast], and you replyed she should have barme shortlie, and soe went your way from the hous; and soe it was quhen some of the family went into the roome qher ther was a barile [barrel] or stand with worte that had never gott barme put in it, they did sie [see] the barme spring furth of it in such a fearfull maner that it tuched [touched] the jeasts [joists] of the roume, and got coogs [wooden vessels] and keeped it, and wer greatlie astonishing, considereing there was never barme putt into it by any persone.'

1678: Catherine was seen at 10pm in the darkness, riding a white-faced calf in the High Street and 'Quhen it was demanded you wher you had bein at such a tyme in such a pouster [position] you answered you had been in the east countrie and had got that stirk at the kirk styll [style]; it was Margaret Liddells, ye was goeing to take it home.' (Clealry the court implied that she was a liar).

1678: One day, at the posthouse in Cockburnspath, about seven miles from Dunbar, Catherine went begging a drink from the postmaster's servant, Helen Paterson. The girl refused her and she went off, muttering to herself. Shortly afterwards, the girl 'did fall doun [as if] deid [dead], and continued a considerable tyme as if she had been deid, and then was in ane high and mightie distemper.' The family were convinced that Catherine had practised 'divilish airts' and sent another servant to fetch her back to the house. When she got there, she gave the servant girl something to drink and she recovered.

1682: On 1st January - Handsel Monday - Catherine went to Ruchlaw's

Close in Dunbar to visit Patrick Ferguson, a mason who lived there. It being a holiday, Patrick was watching some people playing pennystone - a form of quoits played with flat stones - and Catherine offered him some bread and cheese. At first, he refused the food but she insisted he eat it; he tasted it, then handed it back to her. Clearly, he was suspicious but in all probability, the cheese was mouldy. Catherine let it fall to the ground and immediately afterwards, Ferguson's wife 'took seiknes, imediatelie lost all her sences, and within ten or tuelf [twelve] days she deid.'

1682: Catherine went begging to John Lauder's house to seek alms 'and gott a lock [handful] meall from his wyf, thereafter you sought a soup barme, quhich she refused you; ye stood still and would not go away without it; at last she was forced to give you some barme, and you was no sooner gone from the hous, than his wyfe took such ane violent pain in her hand and arme that she was lyk to goe distracted, and ane Doctor McKullo, a stranger being accidentalie in the hous dreu blood of her, bot she being no better of it, he said it was some evill wight [person or creature] that delt with her. And you haveing thereafter comed back to the said James his hous and said that his wyfe would never be weill, till either she or her child deid, and she haveing ane young child soukeing [suckling], tooke seiknes and within a moneth [month] thereafter died and she recovered and greu bet ter daillie thereafter, quhich occasioned such a terrour and fear in that familie that they could never sie you thereafter bot that ther flesh trimbled [trembled].'

1683: At some point in the year, Catherine received alms from James Forrester's wife in Spott; when she asked for some milk and was refused it, she went off angrily 'and the verrie nixt tyme the cou was milked she gave only blood instead of milk to the great astonishment of all who knew it, and continued [to do so] for two or three dayes and then deid.' (The afflicted cow probably died of mastitis)

1683: In August, Catherine was at the seashore when the herring drave was in progress at Dunbar; perhaps she hoped to get some free fish. By now, her reputation as a witch was well-established as'.....there cam a dum [dumb] man to you and put a great and long pin in your shoulder, at quhich tyme ye did not speik on [one] word that ye fand ounie [any] paine, and quhen he took it out and held it up befor severall persones ye called him a dum devill and went away from him.'

145

1684: Perhaps the saddest of the coincidental deaths attributed to Catherine's witchery was that of a Dunbar seaman. Sailors and fishermen are by inclination superstitious because of the hazards they face at sea; Catherine did herself irreparable harm, souring her name in a largely fishing community when she foolishly predicted the man's death. William Henderson, a sailor, was taking leave of his wife Jean Murray on the shore; standing nearby, Catherine was overheard to say "It will be a long goodnight." This was no casual remark; at her trial she is alleged to have 'repeited these words twyce over.' William Henderson was lost in a shipwreck a few days later.

1684: Catherine went to George Colme's house in Spott seeking alms there. His daughter Agnes Colme and a friend Margaret Jackson were so terrified when they saw her coming to the house they 'prayed to God to bliss them, [and] you said they had not prayed soe much till they sau your cannie face, and bade the evill spirite take a list of them, and sliped [slipped] doun your hand by your syde, and diped [dipped] your fingers in the water coog [wooden vessel] and put your fingers upon the sole of your foott, and went your way; and shortlie therefter the said George Colme had three kyn [cattle] and two stirks [steers] deid.'

1684: Not long afterwards, Catherine visited a house in the West Links, near West Barns, where she heard a calf lowing pitifully; she asked its owner, the wife of Thomas Thomson what it was that made it 'rout' or bellow - shades of Isobel Young in 1629 at East Barns. The woman said all it needed was to be fed; Catherine replied 'it was calfed at ane ebb sea, it will rout till it die.' The calf obliged her a few days later.

1685: For some undisclosed reason, Catherine was in the house of Thomas Ross while his daughter was making pottage; she asked if she might have some and the young girl 'answered mirrilie "I wish you worrie [choke] on them then" quherupon you again answered that some of hers should befor long;.....Thomas Ross woried [choked] that same night upon a piece of beef in Patrick Lougan, the wright his hous, of quhilk he deid.'

1685: Catherine approached George, the young son of Maurice Ferguson, a Dunbar mason; the child was 'of age about four years, playeing and casteing his bonnet, you did take up the bonnet and put it

upon the childs head be way of charme with the croun [crown]
dounward. The child went home to his father and told him what
you had done and that his head was braineing [hurting], and cryed
pitifullie for three or four dayes till he deid.'

1685: In November or December, Catherine was buying a sheep's heid
from the wife of William MacKie, a Dunbar butcher. Another
woman in the shop offered more money for it. 'Jean Johnsone,
spouse to George Walker, did buy it and gave more for it than you
bade.' An understandably irritated Catherine told her the sheep's
heid 'should do her familie noe good'. While cooking the heid, Jean
Johnson complained of feeling unwell; people said Catherine had
bewitched her so she 'came to her hous and caused her provyde a
sheeps draught and gave her fyve onions and desired her to take
three of them and boyll with the draught and take some of the
broath [broth] and that it would cure her, quhich accordinglie she
did, and upon the first tasteing of the broath she was weill; quhich is
cleirlie [clearly] a layeing on and takeing of seiknes.'

1687: In August, the eleven and eight years-old daughters of Patrick
Wood, a Dunbar maltman, were walking near Catherine's house
when she 'affrighted them by some strange pouster [position] ye
was lyeing in in the hieway [main street]; you rose up and cheased
[chased] them, they came instantlie home and fell seik both; the
youngest becam speechless and the eldest told to her father how
that ye laye upon the hie street, shot out your head and feett and
then rose and cheased them.' These were the words of two hysterical children. The next day, Catherine went to the house to beg some
milk and the childrens' father understandably drew a knife, threatening to kill her if his child never spoke again. Catherine fell down at
his feet, possibly to distract him, then Wood's wife took her husband
away from the inert woman. Catherine soon came round from her
fainting fit and went home; the little girl found her voice again.

1687: At Michaelmas (29th September), Catherine visited Patrick Mathie's
house in Dunbar, where sitting down, she 'sought some milk and
repeated these words and charmes three tymes over (viz., "If I
break my nose, I spoylle my face, and quhen I spoylle my face, I
break my fortone"). And upon the Sunday therefter, you did come
to the same hous with a piece rau pledden [coarse cloth], and did
offer it in pand [pledge or pawn] for some money, and you haveing

gotten the milk at Patrick Mathies desyre, his daughter Issobell Mathie being verrie offended that you should have gott any milk or comed to the hous with pledden upon such a day [the Sabbath], the said Isobell Mathie hath ever since bein [been] in ane mellancholie conditione and truble of mind and contineues soe to this hour, altho befor she was a persone of inteir [entire] judgment and discretione.'

1688: On 2nd January - Handsel Monday - Catherine sought alms from Thomas Whyte, a Dunbar cooper; on receiving them, she asked for a pint of ale. Whyte replied he would rather 'sie you hanged and brunt before you gott any of that drink, and called you witch and you answered that ye wished a hanged man might be about his hous or [before] long; and soe it was that in the moneth of March last George Lumsdean in the Cove (near Cockburnspath), the verrie nixt nighbour to the said John Whyt, hanged himself and was carried closs be [by] his door.'

The twenty-sixth indictment reads as follows:
'As also on the tent [tenth] day of May instant 1688 years, you being present within the tolbooth of Dumbar, befor the commissioners appoynted be the Lords of his Majestties Privie Counsell for the tryell of you as being most suspect of witchcraft, you did ther publictlie acknouledge that you are ane witch.'

The final indictment speaks for itself:
'As also upon the nyntein [nineteenth] day of the said moneth of May instant, Mr Thomas Wood, minister at Dumbar, being in the prisone hous visiting you, and asked if ye was a witch, you answered that you are, and he asked how long since you became on [one], tuentie [twenty] years? you (sic) answered, Nay not soe long. Then he asked hou ye entered in the service of the devill. You answered ane Highland woman learned you called Margaret McLain. Then he asked hou did she learne you, did ye renunce your baptisme? Ye answered ye did what she bade you. He farder asked, Did she bide you renunce your baptisme? You answered, Yes. Then he said to you, Did you soe then? You answered you did. Then he said, Will you byde by this confessione? You answered you would for God knoues all things........'
In summing up the case for the prosecution, Patrick Brown, procurator fiscal said:
'...it is manifest that you are guiltie of the crymes of witchcraft, sorcerie, necromancie, superstitione and abuseing of the people us-

ing of spells and charmes, layeing on and takeing of seiknesses.... ye aught [ought] to be punished with the paines of death and confiscation of moveables to the terror and example of uthers to comitt the lyk in tyme comeing.'

On 30th May 1688, no fewer than forty-six people from Dunbar and the surrounding district testified against Catherine McTaggart. In her defence, feeble attempts were made to dismiss some of the accusations against her. She said her suggestion that salt be added to the Shirreffs' ale in 1677 was a jest. Perhaps it was her version of an old Scots proverb which described troublemakers as those who 'made the kail [cabbage] salt.' She seemed to be unlucky with those of the name Ferguson. In 1677, she had allegedly caused the death of John Ferguson who struck her for stealing a piece of coal. Her explanation of the encounter with Patrick Ferguson in 1682, when his wife died, was simply that Ferguson had a grudge against her. She was unable to offer an explanation why young George, son of Maurice Ferguson, should have died as a result of her placing the child's bonnet on upside down. Referring to the incident at George Colme's house in Spott in 1684, when she had been refused alms and was thought to have bewitched a pail of water which resulted in the death of several cattle, Catherine said she had dipped her fingers in the water to wet them in order to pull out some whins from her foot, a plausible enough reason, given that she was barefooted and had walked two miles from Dunbar on hot, dusty roads. She admitted she had given sheep's heid broth to Jean Johnston to cure her after she fell ill, but she remained silent on whether she had made the woman ill in the first place after the altercation in the butcher's shop. These were the responses to only five of the twenty-seven charges brought against her.

The court proceeded to hear the depositions of the witnesses. These gave the following evidence:

Isobel Reston, aged 36, testified she was in Thomas Ross' house on the day in 1685 when Catherine attempted to beg some pottage from Ross' daughter; she heard Catherine predict the death by choking of someone in the Ross household. Her testimony was confirmed by Janet Ross, aged 24, servant to Thomas Ross' daughter.

George Wallace, aged 47, baker and burgess, testified that William Brown, Catherine's husband, was in his house to sell a cow to James Reid, butcher, that he heard her threaten Reid, who subsequently died. This was confirmed by George Affleck, aged 66, another butcher.

Richard Merstone, aged 60, said he witnessed the incident with John Ferguson involving the theft of coal in 1677 and that he overheard Catherine threaten Ferguson's life. Marion Bairnsfather, aged 60, Ferguson's widow, confirmed that her husband had come home that evening and told her of the incident.

Patrick Ferguson, aged 46, swore that what Marion had said was the truth; he also confirmed that after refusing bread and cheese from Catherine in 1682, his wife died and was buried less than two weeks afterwards.

James Forrester, aged 39, confirmed that after his wife refused to give Catherine milk in 1683, his cow gave blood instead of milk, a fact his wife confirmed.

Andrew Stevenson, aged 61, testified that in 1674, Catherine had begged some oats from him. When he found her at his house, he said he had struck her because she refused to leave and that his wife died later.

Sarah Aitchison, widow of John Laurie whom Catherine was accused of be-witching in 1676 so that he died, confirmed the details. She also said she had seen a great many crows-about forty-flying over Catherine's and her neigh-bours' houses; that her husband 'took a fearfull distemper that she was necessitat to get some to hold him in the bed, and that for thrie years efter the pannall [prisoner] would never look the deponant [herself] in the face but fled from her.' Her testimony was confirmed by John Smith, aged 40, who said he had seen Catherine go to Laurie's house with the witch hair tether, that he saw a great many crows over Laurie's house that day and that when he was called in to help keep Laurie in bed, the delirious man bit at anything within reach and stared up and said "Ther she is, ther she is !"

Agnes Colme, aged 20, said she was in her father's house in Spott with Margaret Jackson in 1684, when Catherine had asked for alms and on refusal, wet her fingers in a bucket and touched the sole of her foot, after which five of her father's cattle died. Margaret Jackson confirmed Agnes' statement.

Maurice Ferguson, aged 40, confirmed the circumstances preceeding the death of his four year-old son George in 1685.
Jean Boig, aged 24, confirmed the incident at Patrick Mathie's house in 1687; at that time, she was his servant and an eye-witness to the altercation between Mathie's daughter Isobel and Catherine, when the latter attempted to pawn some cloth on the Sabbath day. This was also confirmed by another servant, Christian Dunbar, aged 24.

Lucress Smith, aged 30, wife of William Bryson, confirmed the incident in 1684 concerning the bellowing calf which Catherine had predicted would die. William Bryson, aged 48, confirmed his wife's testimony, as did Thomas Thomson.

George Shirreff, aged 50, in referring to incidents which took place at the Knowes in 1673 and 1677 said he knew nothing other than hearsay. The same response was given by Patrick Shirreff, aged 50. However, Christian Orme, aged 48, wife of George Shirreff confirmed that Catherine had cured her of illness in 1673 and transferred it to her neighbour, Helen Pringle, aged 48, wife of Patrick Shirreff, said that Catherine had offered her onions which Christian Orme had refused to buy; she accepted them and because Christian had slighted her, said that Catherine made her husband ill. Christian Orme also confirmed the tale about the magical yeast that grew in great quantities. Helen Pringle embellished on her testimony; she informed the court that she had allowed Catherine to sleep in the barn, that she lay on chaff which was given to the horses as feed and that within two weeks, two of her best horses died. (This appears to be a deliberate attempt on the part of Helen Pringle to add to an already convoluted story, thus blackening Catherine's character even more. Why did Catherine cure Christian Orme, who had refused to buy her onions and transfer her sickness to Helen Pringle who not only accepted the onions but also offered her a place to sleep, albeit in a stable ?)

James Lauder, aged 48, and his wife Katharine Sandilands, aged 46, both confirmed the incident in 1682, when they gave Catherine a handful of meal but not the soup she had asked for and that shortly afterwards, their child died.

John Home, aged 48, postmaster at Cockburnspath, his servant Helen Paterson, aged 28, John Ker, another servant, aged 38, James Simpson, aged 54, all of Cockburnspath, confirmed the incident in 1678, when Catherine had put a sickness on Helen Paterson; other testimonies were made by eyewitnesses John Hog of Dunglass, the chapman Thomas Lamb and a local farmer, George Lyall.

Jean Johnson, aged 48, wife of George Walker, confirmed the incident of the sheep's heid in 1685. Her husband, aged 56, corroborated her story.

Patrick Wood, aged 50, and his wife Rachel Darra, aged 44, confirmed the incident involving their two young daughters in 1687.

Janet Symington, aged 64, wife of John Affleck, testified about the incident in 1675 when she attempted to beg some barley from Catherine.

Helen Milne, aged 40, confirmed the quarrel which took place between John Milne and Catherine in 1658 which brought about his rapid decline.

James Congalton, aged 50, confirmed the story about Milne's horse breaking its neck from a fall, as Catherine had predicted; he also confirmed the incident in 1671, when Catherine had sat outside his house, refusing to leave until he paid her for plants she'd sold him.

William Smaill, aged 27, said he was present on the foreshore in 1684, when William Henderson was saying his farewells to his wife. He said he heard Catherine say
     "Ye may take leave of each uther for it will be a long goodnight."
Smaill added that it was a very dark night and that he couldn't be sure if the voice was Catherine's; then he said it must have been hers, as Henderson's wife never looked at Catherine again after that.

Alex Affleck, aged 66, confirmed he had been present when a dumb man pricked Catherine at the harbour in 1683.

Thomas Whyte and John Whyte both confirmed the incident concerning the suicide at Cockburnspath in 1688.

Several town officers confirmed they had witnessed the minister Thomas Wood's interrogation of Catherine in the Tolbooth, when she confessed she was a witch. Perhaps not surprisingly, only fifteen of the forty-six witnesses were literate and able to sign their depositions; one of the illiterate, Christian Orme, said she couldn't write but was able to sign her name.
     A jury of fifteen was appointed to consider the charges and the evidence. The court was at pains to ensure that few were from Dunbar itself; the majority lived in small parishes on the periphery - places such as Innerwick or surrounding farms. Only three were resident in Dunbar - William Cockburn, wright, William Cockburn, cooper, and Nicol Kellie, wright. We have of course no details of the length of time it took to reach a verdict but it must have been swift as the proceedings were completed by the end of that day of 30th May 1688. Catherine McTaggart was charged with witchcraft, sorcery and using charms as well as terrifying and abusing the people; the jury found her guilty on the three counts of witchcraft, sorcery and superstitious libel. This verdict should have assured her execution but it is not confirmed by the

Privy Council *Register* for 1688. According to Chambers, *Domestic Annals of Scotland*, she was sent to Dunbar to be burnt 'if her judges pleased.' It is certain they pleased themselves.

Catherine McTaggart was by no means innocent but she wasn't a witch. She was guilty of many personality defects - unable to control her temper, rude and unpleasant at best, vindictive at worst, especially when her efforts to obtain handouts were frustrated. She was, in short, a victim of her temperament. In a more enlightened age, she would have been sent packing with a flea in her ear and told to stop pestering people; perhaps she might have been arrested for vagrancy and cautioned in the local sheriff court as a public nuisance. Undoubtedly, she was possessed of a degree of malevolence; she used peoples' fear of witchcraft to her advantage. She enjoyed the terror the mere sight of her evoked, especially in the young and impressionable. She took a malicious delight in the power that fear and terror gave her over others. Why she turned to begging when she was married to a weaver with good employment and a reasonable standard of living is a mystery. Perhaps her husband William left Dunbar to seek work elsewhere; if that were so, Catherine enjoyed the freedom to do as she pleased, go where she wanted, stay out late at night if she chose. Hers is a typical story of the outcast, the loner who unfortunately vented her spleen openly in an age when it was dangerous to do so. The people she terrified were already afraid of her because of a series of unlucky coincidences; with a reputation of allegedly causing the deaths of five men, two women, two children, a horse, eight cows and bullocks, bringing sickness to four women, three of whom she 'cured', inducing sickness in a cow and finally, interfering in the brewing of ale in two households. It is no wonder she was feared. Such a reputation would be hard to live down anywhere, let alone a small community like Dunbar, where she must have been 'the speak of the place' before and during her trial and for many years after her death. One thing is clear. Whatever else Catherine McTaggart was, she was no witch.

8

Embers

The witch hunt continued sporadically from 1689 until the last unfortunate victim was burnt in Scotland in 1727. By the turn of the century, the few cases brought before the courts were confined largely to the north, as perhaps one might expect, given its relative isolation. There were of course notable outbreaks in East Lothian, Fife and Renfrewshire, areas which were rarely free from the mania.

Following the persecution and martyrdom of the Covenanters and the Glorious Revolution of 1688 which put William of Orange on the throne, the witch hunt was less favourably considered by the secular authorities, an attitude not wholly supported by the Kirk. The lengths to which the justiciary went in the trial of witches have been graphically demonstrated in the previous chapter in the case of Catherine McTaggart of Dunbar, the only person to be tried for witchcraft that year. For its part, the Kirk maintained its stance although increasingly, many in the clergy were dampening down their former enthusiasm for the hunt. Once more, the country appeared to be settling down after James VII was forced to flee the country, taking with him any residual fears about the threat of Popery. By the end of the century, witchcraft had almost ceased to pre-occupy the Kirk, although communities like Dunfermline and Torryburn tried witches well into the eighteenth century. In other parts of Scotland, executions continued, albeit sporadically; by contrast, in England, the last recorded hanging was that of Alicia Molland of Exeter in 1685. In both countries, judges were reluctant to try, let alone sentence suspects. It is thought that the last judicial trial of an English witch occurred in 1712, when Jane Wenham of Hertford was brought to the bar. After hearing the usual preposterous evidence, the judge advised the jury to return a verdict of not guilty, a recommendation they ignored. The law required the judge to impose the death penalty which he reluctantly did, then lodged for a royal pardon, an appeal which Queen Anne granted. The people of Hertford were enraged; Jane Wenham had to be hidden from the mob calling for her blood.

The last reference to witchcraft - and an oblique reference at that - by the Privy Council, occurs in the *Register* for 1689. Ironically, it concerns a minister, William Eason, who was deprived of his living in Auchtergivan, Strathtay - near Dunkeld in Perthshire – because he

> 'actually consulted with a woman who is suspected by every on[e] that knowes her to have ane familiar spirit...'

In short, the woman was considered a witch. Perhaps the Lords in Privy

Council felt it somewhat indelicate to call her a witch outright. Eason had resorted to consulting a witch because his wife was sick.

In 1694, Home of Reston made an impassioned plea to Lord Polwarth that not enough was being done to apprehend witches in the Eyemouth district, as mentioned in Chapter 6. In 1695, two women in Inverness, known only as McRorie and McQuicken were tried for witchcraft; the Privy Council ruled that if they were found guilty, the commissioners appointed to hear their testimonies were authorised to burn or otherwise execute them. One can imagine the result.

One of the most infamous cases in Scotland began in the autumn of 1696; it has all the hallmarks of the New England epidemic of 1692, when a group of hysterical girls in the Puritan-dominated community of Salem, Massachussetts, accused several neighbours of witchcraft and whose trials resulted in the execution of about thirty people. The Scottish Salem occurred in the small parish of Erskine, Renfrewshire, where Christian Shaw, the eleven year-old daughter of the Laird of Bargarran, accused no fewer than twenty-five people of bewitching her; the difference between the tragedies at Erskine and Salem is that Christian managed it all by herself. Whether she was innocent or not, or falsely accused her so-called tormentors, is still the subject of debate today. What is not at issue is that on the strength of her accusations, six people paid with their lives.

It all began with a trivial incident in the kitchen of Bargarran House. Young Christian discovered a servant, Katharine Campbell, stealing a drink of milk from a pail. In those days, milk was a valuable commodity and to steal it was a serious matter - we have seen the lengths to which many accused of witchcraft went in order to to syphon off the precious liquid or bewitch their neighbours' cows so that they ceased to give it. At any rate, Christian confronted Katharine, threatening to tell her mother about the theft. Katharine Campbell came from the Highlands and was known for her quick, fiery temper. She cursed young Christian and said if she told on her, the devil would visit her. A few days later, Agnes Naismith, an old woman with something of a reputation as a witch called at Bargarran House, where Christian spoke to her sharply. The ground was thus prepared for what was to follow, the seeds of a grudge sown in the receptive soil of a young girl's imagination. That night, Christian was beset by sudden and violent fits. At the end of the year, the Presbytery minute book records that the minister, Andrew Turner, had reported the

> 'deplorable case of Christian Shaw, daughter of the laird of Bargarran, in the paroch [parish] of Erskine, who since the beginning of September last, hath been under a very sore and unnatural-like distemper, frequently seized with strange fits, sometimes blood, sometimes deaf and dumb, the several parts of her body sometimes

155

violently extended and other times as violently contracted....and
those several weekes by past she hath degorged....hair, folded-up
straw, unclean hay, wild-fowl feathers, with divers kinds of bones
of fowles and others, together with a number of coal cinders burning
hot, candle grease, gravel-stones etc.....'

In view of all this, the Presbytery felt it was time they acted. Between
January and May 1697, no fewer than twenty-five people - ten men and fifteen women - were accused of witchcraft, named by Christian Shaw. Of these,
the Bargarran Witches, six went to the gallows and another, John Reid, hanged
himself in prison. Katharine Campbell, Agnes Naismith, Margaret Fulton -
deranged by the time of her execution - and Margaret Lang, a matronly, well-
respected woman, were executed along with brothers James and John Lindsay.
Modern medical opinion is that Christian Shaw was particularly vulnerable to
her kind of attacks; her age, puberty, personality and the kind of life she led
were all contributory factors. She was undoubtedly intelligent but she was
also suffering from clinical hysteria, which mysteriously disappeared never to
return after her six so-called tormentors were executed. There are two interesting postscripts to her case. One is that Christian married a minister and
became Mrs Miller for two years, only to lose her husband to illness in 1721,
after which she devoted her energies to establishing the thread-making industry in Paisley. She obtained the jealously guarded secret from the Dutch at
Campvere in Holland in an early example of industrial espionage. The second postscript is that some years after her death, two investigators made a
strange discovery in her bedroom at Bargarran House. They found a hole by
the side of her bed which was hidden by it. The aperture had been made
deliberately and wasn't a natural split in the wooden partition between two
rooms. Was the hole used to conceal the rubbish that Christian supposedly
disgorged during her fits? With some sleight of hand, she could have easily
transferred the objects to her mouth which she vomited during her 'fits'. A
contemporary medical diagnosis was that Christian was suffering from hypo-
chondriac melancholy rather than the effects of black magic; the doctor wasn't
far off the mark. Modern medical experts who deal with hysteria have since
confirmed that hysterics are able to swallow objects and retain them in the
gullet, disgorging them at will. By 1785, Christian Shaw was dead; she never
saw her name in print that year, when she was described as the Bargarran
Imposter. It would seem that Christian Shaw or Miller was not only a spinner
of fine thread.

Between 1696 and 1698, Elspet McEwan of Kirkcudbright appears to have
perfected a variation of Isobel Gowdie's method of extracting milk from cows.
From 1696, she drew off the precious fluid from her neighbours' animals by
means of a pin situated at the bottom of the rafters of her house. Perhaps

stricken with conscience, she was also able to increase the productivity of her neighbours' chickens, although she was equally capable of stopping them from laying. By 1698, her reputation as a witch being well-known, she was brought before the local magistrates to answer for her crimes. A manservant was sent with the minister's mare to her house to bring her in. She mounted the horse and as it approached the manse, the poor brute allegedly sweated droplets of blood. Her guilt thus proven, Elspet McEwan was imprisoned in the local tolbooth to await formal trial. Despite the fact that the Privy Council had outlawed the use of torture thirty years earlier, Elspet was so badly abused she begged her tormentors to end her life. A commission to try her was obtained in March 1698. A verdict of guilty sealed her fate. Her death-wish was fulfilled at the stake.

In 1698 perhaps can be detected a definite softening of attitudes towards suspected witches. In that year, Margaret Polwart in Coldingham was brought before the kirk session to answer a charge of the use of sorcery to cure her ailing child. She was helped by two local woman, Jean Hart, already suspected of witchcraft and Alison Nesbit, the latter having been

> 'lately scratched or had blood drawn [from her] above the breath [mouth or forehead] by some one who had suspectit her of witch-craft.'

An eyewitness looking in the window of Margaret Polwart's house swore she saw Jean Hart hold a candle in her left hand, then move her right hand about, mouthing

> 'a blasphemy, but what she could not say.'

Margaret Polwart was released from custody with a public rebuke. It is not known what happened to her accomplices.

Neck jougs at Spott Kirk, E Lothian

In the same year occurred the case of old Marion Lillie of Spott, near Dunbar. Known as the *Rigwoody Witch* - rigwoody means bony or stick-like - the sobriquet appears to be Marion's only claim to fame. She is remembered today only by the Witch's Stone enclosed by iron railings outside the village, thought to mark the place of her execution. Her career as a witch is unremarkable compared with others in Scotland; all she seems to have been guilty of was to speak roughly to her neighbours and that she had once frightened a pregnant woman

'to a rather unpleasant extremity by handling her rudely'.

One can but speculate on the nature of the unpleasantness. Although the records are incomplete, it is certain that Marion was strangled and burnt at the stake. Today, the Witch's Stone at Spott is hardly noticeable, although this writer and a friend made a curious and eerie discovery there as recently as 1st May 2000, an incident described in Chapter 9.

In 1699, a coven of twelve witches was discovered in Ross-shire. At their ensuing trial, two of them, Margaret Monro and Agnes Heath confessed willingly and received light punishment; the charges brought against John Glass and Mary Keill were declared not proven and the remaining eight suspects were admonished and given arbitrary punishment - probably branding on the cheek and banishment from the parish.

In 1700, Meg Lawson was executed at Selkirk - she allegedly changed herself into a mouse during her time as a witch, as is indicated in *The History of Selkirk*. In that year, Shetland burnt Barbara Tulloch and her daughter Ellen King as witches at Tingwall Loch. These were the only casualties for that year. In 1701, there were no executions, although one of two women arrested was banished from her parish. In 1702, Margaret Myles was the last witch to be burnt in Edinburgh for undisclosed crimes of sorcery. Margaret went to her death defiantly and certainly not penitent; nor at first would she oblige the minister with an eleventh hour return to the faith. When asked to read the Lord's Prayer at the stake, she responded with the following:

'Our Father, who wert in heaven....'

She also refused to say the words

'I renounce the devil and I adhere to my baptism'

All she would repeat was

'I nunce the devil and hered unto my baptism.'

However, as the executioner was covering her face before strangling her, she was heard to say

'Lord, take me out of the devil's hands and put me in God's.'

In 1703, Robert Bainzie of Oyne, Aberdeenshire was accused of charming or witchcraft; he was merely rebuked however, possibly because he was a kirk elder. Once again, Torryburn came to the fore; the minister there, Allan Logan, being noted for his zeal in persecuting witches. Logan, the self-appointed witchfinder of Torryburn , was intent on ridding the community of 'all trafficking with the devil and his invisible world'. He was so obsessed with witches that Helen Kay, one of his parishioners voiced the views of many others, accusing him of being 'daft on witches'. Helen was publicly rebuked before the whole congregation for her impudence

In 1704, a complaint was brought by Jean Neilson, an invalid, against

Lillias Adie, whom she believed had caused her ailment. Lillias was put in prison on 29th July, when the Torryburn minister, Allan Logan and the kirk session 'examined' - tortured - her. Lillias Adie confessed she had been a witch for seven years after she met the devil in a cornfield, where she had renounced her baptism and embraced him; she said she found his skin cold to the touch and remarked that his feet were cloven like those of a bullock. At night, she joined with him and others in dances that were lit by a strange light which came out of the darkness; she said it wasn't as bright as candle-light but enough for her to see the faces of those around her. She named several women as witches but most appear to have escaped punishment. Some accounts say Lillias Adie - known locally as Torryburn Jean - was executed; in point of fact, she died in prison. Denied burial in consecrated ground because of her witchcraft, she was interred within the floodmark of the sands between Torrie and Torryburn; it is recorded that a local antiquarian dug up her remains in the nineteenth century and preserved her skull ! The skull now resides in St. Andrew's University museum. An interesting footnote is that in 1884, a Doctor William Dow examined the skull and, declaring it abnormally small, suggested that Lillias was afflicted by a diseased brain. Although Lillias herself cheated the hangman, two others named by her - Grissel Anderson and Euphan Stirt - did not.

Fife figures yet again in the years 1704-1705, in the particularly tragic case of the Witches of Pittenweem, where the mob took over when the court failed to prosecute two women. It will be remembered that Pittenweem had despatched several witches in the course of the previous century, even demanding payment of the expenses arising from the trial and execution of three women from their families. The case of the Pittenweem Witches of 1704-05 is yet another example of the clergy fanning the flames of prejudice, compounded in this instance by passive consent to mob-rule. The first of the witches was Beatrix Laing, wife of a local burgess and former treasurer of Pittenweem Burgh Council. The story bears some comparison with that of the Bargarran Witches in 1697. It involved a young man, Patrick Morton, who was apprenticed to his father, a local blacksmith. One day, he was working at the forge when Beatrix called and asked him to make some nails for her. The boy said he couldn't oblige her as he was too busy; perhaps Beatrix Laing believed she deserved better treatment in view of her husband's standing in the community. Again, she asked the boy to accommodate her. Again he refused. She lost her temper and cursed him. Beatrix already had the reputation of being a witch and when Patrick saw her the following day, she was doing something which to his mind was very peculiar. He watched her put hot coals in a bucket of water and perhaps heard her muttering to herself. At any rate, he got it into his head that she was bewitching him. Not long after, he

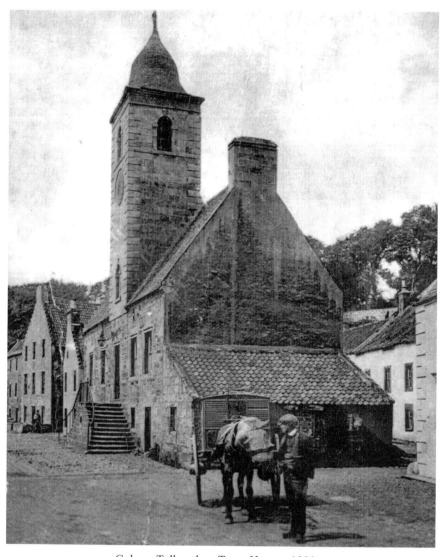

Culross Tolbooth or Town House c1900

complained of weakness in his legs; he grew emaciated and began to show symptoms of epilepsy. His body swelled, his breathing was laboured, his head turned round at an alarming angle and couldn't be put back in place. This could easily have been caused by tetanus, given his occupation. In his delirium, he accused Beatrix Laing and another woman, Janet Corphat or

Cornfoot, of putting a spell on him. He eagerly showed visitors marks on his arms, which he said had been inflicted by the witches. Doctors called in to treat him shook their heads; his stomach was swollen, his chest bulged, his head was permanently twisted to one side. On 19th May 1704, he told the local minister he would never find peace until the two witches were punished. In one of his hallucinatory moments, Patrick Morton said the devil had come to the foot of his bed, saying the following:

'My child, I will give you a silver suit and silver tressing about your hat if you will but confess there is no Saviour; though two of my children [presumably Beatrix and Janet] suffer punishment, yet it shall be well with you hereafter.'

The Privy Council granted a commission for the trial of Beatrix Laing. She was brutally tortured and denied sleep; in her confession, she named Janet Cornfoot, Isobel Adam and Nicol Lawson as her accomplices. She later recanted her confession and was kept in a damp dungeon for five months while the local magistrates and minister attempted to have her tried in Edinburgh. However, through the good offices of two members of the Privy Council, Lords Balcarres and Anstruther, the Council ordered she be released on 12th August on payment of a fine of £8. The local population was outraged. Beatrix was forced to leave Pittenweem; she didn't dare return home and wandered all over Fife like a beggar, finally dying 'undesired' in St Andrews.

Isobel Adam was next to be tried. She paid off her inquisitors with cash - quite illegal - despite making the following confession:

'Confess that about a fortnight after Martinmas [11th November], she came to Beatrix Laing's and saw a little black man with a hat and black clothes sitting at the board end, and Beatrix said "Here is a gentleman that will fee [hire] you"....upon which she engaged and the Devil kissed her, and told her he knew she was disenchanted with her lot, and that in his service she should get riches as much as she could wish. And that upon New Year's Day thereafter, the Devil appeared to her in Thomas Adams' house, and there she renounced her baptism vows; and likewise acknouledges that she was in [Andrew] Macgregor's house with Beatrix Laing, Nicol Lawson, Janet Corphat and Thomas Brown, on a design to strangle the said Macgregor.'

Thomas Brown died in Pittenweem jail not long after his arrest. There is no record of a trial involving Nicol Lawson in 1705 but he was arrested for practising witchcraft in 1709; the outcome is not recorded.

Patrick Morton's third tormentor, Janet Corphat or Cornfoot, was tortured, tried, re-tried and convicted. The boy's story was corroborated by Andrew Macgregor, the group's intended victim. Macgregor accused Janet and the others of attacking him in his bed one night on the promptings of the devil. Janet was put in the burgh jail and flogged by the minister, Patrick Cowper. Perhaps as with Beatrix Laing, sense prevailed; men of influence - probably Balcarres and Anstruther again - helped her to escape from prison. The mob got to her. The minister, Patrick Cowper, did nothing to protect her; she was entitled to sanctuary but presumably he closed the kirk doors on a woman he considered a rank witch. The mob took hold of her, tied her up and dragged her by the heels through the streets of Pittenweem. A local bailie attempted to disperse the mob but was powerless against the vengeful crowd. After he left the scene, the mob tied Janet to a rope which they stretched between the shore and a ship moored in the harbour; they swung her back and forth, all the while pelting her with stones. Some accounts say that the minister and a few bailies stood by and again did nothing. Tiring of the game, they dragged Janet to the shore, placed a wooden door on her and crushed her to death by piling boulders on it.

In 1704, Anna Wood, a young serving wench and five other women were indicted for menacing a sailor, Robert Nimmo,. Their chief accuser, Nimmo, swore under oath that one dark night, walking to Bo'ness from Linlithgow, he was surrounded by Anna and five witches. No matter how hard he ran, they continued to dance round him. As he raced down the slope towards his home on the shores of the Firth of Forth at Carriden, he prayed he would out-run them. When he neared habitation, he said the women changed into 'muckle black crows' to escape detection. Warming to his subject, he claimed that the six crows followed him nearly to his house, where he saw Anna turn back into human form. Anna was tried by the Carriden kirk session and put into ward to await trial. However, she escaped which the townspeople felt was hardly surprising as she was known to change herself into a black cat or take flight as a crow. Anna was never seen in the district again.

In the year of 1705, the small village of Spott, outside Dunbar, rejoiced in the burning of 'many witches' on the top of Spott Loan, as is recorded in the kirk session minute-book. How many? Most covens contained twelve or thirteen witches. On whose authority were these poor people burnt? No commission was granted for their trial, or at least, no records exist which approved it. It seems that with the enlightened attitude prevalent in central authority and the reluctance of judges to try suspects for fear of mockery, if not a waste of the courts' time, local communities kept the fires burning by taking the law into their own hands. By now, defence lawyers were able to dismiss out of hand the ridiculous evidence being brought before the courts and it is certain that many cases never saw the light of day. Also, the medical profession were increasingly asked for opinions about the state of the mental health of some of the accused. Fewer voices in authority were raised at this time, the beginning of what would later become known as the Age of Enlightenment in Scotland. It was not born from any specific concern about the persecution of witches, although its aims were humanitarian. The Age of Enlightenment developed after the founding of several important institutions like the Royal College of Physicians in 1681. About this time, Sit George Mackenzie, the so-called 'Bluidy' Mackenzie, now Lord Advocate, consolidated and published the laws of Scotland, which brought a new coherence to the administration. Many who shared that aristocratic state of mind called intelligence dismissed witchcraft and belief in it as sheer superstition or folklore. And yet as late as 1705, an East Lothian minister, John Bell of Gladsmuir, near Haddington, published anonymously his spuriously titled treatise *An Ingenious and Scientific Discourse of Witchcraft*; removing the words 'and Scientific' makes the treatise more apposite. Bell admitted he had personally pricked suspected witches. His manuscript describes the ways used to detect witches in nearby Samuelston in 1618, 1661 and 1662. One hopes that Bell was simply committing to paper an aspect of Scottish history when he wrote the following:

'....a witch's mark was like a blue or red spot and like flea-biting....'
He solemnly wrote that the witch's or devil's mark was often well-hidden and found only with difficulty on certain parts of the body such as the eyebrows, the hair under the armpits and in the inside of the lips. At least he had the presence of mind to admit that much misery and harm had been done to many an innocent woman through the practice of pricking.

In the following year, Duncan Forbes of Culloden was granted a commission to try George and Lachlan Rattray in Inverness, although he was not given authority to carry out sentence on them. The outcome of the trial was reported to the Privy Council, which ordered the men's execution in September. Between 1706 and 1709, Perth saw two executions while in Thurso, the magistrates despatched six people. In 1708, there were two cases of witchcraft in Orkney. One appears to have its roots in the folklore of the island as there is no record of it in the Privy Council *Register*, nor is the witch named. Perhaps modern Orcadians interested in such matters will be familiar with the witch of Dunross-ness who was known to hate the crew of a particular fishing boat for some reason. Setting off on a calm and cloudless day, the fishermen looked forward to a prosperous and safe trip. The witch raised a storm by floating a small wooden vessel in a tub and while she worked in the house, reputedly chanted an old Norse spell. Every now and then, she asked her child to look at the tub and tell her if the little wooden vessel was still afloat. She sang louder and louder until the child came back and said the vessel had capsized. She called out
'The turn is done!'

The same day, the fishing boat sank with all its crew.

The second case, that of Katharine Taylor, a crippled beggar-woman accused of sorcery and charming, involved the treating of William Stensgar of Southside, Orkney for rheumatism, a common complaint in that inhospitable climate. He asked the beggar-woman if she could cure him. He said Katharine told him to accompany him to a stile at sunrise and for his wife to come along with a pail of water. At the stile, she massaged William's afflicted knee, recited a spell and sang the *23rd Psalm*. The object of this was to draw the rheumatism into the pail of water, which was then emptied over the stile so that the next person to cross it would take the ailment. Although no outcome of her trial is recorded, it is thought that she was executed. In 1709, Elspeth Rule was tried in Dumfries on 3rd May. Oddly enough, no specific charge of witchcraft was brought against her although she had threatened people who afterwards lost cattle and whose friends died; one person was supposedly driven insane by Elspeth's spells. Elspeth Rule, the last witch tried in Dumfries, was branded and banished for life from Scotland.

The last two major trials for witchcraft took place in 1718 and 1727, both occurring in the north of Scotland. The trial in 1718 would not be out of place in a Stephen King horror tale. It is, appropriately, about cats. Lots of them. It happened in Scrabster, near Thurso. The suspected witch went by the name of Margaret Nin Gilbert [Gilbertson] who had a friend, Margaret Olsone [Olsen], described as a woman who 'behaved wickedly.' It transpired that Olsen had been evicted from her house by her landlord, a Mr Fraser, who installed another tenant, William Montgomery, in her place. Margaret Olsen consulted Margaret Gilbertson to see what harm they could do to Fraser. Margaret tried to bewitch him but was unsuccessful as she said Fraser was too wealthy and important and her powers were useless against him. So the pair turned their attention to Montgomery, a mason and the new tenant of Burnside of Scrabster. Shortly after his arrival, his house was overrun with cats. He was away from home at the time and his wife wrote to him five times, threatening to leave him. She said that if he didn't return home to protect his family from the feline invasions, she and their child were going to live in Thurso. Their servant had already left suddenly because one night, five cats came to the fireside where she sat alone. She swore she heard them speaking to each other in human voices. Montgomery returned home to do battle with the erudite cats.

On 28th November, he and his assistant Willie Geddes trapped one of the cats, pinned it down with a dirk and beat it with a sword before throwing it outside. The next morning, the body of the cat was nowhere to be seen. A few nights later, the cats returned and again Montgomery and Geddes attacked them, smothering one in a plaid, stabbing it and smashing its head with an axe.

Again, the body was thrown outside and again it had disappeared by daylight. Montgomery was convinced there was witchcraft about and he petitioned the sheriff-depute at Caithness to enquire if anyone local had been taken ill or wounded recently. The story now takes a macabre twist. Margaret Gilbertson had lost a limb. Eye-witnesses said they had seen her leg dropping off at her cottage door. She was arrested. On 24th March 1719, the depute-sheriff of Caithness submitted Montgomery's complaint to the King's Advocate, Robert Dundas of Arniston. Margaret's black and putrefied leg was brought into court as exhibit number one at her subsequent trial. During the hearings, it transpired that a suspected witch by the name of Helen Andrew had suddenly died; another, known only as McHuistan had drowned herself in the sea. Margaret Gilbertson, who lived less than two miles from Montgomery was seen

'to drop at her own door, one of her leggs from the middle.'

Margaret was examined and confessed she and others had been in Montgomery's house in the form of cats and that he had broken her leg with a dirk and an axe. She confessed she was in league with the devil. She named Margaret Olsen as one of the cats and another woman - probably Helen Andrew - who was so badly wounded by Montgomery she died. Margaret Gilbertson never lived to see the outcome of her trial; she died in prison, obviously a victim of the gangrene which had caused her leg to rot away. The last of the Thurso Witches, Margaret Olsen was pricked and the devil's mark was found on her shoulder. She was strangled and burnt. From that day on, no more cats came to the house of William Montgomery.

In 1720, in Midcalder, Lord Torphichen's son Patrick Sandilands began having hallucinations and blamed them on the Calder Witches - shades of Christian Shaw twenty-three years earlier. Several old women were imprisoned but it appears that none was executed. One of them, Jonet Fogo, confessed that she had given her dead son's corpse to the devil to roast and eat! There was one last act in the witch hunt. In 1726, the Reverend T Woodrow in Eastwood, Renfrewshire was still receiving occasional reports of witches in correspondence from two of his Ross-shire brethren. One of them mentioned a witch who was executed for taking away the sight of an Episcopalian minister. As the writer put it, it had to be witchcraft as there was no other explanation for the sudden onset of the man's blindness. Witches were still scapegoats. In 1727, the year of the last judicial execution for witchcraft in Scotland, the superstitious were alive and well, wreaking their revenge to the very end.

There is some controversy about the actual date of the last witch-burning, which occurred in Dornoch, Sutherland. Some accounts favour 1722; this writer believes it occurred five years later, confirmed by the correspondence of an English gentleman travelling through Scotland that year. Edward Burt's *Letters from the North of Scotland* published years later contains a letter (*Letter xii, vol.i*) to a friend in London, which confirms the date of the last witch burning:

'I am pleased when I reflect, that the notion of witches is pretty well worn out among people of any tolerance, sense and education in England; but here [in Scotland] it remains among some that sit judicially; and witchcraft and Charming (as it is called) make up a considerable article in the recorded acts of the general assembly [of the Church of Scotland]......'

At least Burt is honest; he refers later to an unidentified witch tried in Hertford - in fact, Jane Wenham, whose trial in 1712 is mentioned earlier. As to the last trial in Scotland, Burt is quite specific:

'In the beginning of the year 1727, two poor Highland women (mother and daughter), in the shire of Sutherland, were accused of witchcraft, tried and condemned to be burnt. This proceeding was in a court held by the deputy-sheriff. The young one made her escape out of prison, but the old woman suffered that cruel death, in a pitch barrel, in June following, at Dornoch the head borough [sic] of that county.'

The case to which Burt refers is that of Janet Horn and her daughter who lived in the parish of Loth, near Dornoch in Sutherland. Captain David Ross of Littledean, sheriff-depute of Sutherland had them brought before him. Janet, an elderly woman who showed definite symptoms of what today would be termed dementia, had made a pact with the devil. She attended local Sabbats by changing her daughter into a pony, which the devil himself had shod with horseshoes. It is fact that Janet's daughter suffered from a deformity in her hands and feet, an ailment she passed on to her son. Both mother and daughter were found guilty of practising witchcraft but as Edward Burt says, the daughter managed to escape. As for poor Janet, the story is that on the day of her execution in June 1727 - a chilly one by all accounts - she warmed her hands at the very fire which was about to consume her alive. Sir Walter Scott recorded in his *Letters on Demonology and Witchcraft* that Janet's lame grandson was still living in 1830, receiving

'the charity of the present Marchioness of Stafford, Countess of Sutherland.'

However, the name Horn was long reviled in that part of Scotland.

If further proof of Burt's date of the trial is needed, it can be found in a letter to Thomas Woodrow of Eastwood dated 18th April 1727 from James Frazer of Ross:

'Since I saw you in Edinburgh in May last [probably at the annual meeting of the General Assembly], there has been a great noise in the parish of Loth in Sutherland, by which the minister is said to have suffered. He is not yet recovered; however, the thing has been examined into and the women were, I know, before the presbytery. There were likewise very lately a rumour of that kind in the parrish of Tarbet,'

There is no mention of the Tarbet incident in central records.

We cannot be certain that Janet Horn was the last witch to face death for practising witchcraft but central records are silent on the subject of witchcraft after the turn of the century. Finally, the united parliament of Britain repealed the *Witchcraft Acts* of 1563 enacted by Elizabeth I and Mary, Queen of Scots and that of James VI and I of 1604. Even so, elements of the Scottish Kirk deprecated their repeal. The General Assembly of the Established Presbyterian Kirk had to content itself with a mild protest. Not so the seceding arm which called itself the Associate Presbytery Established Church of Scotland, known colloquially as the Auld Lichts (Old Lights, because they clung to the form of Presbyterianism favoured by the Covenanters, or at least, in their exponents' and supporters' minds, a purer and more rigid form of worship than the Established Church offered). For those grim and oppressive men, witchcraft remained one of the cardinal sins. Their Act of 1743 describes the Confession of National and Personal Sins; witchcraft remained a sin, as evinced by the following:

'The Penal Statute against witches having been repealed by Parliament contrary to the express laws of God.'

This was a reference to *Exodus,* chapter 23, verse 18:

'Thou shalt not suffer a witch to live.'

At last, the persecution of witches was over. Or was it ?

The English were rightly proud of their more enlightened attitude towards witches after 1685. Well, at least the authorities and even the church felt they had shown others the way. But somehow, they failed to get the message across to the common people. In 1751, a man was executed in England for the murder of Ruth Osborne, a suspected witch. Apparently, in 1745 - the year of the Jacobite Rising in Scotland - Ruth had tried to beg some milk from a man called Butterfield. When he refused her, she went away muttering that she wished the Pretender (Charles Edward Stuart, Bonnie Prince Charlie) would soon come and carry off his cattle. Butterfield fell ill and his fortunes failed. He got it into his mind that Ruth had put a spell on him. To counteract her bewitchment, he called in a 'white' witch from Northamptonshire who got to work and attempted to remove the spell. But she was expensive and produced no visible results. In his frustration, Butterfield arranged for Ruth Osborne and her husband John to be ducked in the pond at Tring for their crime. The couple were in their seventies. To protect them from the mob, the parish over-seer took them into the poorhouse, then to the local church. The mob gathered outside intent on revenge, their anger no doubt whipped up by Butterfield's cronies. They broke into the church and took the terrified old couple to the duckpond. Ruth Osborne was murdered in the pond and her husband was tied to her dead body; shortly afterwards he died. The clergy in Tring did nothing to help the Osbornes. One of the mob, Thomas Colley, was tried for the murder of Ruth Osborne and hanged at St Albans on 22nd August 1751.

The authorities in Scotland also failed to get the message across to the common people. Belief in witchcraft could not be swept away overnight and certainly not by men in the remote and foreign capital of England, let alone in Edinburgh. In the same year that Thomas Colley was hanged for murdering Ruth Osborne, the Presbytery of Tain obliged to take action against three men who had mutilated a woman and her daughter. The practice of scoring a witch 'above the breath' continued on both sides of the Border well into the eighteenth century; in Scotland, a case was recorded in 1831. In 1751, the Kirk authorities in Tain did no more than rebuke the culprits who had dragged a woman and her daughter from their beds, two of them holding the women down while the third cut them about the forehead. No charge of common assault appears to have been brought against them.

And yet incredibly, after the the repeal of the *Witchcraft Acts* of 1563 and 1604 by legislation enacted in 1736, at least two women were put in prison on account of witchcraft. While the eighteenth century act abolished the practising of witchcraft, it contained a saving measure which made pretending to be a witch unlawful. The act of 1736 allowed the authorities to prosecute any person who pretended '....to exercise or use any kind of witchcraft, sorcery, inchantment or undertake to tell fortunes....' and that any person convicted of such practices would '....suffer imprisonment by the space of one whole year without bail, or mainprize [release on surety], and once in every quarter of the said year in some market town of the proper county upon the market day there stand openly on the pillory by the space of one hour....' for the population to witness.

As Robin Murdoch indicates in his *Foreword,* it was under the repealing legislation of 1736 that Jean Maxwell of Kirkcudbright was prosecuted for *pretending* to be a witch as late as 1805. A case nearer our own time is that of Helen Duncan in Edinburgh, a spiritualist or medium who was similarly imprisoned for abusing the people by deceit; ostensibly considered a confidence trickster, the real reason was that the authorities believed she was giving military secrets to those sympathetic to the Germans during the Second World War. The act of 1736 was repealed in its entirety by the *Fraudulent Mediums Act,* 1951. Old habits indeed take a long time to die.

9

Festivals, Rites and Charms

Despite Isobel Gowdie's highly informative confession about witch practices in Auldearn, Nairnshire, in 1662, it is necessary to fill in certain gaps in her otherwise colourful tale. For example, Isobel does not tell us about dates in the year which had particular significance for witches. Just as Easter and Christmas are the major events in the Christian calendar, so too were certain festive days held special by witches and warlocks. On these occasions, witches were said to be at their most active and powerful so that the God-fearing people were careful not to go out of doors if they could avoid doing so. As any schoolboy or schoolgirl knows, the most important festival of all was Halloween on 31st October. There were other red letter days - or to be precise - nights, celebrated by witches and warlocks. Many of these originated either in Celtic pagan rituals or those of the early Christian church. Important festivals were celebrated on the following dates:

1st	February	: February Eve or Candlemas Eve
20th	March	: Spring Equinox
30th	April	: May Eve
21st	June	: Summer Solstice, or Midsummer
31st	July	: August Eve, or Lammas
20th	September	: Autumn Equinox
31st	October	: All Hallows' Eve, or *Festival of Souls*
20th	December	: Winter Solstice, or *Festival of Rebirth*

It is by no concidence that the February, May, September and October festivals coincide with those important in the ancient Celtic or early Christian calendars. Candlemas, the *Festival of Light*, took place on 2nd February. It celebrated Jesus' introduction to the house of God and was also a time when candles were lit to ward off evil spirits - hence the importance of the preceding night to witches. The Celtic *Festival of Beltane*, the ancient worship of the sun, occurred on 1st May and required all fires to be dimmed before the

Beltane fires were re-lit on 1st May so that darkness prevailed on May Eve (30th April), a productive time for the powers of darkness. The old customs appear to still linger in secluded country villages in Scotland. At Spott, East Lothian, Robin Murdoch and I visited the Witch's Stone on 1st May 2000. The stone reputedly marks the place of execution of Marion Lillie, known as the *Rigwoody Witch*; that morning, four coins had been placed on the stone, perhaps by way of commemoration, on May Eve or May Day. The two equinoxes in Spring and Autumn were times of wild storms and would have allowed witches to travel freely about the countryside undetected. The Spring Equinox was known to the Celts as *Imbolc,* the Autumn Equinox as *Lugnasadh. Samhain* was the Celtic name for the festival on 1st November, which was the start of the Celtic New Year and the beginning of winter, the time of darkness. All Hallows' was when the early church believed that the gates of heaven and hell were opened so that the souls of the dead could revisit the places they'd known on earth. Good and evil spirits roamed freely on the night preceding All Saints' Day on 1st November; evil spirits would of course be made welcome by witches because they could make mischief for their enemies. These festivals in effect celebrated natural occurrences like sowing, harvesting, the return of the light and the dark, all part of the earth's cycle of death and rebirth.

In addition to these red letter dates, meetings known as Esbats were organised by local covens and attended only by their own members. These were held monthly and timed to occur at the full moon so that in accordance with the lunar calendar, there were thirteen gatherings. More significant were the Sabbats held four or five times a year, occasions when the devil and other covens in the district were present. Sabbats were large affairs of feasting and general merriment - they were in fact an excuse for orgies on a scale which would not have been out of place in the decadent declining years of the Roman Empire. Favoured meeting places for Esbats and Sabbats were deserted churches - Burns put this to stunning use in *Tam o' Shanter,* the old ruined Kirk of Alloway providing an eerie setting for his poem - ruined castles and houses, abbeys and monasteries, remote places by the sea or in lonely hills and unfrequented woods. In Scottish witchcraft lore, crossroads were the most favoured places for witches to foregather before they proceeded to their appointed destination.

All societies and clubs have formal procedures; so too had witches. If the devil was present, he sat at the head of the table, usually with the prettiest witches - young women known as maidens - seated on either side of him. In Scotland, there was usually a piper to play in the food for the banquet and a grace of sorts would be said before the meal commenced. The food eaten, the devil would then enquire what his servants had achieved since he last met with them. If the feast took place in a deserted kirk, the devil sat at the ruined altar, or in the case of working churches, he would occupy the Reader's chair, as Isobel Gowdie pointed out in her confession. Many accounts describe how the devil often had a black book from which he read. Perhaps he also noted in it the names of his servants who had done particularly well.

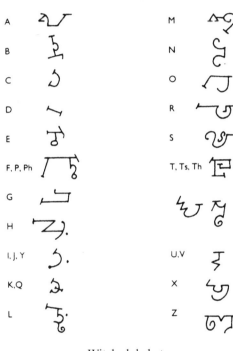

Witch alphabet

As we have seen during the course of this book, the stock-in-trade of witches was the effigy, the wax or clay image made of a victim which was pierced with pins to induce pain, or cast into the fire to bring on the sweating sickness or thrown into the sea to cause death by drowning. Another popular spell was to inflict illness on a person, then transfer it to someone or something else. There are many examples of this in the preceding chapters. An unusual method of visiting sickness on a victim is described in Chapter 1, that used by Agnes Sampson, one of the North Berwick Witches, in 1590. She attempted to make James VI ill by stringing up a toad by its legs for three days to allow her to collect its venom which she then intended to smear on a piece of cloth belonging to the king. Unable to obtain a piece of his clothing, she made a wax image of him, which she then pierced with pins. The 'white' witches claimed to be able to remove sickness by washing the sufferer's clothing in south-running water, as John Neill of Tweedmouth recommended to the wife of an ailing man living there in 1631. Neill was also

171

instrumental in the attempted murder of Sir George Home of Manderston; he met the devil and several witches on Coldingham Moor to decide how best to get rid of Sir George, whose wife wanted him eliminated. The plan was to obtain a dead foal, place it Sir George's stable under his horse's manger so that Sir George would contract a serious illness from which he would recover only in the event of the foal being found. A classic example of transference is that attributed to Marion Layland in Orkney, described in Chapter 2; it may be recalled that in 1633, she was alleged to have caused madness in the skipper of a ship which was transferred to the ship's dog, the unfortunate animal subsequently being cast into the sea.

In the north of Scotland, a cure for epilepsy was of unmistakeable pagan origin; it involved the sacrifice of a black cockerel by burying it along with a lock of the person's hair and some nail parings at the spot where the epileptic first fell to the ground. Another method of curing was by invocation or incantation of certain words arranged in a specific way. A common cure used in Orkney for sick animals went as follows:

'Three things have thee forspoken,
Heart, tongue, and eye, almaist;
Three things shall thee mend again,
Father, Son and Haily Ghaist.'

A similar rhyme used by a Selkirk witch went thus:

'Three bitten, has three bitten
The tongue, the ear, the heart, all the maist;
Three things must ye haill,
The Father, the Son and the Haily Ghaist.'

Belief in the magic properties of certain trees, shrubs and plants stems from early pre-Christian Celtic and Druidic belief - rheumatism-curing apple trees, mistletoe or *allheal,* lightning-deflecting hawthorn and lifespan-enhancing holly. In Scotland, there was one tree considered very unlucky - the elder, the tree upon which Judas Iscariot reputedly hanged himself. To bring elder into the house was to invite the devil in; the elder was the favourite tree for witches to hide in. The rowan was thought to offer protection against witches, especially in the north of Scotland. The presence of a ruined croft house or cottage

172

hidden by growth may be indicated by a nearby rowan. We have seen how in 1618, young Margaret Barclay in Irvine carried about with her a sprig of rowan and a red thread which she said helped her cow to produce more milk; her judges either failed to appreciate the significance of the rowan, a charm against witchcraft, or they deliberately ignored the fact that no witch would carry a sprig of it. Herbs used by witches included monk's hood or wolf bane, from which they distilled the much sought-after poison aconite; hemlock and deadly nightshade (belladonna) were also used in the preparation of poisons. Mandrake was popular, reputed to grow only beneath the gallows and often used to make love potions and increase sexual power. It may be remembered that in 1601, David Roy consulted a witch for a love potion made from an extract of daffodils. Foxgloves, or *witches' thimmles* [thimbles], a source of digitalis, was first used by witches, then by the medical profession; it appears that a Dr Withering treated a patient suffering from of dropsy by administering foxglove tea, a known witch cure. When it could be found, the purple orchis was used in love potions; it had to be plucked before sunrise with the witch facing southwards for full effect. Nettles were used to cure ailments - again, the nettle root had to be pulled before sunrise. Orris root was used in divinations; tied by thread and used as a pendulum, it indicated an affirmative answer to a question when it turned *deasil* [clockwise] or negative if it turned *widdershins* [anti-clockwise].

An essential part of a witch's initiation was physical contact with the devil; this took the form of either copulation or what was known as the *Osculum Infame*, or obscene kiss on his buttocks. At the initiation ceremony, food was taken, followed by dancing in a circle, usually starting from the left; witches met in remote places often with historical connections or the local mercat cross. The coven usually ended the ceremony with mass copulation, a fact made known at the trial of the North Berwick Witches in 1591. The Catholic Church believed sexual intercourse was possible with demons, an aspect of witchcraft the Reformed Church readily accepted because it added scandal to what it considered evil and obscene practices. Sexual undertones were rarely far away in Scottish witch trials particularly when the suspect was young or attractive. Before they went to the stake in 1679, the Bo'Ness Witches confessed their intimacy with the devil in the shape of a deer or other creature; this is quoted in Pitcairn's *Criminal Trials*. Sometimes the devil would appear as a stirk, a bull, a roe deer or a dog. One of the Bo'Ness Witches, Margaret Hamilton, said the devil had entered her in the likeness of a man and withdrew from her in the form of a black dog. At her trial in 1662, Isobel Gowdie said she found the devil's seed cold in her, like spring well-water.

As mentioned earlier, the most important festival of the year was Halloween or as it was called in pre-Reformation times, All Hallows' Eve. In pagan times, the tribal villagers believed it was the night when the dead came back to visit their earthly haunts. The hollowed-out turnip with candle used by children during the past two centuries is a relic of the days when pagan tribes stuck the skulls of people or animals on poles to ward off evil spirits. In seventeenth and eighteenth century Scotland, the superstitious folk were afraid of Halloween as it was the time when the demons of the earth, water, fire and air were particularly active under the command of the Nighthag; Robert Burns used this theme to brilliant effect in *Tam o' Shanter*. Burns admitted that he gained his knowledge of witches and warlocks from Betty Davidson, an old servant friend of his mother's, whom he said knew by heart a fantastic range of tales and songs about the little people and witches.

A vital element of witch folklore was her ability to change her shape. Trials abound with examples of shape-shifting. There is a certain poetic licence in this aspect of witchcraft, as anthropolgists would regard this simply as imitation of the creature's characteristics. Most witches had a familiar, usually a cat and preferably black; some favoured hares, crows, magpies and ravens. In their dances, witches imitated their favourite creatures' movements rather than transformed into them. Marion Pardoun, the Witch of Hillswick, Shetland, unusually chose the porpoise as her favoured familiar, perhaps because she was impressed by its speed and grace. However, when she wanted to bewitch her neighbours' cattle, she chose the *corbie*, or crow. The scavenging habits of that bird have given rise to the belief that there is something inherently evil about it and its related species, the magpie. The raven, another bird of wicked appearance, helped witches to achieve longevity of life and was their representative at funerals. A single magpie flying away from the sun was thought extremely unlucky; it was supposed to be out looking for victims for its witch mistress. Probably this is the basis for the folk belief, reflected in the following rhyme which gives the witches' version in brackets:

> 'Ane for sorrow
> (Ane for the person who's worked me ill)
> Two for mirth
> (Twa for the man I'm going to kill)

174

Three for a waddin' [wedding]
(Three for a droonin'[drowning]
Fower [four] for a birth
(Fower for a curse)
Five for a fiddler
(Five for a minister's even worse)
Six for a dance
(Six for cantrips ower the moor)
Seven for Auld Scotia
(Seven for the bairnie [child] I shall smoor [smother]
Eight for France
(Eight for the Devil I'll meet the morn).

It is of course the cat which is most associated with witches. Venerated and feared for centuries going back to ancient Egypt, the cat has skirted the edges of human society probably for as long as man himself has been around. There are many superstitions associated with cats, particularly black cats. In Dunbar, East Lothian for example, it was said that if a black cat crossed a fisherman's path on a Friday, he would turn back from his boat and remain ashore all day. Perhaps this superstition is not restricted to Dunbar however. As has been seen already, references to cats abound in witch trials; a little-known episode occurred in Currie, Midlothian - not particularly noted for its witches - in the middle of the seventeenth century when a young man, Andrew Ramsay, was walking home one night. The sixteen year-old youth was taking a short-cut through Currie Kirkyard one night when he saw several cats came out of the quire or choir window. Before his eyes, they turned into women. Taking to his heels, he had almost escaped, but one gripped him by his 'gravat' or neckerchief which he lost in his flight. Andrew later identified two of them, Margaret Watson and Margaret Walker from Pentland, near Edinburgh, between Lothianburn and Loanhead. Unfortunately, there is a frustrating gap in the Currie Kirk session minute-book, so it is not possible to describe the outcome. Even today, black cats are considered to bring good or bad luck; some think it lucky for a black cat to cross their path, while others will go to ridiculous lengths to avoid one. Actors used to say that it was unlucky to kick a black cat. Undoubtedly true from the cat's point of view!

Hares and toads were also strong medicine in the witch's range of familiars. Perhaps the hare was favoured because it could run fast; Isobel Gowdie related how she changed herself into one to escape a pack of dogs set upon her.

175

The toad was favoured by the devil and so was important in witch-lore. Not only are toads ugly, they produce venom from their skin when handled roughly. At her trial in 1650, it was said that Maggie Osborne, the landlady of an Ayrshire inn reputedly saved her Communion wafer for the devil who appeared at the kirk door in the form of a toad and took the offering in its mouth.

Before the Industrial Revolution, Scotland, like England, derived its wealth mainly from agriculture. Cattle, especially cows, were an integral part of the economy. Cattle were a source of meat, cows provided milk, an essential commodity for the production of butter and cheese, vital components in an otherwise extremely restricted diet. In small rural communities, cattle were slaughtered on an infrequent basis, generally at Martinmas (November), when winter feeding was very difficult. Meat was salted, as was the humble herring, another important item in the winter diet.. It is not surprising therefore to find witches continuously striving to obtain milk by spells; nor should it be difficult to understand why, when those with livestock crossed a witch, they expected her to take revenge on the animals. Equally, she would attempt to disrupt fishing or even sink the boats of the fishermen who refused her fish or insulted her. Curses laid on cattle and chickens could spell disaster for the small tenant farmer. Another way to create havoc was to burn down hayricks, a scarce and valuable source of fodder for cattle. The witch trials featured many incidents involving cattle; a witch would devise means to syphon off precious milk for her own use or she made the cow stop producing it. Instances where witches were accused of making the cow produce blood or poison instead of milk could be attributed to mastitis, a common ailment.

So, the witch's armoury consisted of wax or clay effigies to induce sickness and death by fever and drowning. potions, incantations, charms, rituals, herbs and poisons. In addition, witches used elf-arrows, or what might be termed witch bullets. Elf-arrows were in fact Neolithic flint arrowheads, common surface finds in Scotland. They were genuine arrow-heads, used by the early hunters. The superstitious people who discovered these 'elf stones' had no idea of their origins; they were regarded as the weapons of the little people, that they fell out of the air and if they found a victim, the person or animal was 'elf-shot'. These so-called elf-darts flew about at night-time, fired by fairies or witches. When a farmer found that his cows were producing less or inferior milk, he would unashamedly inform his neighbours they had been elf-shot. Isobel Gowdie explained the use of elf-arrows in her lengthy confession of 1662; she informed her judges that elf-arrows were sharpened by the devil and given to elf boys who finished them. They then gave them to witches, who fired them from their thumbnails. But witches appear to have been poor shots; the elves were more skilful, carrying their arrows in quivers made from sloughed-off adder skins; the elves fired their deadly darts from small bows made it was said, from the ribs of a man who had died where three lairds' lands met. The arrow shafts were made from the bog-weed plant. During her trial in 1607, Bartie Paterson of Newbattle reeled-off the following charm for curing elf-shot cattle:

'I charge thee for arrow schot,
For door schot, for words schot,
For liverschote, for lungschote
For hertschote, all the maist.'

The purest of doggerel. As commented on earlier, witches were not skilled in poetry or even rhyme.

A look at the Ordnance Survey map will identify places which appear to have connections with witches. Some of these are spurious, although many certainly have genuine connections with the dark past of the witch hunt. Some of the more well-known places are listed below.

Auchtergaven,   At Meikle Obney, the Witch's Stone
Tayside

Auldearn, Nairn: The prehistoric stone where Isobel Gowdie and her
                    coven met

Birnam,   The Witch's Stone, where Macbeth reputedly met
Perth and Kinross   the three witches

Blairlogie,   Witches' Craig, where witches were pushed over the
Stirling   cliff; if they survived they were guilty, a variation of the
                    ducking or 'floating' test
Cardean, Tayside   The Witch's Knowe, where witches gathered for covens

Carlops,   The Witch's Leap, where a witch was said to live at
Berwickshire   the foot of Carlops Hill

Closeburn, Nithsdale	A cairn at Auchencairn known as the Witches' Wa's [Walls]
Colinton, Edinburgh	The Witch's Walk situated between R L Stevenson's cottage and the local kirk
Culross, Fife	Witch Stone, now believed to be in Dunfermline
Dalgety, Fife	Witches' Knowe, now part of Hillend Industrial Estate
Dunfermline,	Witch Loan; the place of execution and the Witch Knowe or place of interment; The Witch Dub at the foot of the Loan was where witches were floated
Fauldshope, Berwickshire	Once known as Falsehope, there is a Witch's Hill nearby
Gask, Perth and Kinross	The Witch's Knowe, where witches were executed
Innerwick, East Lothian	The Witch's Cairn, at Crystal Rig, where the local witches gathered to work magic to sink fishing boats in the North Sea
Innerleithen, Peebleshire	The Witches' Dancing Ground, at Mirchmoor Hill; another site named the same can be found at Traquair, Salter-Sykes
Lamberton, Berwickshire	The Witch's Knowe, west of Lamberton, is at Mordington Hill, an execution site
Marykirk:, Kincardine	The Witch Hillock, an ancient burial barrow was used by witches for their Sabbats
Midcalder, Midlothian	The Cunnigar, or Witches' Knowe

Mordington, Berwickshire	See entry for Lamberton
Musselburgh, East Lothian	The Bogie Hole, where witches were burnt
Oldhamstocks, East Lothian	The Witches' Cairn, supposed site of Sabbats
Ratho, Midlothian	The Witches' Stone, an ancient cup-and-ring marked stone near Tormain Hill
Scalloway, Shetland	The Gallows Hill reputedly shows traces of the ashes of witch burning pyres
South Uist, Outer Hebrides	The Witches' Gravestones, a chambered cairn
Spott, East lothian	The Witch's Stone reputedly marks the place where the *Rigwoody Witch*, Marion Lillie was executed
Torryburn, Fife	Formerly at Windybraes, the Witch Stane, now thought to be one of three in Dunfermline Glen; one of these reputedly marked the burial place of Lillias Adie .
Urquhart, Morayshire	The Nine Deil's Stanes; if walked round three times at midnight, the devil may be seen
Vallay, Outer Hebrides	The Witch's Pit which, according to legend can never be filled.

There are many parts of Scotland with witch associations and locations which are too numerous to mention here. Many sites have been obliterated by urban and suburban development, although names survive in local memory, if not on the Ordnance Survey map. Nowadays, if they are thought of at all, witches and warlocks are no more than a part of Scotland's quaint and colourful folk-

179

lore and viewed with mild amusement. Witches have become sanitised or relegated to children's literature or television cartoons. To the amateur student of mythology, the festivals, customs, rites and charms are part of antiquity, the traditions of a society which has long since disappeared. In Scotland as elsewhere, folklore is an integral part of the rich heritage of the past. However, legends can be deceptively innocent. In the case of the Scottish witches and warlocks, the dreadful reality cannot be ignored. During the course of more than a century, several thousand people in Scotland suffered pain and death, a heavy price to pay for a place in legend. Few who are superficially interested in folklore trouble their consciences with the knowledge that so many women and men were cruelly tortured, then judicially murdered for what were ridiculous reasons. But that, as they say, is history.

10

Conclusion

Summing-up this book is relatively simple in terms of the when and the how of the witch hunt. The why presents certain problems. To some extent, the conditions which gave rise to the persecution of witches in Scotland, with its periodic epidemics over the course of a century and a half. have been identified; the nature and the content of the trials described in the preceding chapters speak for themselves.

As indicated in Chapter 1, witchcraft, sorcery, necromancy, healing and causing illness by spells and potions, charming and divination were an integral part of Scotland's history, stemming from the country's Celtic and pre-Christian origins. During the First Millenium of the Christian Church, belief in witches and wizards or warlocks was accepted along with that in fairies, elves, sprites and other supernatural creatures, a belief which continued until the late fifteenth century. Witches were part of a rich and colourful folklore. When they were singled-out for special and savage treatment because of the religious - political climate which came with the Reformation in 1560, the romance died as it always will in the harsh light of reality.

For long, witchcraft and witches have remained the province of the folklorist or the amateur local historian interested in the legends and traditions of his or her locality. This is not meant to imply that the approach has been fatuous or unscholarly., especially in the past century. Folklore studies are important and now form part of the academic syllabus. The folklorist is concerned with the effects of evil spirits and their powers and the way such powers have given rise to popular myths and legends as well as explaining local customs and traditions. The psychologist also has an interest in the existence - real or imagined - of evil but from the point of view of the power of auto-suggestion and its ability to upset and influence normal or appropriate human behaviour. The serious historian is perhaps interested to a degree in both these aspects but the prime interest is the reason behind belief in such power in the context of the social, political and religious climate prevailing at the time. The history of the witch hunt in sixteenth and seventeenth century Britain in general and Scotland in particular is a subject which deserves a more factual approach than it has sometimes received in the past.

There is absolutely no doubt that in Scotland, as elsewhere, the majority of the population believed in witchcraft and the existence of witches. The Church of Scotland encouraged that belief; its clergy fulminated from the pulpits every Sunday, urging their congregations to be on their guard against witches and to report suspected persons to the kirk session or presbytery. The witch became public enemy No I almost overnight. Witches had been considered more of a nuisance than a threat in pre-Reformation Scotland; then in 1560 and the immediate post-Reformation period, witchcraft and its practitioners were seen as a real threat to the survival of the fledgling Protestant Church, insecure and vulnerable to a possible Roman Catholic backlash which might topple it. Catholics were denounced as heretics who worshipped graven images, muttered and chanted to themselves; the transition from Catholic-heretic to witch-heretic was both logical and understandable. Thus the first victims of the witch hunt were probably predominantly those who clung to the old faith which the Protestant authorities considered little more than superstition masquerading as Christian belief.

Until 1590, there are scant references to the witch hunt or its resulting trials in Scotland. This is due to the fact that by and large, such matters were dealt with by the parish authorities. The parish is the oldest administrative unit in Scotland, introduced in the twelfth century by David I who modelled his burghs on the English equivalent. Parishes were largely self-governing with only occasional interference from central authorities. To a considerable degree, parochialism worked; it satisfied the needs of a predominantly rural population. The parish was responsible for schools and education, poor relief, law and order, the regulation of trade and commerce and even the conduct of the parish church. Parish or burgh councils worked closely with the local church. Those who held offices in both were chosen not for their administrative skills or intelligence but because of their wealth and influence. Although the parish system worked well enough, the scope for nepotism, corruption, mismanagement and official meddling was limitless. Where law and order were concerned, the local magistrates acted much as they pleased, imposing sentences which they considered fit for the crime. As the most serious crimes included murder, witchcraft and sorcery, the death penalty was usually imposed. In time, parishes grew ever more reactionary, particularly during the increase in the number of royal burghs with their isolationist, protectionist policies. That many people were executed for adhering to Catholicism or were considered heretical by refusing to embrace or denying the new religion is without doubt; there are pitifully few records to prove the extent of the persecution; either cases were unrecorded locally or the records have not survived.

After the Reformation, the Kirk supported the parish and burgh authorities, deferring to its 'betters'. The Kirk also exercised a control over its flocks in a way which was unprecedented in the history of the Christian faith; it was in the landowning classes' interest for it to do so and both worked hand-in-glove to keep the population in check by literally putting the fear of God into them. And of course, witches. The Presbyterian form of faith was transfixed by the existence of sin; its clergy waged constant war on sinners of all kinds and witches in particular. Witches were anti-Christ, servants of the devil who was intent on the destruction or submission of the world, God's greatest achievement. All manner of natural disasters such as plague, famine and sudden and unexplained sickness and death in both human beings and livestock were blamed on witches acting on the express orders of their Satanic master. The Kirk reacted predictably, denouncing first the Catholic-heretic, then the witch-heretic. Witches were responsible for blighting crops, destroying valuable animal stock, stealing milk, destroying the mills which ground the flour for bread, scattering and sinking fishing boats and their essential cargoes. The Kirk argued convincingly that witches used their powers to threaten the life of man by destroying his sources of food; they also visited sickness and death on those whom they particularly detested. From time immemorial, man's aspirations have been concerned with his well-being; good health, good fortune, happiness, procreation to ensure the immortality of his line and of course, longevity of life. It is understandable that anything or anyone posing a threat to such things should be regarded as evil or hostile and controlled or eradicated. That witches were the chief scapegoats should come as no surprise; the Kirk used the existence of witches and their evil powers in a way modern day evangelists would envy. In that unsophisticated society witches were a major threat; only the church could offer protection and it was bought at the price of submission to the Kirk's will. A recent account, *The Witch in History*, describes the people of both sexes who were accused of practising witchcraft as those who 'shared characteristics which marked them out as not only abnormal but frightening. ' This of course is true but the whole truth is even more frightening if not out of place in the brutal judicial climate of the time. The truth is that few people accused of witchcraft were active members of pre- or anti-Christian cults; in the majority of cases, the suspects were ordinary women and men who were persecuted for little more than what amounted to anti-social behaviour. Very few of the cases researched for this book support the view of the witch as abnormal or menacing; it was Kirk propaganda which planted the seeds of suspicion and fear in a largely uneducated, superstitious and narrow-minded population. It did not take much to prey on the minds and susceptibilities of such people. However, it is true that a minority of those accused of witchcraft enjoyed the fear they instilled, as in the case of Catherine McTaggart in Dunbar, East Lothian in 1688. Social misbehaviour is hardly new; while it should rightly be controlled and the perpetrators appropriately admonished, it is hard to justify the execution in Scotland of several thousand women and men during the period 1560 to 1727.

As has been argued elsewhere, witchcraft stemmed from the ancient pagan religious system which was supplanted by Christianity, a religion which purported to raise man above his savage state . It is perhaps one of the great ironies of history that the very religion which aimed to civilize mankind restored for a time the savage state it promised to remove. 'To suffer a witch to live' was expressly forbidden by Scripture and to do so was, by extension, a deliberate affront to God. That is if witches did indeed exist. At first, persecution was localised and directed against heretics. Then, suddenly, witches were discovered everywhere, particularly after Bothwell's supposed attempt on James VI's life through witch agents. The king's own interest in witchcraft fuelled the flames so that in the short space of seven years from 1590 to 1597, an epidemic erupted which resulted in the deaths of many innocent people. A major outbreak occurred in Aberdeen in 1596-97; it is now believed that some of the victims were part of an ancient cult but the majority of the twenty-three women and two man were little more than the victims of hysteria. Then matters got out of control, forcing the central authorities to intervene in a hitherto local matter.

The Kirk forcibly argued that the detection and arrest of witches was wholly a matter for them when the Privy Council introduced a ban on local trials. Small presbyteries, too weak to argue their case, appealed to the Kirk's mouthpiece, the General Assembly.. A compromise was reached which allowed the Kirk to continue its crusade but withheld the power to prosecute; even so, the Kirk was allowed to interrogate suspects before trial. The carefully worded questions put to those accused of witchcraft were orchestrated in a way to extract a confession. After that was achieved, the Kirk could hand the suspect over to the civil authorities who applied to the Privy Council for a commission to try the accused.

What is perhaps hard to accept was that once declared a witch, there were no distinctions made. Many victims were little more than herbalists practising alternative medicine-those who today would be termed 'white' witches. Others were fortune-tellers who sold love potions- quacks in other words. Many were social misfits, outcasts like vagabonds and beggars; some were clinically deranged, probably suffering from dementia or hallucination. A few were promiscuous or unmarried mothers who had 'fallen'; many of these women were sexually harassed. Some were outspoken in an age when women were expected to be obedient and docile. Even those who associated with 'known' witches or consulted them were guilty of the crime of witchcraft. For almost half of the sixteenth and practically all of the seventeenth centuries, the wholesale slaughter of innocent people was instigated by the Kirk and condoned by the civil authorities.

The reality is that witchcraft had more to do with minor provocations and disagreements, inevitable between people living in a close-knit, narrow-minded society rigidly controlled by an unforgiving church. Animosity between neighbours was and is unavoidable. When sudden and unexplained personal tragedies followed closely on the heels of some petty animosity between neighbours, matters got out of hand.   Threats and curses were made; an accusation of witchcraft was one way of resolving the problem by obtaining redress in the kirk, then the court. To curse a neighbour could and did have fatal consequences. The Kirk eagerly sprang to the defence of the wronged individual- or at least the individual who made the accusation. Given the failings in human nature, it is perhaps surprising that the number of people punished was as low as the 4,000-plus estimated victims of the witch hunt.

In the preceding chapters, we have seen that to be accused of witchcraft in Scotland was to suffer the unimaginable terrors of a waking nightmare. Once in the hands of the men of God who, in some cases, even seem to have taken a sadistic pleasure in personally torturing their victims to gain confessions, a person suspected of witchcraft had little hope of salvation.   Those who confessed themselves as witches were executed as sure as the sparks that flew upwards from their funeral pyres.   We have seen the effects of individual and mass hysteria and its direct relationship with witchcraft.   That hysteria was already present in the imagination of the victims; it was further inflamed by a superstitious clergy. Sometimes, hysteria existed in the minds of both suspect and alleged victim; it was contagious, like a communicable disease. A single victim could infect others with his or her fantasies and fears until whole communities were convulsed by the sickness. In the case of Catharine McTaggart of Dunbar (Chapter 7), it is clear that mass hysteria was at work. At her trial in 1688, witness after witness misrepresented their experiences or presented them to suit the indictment; for her part, the eccentric and unpleasant old woman made no secret of the fact that she enjoyed being called a witch because it made people - and mainly men - fear her. We have also seen the effects of mass hysteria and anger in the mob which brought about the exceptionally cruel and tragic death of Janet Cornfoot of Pittenweem in 1705. The hunt, apprehension, trial and execution of witches has to some extent a parallel in the management of disease by modern medicine. When disease is present in an individual, doctors take appropriate action; the patient is diagnosed, treated and hopefully, the problem is resolved by such intervention. In the case of a witch, death was usually the only effective remedy.

Of course, prejudice against witches was often solely based on the way they looked or behaved. The popular image of a witch then and now is that of an old hag whose nose and chin conspired to meet in front of her toothless mouth; living alone with only a cat for company, she talked to herself a lot which people interpreted as the chanting of spells. She invariably lived on the fringe of the community in a hovel or dilapidated cottage, where her cooking-pot or cauldron was constantly on the boil, providing her with the soups and porridge which were about all her bare gums would permit her to eat. She made her soups with whatever came to hand - usually herbs and plants from her garden or found in the fields and hedgerows. Often, these old crones turned away from the kirk because it had failed or ostracised them for some misdemeanour. Shunning the kirk was a dangerous way to obtain revenge on it; it is for this reason that so many confessed witches admitted they had renounced their baptism, an admission intended to shock rather than advertise guilt. To do so was to remove the kirk's 'protection' against the devil. But in truth, many so-called witches were respectable people who fell foul of neighbours; arguments grew out of minor incidents - the raking and disposal of dung for example - insults were exchanged and threats and curses were voiced in the heat of the moment. Conflict, prejudice, jealousy and sexual rejection were commonplace in communities where people lived in close proximity, sharing amenities. That some alleged witches were better-off than others had a definite bearing on the attitudes of their less prosperous neighbours.

Nothing paralyses the mind as effectively as fear, ignorance, jealousy and superstition; add pain and physical or mental distress and the result is a lethal cocktail. When the hunt got out of hand, the central authorities, which had been content to leave individual communities to deal with such nuisances as witches, felt it was time to intervene. Even so, the State in the form of the

Privy Council worked closely in tandem with the Kirk since most Privy Councillors were church heritors or churchmen themselves. The heritors made an important contribution to the Kirk's finances through their patronage; in return, the Kirk kept the people under control and as the majority worked the land as employees or tenants of the heritors, it was a vicious circle few could escape. The Kirk looked for support in the witch hunt from its heritors, the local lairds and landowners. We have seen how things could get out of hand, as in the case of the Samuelston Witches of 1661, when the Earl of Haddington was forced to seek a commission from the Privy Council to rid his estates of a number of witches or else lose his tenants who threatened to quit their leases if nothing was done about the menace they believed was present in their midst.

In that society three centuries ago, everyone knew each other, which meant they also knew each other's business. We must also remember that what we see of ourselves in the mirror is seldom what others see. In that claustrophobic, fear-ridden, ignorant and superstitious climate, the Kirk played on the imaginations of their congregations, threatening them with hell-fire and damnation if they did not 'insist' - inform - on their neighbours whom they suspected of practising witchcraft. The Kirk had the last word in practically everything; it baptised infants, it married and buried people. Not to be a member of the Kirk was tantamount at best to self-ostracisation from society or at worst, to be guilty of something the Kirk disavowed. Outcasts, those who did not attend church regularly, murderers, suicides and witches could not be buried in consecrated ground, which brought them just deserts - an eternity in Purgatory. This was graphically illustrated by the General Assembly in 1649, when it complained to the Presbytery of Dunfermline about the interment of Lady Pitathrie in sacred ground, a woman who had not only been accused of witchcraft but had committed the unpardonable sin of suicide. Most societies have always had more to fear from generalisations than generals; in the case of witchcraft in seventeenth century Scotland, those accused of it had more to fear from godliness than god.

It is perverse to argue that the witch hunt had nothing to do with misogyny and everything to do with superstition. It was in fact a mixture of both. It has been estimated that 80% of the victims of the witch hunt were women, a significant number of whom belonged to vulnerable social classes - widows, spinsters and the elderly with no families to look after them; a fair proportion were unmarried mothers -already ostracised for their unclean fornication and 'chance-bairns' or illegitimate children - servants, beggars and vagabonds. It is easy to strip away the veneer of godliness which motivated the witch hunter; beneath it lay self-righteousness, malice, envy, greed and sexual repression as well as sexual rejection. Christian apologists have insisted that the Kirk's role was minimal; that is to be expected. The argument is that in the culture of the time, the Kirk was rightly the arbiter of morality, that it provided the people with spiritual comfort in a uncertain world and that it was a foregone conclusion it would react appropriately towards those who threatened it. It was much more than that. However, the morality preached by the seventeenth century clergy was debunked famously in the next century by Robert Burns' parody *Holy Willie's Prayer* which indicated that hypocrisy still persisted. Burns did not hide his distaste of the way the Kirk was run in his day. The Scottish Kirk was woefully short on love, humour and humanity and not just towards witches; its servants were not above lying, cheating and indulging themselves in the privacy of their own homes. Hypocrisy ruled. Little has changed since then. In the case of the witch hunt, it took well over a century for enlightenment to soften the Kirk's attitude; enlightenment should uphold freedom of speech and action, but it weakens the ability to control and direct. Why for instance did the Kirk fail abysmally to put into practice the exhortation of Jesus of Nazareth who asked that those possessed by demons be brought to him so that he could offer them comfort? The Scottish clergy approached the problem of witches with a bible in one hand and a flaming torch in the other. The scandal of the witch hunt cannot be stated more succinctly.

Much of the witch epidemic was caused by hysteria and paranoia, both in individuals and whole communities. Hysteria is recognised as a clinical condition, as is paranoia; the former often results in the latter. The popular conception of paranoia is that it is a state of mind which convinces the sufferer he or she is being oppressed by hostile forces which induces unreasonable and imaginary fear so that a persecution complex quickly develops. The accepted definition of paranoia is that it is a morbid mental condition characterised by disturbed emotions, sentiments of vanity and fear combined with delusions of grandeur. This is however a somewhat superficial description of paranoia, since those afflicted by it in seventeenth century Scotland were hardly convulsed by thoughts of vanity; in a sense, their paranoiac displays were 'rational' since they were concerned with survival. While the condition is basically rooted in an acute fear of loneliness, paranoiacs are seldom alone. They are conscious of others around them, especially those whom they think are unkindly disposed towards them and are the cause of their torment. It has been said that paranoiacs believe that relief from the condition comes from an acceptance that others are to blame for the misfortunes visited upon them. The truth is that paranoia is only superficially an imagined fear; its true power lies in its capacity to satisfy the sufferer that because others are talking about or plotting against him or her, they are gratifying an over-riding subconscious need to be the focus of others' attention which in turn makes the sufferer feel important. The true relief comes from the satisfaction and even pleasure which derive from the discovery that some kind of order and power exists to effectively contain and even remove those who are responsible for the condition in the first place. We have a classic example of hysterical paranoia in the case of Christian Shaw and the Bargarran Witches (Chapter 8).

In the case of witchcraft, the majority of people in Scotland looked first to the Kirk, then the civil powers for relief from what may be described as collective paranoia induced by the Kirk as it wrestled with sin and the powers of darkness. In addition, a precarious existence and the uncertainty of survival at basic subsistence level in a largely agricultural economy dominated the lives of most people. Sudden and inexplicable disasters that could threaten life were never far from the minds of ordinary people. Such were the stuff of paranoia. Witches were tangible proof that dark forces were at work, conspiring against a basically decent, god-fearing and law-abiding population. Relief came from informing the authorities about witches so that actions could be brought against them by those in whom trust was placed.

There is no doubt that the Scottish Kirk deliberately set out in the same mood as Baron Victor Frankenstein to breathe life into an idea; in the Kirk's case, witches were to blame for many of society's ills. And like Dr Frankenstein, they created a monster - the monster of fear and superstition which, like Frankenstein's creation, inevitably got out of control. Thus the witch became both personification of evil and scapegoat. Once identified, she - and occasionally he - was subjected to a process of mental and physical torture which invariably led to death. That process was virtually standard practice up and down the country.

It is perhaps appropriate to pause here to reflect on similar approaches by the few to protect their interests at the expense of the many. All societies are ruled by a small percentage of their populations; when the elite believe the social structure on which their lives depend is threatened, they resort to devious and draconian measures to preserve their position. History abounds with examples. Among them are the Spanish Inquisition, established to root out heresy - in effect, those who challenged the orthodox religion and the self-interest of those at the top. The slaughter of the Huguenots in seventeenth century France is yet another example. So too were the anti-Jewish riots and massacres encouraged in Russia which began in the Middle Ages and continued until the early twentieth century. In pre-revolutionary eighteenth century France, kings issued *lettres de cachet* or blank forms which authorised magistrates and prison governors to arrest anyone they liked - perhaps that should be disliked. And of course, nearer our own time were the post-revolutionary Russian Communist measures to imprison and execute those who were considered politically incorrect and the persecution of Jews by Nazi Germany. With wooden boxes installed in every kirk to allow people to inform anonymously on those whom they disliked or bore grudges against, the seventeenth-century

Scottish witch hunt would not have been out of place in other regimes before and after its historical time.

As has been seen, the first step in the witch hunt in Scotland was to discover the culprits, then apprehend them. This was done by the Kirk. Suspects were brought before the kirk session, confronted with their supposed crimes and interrogated. At an early stage, a 'brodder' or witch-pricker-often the local minister - was brought in to find the Devil's Mark. The mark was invariably 'discovered' - blemishes like warts, moles, flea-bites, bruises, patches of dead or rough skin, nodules, bumps and growths. In that society, few were free of such blemishes. Women suffered the indignity of a search of their most private parts and their heads were often shaved. Confessions were extracted under beatings while the suspect was 'wardit' or imprisoned in the kirk steeple. When a confession was obtained, the suspect appeared at the next 'doon-sitting' or *sederunt* of the kirk session, a formal occasion which gave the process some air of democracy. Invariably, the *sederunts* supported the minister who was then authorised to approach the civil authorities who in turn applied to the Privy Council in Edinburgh for a commission to try the suspect locally. However good in theory, trial by local commission could hardly fail to be unbiased since the members of the assize and - when appointed - the jury were local people who were as deeply prejudiced as the ignorant and often malicious people who had informed on the suspect in the first place.

Despite having made an initial confession to the kirk authorities, a suspected witch had to endure a further process of 'examination' - a euphemism for torture in the local tolbooth or jail. When the evidence against her was weak, it was often at this point that 'pricking' occurred under the supervision of the minister and possibly a burgh official. Ministers were quick to spot and report anything odd during the process. Unusual reactions were noted, such as when in her embarrassment, a naked suspect looked away or stared into space to avoid the eyes of the man who pricked her; those who looked away were often thought to be in clandestine communication with the powers of darkness and the devil who was of course invisible to the godly.

After initial pricking, a suspect was invariably tortured in the tolbooth. The most common forms were sleep deprivation, known as 'waking'and restriction of diet; visits by families were not allowed. Suspects were often stripped naked, made to lie on the cold stone floor of their jail with only a hair-shirt for covering; if a suspect had been particularly stubborn and whipped - sometimes by the minister - the shirt was steeped in vinegar to add to her discomfort. Fiendish instruments of torture were available to regulate the most stubborn who refused to confess. Commonest was the pilniewinks or thumbscrews which crushed the thumbs; the boot, a wooden contraption which encased the leg and had wedges driven into it to crush the ankles was effective as was the caspieclaws or iron frame applied to the leg and heated over a brazier. One of the worst instruments was the scold's or witch's bridle. It consisted of an iron-framed headpiece which was padlocked in place. A cruciform device projected into the victim's mouth in such a manner that any one of the four points would pierce the roof of the mouth, the tongue or either cheek if the victim attempted to speak. The lash was liberally used, sometimes with the added refinement when the victim was placed in the stocks and iron bars laid on her outstretched legs (Chapter 4). Some victims were strung up by their thumbs from the ceiling of their cells and candles were used to burn the soles of their feet, their heads and were even placed inside their mouths, as the English commissioners sent to Scotland to administer justice learnt after the battle of Dunbar in 1650.

Few witches were 'ducked' or 'floated' in Scotland, a common practice in England. There were instances in the Borders and in Fife but by and large, the Scots did not use this method. Ducking in the village pond or river was a case of heads-you-lose-tails-I-win; if a witch floated, she was guilty and if she sank, she was innocent. It appears that those who were charged with the task could manipulate the ropes securing the victim to achieve the desired outcome.

During the trial, suspects were treated to torture of a different kind, arguably the worst. They had to stand before their judges, listening to the outrageous accusations made against them without recourse to legal counsel. Wit, satire, cynicism and sarcasm - modern defensive weapons we employ to debunk canting hypocrisy and overweening, unyielding and insensitive bureaucracy - would have been of little avail to a seventeenth century woman accused of witchcraft, even had she possessed the necessary intelligence and mental power to use them. The fictitious nonsense which masqueraded as evidence was equalled in its fatuity by the banality, ignorance and superstition of those who sat in judgement. Matters were taken out of context, sinister motives were read into them and attention to the finer points of law were dispensed with or ignored. Often, the procurators fiscal appointed to conduct trials possessed no legal skills; even the competency of court sheriffs was suspect, as in the case of Isobel Falconer in Eyemouth in 1606 (Chapter 2). And the longer a trial took, the more impatient the judges became. Justice had to be done and seen to be done swiftly; the longer a witch lived, the more damage she could inflict. The benighted men who passed judgement on so many women who were half-crazed by the pains of torture and fear of retribution were Lilliputians indeed; their intelligence, thought processes and intellectual properties were in direct proportion to Dean Swift's eight-inch high creations.

Occasionally, spirited women like Agnes Sampson of Nether Keith in 1590, Margaret Barclay of Irvine in 1618 and Margaret Lang of Paisley in 1697 conducted themselves with dignity. It was to no avail. On the final day of her trial in 1618 before sentence was passed on her, Margaret Barclay perhaps felt a glimmer of hope when her husband Archibald Dean appeared in court with a lawyer for the first time. Her brief flicker of optimism was soon extinguished; Dean was too late to save her, a fact she acknowledged in a single bitter sentence that day:

'Ye have been too long in coming.'

The pathos in these few words is only surpassed by their heart-breaking hopelessness.

When trials were completed, the fate of the accused was announced by the doomster or dempster to the court. Sentences were brief and to the point; in the majority of cases, they were carried out immediately. Even those who received non-capital punishment such as branding on the cheek by hot iron or scoring by knives 'above the breath' - about the mouth or forehead - followed by banishment from the parish were dealt with quickly; the guilty were dragged through the streets by sledge for all to see that justice had been done. In most cases, the sentence of death was carried out the day after the trial, the victim's money and goods being 'escheated' or impounded to meet the costs of her stay in jail and the expenses of her trial and execution.

A significant proportion of those accused of witchcraft were not, as has been supposed, elderly, poor or outcast. Appendix 1 gives a snapshot of 85 cases which suggests that the greatest number came from either working-class or lower middle-class backgrounds. About ten per cent belonged to the landowning and titled classes, although in the latter case, few prosecutions ended in conviction, probably because the suspects were well-to-do and could pay for defence counsel. Several who were brought to court were tried before biased juries, usually drawn from their dependents. Exceptions were rare, as in the case of Lady Pitathrie who committed suicide in prison while awaiting trial in 1649. Some of the gentry, like Lady and Laird B. and his sister, B. in the Merse [Berwickshire] were not only acquitted, their identities were protected. Were Laird B's family among those identified in Black's *Calendar* as the 'Ladies of Butt' in 1594 in Berwickshire? It seems reasonable to suggest they were. The reason for maintaining secrecy is obvious; public outcry might have led to the loss of tenants and therefore rents and, as the Laird of B. was probably a church heritor, loss of income to the local church.

As usual, any of the nobility involved in witchcraft were rarely prosecuted, including no less a person than Mary, Queen of Scots, herself. Despite having given her royal assent to the act outlawing witchcraft in 1563, the queen was quite capable of applying a Nelsonian eye to the use of witchcraft when it suited her, During the difficult birth of James VI in 1566, she had no qualms when the Countess of Atholl attempted to transfer her birth pains by means of witchcraft to Lady Reres, one of the ladies - in - waiting. Lady Reres reputedly writhed about in agony, simulating pain beside the queen but it was to no avail.

Of the few titled people who were brought to trial for witchcraft, Katherene Roiss, Lady Foulis in Ross-shire, was able to escape justice for the attempted murder of her eldest stepson and sister-in-law so that her brother George Roiss could inherit land belonging to her late husband, Lord Monro of Foulis. Leaving aside Lady Foulis' crime of consulting witches - an incompetent group by any standards - she was clearly guilty of attempted murder by her own endeavours, which included feeding her sister-in-law food laced with rat poison. Lady Foulis was declared innocent by a jury 'packed with her dependents' in 1590. A similar verdict was returned on her kinsman, Hector Monro. At this time occurred the attempt on James VI's life by Francis, 5th Earl of Bothwell who used the so-called North Berwick Witches in his plot. Bothwell escaped justice without difficulty, although he was obliged to go into voluntary exile, dying in Italy with the accusation of witchcraft against his name. In 1628, an East Lothian woman, Isobel Young of Eastbarns, near Dunbar, was executed for using sorcery to cure cattle of some kind of disease. The man she consulted was Sir James Lockhart of Lee, who gave her water treated by the Lee Penny which supposedly cured such ailments. Lee himself had been brought before the Glasgow Presbytery for using sorcery but he was released with a rebuke. Another case which attracted gossip, if not censure, in well-to-do circles was that of Lady Manderston of Duns, who in 1629, tried to have her estranged husband, Sir George Home of Manderston murdered by using a reputed warlock, John Neill of Tweedmouth. Lady Manderston was found not guilty; Neill was executed for witchcraft in 1631.

The case of Dame Helen Arnot, Lady Manderston, has a bizarre twist in that it involved James Mowat, Writer to the Signet and former sheriff clerk at Berwick. It is a somewhat convoluted tale; not all the facts have survived, nor are the motives clear. The story begins in 1629, during the trial of Alexander Hamilton of Haddington (see p39) about the same time as Lady Home solicited the assistance of John Neill of Tweedmouth to murder her husband Sir George Home by witchcraft. Hamilton was executed for his dealings in witchcraft in january 1630 and it seems that James Mowat was a member of the prosecuting council. Mowat was brought before the Privy council for falsifying part of Hamilton's deposition for which he was put in ward for professional misconduct. A similar charge was brought against Mowat in 1631 by Katharine Wilson and John Smith of Duns who had been named in Alexander Hamilton's deposition as practising witches. Whether John Neill was also mentioned is unclear although at his trial in 1630, he confessed that he had consulted with several witches on Coldingham Moor on Lady Manderston's behalf.

The complaint to the Privy Council by Katharine Wilson and John Smith accused James Mowat of a 'gross oversight' in his treatment of Alexander Hamilton's deposition. Mowat was also accused of tampering with the deposition of one James Home, a convicted murderer who on mounting the scaffold confessed on his knees that he had been bribed by Mowat to perjure himself by accusing Wilson and Smith of witchcraft. Not content wih Home's statement, Mowat had also manufactured depositions allegedly made by several people in Duns, including two ministers; he assured some of them that their 'depositions' would never be challenged. Appearing before the Privy Council for a second time to answer these charges, Mowat had little choice but to admit his errors concerning Hamilton's and Home's testimonies when he was confronted by witnesses from Duns denying any involvement. Mowat was found guilty of attempting to harm the life, credibility and estate of the petitioner Katharine Wilson.

What were Mowat's motives? Had he been coerced by Lady Manderston to shift suspicion from herself to Wilson and Smith during her attempts to murder her husband? We will never know. The only satifactory ending to this sorry tale is that the petitioners Wilson and Smith had all charges against them dropped. Mowat remained in ward until the summer of 1631 for his professional misconduct; having admitted his guilt, he felt he was being illegally held in custody and successfully petitioned the Privy Council for his release without paying the bail-bond of £1000 levied by the Council! A month later, Charles I who had taken a personal interest in Sir George Home's case, ordered that Sir George and his son and heir be protected to allow them to bring charges against certain persons they had lately accused of 'devilish pradtices'. This is yet another example of duplicity when applying the law to the rich and the poor.

A somewhat farcical incident occurred in 1633 involving Sir John Colquhoun of Luss and his German manservant, Thomas Carlips. The pair were accused of consulting witches to obtain love potions to enable them to satisfy their desires for several local women. They took no chances on the outcome of a trial; both fled to London before formal proceedings began and probably because of his influence and wealth, as far as is known, Sir John was never extradited to Scotland.

While possibly not of noble birth, some individuals were highly connected, like William Stewart, Lyon, King of Arms, hanged in 1569 for 'dyvers poyntes of witchcraft and necromancie' at St Andrews. Was he among the 'certain witches' hanged by the Regent Moray on his way north that year? It is entirely possible. It has been suggested that Stewart , a relative of the Regent Moray plotted an attempt on the latter's life. Unlike other witches burnt at the stake that year, William Stewart appears to have been tried in a court of law, so his crime must have been serious. Was it pure coincidence that a year later, Moray was shot in the streets of Linlithgow by Hamilton of Bothwellhaugh, supposedly motivated by private grievances? Being well-connected was no guarantee of immunity. Janet Bell, a close friend of the 8th Earl of Morton who petitioned against her arrest, was executed in 1654. In 1662, the famous Kenneth McKenzie, better known as the *Brahan Seer,* was executed for witchcraft on the accusation of his kinsman's wife, who flew into a jealous rage when Kenneth told her he had 'seen' her husband, the Chief of Clan McKenzie in the arms of another woman in Paris while on business.

Some witches found guilty went to their burnings alive, probably on account of the seriousness of their crimes or the strength of feeling against them Notable among these was Euphame McCalzean in 1591, one of the so-called North Berwick Witches who allegedly attempted to kill James VI. In 1608, several witches in Brechin went to the stake without the usual strangling or hanging; some tried to crawl out of the flames, were cast back in alive, suffering such a lingering and cruel death that it attracted the censure of the Earl of Mar. An unusual execution was that of Robert Erskine or John of Logy who in 1613 was beheaded for witchcraft in Perthshire; death by the axe was usually reserved for persons of quality and breeding, the rope being used on common murderers, witches and thieves.

There were no distinctions made between what would today be termed 'white' witches - faith-healers and herbalists practising alternative medicine. While some concoctions were at best of dubious value, some could be lethal, although it is certain that modern medicine owes something to these early homeopathic cures. A considerable number of women were accused of witchcraft simply because they defended themselves against the unwelcome sexual attentions of men who were often their employers; several were guilty of nothing more than outspokenness, challenging authority or offending against some rule of social etiquette. A witch was a witch and that was that. The majority were innocent of crimes laid at their doors by spiteful and malicious neighbours who coated the bitter pill of their accusations with the sweetness of revenge. And inevitably, as we have seen in the confessions of Isobel Gowdie of Auldearn in 1662, many witches were simply bored women looking for excitement, escaping from tired or uninterested husbands at night to take part in wild dancing and the sexual orgies which followed. It appears that Isobel Gowdie, a reputedly attractive redhead, was her husband's intellectual superior; she sought thrills and excitement in the coven to compensate for the monotony of life on her remote farm, With others, she roamed the country-side after dark, taking part in sex orgies. What led Isobel to freely confess her career as a witch is unclear; perhaps she was tired of it all or felt guilty about her deceptions. If she were indeed physically attractive as has been claimed, perhaps she fell foul of less appealing women in her coven who were jealous of her sexual popularity.

In his interesting and thought provoking *Foreword*, Robin Murdoch has usefully identified the main cause of the witch hunt; he leaves us in no doubt that in his view, the aim was the control of the people by Kirk and by exten-sion, the State, using the people's superstitious beliefs and gullibility to achieve that control. Illusion, self-delusion, auto-suggestion and the hysteria arising from the latter were also main ingredients in the heady brews which were distilled in the witch's cauldron.

It was many years after the Reformation - a century to be precise - before the voices of common sense and reason were raised against the transgressions which disgraced the Church of Scotland, especially the Covenanting Kirk which was all-powerful from about 1638 until 1662. However, to single-out the clergy of a particular stamp could attract a degree of censure for identifying them as sole scapegoats in the same way that witches were scapegoats. Not so in the case of Allan Logan of Torryburn kirk (1695-1717), then Culross Kirk (1717-1733). As we have seen, Logan was obsessed with the idea of witches until about 1720; perhaps he and Walter Bruce of Inverkeithing suffered from monomania. Throughout the period covered by this book, the Kirk was con-cerned not only with promoting the salvation of those whom they considered the Elect of God, but also to identify the national interest with dedication to a godly existence. In the Kirk's view, it was the duty of every single member of the congregation to strive to attain a state of grace by adhering to the strict Calvinist code of ethics in everyday conduct. Not even the most minor devia-tion from the path of righteousness was tolerated or went unpunished. No mat-ter how well-intentioned or motivated, it is virtually impossible to live an existence of complete goodness and obedience. Mankind is human and there-fore fallible. May that long continue. The militant Presbyterianism of the Scottish Kirk did not allow its adherents the luxury of the single most impor-tant tenet of the Christian faith- forgiveness. As in all absolute religions, the emphasis is primarily on control, a fact we are witnessing even today in other equally narrow-minded religions. The Scottish Kirk was in effect a political force which aimed to regulate and supervise - meddle - in the lives of ordinary people in a way which would never be tolerated today. Anything done in the name of god was not only acceptable but morally justified. It was also en-forceable by law.

It is interesting to note that in the majority of church histories written in the period covering the seventeenth to the twentieth centuries - there are a few notable exceptions like Archbishop Spottiswoode's *History of the Church of Scotland* of 1655 - there is no mention of the witchcraft epidemic, nor of the role played by the church. Where the subject is broached, it is usually treated in a revisionist or apologist fashion. For some, the epidemic seems never to have occurred. This explains why the study of witchcraft has been left to local historians who have assiduously harvested the scant details of witch trials from surviving kirk session-books and burgh records. Modern church historians are invariably silent on a disgraceful chapter in the Kirk's history for obvious reasons. It is perhaps not inappropriate here to make a comparison with Communist Russia, where the deliberate policy of successive regimes was to re-write history in the interests of political expediency.

The amateur philosopher may be forgiven for asking the question - was the witch hunt in Scotland one of history's periodic cruel jokes that are visited on every country during its social and scientific development? Or was it a process which had to be lived through so that one element - the Kirk - might modernise itself? The witch hunt was certainly a rung on the ladder to its self-improvement but it was achieved at a great cost of lives - and innocent lives at that. Up till now, witchcraft has not been a popular subject for study - certainly not in terms of Scottish ecclesiastical history - for obvious reasons. I believe that is about to change. After all, while the witch hunt has largely remained the province of the amateur local historian, there is considerable scope for an in-depth study of it on a national scale by not only academics with an interest in sociology but anthropologists and the medical profession who, despite their resistance to new and unorthodox methods in medical treatment, owe much to the witch-herbalists and their potions.

For historians, the momentous battle of Dunbar in 1650 had two definitive consequences; the defeat of the Scottish Army of the Covenant hastened the union of Scotland and England, much more so than the preliminary political feelers which led to the Act of Union in 1707. Modern historians now accept the fact that the battle, rather than the merging of two parliaments, ended the *auld sang*. It is ironic that the small and insignificant royal burgh of Dunbar, the scene of a defeat of Scottish arms in 1296 by Edward I which led to the Wars of Independence and the creation of a sovereign nation, was also instrumental in ending that sovereignty in 1650 in a battle fought over virtually the same ground. *Dunbar Drove*, as the battle subsequently became known, not only ensured the destruction of the tyrannical Covenanter Kirk, it brought about union with England. What is less well-known is that for those accused of witchcraft and awaiting trial, the English victory gave them added years of life and saved many from the stake. If we compute the average number of witches executed in Scotland at 50 per year - and that is a conservative figure

- 500 lives may have been spared between September 1650 and May 1660.

Certain incidents described in this book make depressing if not frightening and chilling reading. It highlights - some may say revels in - the brutal treatment meted out to those accused of practising the black arts. It also draws attention to the farcical and absurd beliefs held not only by an uneducated population but prevalent also in the upper strata of that society. How could sane and reasonably intelligent men sit through depositions and confessions which made ridiculous and outrageous claims? Probably the answer is that their inferiors wanted to believe such wild and unrealistic stories. We will never know the true extent of the witch hunt in terms of the number of its victims. Estimating the number of people tried and punished for allegedly practising witchcraft will always be an inexact science. What is certain is that several thousand women and men went to their deaths unnecessarily. There are no memorials to those who perished in Scotland other than the odd place name, which marks an execution spot or where supposed witches held their covens and Sabbats. Even the Witch's Stone at Spott, near Dunbar, has virtually lost its significance in this writer's lifetime; at one time, it was identified by a small nameplate but now languishes almost hidden by undergrowth so that not only is its purpose obscure - it could be taken for the grave of a pet animal - it can easily be missed by the casual observer. Perhaps these unfortunates deserve a little more in terms of permanent memorial. At least let us hope that lessons have been learnt from their needless deaths.

Reactionaries are alive and well and living in Scotland as elsewhere. The witch hunt has taken new and more subtle forms. What we in a modern society must remember is that if the proper study of mankind is man, the ultimate objective of human society should be humanity.

Appendix 1 - Statistics

Estimated deaths

It must be made clear that because of missing, incomplete or inadequate records, the true number of witches executed during the witch hunt cannot be accurately computed. In the first thirty years of the Reformation, records were not maintained centrally. It was left to local church presbyteries and burgh courts to deal with the witch problem until 1590, when cases began to be recorded by the central administrative machinery in Edinburgh. Even after 1590, when the first full-scale epidemic gripped the nation, records which exist are tantalisingly brief and incomplete, as Christina Larner's extensive study *A Source-Book of Scottish Witchcraft* shows. Her study contains a list of 1,891 trials of named and unnamed individuals; in addition, she has also listed as single cases entries which indicate that 'several persons', 'divers witches', 'sundry persons' or 'certain people' were either treid or mentioned in trials. Where records survive to confirm an execution, this has been noted in the Index (see pages 211-250). However, as the majority of cases were tried locally, it is impossible to state the outcome in every single case. As a rule however, local trials rarely resulted in acquittal; some accused people were branded and/or banished; others were released on bail; a few died or committed suicide in prison. The majority were executed.

Legge, in his article *Witchcraft in Scotland* which appeared in *The Scottish Review* (vol. xviii, October, 1891) considered that a conservative estimate of 3,400 executions could be supported despite incomplete records. He calculated the numbers who met their deaths in each epidemic were as follows:

First epidemic	1590-97	50 witches per annum=	350
Second epidemic	1640-50	100 " " "	= 1,000
Third epidemic	1660-62	150 " " "	= 450
During the whole period from 1580 to 1680			= 1,600

This makes a total of 3,400. For some reason, Legge fails to identify the epidemic which occurred from 1628 to 1632; he has however included the figures in his overall total for 1580-1680. To his total should be added those executed in the first thirty years of the Reformation, Roman Catholics who were regarded as heretic-witches. A figure of 50 per annum for that period would add a further 1,000, giving a grand total of 4,400. This is certainly not an exaggeration.

Types of Trial

Larner gives a breakdown of her figures as follows:

High Court of Justiciary	:	402
Justice Ayres/Circuit Courts	:	165
Local commissions authorised by the Privy Council	:	791
Committee of Estates of Parliament	:	170
Trial by other means	:	264

Only 567 of the cases identified by Larner were heard by the judiciary. Many of these did not result in the death penalty; non-capital punishment or acquittal was more common and many of those identified by name were simply mentioned in various trials, Whether they were proceeded against locally cannot be established with certainty but this is likely.

Occupation or status

From a sample of 85 individuals appearing in Larner, the following illustrates the social class of each individual:

Beggars, vagabonds, the poor, unmarried mothers	:	21
Servants	:	7
Wives of labourers, tradesmen, etc	:	34
Wives of burgesses	:	8
Midwives	:	7
Wives of upper classes, gentry, nobility	:	8

Thus, more than half of those brought to trial were from respectable backgrounds.

The following communities were particular blackspots, where five or more suspects were put on trial during the period of the witch hunt. Numbers relate to named individuals; the totals must be approached with caution however, as records are incomplete or imprecise; for example, in Dunbar, East Lothian, a further 15 unnamed suspects were tried and executed. The letters in brackets indicate shires or counties, (see key in Appendix 5).

* denotes communities which arrested 15 or more suspects

Aberdeen	120*
Aberdour (FI)	11
Alloa(CL)	18*
Auldearn (NA)	46*
Ayr	66*
Ayton (BE)	6
Bo'Ness (WL)	19*
Borthwick (ML)	7
Brechin (AN)	18*
Burntisland (FI)	10
Bute	21*
Caithness	12
Carriden (WL)	11
Coldingham (BE)	5
Collessie (FI)	5
Conveth (IN)	25*
Cousland (ML)	14
Craigie (AY)	11
Crail (FI)	5
Crichton (ML)	16*
Crook of Devon (KN)	27*
Culross (FI)	23*
Dalkeith (ML)	33*
Dumbarton	16*
Dumfries	63*
Dunbar (EL)	18*

Dunfermline (FI)	18*
Dysart (FI)	24*
Edinburgh & suburbs	131*
Edinburgh	38*
Broughton	1
Canongate	1
Colinton	1
Corstorphine	9
Cowgate	1
Duddingston	8
Gilmerton	12
Holyrood	1
Leith	19*
Liberton	28*
Mortonhall	1
Niddrie	11
Elgin	18*
Erskine (RE)	27*
Eyemouth (BE)	24*
Fala (ML)	5
Forfar (AN)	18*
Fortrose(RO)	5
Foulden (BE)	5
Glasgow	34*
Greenock (RE)	5
Haddington (EL)	50*
Innerleithen (PE)	5
Inverkeithing (FI)	51*
Inverkip (RE)	23*
Inverness	8
Jedburgh (RX)	24*
Kilernan (RO)	6
Kinross (KN)	5
Kirkcaldy (FI)	18*
Kirkcudbright	15*
Kirkliston (ML)	6
Lanark	8

Largs (AY)	7	Thurso (CA)	12
Lasswade (ML)	7	Torryburn (FI)	17*
Lauder (BE)	13	Tranent (EL)	54*
Longniddry (EL)	10		
		Wemyss (FI)	8
Midcalder (ML)	9	Whittinghame (EL)	8
Montrose (AN)	6	Wick	7
Moray	11		
Musselburgh (EL)	19*		

Newbattle (ML)   8
Newburgh (FI)   10
North Berwick (EL)   5+

Orkney   48*
Ormiston (EL)   15*

Paisley   12
Peaston/Penston (EL)   30*
Peebles   18*
Pencaitland (EL)   18*
Penicuik (ML)   10
Penninghame (WI)   5
Perth   22*
Pittenweem (FI)   13
Pollockshaws (RE)   6
Preston (EL)   6
Prestonpans (EL)   82*

Renfrew   7
Rhynd (PR)   9
Rothesay   13

St Andrews (FI)   19*
Samuelston (EL)   48*
Selkirk   11
Shetland   19*
South Queensferry   24*
Spott/Pinkerton (EL)   10+
Stenton (EL)   18*
Stirling   26*
Stobo (PE)   5
Strathglass (IN)   7

Tain (RO)   10

Appendix 2   Chronological Table of Events

Date	State and Church control	National disasters/politics	Witch control
1560	Mary, Queen of Scots Reformation, General Assembly	Catholic backlash	Catholic-witch heretics executed locally
1563		Persecution of Catholic witch heretics	*Witchcraft Act* passed
1567	Mary deposed, Regent Moray rules		
1569	James VI, Regent Moray		Witches executed St Andrews, Dundee
1570		Regent Moray murdered; Plague	Few cases of witch trials
1571-90		Problems in James VI's Minority	Few cases
1589	Marriage of James VI and Anne of Denmark	Plot to usurp throne by 5th Earl of Bothwell using witchcraft (1590-91)	Trial of North Berwick Witches
1594-98	Episcopal commissions to try witches locally	Famine; publication of James VI's treatise on witchcraft, *Daemonologie* (1597) Privy Council imposes embargo on local trials getting out of control	First epidemic of witch trials and executions
1600		Plague	Few cases
1603	James VI departs for England, Scotland governed by Privy Council		Few cases
1607		Plague	Few cases
1610	General Assembly and Privy Council argue over right to try witches	Privy Council reserves right to grant local commissions	Increase in trials
1623-24		Famine; plague in Edinburgh	Increase in trials
1625	Charles I Episcopacy strengthened		

1628-32		Plague till 1632	Second epidemic of trials and executions
1633		Charles I's treasure ship sunk off Fife by storm reputedly caused by Lancashire Witches	Execution of Lancashire witches in London
1633-35		Plague continues	Few trials
1637		Unrest due to Charles I's attempt to introduce Laud's Book of Common Prayer in St Giles, riots in Edinburgh	Trials virtually cease
1638	Kirk in dispute with Charles I	Signing of National Covenant	
1640	Covenanters dominate General Assembly		Trials increase
1644-48		English Civil War; Scots support parliamentary cause against Charles; plague in Scotland	Trials increase
1649	Covenanter dominated Kirk Party virtually rule Scotland; General Assembly appoints commission to deal with witchcraft. Rule challenged by parliament's Committee of Estates which issues 170 commissions to try witches locally		Third epidemic of trials and executions
1650	Charles II crowned in Scotland	Battle of Dunbar and defeat of Kirk Party	Trials decrease
1651	Cromwell; Kirk Party disintegrates	Martial law imposed; justice administered by English commissioners	Witches in custody released
1652-58	Commonwealth; General Assembly meets for last time in 1653 until 1690		Few trials until 1657
1656	Cromwell pressurises Long Parliament to pass *Act of General Pardon and Oblivion*	Amnesty given to all who took up arms against English parliamentary forces	Act does not apply to witches; trials increase

1658	Suspension of Scottish parliament lifted; Privy Council reinstated; upper classes restored to public office and JPs judicial powers restored.	Trials increase
1660	Restoration of Charles II	Charles passes *Act of Indemnity and Oblivion* which pardons most Cromwellian supporters and those accused of witchcraft; Act does not extend to Scotland	Fourth epidemic of trials; Witches released in 1650s re-tried
1663-79		Covenanter rebellion, defeat at Rullion Green (1666), victory at Drumclog and defeat at Bothwell Bridge in 1679; assassination of Archbishop Sharp	Few cases confined mainly to East Lothian
1680-84		Persecution of Covenanters; known as The Killing Time due to execution or deportation of 200 Covenanters	King's Advocate refuses to try suspected witches
1688	William and Mary		Few trials
1697		Famine for seven years	Local panic in Paisley
1702	Anne		
1707	Act of Union		Isolated cases to 1727 when last witch executed in Dornoch
1736		Repeal of *Witchcraft Acts* on both sides of the Border	
1737- 1805			Isolated cases of scoring or imprisonment
1800s		Witchcraft and witches become part of Scottish folklore	

Appendix 3

The diagrams which appear below illustrate the intricate process of accusation and counter-accusation in two witchcraft trials which took place in Tranent, East Lothian in 1659. In all, thirty-three people were involved, nine of whom were executed. Diagram 1 clearly indicates that the initial suspect in the first trial was Janet Thompson who identified nine of the others; Barbara Cochrane named four and Elspeth Fouller another four, the total being nineteen.

Diagram 1

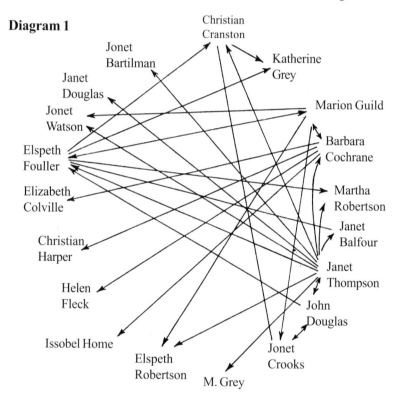

Diagram 2 shows that Marion Lynn was the first to be arrested and examined; she identified thirteen other suspects. One can but speculate on Lynn's nature; perhaps she was a vindictive woman who did not enjoy good relations with her neighbours in Tranent. This diagram also shows that at least one of the women Marion Lynn accused - Marion Logan - made a counter-accusation in retaliation, a commonplace situation in multiple trials.

Diagram 2

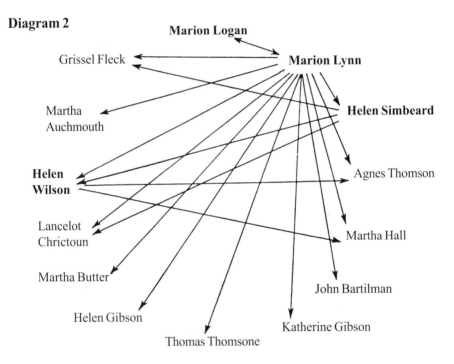

Diagram 3 (overleaf) illustrates the typical format for dealing with suspected witches as indicated in Chapter 1 (pp8-11).

A suspect invariably 'confessed' to practising witchcraft before the Kirk Session, answering carefully worded questions guaranteed to incriminate her.

Diagram 3

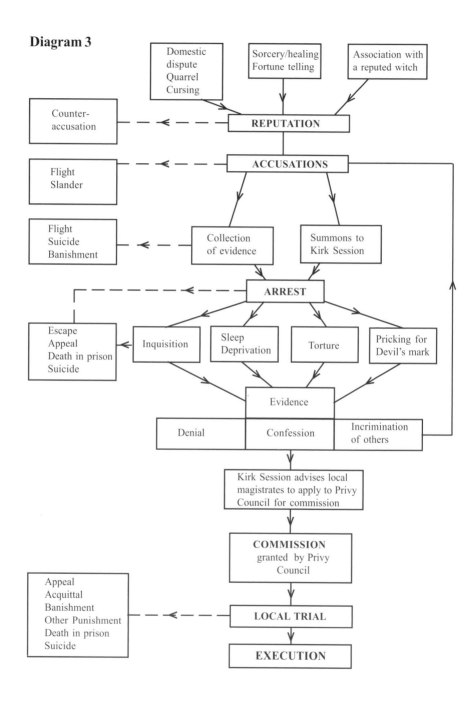

- Domestic dispute Quarrel Cursing
- Sorcery/healing Fortune telling
- Association with a reputed witch

Counter-accusation

REPUTATION

Flight Slander

ACCUSATIONS

Flight Suicide Banishment

Collection of evidence

Summons to Kirk Session

ARREST

Escape Appeal Death in prison Suicide

Inquisition

Sleep Deprivation

Torture

Pricking for Devil's mark

Evidence

Denial

Confession

Incrimination of others

Kirk Session advises local magistrates to apply to Privy Council for commission

COMMISSION granted by Privy Council

Appeal Acquittal Banishment Other Punishment Death in prison Suicide

LOCAL TRIAL

EXECUTION

Appendix 4

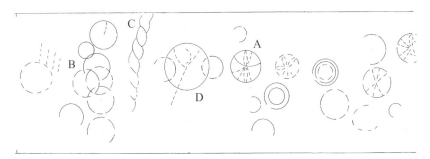

Central section of ritual marks on wooden panel above
fireplace in Culross Palace, Fife

This short appendix acknowledges the work of Timothy Easton and Richard
Harris for background information.

The drawing above illustrates a part of a set of ritual marks from Culross Palace, Fife.   These particular marks are located on a narrow wooden panel
above a fireplace in the Laird's bedroom, immediately outside the strong-
room.   There are marks in at least one other part of the building, the Great
Hall, where they are visible on the mantelpiece but are not yet formally recorded.   Indeed, there may be even more awaiting discovery under closer
scrutiny of the rest of the structure.

Ritual marks can occur in several forms, the most common of which are
simple 'geometric' shapes or letters, sometimes of monogram appearance.   The
marks from the Laird's bedroom at Culross fall into the geometric category,
being mainly derived from circles and arcs.   The circles are typically small,
usually less than 30mm and no more than 50mm.   Many are drawn dotted or
are incomplete, evidently standard practice.   Six petal 'daisywheels' (see A)
are common and again frequently incomplete.   Clusters of circles as at (B) are
also known from English sites but, the rope feature (C) appears to be unusual.
The group of circles at (D) may be a representation of spectacles.

Ritual marks of the type illustrated were used to protect buildings from the
unwelcome attention of witches.   Chimneys, doors and windows were believed to be particulary vulnerable to their access and, while the latter two
could be blocked with wood or glass, the former were permanently open to the

209

elements. Given their penchant for shape-shifting, witches were believed to enter buildings easily by means of the chimney; a situation warned of by no less a person than James VI in his treatise *Daemonologie,* re-published in 1604:

> 'for some of them sayeth that being transformed in the likeness of a little beast or fowl, they will come and pierce through whatsoever house or church, though all ordinary passages be closed, by whatsoever open the air may enter at'.

The practice appears to be far more common in England than in Scotland but the number and the survival rate of sixteenth to eighteenth century buildings in the latter is considerably less. Many ritual marks also had Catholic implications and, given the austerity of the Reformation in Scotland, it is perhaps not surprising that their occurrence is less frequent.

Although many of the ritual marks which occur were made by the occupants of the houses, there is also evidence of the house-builders applying these during the construction phase. It should also not be forgotten that a lot of structural timber was re-cycled and ritual marks can appear far from their intended target.

There has been, to date, only a brief opportunity to examine the marks on the mantelpiece of the Great Hall at Culross Palace and they appear to be predominantly letter type. These letters are normally drawn with straight lines giving them a distinct resemblance to Runic script.

Appendix 5:
Index of persons accused of witchcraft according to surviving records

Each entry gives the name, parish, town or county and year tried; those mentioned in the text are identified by page numbers. The following abbreviations have been used for each shire or county in Scotland:

AB	Aberdeenshire	LA	Lanarkshire
AN	Angus/Forfarshire	ML	Midlothian/Edinburghshire
AY	Ayrshire	MO	Moray
BA	Banffshire	MO	Moray/Elginshire
BE	Berwickshire/Merse	NA	Nairnshire
CA	Caithness-shire	OR	Orkney
CL	Clackmannanshire	PE	Peebles-shire
DM	Dunbartonshire	PR	Perthshire
DU	Dumfriesshire	RE	Renfrewshire
EL	East Lothian/Haddingtonshire	RO	Ross-shire
FI	Fife/Fifeshire	RX	Roxburghshire
GA	Galloway	SE	Selkirkshire
IN	Inverness-shire	SH	Shetland
KI	Kincardineshire	ST	Stirlingshire
KN	Kinross-shire	SU	Sutherlandshire
KR	Kirkcudbrightshire	WI	Wigtonshire
		WL	West Lothian

Key: While it is impossible to indicate the outcome of every case for reasons already given, the following codes have been used to identify known outcomes. It should be borne in mind that the majority of those tried locally were executed.

A = Confirmed execution

B = Tried by local commission authorised by the Privy Council or the Committee of Estates of parliament: some cases may have only been mentioned in trials but it is likely that these also would be investigated at local level, usually executed

C = Non-capital punishment, for example branding and/or banishment

D = Other outcome such as death from torture, suicide or escape from prison.

E = Acquittal, case discontinued, not guilty verdict or release on bail or caution to attend a future trial when requested

* = Death or harassment by mob

A.—, an old Lady (Merse/BE) 1594
Abel, Andrew (Hill of Tillicarie AB)
	1630**B**
Aberdeen, Witches p20
Abernethy, Margret (Aberdeen) 1669**B**
Abbot, Jeane (Lyne PE) 1649**B**
Achesonn, Janet (PE) 1629**B**
Achesoun, Jonnet (Pinkerton /Dunbar EL)
	1624, 1628**A** p37
Acreskine, Robert (Borthwick ML)
	1649**B**
Adair, Eupham (Crichton ML) 1661
Adam, Agnes (Lanark) 1629
Adam, Elspet (Aberdeen) 1606
Adam, Isobel (Pittenweem FI) 1704**E**
	p161
Adame, Agnes (LA) 1629
Adamson, Margret (Clova AN) 1662**A**
	p125
Adamson, Patrick (St Andrews) [No
	Date]
Adamsone, Isobel (Dumfries) 1642**A**
Adamsone, Marjorie (Penston EL)
	1649**B**
Adie, Lillias, known as Torryburn Jean
	(Torryburn FI) 1704**D** pp159, 179
Adinstoun, Margaret (Borthwick ML)
	1649**B**
Affleck, Margaret (DU) 1630**B**
Agnew, Andrew (Dumfries) 1654**A** pp113-
	114
Aitchesoun, Mergarett (Prestonpans EL)
	1590
Aitchesoune, Masie (Prestonpans EL) 1590
Aitken, Bessie (Leith, Edinburgh) 1597**E**
Aitkenheid, Christian (Dumfries) 1628
Aird, Agnes (Prestonpans EL) 1661
Airth, Jonet (PR) 1662**B**
Aitchison, Helen (LA) 1650
Aitkine, Bessie (Swintonhill BE) 1629**B**
Aitkine, Marion (LA) 1629
Aitkyne, Marjorie (Inverkeithing FI)
	1623**A** p33
Alexander, Anna (Ladievrde) 1649**B**
Alexander, Elspet (Forfar) 1661-62,

1662**A**
Alexander, Helen (Forfar AN) 1663**D**
Alexander, Isobell, 1650
Alexander, Jonet (Inverkip RE) 1662**B**
Alexander, Katharene (PE) 1629**B**
Alexander, Margaret (EL) 1629**B**
Alexander, Margaret (Glasgow) 1700**E**
Alexander, Susanna (Aberdour F1)
	1654**A**
Allan, Catherine (Carriden WL) 1649**B**
Allan, Jonet (PR) 1662**B**
Allan, Margaret (Ayr) 1658
Allan, Margaret (Longniddry EL) 1649**B**
Allane, Janet (Lauder BE) 1629**B**
Allane, Janet (Burntisland FI) 1598**E**
Allane, Margaret (Cousland ML) 1630**B**
Allane, Margaret (Duddingston, Edin-
	burgh) 1661**B**
Allane, Robert (Dunbar EL) 1612**B**
Allansone, Issobell (Jedburgh RX) 1649**B**
Allene, Agnes (Crook of Devon KN)
	1662**A**
Alshenour, Katherine (Aberdeen) 1597**A**
Anand, Jonnet (Forgan FI) 1662**B**
Anderson, Bessie (Inverkeithing FI) 1623**A**
	p33
Anderson, Cristian (Newburgh FI) 1662**B**
Anderson, Elizabeth (Glasgow) 1683
Anderson, Elizabeth (Bargarran RE)
	1697**E**
Anderson, Elspeth (FI) 1662**B**
Anderson, Grissel (Torryburn FI)
	c.1703**A** p159
Anderson, Grissell (Torryburn FI) 1666**B**
Anderson, Issobell (Crailing RX) 1662**B**
Anderson, Isobel (Dunnet or Dunmyat PR)
	1714**C**
Anderson, James (Aberdeen) 1670
Anderson, Janet (Aberdeen) 1670
Anderson, Janet (Aberdour FI) 1650
Anderson, Janet (Pittenweem FI) 1643**A**
Anderson, Jonet (Edinburgh) 1658**A**
Anderson, Margaret (Heriot ML) 1649**B**
Anderson, Margaret (Haddington EL)
	1658**A** pp116-117

Anderson, Margaret (Peaston EL) 1678**D**
Andersone, Bessie (Inverkeithing FI)
   1623**A**
Andersone, Janet (Drumalzearton) 1649**B**
Andersone, Johnne (Crailing RX) 1649**B**
Andersone, Marjorie (Prestonpans EL)
   1678**B**
Andersone, Patrick (Peaston EL) 1649**B**
Andersoun, Agnes (Newton ML) 1649**B**
Andersoun, Gowane (AB) 1626**B**
Andersoun, Margaret (Crailing RX)
   1649**B**
Andersoun, Margaret (AB) 1630**B**
Andersoun, Margaret, known as Deiff
   Meg (Eyemouth BE) 1629**B**
Andersoun, Marioun (Cousland ML)
   1630**B**
Andersoune, Jean (Midcalder ML) 1644**C**
Andirsone, Jonet (Stirling) 1617**B**
Andrew, Helen (Thurso) 1718-19 p165
Andro, Bessie (Wick CA) 1655
Angus, Alesoun (Dunbar EL) 1613**B**
Angus, Emie (Inverkeithing FI) 1649
Anstruther, Agnes (Kirkcaldy FI) [No
   date]**D**
Anstruther, Agnes (St. Andrews) 1613
Antonie, Catharine (South Queensferry
   WL) 1643-44**C**
Archer, Bessie (Monifieth AN) 1628**C**
Archibald, Geordie (Selkirk) 1616
Areskine, Michael (Newbattle ML)
   1629**B**
Argyill, Margaret (Samuelston EL)
   1661**B**
Aroane, Marion (Catloch) 1630
Asflack, Agnes (Tranent EL) 1649**B**
Aslowane, Mawsie (Dumfries) 1630**A**
Atkin, Margaret, known as the Great Witch
   of Balweary, (Balweary FI) 1597**A**
   pp22-23
Auchinmoutie, Margaret (Prestonpans EL)
   1661
Auhinlek, Violat (Crichie AB) 1590
Aunchtie, Katharine Nein Rob (RO)
   1629

Auchmouth, Martha (Tranent EL) 1659
   Appendix 3 p207
Aytoune, Margaret (Inverkeithing FI) 1649

B., Lady (Merse/BE) 1594 p192
B., The Laird of (Merse/BE) 1594 p192
B.——, sister of Laird B above, 1594 p192
Baigbie, Jonet (EL) 1661**B**
Bailie, Elspeth (Haddington EL) 1661**A**
Baillie, Elspeth (EL) c.1649**B**
Baillie, Susanna (Liberton, Edinburgh)
   1661
Bailzie, Marioun (Prestonpans EL) 1590
Bain, Margaret (Canisbay CA) 1724
Baine, Margaret (Longniddry EL) 1628**B**
Bainzie, Robert (Oyne AB) 1703**C** p158
Baird, Archibald (EL) 1662
Baird,——, wife of above, 1662
Baird, Elspeth (Leith, Edinburgh) 1628**B**
Baird, Jonet (Keith EL) 1649**B**
Baird, Walter (Aberdeen) 1626, 1627**B**
Baird, Walter (BA) c.1630**A**
Bairdie, Isobel (Burntisland FI) 1649**A**
   p249
Bairsie, Isbell (St Andrews) [No Date]
Baleny, Margaret (BE) 1629**B**
Balfour, Alesoun (Orkney) 1594**A**
Balfour, Christiane (Inverkeithing FI)
   1623**B** pp33-34
Balfour, Helen (Kinross) 1662**B**
Balfour, Janet (Tranent EL) 1659
   Appendix 3 p206
Balfour, Margaret (St. Andrews) 1643
Balfour, Margaret (Elgin) [No Date]
Ballamie or Bellamie, Margaret
   (Ayton BE) 1634 p46
Ballantyne, Cristine (Bute) 1662**B**
Balliem, Margaret 1628-29**B**
Bane, Margrat (Aberdeen) 1597**A**
Bane,——, wife of John 1590
Bankes, Marion (Cousland ML) 1630
Bannatyne, Margret (Samuelston EL) 1661
Bannatyne, Susanna (EL) c.1649
Bannatyne, Susanna (Samuelston EL) 1661
Bannerman, William (Elgin) 1671**C**

Bapae, Agnes (Haddington EL) 1662
Baptie, Margaret (Samuelston EL) 1661**B**
Barbour, Jean (Tongland KR) 1642**A**
Barbour, Margaret (Woolmet ML) 1649**B**
Barclay, Janet (Fisherrow/Musselburgh EL) 1629**B**
Barclay, Margaret (EL) 1661
Barclay, Margaret (lrvine RE) 1618**A**
 pp30-32, 173, 191-192
Bargans, ----, male (Renfrew) 1650
Bargarran, Witches p156, 159, 189
Barhill, Agnes (Duddingston, Edinburgh) 1661
Barker, Janet (Edinburgh) 1643**A**
Barnweil,——, Witch of (Ayr) 1587
Barnett, Patrick (Balbugie PR) 1655
Barnie, Adam (Caithness) 1655
Barny, Janet (Perth) 1623
Barrie, Lillies (Leith, Edinburgh) [No Date]**E**
Barroun, Issobell (Aberdeen) 1596**A**
Barrowman, Margaret (ML) 1628**B**
Bartan, Margaret (Queensferry WL) 1661**B**
Bartilman, John (Tranent EL) 1659
 Appendix 3 p207
Bartilman, Jonet (Tranent EL) 1659
 Appendix p206
Bartilman, Margaret (Haddington EL) 1649**B**
Bartilman, Margaret (Samuelston EL) 1661
Bartleman, Euphame (EL) 1661**B**
Bartleman, Jon (Samuelston EL) 1662
Barton, William (Kirkliston ML) c.1655**A** p113
Barton,——, wife of above c.1655**A** p113
Bathcat, Marion (Dunbar EL) 1628**B**
Bathgate, Elizabeth (Eyemouth BE) 1634**E** pp45-46
Bathgate, Issobell (Queensferry WL) 1661**B**
Bathlat, Begis (EL) c. 1649
Baxter, Janet (Moray) 1629**B**
Baxter, Margaret (Dunbar EL) 1628**B**

Baylie, ——, wife of Thomas (EL) 1662
Bayne, Isobel (Caithness) 1629**B**
Bayne, Jon (Nigg KN) 1652
Beatie, Helen (Menner PE) 1629**B**
Bell, Alexander (Auldearn NA) 1662
Bell,——, wife of above, 1662
Bell,——, wife of Alexander (EL) 1662
Bell, Bessie (Ayr) 1613**A**
Bell, Bessie (Lasswade ML) 1678
Bell, Christian (Gilmerton, Edinburgh) 1661**B**
Bell, Cristina (Liberton, Edinburgh) 1661**A**
Bell, Elspeth (BE) 1662**B**
Bell, Janet (Aberdour FI) 1654**A**
 pp 113, 195
Bell, Margaret (Corstorphine, Edinburgh) 1649**A**
Bell, Margret (Abdie FI) 1662**B**
Belshes, Helen (Eyemouth BE) 1661**B**
Bennet, Issobell (Stirling) 1659**C**
Bennett, Isable (Roxburgh) 1659
Bennett, Janet (Leith, Edinburgh) 1649
Berdock, Margaret (Cousland ML) 1630
Bertram, Lillias (Culter AB) 1640
Bessie [no surname] (Burgon, Scalloway, Shetland) 1673
Beverage, Janet (Dysart FI) 1630**D**
Beverage, Margaret (Dysart FI) 1658
Beveridge, Agnes (Crook of Devon KN) 1662**B**
Beveridge, Margaret (Crook of Devon KN) 1662**B**
Beveridge, Margaret (Broughty Ferry AN) 1662**E**
Beverley, James (Aberdeen) 1671
Bezok, Margaret (Fortrose RO) 1699
Bigham, Isobell (Stranraer WI) 1644**B**
Bigland, Kathcrene (Orkney) 1615**A**
Bigland, Margret (Scalloway, Shetland) 1673**B**
Bining, Jonet (PR) 1662**B**
Binnie, George (Stenton EL) 1662
Binning, Jean (Carriden WL) 1649**B**
Birkinrig or Brinkinrig, Helen (Crichton

ML) 1661**D**
Birks, Helen (Haddington EL) 1662
Birnie, Jonet (Crawford LA) 1650**D**
Bischope, Agnes (Midcalder ML) 1644**A**
Bishop, Janet (Pcnicuik ML) 1629**A**
Bissat, Helen (Dysart FI) 1630**B**
Bizet, Jean (Torryburn FI) 1704
Black, Adam (Larnanadie DU) 1708
Black, Christian (Dalkeith ML) 1650**C**
Black, Elizabeth (Stirling) 1659
Black, Elspeth (Stirling and Alloway)
    1659**C** 1661**B**
Black, John (Berwick) 1683
Black, Kathrin (Stirling) 1681
Black, Thomas, (Liberton, Edinburgh)
    1661**A** p123
Blackie, Elspett (Liberton, Edinburgh)
    1661**A** p123
Blackie, Janet (Dalkeith ML) 1661
Bladderstouns, Elspet (Torryburn FI)
    1630**B**
Blaik, Helen (Dumfries) 1628**B**
Blaik, Marion (EL) 1662
Blaikburne, Margaret (Inverkeithing FI)
    1649
Blaikie, Christian (Prestonpans EL) 1661
Blaikie, Meriory (Cairnie) 1588
Blair, Katherene (Glasgow) 1622**A**
Blair, Katherine (Bo'ness WL) 1624**B**
Blair, Magdalen (Stirling) 1659**E**
Blair, Margaret (Carriden WL) 1649**B**
Blak, Cristine (Samuelston EL) 1661
Blak, Elspit (Alloa CL) 1658
Blak, Jonet (Alloa CL) 1658
Blak, Katharine (Stirling) 1659**B**
Blak, Kathren (Alloa CL) 1658
Blak, Kathrin (Easter Flisk FI) 1662**B**
Blak, Margaret (EL) c.1649**E**
Blak, Samwell (Dumfries) 1658
Blek. Christian (EL) c.1649**E**
Blyth, Elspeth (BE) 1662**B**
Blyth, George (BE) 1628**B**
Blyth, Isobell (Auchtermuchty FI)) 1662**B**
Blyth, Jonet (Haddington EL) 1662
Bog, James (Inverkip RE) 1662**B**

Bogtoun, Meg (Prestonpans EL) 1590
Boig, Jon (Inverkip RE) 1662**B**
Boill, Grissell (Glasgow) 1629**B**
Bonar, Cristian (Newburgh FI) 1662**B**
Bo'Ness, Witches pp 137, 173-174
Bonie, Catherine [No Date}**B**
Bonn, Christian (Cluny AB) 1709?
Borthuick, Alison (Haddington EL) 1629**B**
Borthuick, Margaret (Cousland ML)
    1630**B**
Bothwell-see under Stewart, Francis, 5th
    Earl of
Bowar, Kathrin (Rhynd PR) 1662**D**
Bowie, Agnes (Gilmerton, Edinburgh) 1661
Bowis, Janet (Biggar LA) 1649
Bowmaker, Janet (Duns BE) 1629**B**
Boyd, Agnes (Paisley RE) 1630**D**
Boyd, Janet (Dumbarton DN) 1628**B**
Boyd, Janet (Prestonpans EL) 1628**B**
Boyd, Janet (Glasgow) 1700**E**
Boyd, Jonnet (Ayr) 1658
Boyd, Marion (PE) 1629**B**
Boyd, Marioun (Spott EL) 1624**B**
Boyd, Robert (Dunkeld PR) 1598**E**
Boyman, Janet (Cowgate, Edinburgh)
    1572**A**
Boyndie, Thomas (AY) 1583
Braidheid, Jonet (Auldearn NA) 1662**B**
    pp 128, 130-131
Brake, Cristian (Aberdeen) 1670
Brand, Isobell (Duddingston, Edinburgh)
    1661
Brand, Margaret (Dunfermline FI) 1643**A**
Brand,—— (Crook of Devon KN) 1662**B**
Brauckinrigg, Issobell (Crichton ML)
    1649**B**
Brodie, Agnes (Auldearn NA) 1662**B**
Brodie, Janet (Moray) 1629**B**
Brodie, Margret (Auldearn NA) 1662**B**
    pp 128-129, 131
Bronne, John (Bourhouse, Dunbar EL)
    1649**B**
Brotherstane, Isobel (Birkinside BE)
    1649**B**
Brotherstanes, Janet (BE) 1629**B**

Broun, Agnes (Kilmeny AR) 1662**B**
Broun, Agnes (Torryburn FI) 1666**B**
Broun, Bessie (Dalkeith ML) 1627**B**
Broun, Elizabeth (Inverkeithing FI)
    1623**B** p34
Broun, Helen (Penston EL) 1649**B**
Broun, Jon (Kilmeny AR) 1662**B**
Broun, Jonnet (Dumfries) 1683
Broun, Katherine (Innerleithen PE)
    1629**B**
Broun, Margaret (Liberton, Edinburgh)
    1661
Broun, Marion (Samuelston EL) 1662
Broun, William (Dysart FI) 1630**B**
Broune, Barnard (Dalkeith ML) c.1660**A**
Broune, Bessie (Prestonpans EL) 1590
Broune, Issobell (Eyemouth BE) 1649**B**
Broune, Janet (Nethervrile) 1649**B**
Broune, Marion (Pencaitland EL) 1649**B**
Broune, Marioun (Woodhall ML) 1649**B**
Brounhill, Thomas (Prestonpans EL) 1590
Brounhill,——, wife of above, 1590
Brown, Agnes (Liberton, Edinburgh) 1661
Brown, Issobel (Duddingston, Edinburgh)
    1661
Brown, Janet (Burntisland FI) 1649**A**
    p249
Brown, Janet (Markinch FI) 1643
Brown, Jean (Edinburgh) 1661**D**
Brown, Jean (Penninghame WI) 1706
Brown, Jean (Penninghame WI) 1706**D**
Brown, Margaret (South Queensferry WL)
    1643-44**E**
Brown, Marion (Kilmarnock) 1709
Brown, Thomas (Pittenweem FI) 1705**D**
    p161
Browne, Katherine (Lauder BE) 1628**B**
Bruce, Elspeth (Abdie FI) 1662**B**
Bruce, Elspeth or Elizabeth (Cortachy AN)
    1661,1662,1664**B**
Bruce, Janet (Tranent EL) 1657
Bruce, Jonet (Nether Williamston ML)
    1644**A**
Bruce, Jonet (Midcalder ML) 1644**A**
Bruce, Marioune (Awldrain AB) 1590

Bruce, Robert (Mearns AB) 1650
Brugh, Agnes (Crook of Devon KN)
    1662**A**
Brugh, Janet (Crook of Devon KN)
    1662**A**
Brughe, Johnne (Fossoway PR) 1643**A**
Brunton, Margaret (Dalkeith ML) 1661
Bryce, Matthew (AY) 1583
Bryis, Watty (Dunblane ST) 1615**B**
Bryson, Margaret (Edinburgh) 1661**A**
    p123
Buchan, Margaret (Aberdeen) 1630**B**
Buchanan, Nicholas (Croy, Orkney)
    1680**E**
Buchane, Jeane (Creich FI) 1645
Buchane, Margaret (Aberdeen) 1630**B**
Buchquhannane, Duncan (Prestonpans
    EL) 1590
Budge, Jonnett (Caithness) 1626**B**
Bull, Margaret (Inverkeithing FI) 1623**B**
    p34
Burges, Margaret (Nether Cramond, Edin-
    burgh) 1628**B**
Burges, Marjorie (Culross FI) 1643**D**
Burges, Mary (Strathspey) 1661
Burgess, Katherine (Cromdale MO)
    1643**A**
Burghie, ——, spouse of Alexander
    (Dunbar EL) 1612-13**B**
Burnes, Janet (Dumfries) 1659**C**
Burnes, Janet (Dumfries) 1664**C**
Burnet, Janet (Auldearn NA) 1662
Burnett, Geilis (Aberdeen) 1671**E**
Burnett, Issobell (Aberdeen) 1597**E**
Burnett, Mareon (BE) 1662**B**
Burnlie, ——, female, 1709?
Burrell, Jonet (Kinross) 1662**B**
Burton, Janet (Peaston EL) 1678
Burton, Margaret (Liberton, Edinburgh)
    1661**E**
Butt, the ladies of (Merse/BE) 1594 p192
Buttar, Jonnett (Kinloch PR) 1700**C**
Butter, Margaret (Prestonpans EL) 1661
Butter, Martha (Prestonpans EL) 1659
    Appendix 3 p207

Caffidonisch, Thomas (Tain) 1590
Cairll or Carle, Agnes (AB) 1626, 1627**B**
Cairnes, Bigis (Dumfries) 1659**A**
Cairnes, Alisone (Eyemouth BE) 1649**B**
Cairnes, Issobell (EL) c.1649E, 1661**B**
Cairns, Agnes (Pencaitland EL) 1649**B**
Calder, Witches p165
Callander, Margaret (St. Andrews) 1630**B**
Callon, Janet (Dumfries) 1659**A** p117
Callum, Margaret (Thurso) 1718**B**
Campbell, Agnes (Ayr) 1629**B**
Campbell, Catherine or Katherine (Paisley
    RE) 1697**A** p155-156
Campbell, Gilbert (PR) 1613**B**
Campbell, James (Peaston EL) 1678**D**
Campbell, James (AY) 1583
Campbell, Janet (Perth) 1612**B**

Campbell, Jean (Bute) 1660
Campbell, Jonett (Prestonpans EL) 1590
Campbell, Marion (Peaston EL) 1678**D**
Cant, Elspet (Elgin) 1604**C**
Cant, Elspeth or Elspat (South Queens-
    ferry WL) 1644**A**
Cant, Margaret (Aberdour FI) 1654E,
    c.1661**A** p113, 123
Capae, Robert (Hogel EL) 1662
Caray, Katherine (Orkney) 1616
Carfa, Bessie (Haddington EL) 1629**A**
Carfa, Thomas (Haddington EL) 1629**B**
Carfa,——, brother of above 1629**B**
Carfrae, Jonet (Samuelston EL) 1661**B**
Carlips, Thomas (Luss PR) 1633**D** p194
Carnecroce or Cairncross, Janet (Lystoun)
    1649**B**
Carnochan, Bessie (Dumfries) 1628**B**
Carrick, Alesoun (EL) 1629B, 1630**B**
Carrilie, Bessie (Dumfries and Twynholme
    KR) 1628**B**
Carse, John, 1658**A**
Carvie, Margaret (Falkland FI) 1661**E**
Caskie, Mareon (Lanark) 1670**B**
Cass or Casse, Heleen (Dalkeith, Fisher
    row/Musselburgh EL) 1661**A**
Castell, Janet (Fraserburgh AB) 1649
Cathie, Issobell (EL) c. 1649**E**

Cathie, Issobell (Samuelston EL) 1661**B**
Cathie, Patrik (Samuelston EL) 1661**B**
Cattenhead, Annabell (AB) 1626, 1627**B**
Cechie, Christian (Jedburgh) 1671
Chalmers, Agnes (PE) 1629
Chalmers, Bessie (Inverkeithing FI)
    1621**B** p32
Chalmers, Elspeth (Orkney) 1643
Chalmers, Giles (Oathlaw AN) 1633-34
Chancelar, Susanna (Lanark) 1630
Chansie, Marion (Dalkeith ML) 1650
Chapman, Agnes (Aberdeen) 1608
Chapman, Alesoun (ML) 1628**B**
Chapman, Margaret (Stirling) 1633
Charters, Agnes (Dumfries) 1628
Chatto, Margaret (Inverkeithing FI)
    1621**B** p32
Chattow, Barbara (Inverkeithing FI) 1649
Cheuslie, Elspeth (Prestonpans EL) 1679
Chib, Elspeth (Liberton, Edinburgh) 1661
Chirnesyde, Niniane (Edinburgh) 1591**D**
    p18
Chisholm, Agnes (Kilernan RO) 1697**B**
Chisholm, Mary (Lilliesleaf RX) 1650
Chisolme, Elsbet (Auldearn NA) 1662
    p129
Chousley, Elspeth (Haddington EL)
    1679**E**
Chrystie, Agnes (Stirling) 1634
Chrystie, Katharine (Dysart FI) 1630
Chrystison, John (Brechin AN) 1650**C**
Clacherty, Katharine (Kirkcudbright)
    1658**A**
Clark, Agnes (Dumfries) 1659**A**
Clark, Janet (Dalkeith ML) 1661
Clark, Jonett (Blalach AB) 1590**A**
Clark, Margaret (Carkmuir) 1709
Clark, Michael (Lasswade ML) 1597
Clarkson, or Clerkson Agnes (Dirleton
    EL) 1649
Cleghorne, Jonnet (Niddrie, Edinburgh)
    1661
Cleilland, Jean (LA) 1629
Clench or Cleuch, Aliesone (Clockpen)
    1649**B**

Clerauche, Margaret (Aberdeen) 1597
Clerk, Agnes (Dumfries) 1659**A** p117
Clerk, Agnes (Largs AY) 1662**B**
Clerk, Alexander (Culross FI) 1624**B**
Clerk, Helen (Newhaven, Edinburgh)
    1645**D**
Clerk, Janet (DU) 1630**B**
Clerk, Margaret (Kirkcudbright) 1644
Clerk, Margaret (Dumfries) 1659**A** p117
Clerk, Margaret (Aberdeen) 1597**A**
Clerk, Margaret (Seton of Cullen BA)
    1674**E**
Clerksoun, Janet (LA) 1629**B**
Cleroch, Margaret (AB) 1626**B**
Clow, Elizabeth (Forgan FI) 1662**B**
Cochran, Bessie (Glasgow) 1700**E**
Cochrane, Barbara (Tranent EL) 1659
    Appendix 3 p206
Cochrane, Bessie (Tranent EL) 1659
Cock, Janet (Dalkeith ML) 1661**E**, 1661**A**
    p124
Cock, Jean (Dalkeith ML) 1661**A**
Cockburn, Janet (Pencaitland EL) 1649**B**
Cockburn, Thomas (Prestonpans EL) 1591
Cockie, Isobel (Aberdeen) 1597**A** p20
Coell or Cheill, Janet Ninian (=Nein Ean)
    (Conveth IN) 1662**E**
Coke, William (Kirkcaldy FI) 1633**A** p43
Coldane, Janet (Dalkeith ML) 1661
Collie or Kellie, Margret (Elgin) 1662**A**
Colquhoun, Sir John of Luss (PR) 1633**D**
    p194
Colvill, Elspeth (Tranent EL and West Port,
    Edinburgh) 1659**A**
Colville, Elizabeth (Tranent EL) 1659
    Appendix 3 p206
Colvine, Grissel (Colinton, Edinburgh) 1686
Comb, Margaret (Bo'Ness WL) 1680**E**
Comb, Margaret (Edinburgh) 1680
Comenes, Agnes (Dumfries) 1659**A** p117
Common, George (Overton LA) 1649**B**
Congiltoun, Marioun (Prestonpans EL)
    1590
Conochie, Janet (Bo'Ness WL) c. 1670**A**
Contes, Janet (Peebles) 1649**B**

Cooper or Coupar, Jonat (Brechin AN)
    1650**A**
Cooper, Margaret (Irvine RE) 1650
Cootis, Issobell (Bo'Ness WL) 1624**A**
Coran, Marion (Liberton, Edinburgh) 1661
Corphat or Cornfoot, Janet (Pittenweem
    FI) 1705* pp 160-162, 186
Cors, Thomas (Orkney) 1643 p52
Corsan, Elizabeth (Dumfries) 1650
Corsan, Marione (Dumfries) 1659
Corsane, Janet (Dumfries) 1659**A** p117
Corsar, Marion (Dumfries) 1650
Cothall or Cothills, Helen (Forfar AN) 1661
Coull, Marie Nein Innes Vic, 1669
Coupar, Marable (Orkney) 1624**A**
Couper, Cristiane (Culross FI) 1621**B**
Couper, Janet (Brechin AN) 1650**A**
Coupere, Janet (Brechin AN) 1649
Coupland, Catherine (Samuelston EL)
    1661**B**
Cousing, Robert (Culross FI) 1650
Coutts, Janet (PE) 1650**A** p110
Cowan, William (Innerwick EL) 1662**B**
Cowane, Bessie (Prestonpans EL) 1590
Cowane, Margaret (Edinburgh) 1628**B**
Cowie, Agnes (Liberton, Edinburgh)
    1661**A**
Cowie, Margaret (Torryburn FI) 1666**B**
Cowie, Meggie (Montrose AN) c. 1670**A**
Cowper, Mallie (Aberdeen) 1630**B** p39
Crafford, Elizabeth (Samuelston EL)
    1661**B**
Crafford, Robert (Fisherrow/Musselburgh
    EL) 1661
Craiche, Elspeth or Eppie (Culross FI)
    1656**E**, 1662**B** pp 114, 123
Craig, Christiane (Turriff AB) 1627**B**
Craig, Marion (Liberton, Edinburgh) 1661
Craig, Marjory (Pollockshaws RE) 1677**A**
    p137
Craigie, Katherine (Orkney) 1640, 1643**A**
    pp 52-53
Cranston, Christian (Tranent EL) 1659
    Appendix 3 p206
Cranston, Sarah (Peaston EL) 1678

Cranstoune, Jonet (Edinburgh) c. 1642, 1643

Craufurd, Jeane (Renfrew) 1650**A**

Craufurd, Jonet (Largs AY) 1662**B**

Craw, William (Bo'Ness WL) 1679**A** p137

Crawford, Isobel (Irvine RE) 1618**A** pp 31-32

Crawfurd, Elspeth (Samuelston EL) 1661**B**

Crichton, John (Aberdeen) 1596 p21

Crichtoun, Beatrix (LA) 1629**B**

Crichtoun, William (Dunfermline FI) 1648**A**

Crictoun, Lancelot (Tranent EL) 1659 Appendix 3 p207

Cristell, Kathrine (Bute) 1662**B**

Croket, Bessie (Forfar AN) 1661

Crokett, Issobell (Stirling) 1661

Crombie,——, wife of Thomas Crombie (Pittenweem FI) 1643**A** p22

Crooks, Jonet (Tranent EL) 1659 Appendix 3 p206

Crose or Cause, Margret (PR) 1662**B**

Croser, Marion (PE) 1629**B**

Cruikshank, Katherine (Fisherrow/Mus-selburgh EL) 1661

Crystie, Jonet (Abernethy PR) 1662**B**

Crystie, Kathrene (Dysart FI) 1627**A**

Cuj [Cowie?], Janet (Elgin) 1646**D** p56

Cumlaquoy, Mareoun (Birsay, Orkney) 1643

Cumming, Marion (EL) 1662

Cummyng, Helene (Aberdour FI) 1622**B**

Cumroy, Bessie (Selkirk) 1629**B**

Cuninghame, Isabel, called 'Blewsleaves' or Bluesleeves (Paxton BE) 1629**B** p252

Cunningham, Mary (Culross FI) 1644**B**

Cunnynghame, Marion (Dunfermline FI) 1650

Cunyngham, Katherine (Samuelston EL) 1612**B**

Cuper, Bessie (Creich FI) 1645

Currie,—— (Dunfermline FI) 1677**E**

Currie, Andro (Dunfermline FI) 1677**E**

Currie, Janet (Crimond AB) 1630**B**

Currie, Margaret (Aberdour FI) 1654**E**, 1661**A** pp113, 123

Curry, Jonet (Pentland ML) 1661**B**

Cursetter, Elspeth (Orkney) 1629

Cuthbertson, Christian (Queensfery WL) 1662**B**

Cuthbertson, Isabel (Culter LA) 1640

Cuthbertsone, Agnes (EL) 1661

Cuthbertsoun, Beatrix (Prestonpans EL) 1628**B**

Cuthbertsoun, Margaret (Penicuik ML) 1629**A**

Cwnngham, Jonet, known as Lady Both-well (Edinburgh) 1572 p18

D——, Bessie (Haddington EL) 1662

Dageris, William (Jedburgh) 1628**B**

Daglas, Jean (EL) 1662

Daill, Janet (Moffat DU) 1661

Daill, Janet (Musselburgh EL) 1661**A**

Dairsie, Ishbell (St Andrews) [No Date]**D**

Dalgleish, James (Pencaitland EL) 1649**B**

Dalgleish, Margaret (Peebles) 1627**C**

Dalgleish, Margaret (Lauder BE) 1649**B**

Dalgleish, Margaret (Peaston EL) 1678**D**

Damiet, John (Canongate, Edinburgh) 1593

Darlig, Janet (Prestonpans EL) 1628**B**

Darumpill, Helene (Dysart FI) 1626**B**

Dason, Elspeth (RO) 1671

Dasoun, Margaret (Dysart FI) 1630**B**

Dauidsone, Jonat (Aberdeen) 1597

Dauline, Margaret (South Queensferry WL) 1643-44

Dauline, Marion (South Queensferry WL) 1643-44**E**

Dauling, Eupham (Dysart FI) 1627

Dauling,——, mother of above 1627

Davidson, Isobel (Belhelvie AB) 1676**D** p134

Davidson, James (Waterhaugh) 1709

Davidsone, Marion (Lesmahagow LA) 1646**D**

Davidsonne, Agnes (Jedburgh) 1649**B**

Davidsoun, William (Saltoun EL) 1628
Davie, Johnne (Aberdeen)
    1626,1627**B**
Dawson, ——, wife of John (Pittenweem
    FI) 1643**A** p22
Dawsoun, Bessie (EL) 1661**B**
Deanes, Christiane (Samuelston EL) 1661
Deanes, Helen (East Lothian) c. 1649
Deanes, Helene (Sarnuelston EL) 1661
Deanes, Jeane (EL) c. 1649**B**
Degeddes, Janet (Aberdeen) 1597**A**
Dempherstoun, Margret (Alloa CL) 1658
Dempstar, Agnes (Prestonpans EL)
    1628**B**
Dempstar, Alesoun (Leith, Edinburgh)
    1628**B**
Dempstar, Jonnet (West Wemyss FI)
    1626**B**
Dempster, Elizabeth (Crook of Devon KN)
    1662**B**
Denis or Deans, Alesoun (Dunbar EL)
    1613**B**
Desk, Agnes (Kilrain RO) 1699**B**
Dess, Agnes (Kilernan RO) 1697**B**
Dewar, Jonet (Haddington EL) 1662
Dewart, Alexander (Dumfries) 1707
Dick, Alison (Kirkcaldy FI) 1633**A** p43
Dick, Elizabeth (Anstruther-Easter FI)1701
Dick, ——, sister of (Waughton RX) 1594
Dick,——, mother of above, before 1594**A**
Dick, Margaret (Borthwick ML) 1649**B**
Dickson, Edward (Haddington EL) 1662
Dickson, Isobel (Dumfries) 1692
Dickson, Margaret (Penston EL) 1649**B**
Dickson, Marion (Dumfries) 1692
Dicksoun, Margaret (PE) 1629**B**
Dikson, Jeane (EL) 1662
Dikson, Marion (EL) 1662
Diksone, Janet (Dumfries) 1650
Dobie, Margret (Torryburn FI) 1666**B**
Dobson, Margaret (Eyemouth BE) 1649**B**
Doddes, James (Linton RX) 1649**B**
Dodds, Isabel (Musselburgh EL) 1661
Dodis, Issobell (Liberton, Edinburgh)
    1661**E**

Dods, Margaret (Peaston EL) 1678**A**
Dollour, Mary (Strathglass IN) 1662**B**
Donald, Agnes Nein (Tain RO) 1628**B**
Donald, Christian (Dumbarton) 1677**B**
Donald, Janet (Dumbarton) 1629**A**
Donald, Marg (Dunfermlinc FI) 1645
Donald, Agnes Nein (Logie, Tain) 1662**B**
Donald Vic William Vic More, Jonet Neill
    [Nein?] (Scatwell RO) 1662B**B**
Donaldson, Adam (Culross FI) 1644
Donaldson, John (Brechin AN) 1649
Donaldson, Margaret (Dunfermline FI)
    1643**A**
Donnald, Janet (Dumbarton) 1629**A**
Dote, Christine (St Andrews) [No Date]**D**
Dougall, John (Inverkip RE) 1695
Dougall, John (Glasgow) 1700**E**
Dougall, Margaret (Ayr) 1682
Dougan, Janit (Partoun DU) 1708
Doughtie, Bessie (Fisherrow/Musselburgh
    EL) 1661
Douglas, Beatrix (Inverkeithing FI) 1645
    p58
Douglas, Elspet (Haddington EL) 1649**B**
Douglas, Hellen (Inverkeithing FI) 1649
Douglas, Issobell (Dunkeld PR) 1698**E**
Douglas, Janet (Edinburgh) 1679**C**
Douglas, Janet (Tranent EL) 1659
    Appendix 3 p206
Douglas, John (Tranent EL) 1659-1660**A**
    Appendix 3 p206
Douglas, Jonnet (Fisherrow/Musselburgh
    EL) 1661
Douglas, Margaret (Crichton ML) 1678**A**
Dougleish, Jon (Flisk FI) 1662**B**
Doul, Mary Man Innes du, 1670**E**
Doulson, Beatrix (Whittingehame EL)
    1649**B**
Dovertie, Jonnet (Aberdeen) 1627**B**
Dow, Janet (Preston EL) 1629**B**
Dow, Janet (Wick CA) 1655
Dow, Meg (Gilmerton, Edinburgh)
    1590**A**
Drewer, Jonet (Orkney) 1615**D**
Dron, Margret (Rhynd PR) 1662**B**

Drummond, Alexander (Auchterarder PR) 1629A

Drummond, Barbara (Kilbride ST) 1664, 1665A p133

Drummond, Jean (Glasgow) 1700E

Drummond, Jonat (Nether Keith EL) 1591

Drummond, Margaret (Linton RX) 1723

Dryburgh, Helene (Wemyss FI) 1626B

Dryburgh, Isabel (Penicuik ML) 1629A

Dryburgh, Margret (Falkland FI) 1662B

Drysdaill, Euphame (Cairdie) 1649B

Drysdaill, Jonet (Inveresk EL and Crichton ML) 1609E p28

Drysdale, Agnes (Crook of Devon KN) 1662B

Duchall, Margret (Alloa CL) 1658D

Duff, Issobell (Margret?) (Inverness) 1662A p127

Duff, Margret (Inverkip RE) 1662B p125

Dumbar, Jean (Largs AY) 1662B

Dun, Meg 1590A

Dunbar, Elspet (Moray) 1629B

Dunbar, Hew (Craigie AY) [No Date]

Dunbar, Jonnet (Bo'ness WL) 1624B

Dunbar, Marjorie (Auldearn NA) 1662

Duncan, Bessie (EL) 1629, 1630B

Duncan, Bessie (Creich FI) 1662B

Duncan, Elspitt (ML) 1628B

Duncan, Gelie (Prestonpans EL) 1590-91 pp 13, 17-18

Duncan, Margaret (Glasgow) 1700E

Duncane, Andrew (Shetland) 1604

Duncane, Catherene (Prestonpans EL) 1590

Duncane, Margaret (AY) 1605

Dundas, Ewfame (Caithness) 1629B

Dungalson, Agnes (Dumfries) 1628B

Dunham, Margaret (Lauder BE) 1649A pp 57-58

Dunholme, Margaret (Stow ML) 1649

Dunlop, Elizabeth or Bessie (Lyne AY) 1576A pp 11-12

Durie, Agnes (AB) 1626A

Durie, Janet (Kirkcaldy FI) 1638, 1639

Durie, Margaret (Aberdeen) 1627B

Durie, Margaret (Inverkeithing FI) 1649B p58

Durie, Margaret (Aberdeen) 1671B

Durie, Marion (Innerleithen PE) 1649B

Durie, Marion (Dunfermline FI) 1649B

Durie, Nanse (Aberdeen) 1627

Dury, Margaret (Aberdeen) 1669

Dwne or Dun, Margaret (Longniddry EL) 1594A

Dykis, Walter (Haddington EL) 1662

Dyneis, Jonka (Shetland) 1616

Ean Vane, Agnes Nic (Nairn) 1662

Eanglaish, Agnes Mor Nin Vick (Dingwall RO) 1675

Eason, William (Strathtay PR) 1689C pp 154-155

Edie, Elspeth (Auchtergaven PR) 1689

Edingtoun, Margret (Foulden BE) 1662B

Edward, Jonet (Flisk FI) 1662B

Ego, Thomas (Aberdeen) 1597

Elam, Africk (WI) 1644B

Elder, Alexander (Auldearn NA) 1662

Elder, Issobell (Dyke, Forres MO) 1662, 1663A

Elder, Katherine (Dunfermline FI) 1643A

Elder, Moress (Aberdeen) 1597

Elder,——, wife of above 1597

Elies, George (Forfar AN) 1662B

Eliot, Helen (Culross FI) 1684A

Eliot, Isobell (Peaston EL) 1678A

Elleot, Margaret (Spott EL) 1661B

Ellot, Helene (Jedburgh) 1586-87 p11

Ellote, Manie (Jedburgh) 1613B

Elphinston, Agnes (Penicuik EL) 1662E

Elphinstoun, Susanna (Peebles) 1629B

Elspethie,—— (Newhaven, Edinburgh) 1645

Endor, Witch of p2

Ersche (Irish), Marioun (Longniddry EL) 1608A

Erskin, Barbara (Alloa CL) 1658

Erskine, Annas (PR) 1613, 1614A

Erskine, Barbara (Stirling) 1659E

Erskine, Helene (PE) 1613, 1614C

Erskine, Issobell (PR)   1613, 1614**A**
Erskine, Jonet (Culross EL)   1644**B**
Erskine, Michael (Gorebridge ML)
    1630**A**
Erskyn, Robert, called Johnne of Logy
    (PR) 1613**A** p195
Eumond, Bessie, 1649-50**C**
Ewart, Johnne (Selkirk) 1621**B**
Ewart, Jonet (Gilmerton, Edinburgh) 1661
Ezatt, Helene (Culross FI) 1624**B**

F—, Issobell (Dalkeith ML) 1661
Fairlie, Janet (Kelso) 1649**B**
Fairlie, Jonet (Nether Keith EL) 1591
Fairlie, Samuell (Foulden BE) 1629**B**
Fairweill, Marjorie (Duddingston, Edin-
    burgh) 1661
Falconer, Agnes (BE) 1629**B**
Falconer, Elspet (Auldearn NA) 1662**B**
Falconner, Issobell (Eyemouth BE) 1606,
    1618?, 1624**B** pp 34-35, 191
Falconner, William (WL) 1624**B**
Farquhar, Archie (Nether Keith EL)   1591
Faw, John (Orkney) 1612
Fean, Thome (Prestonpans EL) 1591
Fentoun, Jonett (Dunfermline FI) 1643**D**
Fergie, Marjorie (Inverkeithing FI) 1649
Fergus, Katherine (Aberdeen) 1596,
    1597**A**
Fergusone, Issobell ((Dalkeith ML) 1661**A**
    p123
Fergusson, Agnes (Arbroath AN) 1568**D**
Fergussoun, Elspett (WL) 1624**C**
Fergussoun, Janet (Dumfries)
    1630, 1631**B**
Fermor, Elspeth (EL) 1662
Fernsche or Ferries, Kathrene (Aberdeen)
    1597
Fian or Fiene, Johnne (Prestonpans EL)
    1590**A** pp 14-16, 18
Fidlar, Gilbert (Aberdeen) 1597**E**
Findlaw, James, 1586
Findlaw, Johnne (Aberdeen) 1626
Finlasoun, Jonet (Burntisland FI)   1597**E**
    p22

Finlasoune, Margaret (Renfrew)   1650**A**
Finlason, Thomas (EL) 1662
Finlason,——, wife of above 1662
Finlasoun, T (EL) 1662
Finlasoun,——, wife of W Finlasoun (EL)
    1662
Finlay, Janet (Auldearn NA)   1662
Finlaysoun,——, (Mearns AB) 1650
Finlaysoune, Bessie (Logie PR)   1618
Finnie, Agnes (Edinburgh) 1644**A**
    pp 54-55
Finnie, Janet (Paisley)   1667**D**
Fisher, Margaret (Lanark)   1629**B**
Fisher, Janet (Ayr) 1683**E**
Fisher, Katherine (Galashiels BE)   1649**B**
Fisher, Margaret (Peterhead AB) 1630**B**
Fisher, Marion (Edinburgh) 1643**D**
Flayer, Bigs (Carrington ML)   1649**B**
Fleck, Agnes (Hunterston AY) 1649**B**
Fleck, Grissel (Tranent EL)   1659
    Appendix 3 p207
Fleck, Helen (Tranent EL)   1659
    Appendix 3 p206
Fleck, William (Humbie EL)   1659
Fleming, Margaret (Kirkcudbright)   1671
Flinker, Bessie (Liberton, Edinburgh)
    1661**E**
Flint, Barbara (Eyemouth BE)   1624,
    1629**B**
Flint, Katheren (Edinburgh)   1606
Flowan, Jonet (Ayr)   1658
Fogo, Jonet (Midcalder ML) 1720 p165
Foord, Christian (Aberdeen)   1671**E**
Forbes, Agnes (Aberdeen) 1597**B**
Forbes, Agnes (AB)   1626**B**
Forbes,——, sister of above   1626**B**
Forbes, Elspett (Aberdeen)   1597**E**
Forbes, Issobell (Aberdeen)   1597**E**
Fordell, Issobell (Brechin AN) 1650
Forres, Witches p3
Forrest, Bessie (PE)   1649-50
Forrest, Cristian (Pencaitland EL)   1649**B**
Forrester, Helen (Crichton ML)   1678**A**
Forrester, Joane (Kirkcaldy FI)   1649**B**
Forrester, John (Larstoun)   1649**B**

222

Forrester, Rachael (Haddington EL)
1649**B**

Forsyth, Agnes (Borthwick ML) 1649**B**

Foster, Jeane (EL) 1662

Fothringhame, Margaret (Keith EL)
1649**B**

Forsyth, Jonet (Westray, Orkney) 1629**A**

Fouller, Elspeth (Tranent EL) 1659
Appendix 3 p206

Fowler, Bessie (Fisherrow/Musselburgh
EL) 1661**A**

Fowlis, Lady - see under Roiss,
Katherene

Frame (Fren or Frem), Agnes (Aberdeen)
1597**E**

Frame, James (LA) 1629**B**

Fraser, Bessie (Moray) 1629**B**

Fraser, George (Oathlaw AN) 1633-34**B**

Fraser, Janet (DU) 1691

Fraser, Juenit or Janet (Shetland) 1643**A**

Fraser, Margaret (Aberdeen) 1636

Fraser, Margaret (Turriff AB) 1650

Frasser, Helene (Aberdeen) 1597**A** p20

Frater, Katherine (Mellerstain BE)
1649**B**

Friece, Barbara (Auldearn NA) 1662

Frisell, Katharine (Rothesay, Bute) 1662**B**

Frissell, Geilis (Kingarth, Bute) 1649

Fulkhart, Margaret (EL) 1662

Fullertoun, Bessie (Ayr) 1658

Fulton, Margaret (Paisley), 1697**A** p156

Fyfe, Margaret (Crook of Devon KN)
1662**B**

Fynnie, Malye (Aberdeen) 1597

Gairdner, Grissell (Newburgh FI) 1610**A**

Galbraith, Janet (Dysart FI) 1630**B**

Galbraith, Janet (Greenock RE) 1649

Gall, Jonett (Prestonpans EL) 1590

Galloway, Janet (Kirriemuir AN) 1650

Galvitas,——, wife of Richard (Haddington
EL) 1662

Garner, Robert (Crichton ML) 1649**B**

Gaut, Mauld (Kilbarchan RE) 1649**B**

Gardiner, Jonnett (Aberlemno AN)
1618**B**

Gastoun, Agnes (Melrose RX) 1650**D**

Gastoun, Helene (RX) 1629**B**

Gaylol, Jeane, 1661

Geddie, Malie (Prestonpans EL) 1590

Gely, John (Bute) 1662**B**

Gentleman, Jannet (Glasgow) 1700**E**

George, Helen (AB) 1671

George, Helen (Inverary AR) 1671

Gerard, Janet (Aberdeen) 1596**A** p21

Gerard, Katherine (Aberdeen) 1596**A**
p21

Getwood, Jean (Ormiston EL) 1661**B**

Gib, Anne (Montrose AN) 1580**E**

Gib, Helen (Aberdeen) 1604**B**

Gibb, Bessie (Bo'Ness WL) 1680**E**

Gibb, Kett (Corstorphine, Edinburgh)
1649**A**

Gibesone, Heleen (Prestonpans EL) 1661

Gibesone, Jeane (Niddrie, Edinburgh) 1661

Gibson, Agnes (Inverkip RE) 1662

Gibson, Bessie (Carden PE) 1649**B**

Gibson, Helen (Tranent EL) 1659
Appendix 3 p207

Gibson, Jonet (Niddrie, Edinburgh) 1661

Gibson, Jonet (Liberton, Edinburgh)
1661**A** p123

Gibson, Katherine (Tranent EL) 1659
Appendix 3 p207

Gibson, Margaret (Tranent EL) 1649**B**

Gibsone, Katharine (Tranent EL) 1659

Gibsoun, Marjorie (Inverkeithing FI)
1623**A** p34

GIbsoune, Marion (Midcalder ML)
1644**A**

Gilash, Christian (RO) 1699**B**

Gilbert, Elspet (Auldearn NA) 1662

Gilbert, Margaret Nin (Thurso)
1718-19**D** pp 164-165

Gilchrist, Elspot (St. Andrews) 1595**A**

Gilchrist, Geillis (Leith, Edinburgh) 1649

Gilchrist, Margaret (Bownes, Aberdeen)
1612**B**

Gilchrist, Mary Nein Jon Vic (Scatwell
RO) 1662**B**

Gillaspie, Grissall (Stirling) 1614
Gillespie, Jonnet (Ayr) 1658
Gillies, Adam (North Berwick EL) 1663
Gillies,——, wife of above 1633
Gillimichaell, Marion Nein (Tain) 1628**B**
Gillivory, Jonet (Methven PR) 1662**B**
Gilmore, Jean (Glasgow) 1700**E**
Gilmour or Gilmur, William (AY) 1582, 1583**D**
Gingell, Margaret (Salisbury) 1655**E** p113
Glass, John (Kilernan RO) 1699**E** p158
Glass, Mary (RO) 1699**C**
Gledd, George (Winton EL) 1662
Glenluce, Devil p113
Goodaile, ——, wife of (Carron ST) c.1670**A**
Goold, Issobell (PR) 1662**B**
Gourdie, Bessie (Fala ML) 1678**A**
Gordoun, John (AB) [No Date] **C**
Gordoun, Johnne (Prestonpans EL) 1590**A**
Gott, Mauld (Glasgow) 1649
Gottray, Annabell (Ayr) 1658
Gourlay, James (Pencaitland EL) 1649**B**
Gourlay, Margaret (Stirling) 1659**E**
Gourley, Agnes (Humbie EL) 1649
Govan, Katharine (Wray) 1649**B**
Gow, Christian (Orkney) 1624
Gow, Helen (Tain) 1628**B**
Gow, Jonat Nein Giblie (Tain) 1663
Gowanlocke, Margaret (PE) 1629**B**
Gowdie, Issobell (Auldearn NA) 1662**B** pp 125, 127-131, 156, 169, 171, 176-177, 195-196
Graham, ——, a witch (Peebles) 1640**A**
Graham, Bessie (Kilwinning AY) 1649**A** pp 59-60
Graham, Bessie (Dumfries) 1650**A**
Graham, Christian (Glasgow) 1622**A** p33
Graham, Cristiane (Culross FI) 1621**B**
Graham, Elspet (Dalkeith ML) 1661**A** p123
Graham, Elspeth (PE) 1649-50**A**
Graham, Joan (Ayr) 1683**E**

Graham, Richard (Edinburgh) 1592**A** pp 15, 18
Grahame, Elizabeth (Kilwinning AY) 1649**B**
Grahame, Elspet (Stobo PE) 1649**B**
Grahame, Johne (Peebles) 1629**B**
Grahame, Jonet (Ayr) 1658
Grahame, Jonet (Dalkeith ML) c. 1660**D**
Grant, Agnes (Auldearn NA) 1662**A** pp 128, 131
Grant, Agnes (Elgin) 1643**D**
Grant, Alex (RO) 1671
Grant, Gormyle (Conveth IN) 1662**B**
Grant, Jonat (Aberdeen) 1597**A**
Grant, Jonett (Colquhatstane) 1590**A**
Grant, Katherine (Orkney) 1623**A**
Grant, Marioun (Aberdeen) 1597**A**
Grant, William (Bellie MO) 1650
Grawie, Jonet, 1596**E**
Gray, ——, a witch (Rhynd PR) 1662**C**
Gray, Agnes (Ormiston EL) 1649**B**
Gray, Catherene (Prestonpans EL) 1590**A**
Gray, Christian (Kinross) 1662**B**
Gray, Ellen (Aberdeen) 1597
Gray, Elspet (Beigend PE) 1649**B**
Gray, Elspit (Balwyllo AN)) 1650
Gray, Geillis (Crail FI) 1599**D**
Gray, Gelis (Elgin) 1604**C**
Gray, Isobel (Lanark) 1629**A**
Gray, Janet (Chirnside BE) 1649**B**
Gray, John (Barloch ST) 1677**B**
Gray, Jonnet (Prestonpans EL) 1661
Gray, Katharine (Tranent EL) 1659
Gray, Marion (Tranent EL) 1659
Gray, Vylet (Inverkip RE) 1662**B**
Graye, Elspet (Deskford BA) 1597
Greave, Thomas (Inverkeithing FI) 1623**A** p33
Grebok, .Jonet (Orkney) 1643
Greene, Isobel (Overhartsame) 1649**B**
Greinscheill or Greinscheills, John (Lanark) 1629**B**
Grege, Joannet (Inverkeithing FI) 1649
Grege, Mart (Inverkeithing FI) 1649

Greif, Marion (Ayr) 1595**A**
Greig, John (Grange FI) 1649**B**
Greir or Grieve, Jon (Lauder BE) 1662**B**
Greirsoun, Robert (Prestonpans EL) 1591
Greirsoune, Issobell (Prestonpans EL)
   1607**A** p27
Grey, Katherine (Tranent EL) 1659**B**
   Appendix 3 p206
Grey, M (Tranent EL) 1659
   Appendix 3 p206
Grey-meill, Johnne (Longniddry EL)
   1608**A**
Grieve, Christian (Crook of Devon KN)
   1662**A**
Grieve, Katherine (Orkney) 1633**C**
   pp 44-45
Grieve, Katharine (Inverkeithing FI) 1649
Grieve, Margaret, 1661
Grieve, Robert or Hob (Lauder BE)
   1649**A** p57
Grieve, ------, wife of above 1629**A** p57
Grig, Marion (Dysart FI) 1638
Grig, Thomas (AB) 1630**B**
Grige, Marion (Peebles) 1629**B**
Grinlaw, Elspeth (Queensferry WL)
   1661**B**
Grinlaw, Mareon (Ormiston EL) 1661**E**
   p124
Grintoun, Christian (Eastbarns EL)
   1612**A** p38
Groat, Janet (Caithness) 1655
Grot, Grissel (RO) 1671
Guddal, ------, wife of Richard Watson
   (Tirseppie AN) 1589**E**
Gude or Guide, William (Orkney) 1616
Guiddale, Bessie (Dysart FI) 1630**B**
Guidfellow,------ (EL) 1662
Guild, Elspeth (Torryburn FI) 1666**B**
Guild, Marion (Tranent EL) 1659**A**
   Appendix 3 p206
Guillielaw, John (Ayr) 1658
Guislet, George (Jedburgh) 1671**E**
Guisset, Jannet (Aberdeen) 1597
Gune, Agnes (Wick) 1655
Gutherie, Elspeth (Forfar AN) 1661**A**

Guthrie, Elizabeth (Montrose AN) 1662**B**
Guthrie. Helen (Forfar AN) 1661**A**
Guthrie, Issobell (Inverkeithing FI) 1649
Guthrie, Margaret (Montrose AN)
   1662**B**
Guthrie, Margaret (Carnbee FI) 1666**B**
Gylloun, Issobell (Prestonpans EL) 1590

Hadden, Isobel (Perth) 1623**C**
Haddock, Isobel (PE) 1629**B**
Hadron, Gean (Glasgow) 1699**E**
Hairstains, Janet, 1709**E**
Haistie, Margaret (Lanark) 1629**B**
Haldane. Halden, or Hadden, Isobell
   (Perth) 1623**A**
Haliburton, Euphame (EL) c. 1649**B**
Hall, James (Aberdeen) 1630
Hall, Jonet (Liberton, Edinburgh) 1661**E**
Hall, Margaret (Prestonpans EL) 1661
Hall, Martha (Tranent EL) 1659
   Appendix 3 p207
Halliburtoun, Elspeth (Ormiston EL)
   1661**B**
Halyburton, Menie (Dirleton EL) 1649**A**
   p62
Halyday, Katherine (Peaston EL) 1678
Halyday, Margaret (Craigton AN) 1630**B**
Halywall, Richard (Selkirk) 1679
Hamilton, Alexander (Haddington EL)
   1630**A** pp 39, 193-194
Hamilton, Alexander (Pencaitland EL)
   1628
Hamilton, Helen (Leith, Edinburgh) 1632
   p42
Hamilton, Margaret (Pencaitland EL)
   1649**B**
Hamilton, Margaret (Bo'ness WL)
   1679**A** pp 137, 174
Hamilton, Margaret *secundus* (Bo'Ness
   WL) 1679**A** p137
Hamilton, Margaret (Fala ML) 1629**A**
Hamiltoun, Helene (Leith, Edinburgh)
   1632**B**
Hamiltoun, Margaret (Haddington EL)
   1629**A**

Hamiltoune, Jonet (Ayr) 1658
Hammiltoun, Katherine (Dunbar EL)
1612**B**
Hammyltoun, Christian (Inverkeithing
FI) 1621**B** p32
Hammyltoun, Jonnet (Hamilton LA)
1616**B**
Handesyd, Margaret (Liberton, Edin-
burgh) 1661
Hannay, Marion (DU). 1630**B**
Hardie, Janet (Fisherrow/Musselburgh EL)
1629**B**
Hardie, Marion (Fraserburgh AB) 1630**A**
p39
Hardie, Marion (Eyemouth BE) 1629**D**
Harla, Bessie (Alloa CL) 1658
Harlaw, Adam (EL) c. 1649**E**
Harlaw, Bessie (Inverkeithing FI) 1621**B**
p32
Harlaw, Christian (Inverkeithing FI)
1623 p34
Harlaw, Jon (Ormiston EL) 1661**B**
Harlaw, Jonet (Innerwick EL) 1613**B**
Harper, Christian (Tranent EL) 1659**D**
Appendix 3 p206
Harper, John (Wick) 1655
Hart, Jean (Coldingham BE) 1698 p157
Hart, Margaret (Dalkeith ML) 1661
Harvie, Margaret (Stirling) 1659**E**
Hasben, John (Moray) 1629**B**
Haskerstoun, Margaret (Carriden WL)
1649
Hawie, Margret (Ormiston EL) 1661**B**
Hay, Alexander (Kinmudie AB) 1629**B**
Hay, Anna (Romanno PR) 1649**B**
Hay, Bessie (Auldearn NA) 1662**B**
pp 130-131
Hay, Christiane (WL) 1624**B**
Hay, Elspeth (BE) 1662**B**
Hay, Margaret (Lasswade ML) 1598**B**
Hay, Margaret (Elgin) [No Date]
Hay, Thomas (Winton EL) 1662
Hay,——, wife of above 1662
Heath, Agnes (RO) 1699**C** p158
Henderson, Bessie (Crook of Devon KN)

1662**A**
Henderson, Isobell (Ayr) 1658
Henderson, Margaret, Lady Pitathrie (In-
verkeithing FI) 1649**D** pp62-64,
187, 192
Hendersone, Issobell (Ayr) 1658
Hendersone, Janet (Wlyth or Alyth? AN)
1649**B**
Hendersone, Margaret (Wemyss FI)
1627**B**
Hendersone, Marioun (Inverkeithing FI)
1623**B** p34
Hendersoun, Agnes (ST) 1628**B**
Hendersoun, Elspet (Aberdeen) 1597**A**
Hendersoun, Janet (PE) 1629
Hendersoun, Janet (Selkirk) 1629**B**
Hendersoun, Katharine (Chirnside BE)
1649**B**
Hendirsoun, Bessie (Kidlaw EL) 1612**B**
Hendirsoun, Marioun (Jedburgh) 1613**B**
Hendrie, Agnes (Culross FI) 1675**A**
Hendrie, Janet (Culross FI) 1675**A**
Henreis,—— daughter of Janet (Caithness)
1629**B**
Henrie, Jonnet (Skateraw, Dunbar EL)
1612-13**B**
Henrison, James (Stow ML) 1649
pp61-62
Henrison, Marion (Stow ML) 1649**A**
pp61-62
Hepburne, Bessie (Haddington EL) 1629**B**
Herald, Elspet (AB) 1626**B**
Herbertson, Marion (Dumfries) 1692
Heriot, Margaret (Carrington ML) 1630**B**
Herreis, Janet (DU) 1630**B**
Herring, Captain Patrick (Stirling?)
1597**E**
Heswith, Elizabeth (Stirling) 1683
Hewat, Jonet (Liberton, Edinburgh) 1660
Hewison, Janet (Killallan RE) 1650
Heyman, Annie (Rothesay) 1662**B** p126
Hil, Jannet (Leith, Edinburgh) 1679
Hill, Agnes (Niddrie, Edinburgh) 1661
Hill, Anna (Glasgow) 1700**E**
Hill, Helene (South Queensferry WL)

1644**A**

Hill, Janet (Preston EL) 1629**D**

Hill, Katherine (Queensferry WL) 1615**B**

Hill, Margaret (Liberton, Edinburgh) 1661

Hird, Janet (Crook of Devon KN) 1662**B**

Hislop, Elspitt (Longniddry EL) 1628**B**

Hislop, Isobell (Edinburgh) 1683**E**

Hislop, John (Crichton ML) 1679

Hislop, John (Edinburgh) 1683**E**

Hislop, Marion (Crichton ML) 1679

Hislop, Marion (Edinburgh) 1683**E**

Hislope, Issobell (Crichton ML) 1679

Hog, Gilbert (PE) 1629**B**

Hog, Johne (Dunblane ST) 1629**B**

Hog, Jonet (Linton EL) 1661

Hog, Margaret (Haddington EL) 1649**B**

Hog, William (Ormiston EL) 1661**B**

Hoggen, Christian (Crichton ML) 1678**E**

Holm, Jonet (Inverkip RE) 1662 p125

Holmes, Jonnet (Ayr) 1658

Home, Barbara (Kilpont) 1622**B**

Home, Isobel (Tranent EL) 1659
       Appendix 3 p206

Home, Johne (EL) c. 1649**E**

Home, Jonnet (EL) 1661

Home, Margret (Torryburn FI) 1666**B**

Hongman, Marion (Whittingehame EL)
       1649**B**

Hood, Barbara (Eyemouth BE) 1661**B**

Hopkin,——, a female (Ayr) 1683**E**

Hopkirk, Helen (Crailing RX) 1662**B**

Hormscleugh, Margaret (Perth) 1623**A**

Horn, Janet (Dornoch SU) 1727**A**
       pp166-167

Horn,——, daughter of above 1727**D** p166

Horniman, Barbara (Falkland FI) 1661**E**

Horsburgh, Margaret (Pittenweem FI)
       1643**A** p22

Horsburgh, Rachael (Pencaitland EL)
       1649**B**

Hougan or Hoggan, Eupham (Rhynd PR)
       1662**A**

Houston, Issobell (Glasgow) 1700**E**

Howat, Jonat (Forfar AN) 1662, 1666**E**
       p133

Howat, Jonet (Kirkcudbright) 1672**B**

Howatsoun, Issobell (RX) 1628**B**

Howe, Issobel (Tranent EL) 1659

Howison, Jean (Ormiston EL) 1661**E**
       p124

Hoy, Marjorie (Pencaitland EL) 1649**B**

Hucheons, Bessie (Auldearn NA) 1662

Hucheons, Margret (Auldearn NA) 1662

Hudston, James (Alloa CL) 1658

Huggon, Margaret (Crook of Devon KN)
       1662**B**

Hugo, James (Borthwick ML) 1649**B**

Huit, Joanet (Forfar AN) 1661-62

Huldie, Helen (Coldingham BE) 1629**B**

Humbell, Thomas (Brechin AN) 1650**C**

Hume,——, mother of Cuthbert (Duns
       BE) 1594**A**

Huntar, Alexander (EL) 1662

Huntar, Cristian (Craigie AY) 1658

Huntar, Jean (Ormiston EL) 1661**B**

Huntar, Kathrin (Dalkeith ML) 1661**E**

Hunter, Agnes (Penston EL) 1649**B**

Hunter, Alexander (Haddington EL)
       1629**B**

Hunter, Anna (EL) 1662

Hunter, Helen (Orkney) 1643 p52

Hunter, Jonet (Hailie AY) 1605**A** p27

Hunter, Margaret (Dumbarton) 1629**B**

Hunter, Marion (LA) 1650

Hutchesoun, Margaret (LA) 1629**B**

Hutchesoune. Alesoune (Aberdeen)
       1622**B**

Hutchison, Margt. (Dalkeith ML) 1641**A**

Hutson, George (EL) c. 1649**B**

Hutson, Issobell (EL) c. 1649**B**

Hutson, Marion (EL) c. 1649**B**

Hutsone, Agnes (PR) 1662**B**

Hutton, Helen, 1632

Huttoun, Margaret (Culross FI) 1643**A**

Hyslop, Katherine (Stainhope PE) 1649**B**

Hyndman, Finwell (Bute) 1650

Hynman, Jonet (Inverkip RE) 1662**B**
       p125

Ilson, Helen (PR) 1662**B**

lmelie (Smelie?), Agnes (Aberdeen) 1597**A**

Indrie, Margaret (Liberton, Edinburgh) 1661**A**

Inglis, Helen (Auldearn NA) 1662

Inglis, Issobell (Culross FI) 1675**A**

Inglis, Marion (Corstorphine, Edinburgh) 1649

Ingrahame, Marion (EL) 1661

Innes, Barbra (Elgin) 1662**A**

lnnes, Margrat (Aberdeen) 1597

lnsh, Isobel (Irvine RE) 1618**D** pp31-32

Inverkip, Witches p126

Ireland, Bessie (Perth) 1598**A** p23

Ireland, Janet (Dumfries) 1628**B**

Irvine, Witches p32

Irving, Jonet (Logy PR) 1613

lrving, Jonet (Orkney) 1616

Irwing,—— 1613**B**

Isbuster, Helene (Orkney) 1635 p47

Jackson, Margret (Pollockshaws) 1677**A** p137

Jaffray, Grissell (Dundee) 1669**A** p134

Jamesone, Elizabeth (Bo'ness WL) 1624**B**

Jamesonne, Margaret (Ayr) 1658

Jamesoun, Elspett (Bo'Ness WL) 1624**B**

Janet, a witch (Dysart FI) 1626**D**

Jhonestowne, Isobell (St. Andrews) 1614

Jo, Margaret (Musselburgh EL) 1628**B**

Johnestoun, Margaret (Traquair PE) 1629**B**

Johnestoun, Marie (Peebles) 1629**B**

Johnestoun, Marion (Dumfries) 1630**B**

Johnson, Sarah (Perth) 1715**A**

Johnston, Agnes (Pencaitland EL) 1649**B**

Johnston, Bessie (Humbie EL) 1649**B**

Johnston, David (Musselburgh EL) 1661**A**

Johnston, Margaret (Borthwick ML) 1649**B**

Johnstone, Janet (Newbattle ML) 1649**B**

Johnstoun, Andrew (Humbie EL) 1649**B**

Johnstoun, Geilis (Musselburgh EL) 1609**E** p29

Johnstoun, Issobell (Gullane EL) 1661**B**

Johnstoun, Jonet (Queensferry WL) 1615**B**

Jollie, Alesoune (Fala ML) 1596**E**

Jones, ——, daughter of Katherine (Shetland) 1616

Jonking, Margaret (Elgin) 1671

Jonstoun, Elspeth (Methven PR) 1662**B**

Jonstoun, James (Spott EL) 1661**B**

Jonstoun, Katherin (Ormiston EL) 1661**B**

Jonstoun, Malie (Roxburgh) 1662**B**

Jonstoun, Margret (Ayton BE) 1662**B**

Katie or Kaite, the Witch (Edinburgh) 1585**B**

Kay, or Key, Katharine (Newburgh FI) 1653**E**, 1661**B**

Keand or Card, Barbara (Aberdeen) 1590**A**

Keg, Katharine (Alloa CL) 1658

Keill, Mary (RO) 1699**E** p158

Keir, Isabell (Stirling) 1562**C**

Keir, Isobel (Stirling) 1659

Keirie, Jonat (Inverkeithing FI) 1623**B** p34

Keith, Isobel (Keith Marischal EL) 1649**B**

Keith, Sara (Pencaitland/Winton EL) 1628, 1629**B**

Kellie or Collie, Margret (Elgin) 1662**A**

Kelloch, Issobell (Dalgety FI) 1649**A** pp55-56

Kelly, Agnes (Prestonpans EL) 1678**B**

Kelman, Isoble (Old Aberdeen) 1649**E**

Keltie, Margaret (Crook of Devon KN) 1660**B**

Kemp or Kempe, Anna (Dunbar EL) 1661

Kemp, Isobel (Stenton EL) 1659**A**

Kempe, Jonet (Belton, Dunbar EL) c. 1649**B**

Kennedie, Margaret (Ayr) 1629**B**

Kennedy, Margaret (Linlithgow) 1618**B**

Kenoch, Marione (CA) 1655

Kent, Margaret (Inverkeithing FI) 1621**B** p32

Ker, Isobel (Stirling)   1659**E**
Ker, Issobell (EL)   1661
Ker, Issobel (Dalkeith ML)   1661**E**
Ker, Jonet (Gordon BE)   1630**B**
Ker, Jonet (Dalkeith ML)   1661**A**
Ker, Margaret (EL)   1661.
Kerington, Cristian (Prestonpans EL)
   1590
Kerse, Jean (EL)   1662
Kerse, Katherine (ML)   1657
Key, Issobell (St. Andrews)   1666**B**
Key, Katherine (Newburgh FI)   1653
Kinard, Margaret (PR)   1643
King, Ellen (Shetland)   c. 1700**A** p158
King, Jean (Inverkip RE)   1662 p125
Kingow, Margaret (Pittenweem FI)   1643
Kinnell, Margaret (Inverkeithing FI)
   1623**B**
Kirk, Agnes (Dunfermline FI)   1643**A**
Kirk, George (PR)   1613**B**
Kirk, James (Stirling)   1658**D**, 1659**E**
Kirk, Johnne (PR)   1613**B**
Kirkland, Agnes (Tyninghame EL)
   1650**A**
Kirkland, Elspeth (Aberdour FI)   1681**E**
Kirkpatrik, Agnes (DU)   1630**B**
Kirktoun, Adam (Jedburgh)   1649**B**
Kirktoun, Katharine (EL)   1629,
   1630**B**
Kirktoun, Margret (Langton BE)   1662**B**
Kirkwood, Jeane (Samuelston EL)   1662
Kirkwood, Margaret (Haddington EL)
   1677**D** p134
Knarstoun, James (Orkney)   1633
Knight, Helen (Grange, Aberdeen)
   1629**B**
Knok, William (Dalkeith ML)   1650
Knox, Agnes (Bathgate WL)   1617**B**
Knox, Bessie (EL)   1661
Knox, Elspeth (Peaston EL)   1678**D**
Knox, Jean (Ormiston EL)   1661**B**
Knox or Knock, Maig (Largs AY)   1622**B**
Kowie, Janet (Elgin)   1645
Kylie, ——, a witch (Auldearn NA) 1662
Kyneir, Thomas (Brechin AN)   1650**C**

Kyninmonth, Eduart (Angus?)   1577
Kynnell, Margaret (Inverkeithing FI)
   1623 p34

Lachlane, Jeane (Carnwath LA)
   1643, 1644**A**
Lacost, George (Newmilne EL)   1662
Lacost, George (Waltoun EL)   1662
Laidlaw, Janet (Tweedhopefoot BE)
   1649**B**
Laidlaw, Mali or Marion (Crawford LA)
   1650
Laidlaw, Marion (Stainhope)   1649**B**
Laidly, Andrew (Edinburgh)   1671**E**
Laing, Beatrix (Pittenweem FI)   1705**E**
   pp159-162
Laing, Bettie (Pittenweem FI)   1709
Laing, Jannet (Glasgow)   1700**E**
Laing, Margaret (Lasswade ML)   1678**B**
Lair, Elspet (Auldearn NA)   1662
Laird, Margaret (Kilmalcolm RE)   1698**E**
Lamb, Bessie (EL)   1662
Lamb, Mamie (EL)   1662
Lamont, Marie or Mary, known as Clouts
   (Inverkip RE)   1662
   pp125-126, 128
Lancashire, Witches 1633 pp47, 204
Landrok, Patrik (Wemyss FI)   1626**B**
Lang, Margaret (Paisley)   1697**A**
   pp156, 191
Langlandis, David (WL)   1624**B**
Lason, Agnes (Queensferry WL)   1649**B**
Lauchtie, Marie (Thurso CA)   1626**B**
Laudar, Helen (Crook of Devon KN)
   1662**B**
Lauder, Helen (Dalcove)   1662**B**
Lauder, Helene (Prestonpans EL)   1590
Lauder, Issobell (Prestonpans EL)   1590
Lauder, Margaret (Edinburgh)   1643**A**
Laurie, Johne (Craigie AY)   1659
Laurymer, Margrat (Ayr)   1658
Lauson, Helen (Haddington EL)   1649**B**
Lauson, Issobell (Ayton BE)   1662**B**
Lauson, Jonet (Ayton BE)   1662**B**

Lauson, Margret (Selkirk)   1662**B**
Law, Anna (PR)   1662**B**
Lawder, Bessie (Haddington EL)   1629**B**
Lawder, Katharine (EL)   1629, 1630**B**
Lawrie, Marion (Humbie EL)   1649**B**
Lawson, Elizabeth (EL)   c. 1649**B**
Lawson, Meg (Selkirk)   c. 1700**A**   p158
Lawson, Nicol (Pittenweem FI)   1705,
     1709   p161
Lawsone, Elspeth (Haddington EL)   1661
Laying, Helen (Peaston EL)   1678**A**
Laying, Jean (AB)   1670
Layland, Marrione (Orkney)   1633**A**
     pp44-45, 172
Layng, Issobell (Dumbarton)   1677**B**
Leask, Oliver (Orkney)   1616
Ledy, Alexander (Auldearn NA)   1662
Ledy, Walter (Auldearn NA)   1662
Lees, Catie (Lauder)   1630**D**
Leiges, Marion (Ayr)   1658
Leishman, John (Strikefield)   1649**B**
Leisk, Cristane (Orkney)   1643
Leisk, Jonat (Aberdeen)   1597**E**
Leitch, Issobell (Inverkeithing FI)   1649
Leithame, Katharine (Selkirk)   1628**B**
Leslie, Beatrix (Newbattle ML)   1661**A**
Leslie, Issobell (AB)   1626**B**
Leslie, Williame (Crichie AB)   1590**D**
Letch, Margret (Inverkip RE)   1662**B**
     p125
Lewers, Marion (Kirkcudbright)   1658**E**
Lewing, Marioun (Orkney)   1615
Lewingstoun, Christian (Leith, Edinburgh)
     1597**A**
Leyis, or Lees, Elspet (Aberdeen)
     1596**C**   p20
Leyis, John (Aberdeen)   1596**C**   p20
Leyis, Jonet (Aberdeen)   1596**C**   p20
Leyis, Thomas (Aberdeen)   1596**A**   p20
Leyis, Violat (Aberdeen)   1596**C**   p20
Liddell, Agnes (Prestonpans EL)   1628**B**
Liddell, Archibald (Eyemouth BE) . 1624,
     1629**B**
Liddell, Janet (Eyemouth BE)   1629**B**
Liddell, Jonet (Pencaitland EL)   1662

Liddell, Katharine (Prestonpans EL)
     1678**E**   p137
Liddell, Margaret (Lasswade ML)   1678**B**
Liddell, Margret (Newburgh FI)   1661**B**
Lillie, Marion, known as the Rigwoody
     Witch (Spott EL)   1698**A**
     pp157-158, 179
Linday, Magnus (Orkney)   1616
Lindsay, James (Paisley)   1697**A**   p156
Lindsay, Janet (Eastbarns EL)   1629
Lindsay, John (Paisley)   1697**A**   p156
Lindsay, Jonet (Stirling)   1562**C**
Lindsay, Marion (Haddington EL)   1662
Lintoun, Patrick (Peebles)   1629**B**
Lithgow, Mali (Skirling PE)   1641
Litstar, Jennet (Innerwick EL)   1612-13**B**
Litster, Margaret (Crook of Devon KN)
     1662**A**
Littill, Bessie (Longniddry EL)   1628**B**
Little, Bessie (Glasgow)   1700**E**
Little, Marion (South Queensferry WL)
     1643-44, 1644**A**
Locan, Margaret (Edinburgh)   1683**E**
Loch, Agnes (Musselburgh EL)   1661**A**
Loche, Margaret (Eyemouth BE)   1629**B**
Lochequoir, Jonet (St. Andrews)   1595**A**
Lockhart, Christian (Haddington EL)
     1679**D**
Lockhart, Sir James of Lee and Carnwath
     (AY) before 1629**C** pp37-38, 193
Lockie, Jonet (Carnwath LA)   1644**B**
Logan, Marg (Crichton ML)   1679
Logan, Marion (Tranent EL)   1659**A**
     Appendix 3 p207
Logane, Jonett (Prestonpans EL)   1590
Logie, Bessic (Inverkcithing FI)   1623**B**
     pp33-34
Logie, Catherine or Kathrin (South
     Queensferry WL)   1643-44,
     1644**E**
Lorimer, Catharin (Ayr)   1683**E**
Losk, Jonet (Ayr)   1683**E**
Loudon, Janet (Inverkip RE)   1649
Love, Janet (Greenock and Renfrew)
     1632**D**

Lovie, Janet (Brechin AN) 1639
Lowis, Margaret (Peaston EL) 1678**A**
Lowrie, Janet (South Queensferry WL)
  1643-44**A**
Lowrie, Jonet (EL) 1662
Lowrie, Marioun (Tranent EL) 1659
Lowrie, Patrick (Hailie AY) 1605**A** p27
Lucas, Jonat (Aberdeen) 1597**C**
Luddes, Helen (Craigford ST) 1629**B**
Lukell, Thomas (SU) 1655**E**
Lumsdeall, George (Innerleithen PE)
  1661**B**
Lumsden, Margaret (Aberdeen) 1630**B**
  p39
Lumsden, Marioun (Leith, Edinburgh)
  1632**E** p42
Luost or Lacost, Bessie (Stenton EL)
  1659**A**
Lyall, Catharin (Montrose AN) 1649
Lyall, Catharin (Brechin AN) 1650
Lyell, Henrie (Wick) 1655
Lyell, Marjorie (Jedburgh) 1613**B**
Lyes, Janet (Wedderlie) 1649**B**
Lyil, Jon (EL) 1662
Lyis, Margaret (Galashiels BE) 1649**B**
Lyis, Marioun (Galashiels BE) 1649**B**
Lylburne, Jeane (WL) 1624**B**
Lyle, Alexander (Glasgow) 1700**E**
Lyle, Margaret (Musselburgh EL) 1661**A**
Lyon, Beatrix (Inverkip RE) 1662**B**
Lyndsay, Jonet (Prestonkirk EL) 1593**E**
Lynn, Marion (Tranent EL) 1659**A**
  Appendix 3 p207
Lyon, Janet (Inverkip RE) 1671

McAlester, Giddoch (Boyne) [No Date]
McAlester, Marioune Neynnane Adame,
  known as Losky Loncart (RO)
  1577, 1589 p12
McAllexander,——, wife of Soirle (Bute)
  1662**B**
McAngus, William (SU) 1655**E**
McBirnie, Janet (Lanark) 1650**E**
McCalzeane, Ewfame (Prestonpans EL/
  Cliftonhall ML) 1590, 1591**A**

pp15, 17-18, 195
McCall, Marion (Mauchline, Ayr) 1671**C**
McCan, Issobell (Bute) 1662**B**
McChereich, Donald (SU) 1655**E**
McCheyne, Katherinc (DU) 1630**B**
McClean, Donald (Strathglass IN) 1662**B**
McClean, Hectour (Strathglass IN) 1662**B**
McClean, Jonet (Strathglass IN) 1662**B**
McClean, Margret (Strathglass IN) 1662**B**
McConachie, Jonat (Rothesay) 1662
McConel, Malcolm (Inverness) 1655**C**
McConchy (Vic Conchy), Mary Nein Al-
  laster (Conveth IN) 1662**B**
McConneilear, John 1590
McConneilear,——, wife of above, 1590
McConnochie, Margaret, wife of Johnne
  (AB) 1626
McCoskrie, Rosina (Kirkcudbright) 1644
McEan (Ninian) Dowie Vic Finley, Baike
  (Conveth IN) 1662**B**
McEan (Nean Ean) Duy Vic Conchie Vic
  Goune, Cormule (Conveth IN)
  1662**B**
McEan (Vic Ean), Cristian Neil (Nein)
  Ferquhar (Conveth IN) 1662**B**
McEan (Nein Ean) Cheill, Jonet (Conveth
  IN) 1662**B**
McEan (Ninian) Ean Vic Ean Culleam
  (Vic Connell, Vic William), Kathrin
  (Strathglass IN) 1662**B** p126
McEan, Kathrin Nein Ferquhar (Conveth
  IN) 1662**B**
McEvoch, Thomas McKane Moire McAl-
  lane (RO) 1590**A**
McEwan, Elspeth (Dalry AY) [No Date]
McEwen (Vic Ewin), Cristian Nein Ferqu
  har (Conveth IN) 1662**B**
McEwen, Elspet (Kirkcudbright) 1698**A**
  pp156-157
McEwen (Nyn Owan) Vic Omnoch,
  Kathrin (Conveth IN) 1662**B**
McFersane, Helen (Ayr) 1629
McFinlay (Nean Finlay) Vic Ean Vic
  Homas, Beak (Conveth IN) 1662**B**
  p126

McFinlay Vic Comes, Mary (Conveth IN) 1662**B**

McFinley (Vic Finley), Beak Nein Ean Duy (Conveth IN) 1662**B**

McGhie, Neveine 1590**C**

McGibbone, Andro (Inverness) 1655**D**

McGill, Catherene (Prestonpans EL) 1590

McGill, Gilbert (Prestonpans EL) 1590**A**

McGill, Johnne (Prestonpans EL) 1590**A**

McGillichoan, Janet (Fortrose RO) 1630**B**

McGilliewareycht-dame, Williame, 1590**A**

McGilliphadrick (Nein Giliphadrick), Muriall Duy (Conveth IN) 1662**B**

McGillivorich, Agnes (Nairn) 1662**B**

McGillivray, William (RO) 1590 p12

McGowane, Janet (Kirkcudbright) 1644

McGowane, Janet (Dumfries) 1659**A** p117

McGown, (Nein Goune), Mary (Conveth IN) 1662**B**

McGregor, John (Greenock) 1676**C**

McGueirle, Patrick (Midcalder ML) 1592

McGuffock, Margaret (Kirkcudbright) 1672**D**

McHuistan, ——, a witch (Thurso) 1718-19**D** p165

McIllivein, Margret (Bute) 1662**B**

McIlmartin, Jonet, daughter of Alexander (Bute) 1662 p126

McIllwhichill ,—— (Ardoch PR) 1622**B**

McIlney, Grissel (Dumfries) 1671

McIlvorie, John (Kinross) 1643

McIncaruch, Marioune (RO) 1590

McInlay, Margaret (Dumbarton) 1650**A**

McInnes (Vic Innish), Mary Muarn (Conveth IN) 1662**B**

McIntoshe, Marie Nein Eane Eir (RO) 1629**B**

McIvers, More Nain Duy (IN) 1669**B**

McKaw, Isobel (Kingarth, Bute) 1649

McKaw, Isobell (Rothesay) 1662**B**

McKaw, Patrick (Rothesay) 1662**B**

McKendley, Issobell (PR) 1662**A**

McKendrick, Thomas McAllan (RO) 1577**A** p12

McKendrig, Janet (Dumfries) 1659**A** p117

McKennan, Jonnet (WI) 1644**B**

McKenzie, Kenneth, the Brahan Seer (Fortrose RO) 1662**A** p131-133, 195

McKenzie, Margret (Greenock) 1662**B** p125, 195

McKeoner, Janet (Penninghame WI) 1707**A**

McKessock, Issobell (Rhynd PR) 1662**A**

McKie, Issobell (Stirling) 1611**B**

McKie, John (Craigie AY) 1658

McKirdy, Lachlan (Kingarth Bute) 1649

McKirdy, Margret (Bute) 1649

McKnight, Jennet (Dumfries) 1659

McKulkie, Donald (RO) 1699**B**

McLintok, Marioun (Dumbarton) 1628

McMuldritche, Janet (Dumfries) 1671**A** p136

McMurdoch, Janet (Dumfries) 1671**A**

McMurich, Margaret (Dumbarton) 1650**A**

McMurray, Janet (Dumfries) 1703**C**

McNab, Marione (Stirling) 1649

McNair, Janet (Barloch ST) 1677**B**

McNairn, John (Penninghame WI) 1706

McNarin, Mary (Penninghame WI) 1705**C**

McNaucht, Isobel (Auchlang KI) 1630**B**

McNaught,——, wife of John (Kirkcudbright) 1644

McNeill, Jonet (Rothesay) 1662**B**

McNickell, Margaret (Rothesay) 1662**B**

McNicol, Janet (Bute) 1673**A**

McNicoll, Issobell (Rothesay) 1662**B**

McNicoll, Jonet (Rothesay), 1662

McNillan, John (RO) 1590 p12

McNish, Baik (Conveth IN) 1662**B**

McNish, Margaret (Crook of Devon KN) 1662**B**

McNiven, Catherine (Crieff PR) .1615**A**

Maconachie, Janet (Botary AB) 1643

McPhail (Nein Phaill), Cristian (Conveth

IN) 1662**B**

McPhail (Vic Phaill), Donald (Conveth IN) 1662**B**

McPhee, James (Kingarth, Bute) 1670**E**

McQueen, John (Edinburgh) 1684**C**

McQuicken, ——, a witch (Inverness) 1695**A** p155

McRae, Marion (Ayr) 1683**E**

McReadie, John (BE) 1628**B**

McRobert, Janet (Dumfries) 1701**C**

McRorie, ——, a witch (Inverness) 1695**A** p155

McRory (Ninian Rory) Mie Buy, Jonet (Conveth IN) 1662**B**

Mactargett or McTaggart, Catharin (Dunbar EL) 1688**B** pp139-153, 184, 186

McTeir, Catherine (Dundonald AY) 1602**D**

McTeir, Katherine (AY) 1605

Macwatt, Malie (Culter LA) 1640**E**

McWilliam, John (Dumbarton) 1656**A** p115

McWilliam, Margret (Bute) 1645, 1649, 1662**B** p126

McWilliame, John (Dumbarton) 1650**A**

Macause, Marion (Perth) 1598**A** p23

Mackbeath, Marion (Canisbay CA) 1652

Mackskinning, Jonnet (Ayr) 1658

Maglene, Jonet (Tranent EL) 1622**B**

Maguate, Marion (Coulternisbit LA) [No Date]

Mairshell, Katharine (PE) 1629**B**

Mairtine, Margaret (Inverkeithing FI) 1641

Maislet, Margaret (EL) 1661**B**

Maisson, Jonet (Samuelston EL) 1661

Maitland, Meg (Tranent EL) 1659**B**

Major, Katharine (Dundrennan KI) 1630

Makbeith, Elspet (Auldearn NA) 1662

Make, Bessie (Haddington EL) 1629**B**

Makhomie, Elspet (Auldearn NA) 1662

Makkie, Helene (Aberdeen) 1597**D**

Malcolme, Isobell (Moray) 1643

Malcolme, Issobell (Botary AB) 1637**E**

Malcolme, Steven (ST) 1628**B**

Malcolmie, Patrik (Botary AB) 1644

Man, Andro (Aberdeen) 1597**A** p21

Man, Archibald (Auldearn NA) 1662

Man, Jennet (Auldearn NA) 1662

Man, Jonet (Stenton EL) 1659**D**

Man, Mariorie (Auldearn NA). 1662

Manderston, Lady (Duns) 1629**E** pp193-194

Manners,——, wife of Archibald (EL) 1662

Mansoun, Hucheoun (Caithness) 1629**B**

Mar, Jonet (Collessie FI) 1662**B**

Mar, Violat (Kildeis) 1577

Markirdon, Janet (Nether Williamson ML) 1649**B**

Marnow, Marion (Brechin AN) 1619**A**

Marr, Isobell (Inverkeithing FI) 1643**D** p63

Martha,——, (Tranent EL) 1659

Marshall, Issobell (Rhynd PR) 1662**A**

Marten, Jean, known as Over-The-Dyke-With-It (Auldearn NA) 1662 p128

Martin, Jonet (PR) 1662**A**

Martin, Jeane (Dunbar EL) 1662

Martin, William (Haddington EL) 1662**B**

Martine, Marion (DU) 1630

Marwick, Cirstain (Orkney) 1643 p52

Mason, Bessie (St. Andrews) 1644

Mather, Issobell (Langton BE) 1662**B**

Matheson, Jonnet (Gilmerton, Edinburgh) 1661

Mathesoun, Margaret (Preston EL) 1629**A**

Mathesoun, William (Peebles) 1629**B**

Mathie, Barbara (Prestonpans EL) 1628**B**

Mathie, Helen (Liberton, Edinburgh) 1661

Mathie, Jean (Liberton, Edinburgh) 1661

Mathie, Jonet (Pollockshaws) 1677**A** p137

Mathie, Margaret (Abernethy PR) 1662**B**

Mathiesone, William (Peebles) 1629

Mawer, Issobell (Wemyss FI) 1626**B**

Maxwell, Elizabeth (Dumfries) 1650

Maxwell, Margaret (Dumfries) 1629, 1630**D**

Maxwell, Robert (Little Fordell FI)
  1649A pp55-56
May, Cristian (Torryburn FI) 1666B
Mearns, William (Eyemouth/Ayton BE)
  1634D p46
Meason, Jonet (Alloa CL) 1658
Meikkie, Patrick (EL) c.1649E
Meikle, David (Samuelston EL) 1662
Meldrum, Agnes (Monifieth AN) 1628C
Melros, Janet (Chattill BE) 1629B
Melross or Mewross, Margaret (Pinkerton,
  Dunbar EL) 1624, c.1628A p37
Meluill, Agnes (St. Andrews) 1588,
  1595A
Melvill, Alison (Collessie FI) 1662B
Melvill, Christiane (Abercorn WL)
  1644A
Memphersoun, Katharine (RO) 1629
Menteith, Issobell (Aberdeen) 1596D p21
Merchant, Marat (Brechin AN) 1650A
Mergie, ——, a fugitive (Aberdeen) 1597
Merschell, Margaret (Inverkeithing FI)
  1623B p34
Mertin, Jonet (PR) 1662B
Meslet, Sara (Foulden BE) 1629B
Methven, George (Methven's Coble PR)
  1601B
Methven, Hew (Methven's Coble PR)
  1601B
Meving, Cristian (Ayr) 1658
Meyne, Bessie (Selkirk) 1629B
Michell, Christen (Aberdeen) 1597A
Midleinst, Adam (Jedburgh) 1649B
Millar, Elspeth (Collessie FI) 1662B
Millar, Isobel (Dunfermline FI) 1643A
Millar, Issobell (Longniddry EL) 1628B
Millar, Jenet (Kirkliston ML) 1661
Millar, Jonet (Alloa CL) 1658
Millar, Jonet (Kirkliston ML) 1661,
  (Dalkeith ML) 1661
Millar, Mary (Kirkcudbright), 1698B
Miller, Christen (Aberdeen) 1597A
Miller, Isobel (Dunfermline FI) 1643A
Miller, Janet or Jean (Glasgow) 1629B
Miller, Janet (Dundrennan KR) 1656

Miller, Jonet (Dumfries) 1658A
Miller, Jonet (Tullibodie, Alloa) 1658
Miller, Jonet (Dumfries) 1671A
Millikene, Marion (Craigie AY) 1658
Milnetowne, George (Samuelston EL)
  1649, 1661B
Miltoun, George (EL) c.1649B
Minto, Janet (Selkirk) 1629B
Mirrilies,—— (EL) 1662
Mitchell, Bessie (Crichton ML) 1630B
Mitchell, Christen (Aberdeen) 1596A
Mitchell, Issobell (Inverkeithing FI) 1649
Mitchell, Janet (Cardross DN) 1630B
Mitchell, Janet (Kilmenny FI) 1646E
Mitchell, Marie (Kilmenny FI) 1646E
Mitchell, Jeane (Elgin) 1644
Mitchell, Katherine (Culross FI) c.1641A
Mitchell, Margaret (EL) 1629B
Mitchell, Marion (Leith, Edinburgh)
  1628B
Mitchell, Mary (Barloch ST) 1677B
Mitchell, Thomas (Barloch ST) 1677B
Moffat, Isobel (Dumfries) 1630., 1631B
Moffat, Lillias (LA) 1650
Moffat, Marion (LA) 1650
Moffatt, Bessie (Dalkeith ML) 1661B
Moffatt, Margret (Spott EL) 1661B
Mogersland, Catheren (Ayr) 1658
Moinness, Erss [Irish] Elspett (Aberdeen)
  1597A
Moir, Donald (Inverness) 1603A
Moir, Donald (Kilernan RO) 1696-97D
  p251
Moir, Janet (Tain) 1630B
Moir, Siackc Nine Dod (Tain) 1630B
Moitis,—, wife of George (Prestonpans
  EL) 1590
Molland, Alicia (Exeter) 1685A p154
Mongomerie, Marjorie (Moray) 1611B
  p29
Monro, Barbara (RO) 1699C
Monro, Hector (RO) 1590E pp12, 193
Monro, Issobell (Edinburgh) 1656
Monro, Issobell (Strathspey) 1661B
Monro. Margaret (RO) 1699C p158

Montgomerie, Catherine (Irvine)   1650
Moore, Katharine (Bute)   1662**B**
Moore,——, son of Katharine   1662**B**
Moore, Margaret (Kingarth Bute)   1649
Moorhead, Helen (Dumfries)   1659**A** p117
Mordington, Witches p111
More, Isobel (Auldearn NA)   1662   p129
Moreis, Easter (Foulden BE)   1629**C**
Morison, Bessie (Bowden RX)   1662**B**
Morison, Christian (Stirling)   1672**D**
Morison, Jonet (Inverkip RE)   1662**B**
Morisone, Mary (Glasgow)   1709**E**
Morisoune, Jonet (Bute)   1662**B**
Morris, Grissel (Dunfermline FI)   1643**A**
Mortoune, Agnes (Ayr)   1658
Mosse, Katharine (Ledgerwood BE)
      1628**B**
Mountgomerie, Jeanet (Renfrew)   1650**A**
Mowat, Alexander (Turriff AB)   1627**B**
Mowat, Gilbert (Wick)   1655
Mowat, Elspeth (Liberton, Edinburgh)
      1660E
Mowbray, Janet (South Queensferry WL)
      1643-44**E**
Mudie, Beatrix (Inverkeithing FI)   1621**B**
      p32
Mudie, Lizzie or Elizabeth (Haddington
      EL)   1677**A** p134
Muir, Jonet (Inverkip RE)   1662**B**
Muircone, Agnes (Elgin)   1641
Muirhead, Katherine, 1593**A**
Muirhead, Margaret (ML)   1628**B**
Mullikine, Agnes (Dunfermline FI)
      1563**C** p11
Mun, Jonet (Dumbarton)   1677**B**
Munk, Annas (Dysart FI)   1626**B**
Murdoch, Marion (Perth)   1615
Murdoche, John (Dunfermline FI)   1649
Murdock, Jonnet (Craigie AY)   1658
Mure, James (Minihagan)   1609**D**,
      1610**A**
Mure, Marion (Leith, Edinburgh)   1632**A**
      p42
Muresone, Agnes (Elgin)   1644
Murie, Agnes (Crook of Devon KN)

1662**A**
Murray,——, a witch (Skirling PE)   1659
Murray, Agnes (Haddington EL)
      c.1649**B**
Murray, Grissell (Bowden RX)   1662**B**
Murray, Issobell (Haddington; Penston
      EL)   1649**B**
Murray, James (Innerleithen PE)   1662**B**
Murray, Jonet (Burntisland FI)   1649**B**
Murray, Margret (Spynie MO)   1646   p56
Murray, Margaret (Humbie EL)   1649**B**
Murray, Thomas (Inverkeithing FI)   1631
Murray, William (Leith, Edinburgh)   1599
Murray, ----, wife of Nicol (Prestonpans
      EL) 1590
Murrey, Patrick (Haddington EL)   1630**B**
Murriache, Jonnet (Dunblane ST)   1615**B**
Mutche, Meriore (Aberdeen)   1597**A** p21
Muttoun, Cummer (Aberdeen)   1626**B**
Mwere or Mure, Helene (Tranent EL)
      1622**B**
Myles, Margaret (Edinburgh)   1702**A**
      p158
Myllar, Johnne (PR)   1588**D**
Mylne, Barbara (Edinburgh)   1661**A**
Myrton, Margaret (St Andrews)   [No
      Date]

Nairn, Ane (Prestonpans? EL)   1591
Naismith, Agnes (Paisley)   1697**A**
      pp155-156
Nakoch, Margaret (Wick)   1655
Napier, Barbara (Edinburgh)   1590**E**
      pp15, 18-19
Nethomas, Mary (Rothesay Bute)   1673**A**
Neil, Bessie (Crook of Devon KN) 1662**A**
Neill, Janet (Dumbarton)   1628, 1629**B**
Neill or Niel, John (BE)   1630**B**;
      (Tweedmouth BE)   1630, 1631**A**
      pp172, 193
Neilsoun, Elspet (Dysart FI)   1626**B**
Neinechat, Gradoche (RO)   1629**B**
Nemo, Agnes (Liberton, Edinburgh)
      1656, 1658
Nesbit, Alison (Coldingham BE)   1698**C**

p157

Nesbit, Elie (Hilton BE) 1630**B**

Neveing, Bessie (Renfrew) 1658

Neveing, Bessie (Lanark) 1658

Neville, Nic (St. Andrews) 1569**A**

Neving, Alison (Dysart FI) 1630**B**

Neving,——, a woman (Saltoun EL) 1662

Nicole,—— (Culyeasetter, Shetland) 1603

Nicinnarich, Mary (Fortrose RO) [No Date]

Nicoll, Issobell (Auldearn NA) 1662

Nicoll, Margaret (Banff) 1636

Nicoll, William (Ayr) 1618**B**

Nicolson, Helen (EL) 1662

Nicolsone, Jonet (Prestonkirk/Nether Hailes EL) 1649**A**

Nicolsone, Margaret (Dunblane ST) 1629**E**

Nicolsoun, Jonett (Prestonpans EL) 1590

Nicolsoun, Margaret (Birgham BE) 1615**B**

Nicolsolin, Marioun (Prestonpans EL) 1590

Nicoson, Bessie (Liberton, Edinburgh) 1661**A**

Nidrie, Jonnet (Gilmerton, Edinburgh) 1661

Niklerich,—— 1643

Nisbet, Alison (Hilton BE) 1632**A** pp43, 45

Nisbett, Margret (Spott EL) 1661**B**

Nisbit, Anna (Tranent/Elphinstone EL) 1659

Nisbitt, Bessie (BE) 1630**B**

Nisbitt, David (BE) 1629**B**

Nishie, Elspet (Auldearn NA) 1662

North Berwick, Witches, pp13, 16, 18-19, 126, 139, 171, 173, 193, 195 Appendix 2, p203

Nymmo, Violet (Haddington EL) 1662

Og, Margaret (Aberdeen) 1597**A**

Ogg, Margaret (Insch AB) 1650**D**

Ogilvy, Margaret (Perth) 1715**A**

Oige, Issobell (Aberdeen) 1597**A**

Oliphant, Dorathie (Kirkcaldy FI) 1604**C**

Olipher, Jeane (Jedburgh) 1649**B**

Oliver, Margaret (Prestonpans EL) 1628**B**

Olsone, Margaret (Thurso), 1718-19**A** pp164-165

Olvertheu, Marc (Peaston EL) 1649**B**

Osborne, Maggy (Ayr) c.1650**A** pp107-109, 176

Osborne, Ruth (Tring) 1751* pp167-168

Osborne,——, husband of Ruth, 1751* pp167-168

Osit, Rossina (Inverkeithing FI) 1649

Oswald, Katharine (Niddrie, Edinburgh) 1629**A** pp38-39

Page, Issobell (Newburgh FI) 1662**B**

Pain, Bessie (Kirkcudbright) 1671

Paine, Bessie (Dumfries?) 1671

Paistoun, Jonet (Dalkeith ML) 1661

Pardoun, Marion, known as the Witch of Hillswick (Shetland) 1644 p174

Paris, Elspet (WL) 1624**B**

Parker,—— (Edinburgh) 1646

Partill, Agnes (Dalkeith ML) 1661

Paterson, Barbara (Drumlanrig DU) 1607**A**

Paterson, Christian (Hermiston EL) 1631**A** pp41-42

Paterson, Ellesoun (Dumfries) 1607**A**

Paterson, Janet (Inverkip RE) 1649

Paterson, John (Glasgow) 1700**E**

Paterson, Jonet (Alloa CL) 1658

Paterson, Margaret (Samuelston EL) 1662

Paterson, Margaret .(Dumbarton) 1677**B**

Paterson, Marjory (Dalkeith ML) 1650

Patersone, Agnes (Fisherrow/Musselburgh EL) 1661

Patersone, Barbara (Hunterston AY) 1649**B**

Patersone, Christian (Newbattle ML) 1661**A** p123

Patersone, George (Melrose) 1662**D**

Patersone, Janet (Humbie EL) 1649**B**

236

Patersone, Marjorie (Crail)   1625**B**
Patersonne, Agnes (Ayr)   1658
Patersoun, Bartie (Newbattle ML)
   1607**A** pp27-28, 177
Patersoun, Janet (Cousland ML)   1630**B**
Patersoun, Margaret (Longnewton RX)
   1629**B**
Patersoune, Marie (Prestonpans EL)   1590
Paton, Bessie (Alloa CL)   1658**A**
Paton, Janet (Crook of Devon KN)
   1662**A**
Paton, Janet *secundus* (Crook of Devon
   KN) 1662**A**
Paton, Jonet (Peaston EL)   1649
Paton, Thomas (Dumfries)   1650**A**
Patoun, Jonet (Eastwood, Glasgow)
   1663**B**
Patoune, Margaret (Ayr)   1658
Patowne, John (Dysart FI)   1637
Pattersone, Mailie (Carnwath LA)   1644**B**
Paull, Bessie (Aberdeen)   1597
Paull, Bessie (Cromar AB)   1590**D**
Peacock, Isabell (Dunfermline FI)   1649
Pedie, Jonnet (Wemyss FI)   1626**B**
Peebles, Marion (Shetland)   1644**A**
Peirsoun, Alesoun (Byrehill)   1588**A**
Penman, Gideon (Edinburgh)   1678**B**
   p137
Pennie, Hellie (Aberdeen)   1597**A**
Penny, Kathren (Alloa CL)   1658**A**
Pennycuick, Janet (Penicuik ML)   1629**A**
Peterkin, Bessie (Auldearn NA)   1662
Petersone, Patrick (Shetland)   1616
Phenick, Agnes (Cousland ML)   1630**B**
Phenick or Phinnick, John (Cousland ML)
   1630**B**
Philip, John (Banff)   1631**A** pp40-41
Philp, Margret (Newburgh FI)   1662**B**
Phin, Margaret (Haddington EL)   1677**B**
Pilmure, Anna (Samuelston EL)   1661,
   1662**B**
Pipper,——, (Saltoun EL)   1662
Pipper,——, wife of above   1662
Pitathrie, Lady- see under Henderson,
   Margaret

Pittendreich, Agnes, (Crook of Devon KN)
   1662**E**
Pittenweem, Witches p159
Player, Bigs (Carrington ML)   1649**B**
Pogavie, Agnes (Liberton, Edinburgh)
   1661**A** p123
Polwart, Margaret (Coldingham BE)   1698
   p157
Poock (Pollok), Cristine (Orkney)   1643**B**
Pook, Janet (Falkirk WL)   1590
Portar of Seton, wife of (Preston-
   pans EL)   1590
Porteous, Margaret (Liberton, Edinburgh)
   1661**E**
Porteous, Marion (Preston EL)   1629**B**
Porteous, ——, daughter of Molphrie
   (Scalloway, Shetland)   1673**B**
Portour, Kathren (Forfar AN)   1661-62
Pothif, Effie (Liberton, Edinburgh)   1661
Pringall, Alesoun (Hirsell BE)   1629**B**
Pringle, Margaret (Peaston EL)   1649**B**
Pringle, Margaret (Bo'ness WL)   1679**A**
   p137
Proffit, Bessie (BE)   1662**B**
Propter, Johnne (Ellon AB)   1626**B**
Provost, Margaret (Fortrose RO)   [No
   Date]
Pryde, Agnes (Cupar FI)   1656
Pryde, Agnes (Perth)   1656**E**
Pumphersone, Janet (Liberton, Edinburgh)
   1661
Purcell, Bessie (Edinburgh)   1631**B**
Purdie, Annie (Newhall, Penicuik ML)
   1629**B**
Purdie, Barbara (Haddington EL)   1649**B**
Purdie, Christian (Penicuik ML)   1662**E**
Purdie, Katherine (Niddrie, Edinburgh)
   1661
Purdie, Maly (Skirling PE)   1659
Purdie, Marion (Edinburgh)   1684**D** p138
Pursell, Janet (Preston, Edinburgh)
   1629**B**
Pyper, Jannet (Thurso)   1718-19
Pyper's Mother, The (Dirleton EL)
   1649**A**

Quarie, Agnes (Roxburgh) 1662**B**
Quarrier, Agnes (Aberdour FI) 1622**B**
Quheitt, Mareoun (Samuelston EL) 1661
Quhite, Marioun (AB) 1626**B**
Quhyte, Helene (Prestonpans EL) 1590
Quhyte, Isobel (Lanark) 1629**B**
Quhytelaw, Alexander (Prestonpans EL) 1590

Rae, Grissell (Kirkcudbright) 1672**D**
Raeburn, Marion (Haddington EL) 1662
Raich, Issobell (Lauder BE) 1649**B**
Ramage, Sarah (Niddrie, Edinburgh) 1661
Rammage, Margaret [No Date]**E**
Ramsay, Agnes (PR) 1662**B**
Ramsay, Bessie (Mortonhall, Edinburgh) 1677
Ramsay, Isobal (Dalkeith ML) 1661**A**
Ramsay, John (Niddrie, Edinburgh) 1661
Ramsay, Jon (Ormiston EL) 1661
Ramsay, Margaret (Leith, Edinburgh) 1644
Ramsay, Marioun (Leith, Edinburgh) 1644
Ramsay, ----, wife of John (Prestonpans EL) 1590
Ranie, Margaret (Orkney) 1643**B**
Rankein, Agnes (Prestonpans EL) 1628**B**
Rankin, Margret (Inverkip RE) 1662**B** p125
Rankin, Margret *secundus* (Inverkip RE) 1662**B** p125
Ranking, Marion (Prestonpans? EL) 1591
Rannald, Katharene (Kilpont) 1622**B**
Rannaldsone, Elspeth (Burntisland FI) 1649**B**
Rannick, Agnes (Clerkington EL) 1629**B**
Rassa, Barbara (RO) 1699**B**
Rattray, George (Inverness) 1706**A** p163
Rattray, Lachlan (Inverness) 1706**A** p163
Ray, John (Dumfries) 1630, 1631**B**
Reamy, Isobel (Brechin AN) 1650**D**
Reany, Jonnet (Dunfermline FI) 1628**B**
Reauche, Margrat (Aberdeen) 1597

Redmond, Molly (Minnigaff KI) 1702**C**
Reid, Annabill (Glasgow) 1700**E**
Reid, Christian (Aberdeen) 1596**A** p21
Reid, Elspeth (PR) 1662**A**
Reid, Helen (EL) c.1649**E**
Reid, Helen (Samuelston EL) 1662
Reid, Issabell (Ayr) 1683**E**
Reid, James (Musselburgh EL) 1603**A**
Reid, Janet (Prestonpans EL) 1628**B**
Reid, Janet (Alloa CL) 1658
Reid, John (Paisley) 1697**D** p156
Reid, Jonet (Orkney) 1643**A**
Reid, Jonnet (Ayr) 1630**B**
Reid, Jonnet (Ayr) 1658
Reid, Margaret (Ayr) 1596**C**
Reid, Margaret (Carnwath LA) 1644**B**
Reid, Margaret (Kirkcaldy FI) [No Date]
Reid, Tom (Pinkie, Musselburgh EL) 1547 p11
Reidfoord, ——— (Stobo PE) 1649
Rendall, Jonet (Orkney) 1629**A**
Rennick, Christian (Hunterston AY) 1649**B**
Rennick, Jeaine (Grange FI) 1649**B**
Reoch, Elspeth (Orkney) 1616**A**
Reoch, Margaret (Aberdeen) 1613**B**
Richardson, Issobell (Pilmore EL) c.1649**B**
Richardson, Janet (Cousland ML) 1630**B**
Richart, John (AY) 1583
Richartsoun, Thomas (Maxton RX) 1629**B**
Richesone, Marion (Penston EL) 1649**B**
Richie, Issobell (Aberdeen) 1597**A**
Richie, Marjorie (Inverarity AN) 1662**B**
Rid, Euphame (Caithness) 1626**B**
Rid, Helene, wife of Alexander (AB) 1626**B**
Rid, Margaret (Bathgate WL) 1617**B**
Rid, Margaret (Crimond AB) 1630**B**
Rid, Margaret (Gilmerton, Edinburgh) 1661
Rid, Patrick (Bathgate WL) 1617**B**
Riddell, Bessie (Prestonpans EL) 1628**B**
Ridpeth, Margaret (Prestonpans EL)

1628**B**
Rind, John (Elgin) 1661
Ritchardsone, Issobell (Haddington EL)
    1661
Ritchie, Margaret (Aberdeen) 1630**B**
Ritchie, Margaret (Peterhead AB) 1630**B**
Ritchie, Marion (Newton of Ayr AY)
    1630**B**
Ritchie, Marjorie (Forfar AN) 1661- 2**A**
Ritchie, Marjorie (Shetland) 1616
Rob, Jean (Perth) 1643**A**
Rob, Thomas (Perth) 1643**A**
Robbie, Beatrix (Aberdeen) 1597**C**
Robbie, Jonnet (Newmiln AB) 1626**B**
Robe, Jonet (PR) 1662**B**
Robert, Agnes (Linlithgow) 1657
Robertson, —, a witch (Perth) 1612**B**
Robertson, Adam (Eyemouth BE)
    1661**E**
Robertson, Catherine (Aberdeen) 1654,
    1661**A**
Robertson, Elspeth (Tranent EL) 1659
    Appendix 3 p206
Robertson, Grillies (Crail FI) 1675
Robertson, Janet (Perth) 1597, 1598**A**
Robertson, Janet (Stenhouse ST) 1681
Robertson, Janet (Glasgow) 1700**E**
Robertson, Johne (Auldearn NA) 1662
Robertson, Margaret (Tranent EL) 1659
Robertson, Marion (Fisherrow/
    Musselburgh EL) 1679
Robertson, Martha (Tranent EL) 1659
    Appendix 3 p206
Robertsone, Janet (Aberdour FI) 1622**B**
Robertsone, Janet (Carriden WL) 1649**B**
Robertsoun, Bessie (St. Andrews) 158I
Robertsoun, Jonnet (Inverkeithing FI)
    1623**B**
Robertsoune, Marioun (Chirnside BE)
    1649**B**
Robeson, Agnes (Craigie AY) 1658
Robeson, Jonet (Samuelston EL) 1662
Robesone, Geillie (Dumfries) 1629**A**
Robesonis,—, (EL) 1662
Robesoun, Agnes (PE) 1629**B**

Robesoun, Jonnet (Inverkeithing FI)
    1623**B** p33
Robie, Issobell (Aberdeen) 1597
Robiesone, Isobell (Duddingston, Edin-
    burgh) 1661**E**
Robiesoune, Marioun (PE) 1649-50
Robinson, Donald (Prestonpans EL) 1590
Robison, Isobell (Jedburgh) 1671
Robison, Janet (Irvine RE) 1650
Robison, Jonet (Gilmerton, Edinburgh)
    1661
Robison, Margret (BE) 1662**B**
Robison, Masie (Lauder BE) 1662**B**
Robisone, Gilbert (Culter LA) 1640
Robisone, Marg (Skirling PE) 1659
Robsone, —, father of James (Peebles)
    1641
Robsoun, Janet (Dumfries) 1630**B**
Roch, Christian (Pittenweem FI) 1644**A**
Rodgie, Marion (Aberdeen) 1630**B** p39
Rogie or Rodgie, Helene (Aberdeen)
    1597**A**
Roiss, Cristiane (RO) 1577**A** p
Roiss, Katherene, Lady Foulis (RO)
    1590**E** pp12, 193
Ronaldson, Elspet (Burntisland FI)
    1649**B**
Ronaldsone, Walter (Aberdeen) 1601
Ronaldsoun, Margaret (Aberdeen)
    1627**B**
Rosie, Effie (Stroma, Pentland Firth) 1658
Ross, Christian (RO) 1577**A** p12
Ross, Elspet (Wemyss FI) 1626**D** p35
Ross, Janet (Ayr) 1658
Ross, Jean (Aberdeen) 1671
Ross, Jean (Glasgow) 1700**E**
Rosse, Jean (Anford) 1671
Roughhead,— (Merse/BE) 1594**A**
Rowa or Rwna, Anie Tailzeour (Orkney)
    1624**A**
Rowand, Marjorie (Culross FI) 1624**B**
Rowane, Catherine (Culross FI) 1643
Roy, Agnes (Tain RO) 1590 p12
Roy, Bessie (Fetternear AB) 1590**E**
Roy, David (PR) 1601**D** pp23, 173

Roy, More (IN) 1669
Rule, Elspeth (Dumfries) 1709**C** p164
Russel, Margaret (Peaston EL) 1678**D**
Russell, James (Dreva) 1679**E**
Russell, John (Nisbet BE) 1662
Russell, Katharine (Anford) 1671
Russell, Margaret (Penston EL) 1649**B**
Russell, Marion (Glenluce WI) 1644**B**
Rutherd, Jean (Jedburgh) 1671
Rutherford, Isabel (Crook of Devon KN)
   1662**A**
Rutherfurd, Marion (Kirkcaldy FI)
   1621**B**
Rutherfurde, Isobel (Peebles) 1629**B**
Rychesoun, Anny (Prestonpans EL) 1590
Rynd, Mary (Forfar AN) 1663**D**

Saers, Janett (Ayr) 1658**A** p115
Saidler, Christian (Edinburgh) 1597**A**
Salber, Jonat (Ayr) 1658**A**
Sampsoun,——, daughters of Agnes
   (Prestonpans EL) 1590
Sampsoune, Agnes (Nether Keith, Pre-
   stonpans EL) 1590-91**A** pp15-17,
   139, 171, 191
Samuel, Agnes (Warboys, Cambridge-
   shire) 1591**A** p103
Samuel, Alice (Warboys, Cambridgeshire)
   1591**A** p103
Samuel, John (Warboys, Cambridgeshire)
   1591**A** p103
Samuelston, Witches pp124, 187
Sandersoun, Marion (Coldingham BE)
   1629**B**
Sandeson, Beigis (Samuelston EL) 1662
Sandie,——, wife of George (EL) 1662
Sandieson, Margaret (Sanday, Orkney)
   1635 p47
Sands, Kaitherin (Culross FI) 1675**A**
Sauer, Jonnet (Ayr) 1656
Saythe, Maige (Aberdeen) 1597
Schailer, Marion (LA) 1629**B**
Schankis, David (EL) 1662
Scharpe, Helen (EL) c.1649
Scherswood, George (Samuelston EL)

1662
Schaw, Katherein (Carnwath LA) 1644**A**
Schaw, Marioune (Prestonpans EL) 1590
Scheirar or Sherer, Marioun (ML)
   1628**B**
Scherar, Janet (Preston EL) 1629**B**
Schitlingtoun, Janet (Newbattle ML) 1628
   p36
Schort, Jonet (Holyrood, Edinburgh) 1617
Sckogie, Elspet (Cupar FI) 1654**E**
Sclaitter, Geillis (Orkney) 1616
Scobie, Agnes (Moray) 1649**B**
Scoby, Kathrin (Methven PR) 1662**B**
Scongall or Scougal, Elspet
   (Whittingehame EL) 1649**B**
Scot, Barbara (Samuelston EL) 1661
Scot, Helene (RX) 1620**B**
Scot, Janet (Dysart FI) 1630**B**
Scot, Janet (LA) 1629**B**
Scot, Margaret (Selkirk) 1607
Scot, Robert (Samuelston EL) 1662
Scot, Rot (Samuelston EL) 1661
Scotland, Elizabeth (Bo'Ness WL) 1680**E**
Scots, Bessie (Corstorphine, Edinburgh)
   1649**B**
Scots, William (Corstorphine, Edinburgh)
   1649**B**
Scott, Alexander (Corstorphine, Edin-
   burgh) 1649
Scott, Bessie (Corstorphine, Edinburgh)
   1649
Scott, Janet (Ayr) 1622**B**
Scott, Janet (Dumfries) 1658**C**
Scott, Janet (Gourock) 1662 p125
Scott, Jean (Inverkip RE) 1649
Scott, John (Leith, Edinburgh) 1671
Scott, John (Leith, Edinburgh) 1679
Scott, Johne (Dalkeith ML) 1661
Scott, Jonett (Innerleithen PE) 1661**B**
Scott, Kathrin (Inverkip RE) 1662**B** p125
Scott, Marjory (Largs AY) 1662
Scottie, Agnes (Orkney) 1616
Scottie, William (Orkney) 1643 p52
Scrogges, Jonet (Rhynd PR) 1662**D**
Scroggie, Elspeth (Cupar FI) 1656

Scrogie, Elspeth (Perth)   1655**E**
Seatoun, Elspeth (Abdie FI)   1662**B**
Seith or Seath, Elspet (Balmerino FI)
   1649**E** p60
Selkirk, Elizabeth (Cousland ML)   1630
Semill, George (Paisley)   1630**B**
Sempill, Margaret (LA)   1629**B**
Semple, George (Killalan RE)   1613
Semple, George (Paisley)   1630**C**
Sesbie, Issobell (Perth)   1655**E**
Seweis, ----, a woman called (St.
   Andrews)   1645
Shand, Isobel (Peaston EL)   1678**A**
Shand, John (Moray)   1643
Shanks, James (Brechin AN)   1650**C**
Shanks, Thomas (PE)   1649-50
Sharp, Agnes (Crook of Devon KN)
   1662**B**
Shaw, Kathren (Carnwath LA)   c. 1644**A**
Shaw, Ketherine (Kirkcaldy FI)   [No
   Date]
Shayme, Erick (RO)   1699**B**
Sheipheard, Alexander (Auldearn NA)
   1662
Shenan, Marion (WI)   1644**B**
Sherare, Margrat (Kincardine AB)   1597
Shevies, Robert (Aberdeen)   1669**B**
Shyrie, Isobell (Forfar)   1661-62
Siatoun, Issobel (Jedburgh)   1649**B**
Sibbald, John (Ladievrde)   1649**B**
Simbeard, Helen (Tranent EL)   1659
   Appendix 3 p207
Sime, Florence (Dalkeith ML)   1650
Simpson, Robert (Lasswade ML)   1630
Simpson, William (Broughton, Edinburgh)
   1691**C**
Simpsone, Elizabeth (Dysart FI)   1649**B**
Simpsone, Joan (Kirkcaldy FI)   1649**B**
Simson, Ane (Prestonpans? EL)   1591
Simson, Bessie (Flisk FI)   1662**B**
Simson, Christian (Penicuik ML)   1662**B**
Simson, Issobell (Dyke, Forres)   1662,
   1663**A**
Simson, Margret (Cromarty)   1662**B**
Simsoun, Elspeth (Tain)   1628**B**

Simsoun, Helen (Craigneuk, Wishaw LA)
   1629**B**
Sinclair, Elizabeth (Samuelston EL)   1661
Sinclair, George (Caithness)   1629**B**
Sinclair, Isobel (Eyemouth BE)   1634**E**
   p46
Sinclair, Issobell (Orkney)   1633**A**
Sinclair, John (Hoy, Orkney)   1633
Sinclair, Margaret (Kirkcudbright)   1644
Sinclare,---- (EL)   1629**B**
Sinclare, Janet (Dumfries)   1630, 1631**B**
Sinklar, Grisall (Auldearn NA)   1662
Skair, Catherine (Brechin AN)   1650**A**
Skaitsone, Susanna (Clerkington EL)
   1629**B**
Skebister, Bessie (Orkney)   16J3**A**
Skein, Maly (Aberdeen)   1597
Sleigh, Bessie (Duns BE)   1629**B**
Slobane, Jonet (Ayr)   1658
Slowane, Janet (Ayr)   1658**D**
Slowland, Jonnet (Ayr)   1656
Smaill, Margaret   1678
Smaillie, Jonnet (Ayr)   1630**B**
Small, Cristian (Largs AY)   1662**B**
Small, Helen (Monimail FI)   1648**E**
Small, Janet (Carriden WL)   1649**B**
Small or Smail, Margaret (Penicuik ML)
   1629**A**
Small, Margaret (Aberdeen)   1630**B**
Smart, Tibby   1586
Smellie, Jonet (Ayr)   1650**D** p108-109
Smetoune, Joannet (Inverkeithing FI)   1649
Smiberd, Jonet (ML)   1628**B**
Smith, Christian (Lauder BE)   1649**B**
Smith, Elspet (Hoy, Orkney)   1672**D**
Smith, Isabell (Banchory AB)   1607
Smith, Issobell (Forfar)   1661. 1661-22
Smith or Smythe, Issobell (Belton, Dunbar
   EL)   1661
Smith, Janet (Auldearn NA)   1662
Smith, John (Duns BE)   1631**E** pp193-194
Smith, Johnne (North Berwick EL)
   1630**D**
Smith, Katherine (Inverkeithing FI)   1649
   p58

241

Smith, Katharin (Mortonhall, Edinburgh) 1679
Smith, Narriles (EL) 1662
Smith, Patrick (Eyemouth BE) 1634**B**
Smithe, Elspet (Aberdeen) 1597
Smithe, Jannet (Aberdeen) 1597
Smybeard, Christian (Queensferry WL) 1649**B**
Smyth, Agnes (Skateraw, Dunbar EL) 1612-13**B**
Smyth, Anna (Torryburn FI) 1624**B**
Smyth, Cristiane 1577
Smyth, Issobell (Aberdeen) 1627**B**
Smyth, Janet (Burntisland FI) 1597
Smyth, Katharine (Inverkeithing FI) 1649
Smyth, Kathrene (Inverkeithing FI) 1652
Smythe, Bessie (Lesmahagow LA) 1623
Smythe, Issobell (Pilmore EL) 1661
Smythe, Jonnet (Kinghorn FI) 1643
Smythe, ___, wife of (Prestonpans EL) 1590
Smytht, Mariorye (St. Andrews) 1575**D**
Snyp, Agnes (Glasgow) 1700**E**
Sommerveil, Mary (Edinburgh) 1671**E**
Sommervell, Margaret (Moray) 1649**B**
Somerville, Agnes (Fala ML) 1678**A**
Sonnes, Margaret, 1678**A**
Sonns, Margaret (Fala ML) 1678**A**
Soutar, Elizabeth (Oathlaw AN) 1662**B**
Sowtar, Keathren, known as the Witch of Bandon (Auldearn NA) 1662**A** pp128, 131
Spaldarg, Jonet (Aberdeen) 1597**A**
Sparke, Agnes (Forfar AN) 1661-62
Spears, Helen (Gilmerton, Edinburgh) 1661
Speid, Jonet (Dalkeith ML) 1649**B**
Spens, Agnes (Samuelston EL) 1662
Spens, Issobell (Aberdeen) 1669**B**
Spreull, Margaret (Glasgow) 1629**B**
Sprott, Marione (Dumfries) 1650
Staig, Jonet (Collessie FI) 1662**B**
Staig, Margaret (Penston EL) 1649
Stanhous, Hellene (Inverkeithing FI) 1649
Stark, Thomas (Drongan WI) 1622**B**
Steidman, Christian (Kinross) 1662**B**

Steik, Jonet (Ayr) 1658
Steil, Janet (Ayr) 1658
Steill, Christian (Cousland ML) 1630**B**
Steill, Christiane (Borthwick ML) 1649**B**
Steills, Issobell (Haddington EL) 1661
Steills, John (Peaston EL) 1649**B**
Steill, Nicall (Haddington EL) 1661
Stein, Marion (South Queensferry WL) 1643-1644**A**
Steivinstene, Margaret (Ormiston EL) 1661
Steven, Elizabeth (Prestonpans EL or Niddrie, Edinburgh) c.1629**A** p38
Stevenson, Bessie (Stirling) 1659
Stevenson, Bessie (Dumfries) 1659**A** p117
Stevinsoun, William (Hirsell BE) 1629**B**
Stevinstoun, Marioun (EL) 1662
Stewart, ——, daughter of Black Heug (Rothesay) 1662 p126
Stewart, Agnes (Bo'Ness WL) 1680**E**
Stewart, Annabell (Pollockshaws) 1677**C** p137
Stewart, Cristian (Nokwalter) 1596**A**
Stewart, David (Tyninghame EL) 1650**A**
Stewart, Francis, 5th Earl of Bothwell 1590-94**D** pp16-20, 184, 193 Appendix 2 p203
Stewart, Helen (Cadder LA) 1643-44**A**
Stewart,. Helen (Shetland) c.1675**A**
Stewart,——, mother of above c.1675**A**
Stewart, James (Perth) 1620
Stewart, James (Stobo PE) 1679**E**
Stewart, John (Orkney) 1596**E**
Stewart, John (Irvine RE) 1618**D** pp30-32
Stewart, John (Pollockshaws) 1677**E** p137
Stewart, Jonet (Edinburgh) 1597**A**
Stewart, Kathrene (Jedburgh) 1628**B**
Stewart, Kathrine (Rothesay) 1662**B**
Stewart, Margaret (Dunkeld PR) 1598**E**
Stewart, Marie (Rothesay) 1662**B** p126
Stewart, Mary (Kilbride RE) 1705**C**
Stewart, William (St. Andrews) 1569**A** p194
Stewart, William (Stobo PE) 1679**E**

Stewinsone, Bessie (Hamilton LA) 1616**B**
Stillie, Issobell (EL) c.1649
Stillie, Nicoll (EL) c.1649
Stirk, Marioun (Culross FI) 1624**B**
Stirt, Euphan (Torryburn FI) c.1704**A**
  p159
Stoddart, Jonet (Inveresk EL) 1661
Stoddart, Thomas (PE) 1629**B**
Stout, Jonet (Forfar AN) 1661-1662
Stowane, Mawsie (Dumfries) 1628**B**
Strachan, Margaret (Tranent EL) 1649**B**
Straittoun, Jonett (Prestonpans EL) 1590
Stramby, Junet 1591
Strath, Margaret (Aberdeen) 1629
Strathauchyn, Elspett (Aberdeen) 1597
Stratoune, Jonet (incorrectly called Hep-
  burn in Mackenzie, *Laws and
  Customs* etc) 1596**A**
Strauchane, Janet (Prestonpans EL)
  1628**B**
Strauthaquhin, Isobell (Aberdeen) 1596**A**
Strauthaquhin,——, daughter of above
  1596**A**
Studgeoun, Margaret (Lanark) 1629**B**
Sumner, Helen (Aberdeen) 1671
Sunderlang, Margaret (Ayr) 1658
Sutherland, Marshall (CA) 1659
Swinton, Giles (Cousland ML) 1630**B**
Sydserf, Jean (Stenton EL) 1659**A**
Sym, Janet (Brechin AN) 1659
Symen, Helen (Aberdeen) 1671
Sympson, Janet (Ormiston EL) 1649**B**
Symson, Jonnett (Craigie AY) 1658
Symson, Janet (Samuelston EL) 1662
Symsone, Marion (Craigie AY) 1658
Symsoun, Marion (Kinneil AN)) 1624**B**
Syrie, Issobell (Forfar AN) 1661**E**

Tailyeor, Margaret (EL) 1662
Tailyeour, Alesoun (Pencaitland EL)
  1628**B**
Tailyeour, Andro (Brechin AN) 1620**B**
Tailyeour, Christian (ML) 1628**B**
Tailyeour, Marioun (Moray) 1611**B** p29
Tailyour, Marion (Brynhainye) [No Date]

Tailzear, Helene (Eyemouth BE) 1649**B**
  p62
Tailzefair, Marion (Nenthorn BE) 1629**B**
Tailzeor, Agnes (Bo'Ness WL) 1649**B**
Tailzeor, Elspet (Samuelston EL) 1661
Tailzeor, Margrat (Alloa CL) 1658**A** p116
Tailzeor, Marion (Orkney) 1615
Tailzour, John (Forfar AN) 1661-1662
Taiss, Beak (Aberdeen) 1597
Tait, Helen (Dumfries) 1659**C** p117
Tait, Jonnet (Craigie AY) 1658
Tamsone, Margaret (Elgin) 1664**C**
Tarbat, Elspeth (Glasgow) 1700**E**
Task, John (Eastbarns EL) 1662
Tasker, Margaret (Dalkeith ML) 1650
Taylor, Janet, known as the Witch of
  Monza (Stirling) 1643**C**
Taylor, John (Auldearn NA) 1662 p130
Taylor, Katharine (Stromness, Orkney)
  1708 p164
Taylor, Mariore (Auldearn NA) 1662
Temple, Marjorie (Pencaitland EL)
  1649**B**
Thom, Bessie (Aberdeen) 1596**A**
Thom, Heline (Ayr) 1658
Thomas, ----, daughter of Barbara
  (Shetland) 1616
Thomassone, Donald (Caithness) 1629**B**
Thomesone, Christian (Linton RX) 1649**B**
Thomesone, Christian (Lyne AY) 1649**B**
Thomesone, Isobel (Craigsford BE)
  1628**B**
Thomesone, Helen (Glasgow) 1649**B**
Thomesone, Janet 1649**B**
Thomesone, Jean (Dumfries) 1629,
  1630**B**
Thomesone, Jonet (Orkney) 1643 p52
Thomesoun, Agnes (PE) 1629**B**
Thomesoun, Christian (Penicuik ML)
  1629**A**
Thomesoun, Isobel (Ryslaw BE) 1629**B**
Thomesoun, Janet (Ayr) 1629**B**
Thomesoun, Nicoll (Dumfries) 1630**E**
Thomesoun, William (PE) 1629**B**
Thompson, Annabell (Bo'ness WL)

1679**A** p137

Thompson, Bessie (Pencaitland EL) 1662

Thompson, Jonet (Tranent EL) 1659
Appendix 3 p206

Thompson, Thomas (Preston/Tranent EL)
1659

Thomsen, Issobell (Samuelston EL) 1662

Thomson or Antonie, Catherine (South
Queensferry WL) 1643-44

Thomson, Agnes (Crichton ML) 1649

Thomson, Agnes (Tranent EL) 1659
Appendix 3 p207

Thomson, Agnes (Peaston EL) 1678**D**

Thomson, Bessie (Roxburgh) 1662**B**

Thomson, Christine (Liberton, Edinburgh)
1661

Thomson, Elspeth (Banff) 1671

Thomson, Elspeth (Fortree BA) 1671

Thomson, Grissel (Cupar FI) 1646**A**

Thomson, Helen (South Queensferry WL)
1643-44**A**

Thomson, Isabel (Stow ML) 1649**A** p61

Thomson, Jean (Dumfries) 1659**A** p117

Thomson, Jonot (Edinstoun or Edmon-
stoun ML) 1649**B**

Thomson, Margaret (North Berwick EL)
1591**D** p18

Thomson, Robert (Laidlawsteel SE) 1629

Thomsone, Beatrix (Inverkeithing FI)
1623**B** p33

Thomsone, Christiane (Inverkeithing FI)
1649

Thomsone, Elspeth (Dumfries) 1671**A**
p136

Thomsone, Issobell (Samuelston EL) 1661

Thomsone, Margret (Midcalder ML)
1644**E** p53

Thomsone, Thomas (Tranent EL) 1659
Appendix 3 p207

Thomsoun, Isobel (Crailford BE) 1629**B**

Thomsoun, Issobell (ML) 1628

Thomsoun, James (AY) 1583

Thomsoun, Margrett (Prestonpans EL)
1590

Thomsoune, Bessie (Prestonpans EL) 1590

Threipland, Jeane (Bolton EL) 1649**B**

Thurso, Witches p165

Thyn, Marionn (Legerwood BE) 1649**B**

Tod, Beigis (Longniddry EL) 1608**A**

Tod, Cristiane (Longniddry EL) 1594**A**

Tod, Elspeth (Rhynd PR) 1662**D**

Tod, Patrick (Ecclesgreig, St Cyrus KN)
1630**B**

Todrig, Bessie (EL) 1661**B**

Todry, Jonet (Haddington EL) 1662

Toir, Malcome (Stirling) 1610**C**

Tomson, Jean (Dumfries) 1659**A**

Tonderghee, Lady (Minnigaff KR)
1702**C**

Tor, Jonnett (Langside FI) 1624**B**

Torrie, Agnes (Auldearn NA) 1662

Toshe, Kathrene (Jedburgh) 1628

Toyes, Jonet (PR) 1662**A**

Trail, Janet (Perth) 1623**A**

Trail, Telis (Aberdeen) 1603

Tranent, Witches p117

Traye, Issobell (Inverkeithing FI) 1631

Trottar, Helen (Samuelston EL) 1662

Tucidie, Janet (Corstorphine, Edinburgh)
1662

Tullie, David (Jedburgh) 1649**B**

Tulloch, or Yulloch, Agnes (Orkney) 1616

Tulloch, Barbara (Shetland) c.1700**A**
p158

Tulloch, Jonet (Renfrew) 1657

Turnbull, Andro (Hillhouse WL) 1617**B**

Turnbull, Bessie (Ormiston EL) 1661**B**

Turnbull, Malie (RX) 1662**B**

Turnbull, Margaret (Lilliesleaf RX) 1650

Turnbull, Marionn (Jedburgh) 1649**B**

Turnour, Malie (Stobhill ML) 1628**B**

Turnour, Margaret (AB) 1626**B**

Twedie, Marion, 1649**B**

Twedy, Marioun (PE) 1649-50

Tweedie, Marioun (Penicuik ML) 1662**E**

Udny, Margaret (Aberdeen) 1627**B**

Umphra or Humphrey, Jonnet (Culross FI)
1624**B**

Umphra or Humphrey, Mayse (Culross FI)

1624**B**

Unchach, Gretchach (Wick) 1655
Unes or Middeltoun, Janet (ML) 1628
Unes, Margaret (Dalkeith ML) 1628**B**
    p36
Ur, Bessie (PE) 1629**B**
Urich, Agnes (Kilernan RO) 1697**B**

Vaith, Margrat (Haddington EL) 1649
Vallandge, Cristian (Rhynd PR) 1662**D**
Vane, Agnes Nic Ean (Nairn) 1662**B**
Vassie, Agnes (Midcalder ML) 1644**A**
Vatsoune, Couper (Aberdeen) 1597**A**
Vaus, Sunna (Scalloway, Shetland) 1673
Vayne, Margret Neill (IN) 1669**B**
VcClerich, Neane (KN) 1643
Veitch, Barbara (Crichton ML) 1678
Veitch, Bessie (Milne of Stobo PE)
    1649**B**
Veitch, Catharine (Keith Marischal EL)
    1649**B**
Veitch, Marion (Peaston EL) 1678**A**
Veitche, Margaret (Cousland ML) 1630
Veitch, Marion (Nether Williamston ML)
    1649**B**
Vertie, Katherene (Corhouse EL) 1612-
    1613**B**
Vicker, or Vicar, Bessie (Bo'ness WL)
    1679**A** p137
Voe, Suna (Scalloway, Shetland) 1673**B**

Waderstoun, Cristine (EL) 1661
Wadie, Nicoll (Haddington EL) 1662
Waldon, Margaret (Liberton, Edinburgh)
    1661**A**
Walenge or Wallenge, Katharine
    (Kinghorn FI) 1643
Walker,—, the Witch (Inverkeithing FI)
    1631
Walker, Catharin (Brechin AN) 1650
Walker, Grissell (Peaston EL) 1678**D**
Walker, Janet (Kirriemuir AN) 1662**A**
Walker, Jeane (Carriden WL) 1649**B**
Walker, Johne (Ayr) 1658
Walker, Margret (Pentland ML) 1661**B**

p175

Wallace,—— (Ayr) 1658
Wallace, Agnes (Ayton BE) 1629**B**
Wallace, Agnes (Crail FI) 1643
Wallace, Agnes (Ayr) 1658
Wallace, Beigs (Preston EL) 1629**B**
Wallace, Janet (Ochiltree AY) 1630**B**
Wallace, Janet (Dalswinton DU) 1649**B**
Wallace, Katherene (Prestonpans EL) 1590
Wallace, Margaret (Ayr) 1629**B**
Wallace, Margaret (Glasgow) 1622**A**
    pp32-33
Wallace, Margaret (Langton BE) 1629**B**
Wallas, Helen (Orkney) 1616
Wallas,—— (Ayr) 1658
Wallenge, Katherine (Kinghorn FI) 1644
Wanderson, ——, wife of Archibald
    (Pittenweem FI) 1644**A** p
Wanderson, ——, wife of Thomas
    (Pittenweem FI) 1644**A**
Warboys, Witches 1591**A** p103
Wardrop, Janet (Inverkip RE) 1629**B**
Warrock, Alexander (Bolton EL) 1644**B**
Wasoun, Alexander (AY) 1583
Wasoune, Agnes (Craigie AY) 1658
Wast, Jonet (EL) c.1649**B**
Wast, Jonet (Samuelston EL) 1661
Wastel, Jeane (Carriden WL) 1649
Wat, Charles (Prestonpans EL) 1591
Waterson, Agnes (Burntisland FI) 1649**B**
Waterstoun, Agnes (Burntisland FI)
    1649**B**
Watherstoun, Cristine (Samuelston EL)
    1661
Watson, Bessie (Cromarty) 1662
Watson, Cruddal (Perth) 1589
Watson, George (Spott EL) 1661**B**
Watson, Janet (Tranent EL) 1659
    Appendix 3 p206
Watson, Jonet (Haddington EL) 1662
Watson, Margaret (Pentland ML) 1661
    p175
Watson, Margaret (Gilmerton, Edinburgh)
    1661
Watson, Marion (Peebles) 1649**B**

Watson, Marion (Peebles) 1650**E**
Watson, Marion (LA) 1650
Watson, Patrik (Dirleton EL) 1649
Watsone, Beatrix (Corstorphine, Edinburgh) 1649**D**
Watsone, Elspet (Elgin) 1631-32**C**
Watsone, Jonet (Dalkeith ML) 1661**B**
Watsone, Margaret (Stroma, Pentland Firth) 1659
Watsone, Marion (Carriden WL) 1649**B**
Watsone, Mariown (Peebles) 1650**D**
Watsoun, Elspet (Dysart FI) 1630**B**
Watsoun, Jean (PE) 1629
Watsoun, Margaret (Carnwath LA) 1644**A**
Watt, Agnes (Futtie, Aberdeen) 1627**B**
Watt, Archibald, known as Sole the Paitlet (Douglas LA) 1650
Watt, Jonnet (Culross FI) 1624**B**
Watt, Jonet (Ballgillo FI?) 1709
Watt, Libra (Grangepans FI) 1649**B**
Watt, William (ML) 1628**B**
Wauch, Agnes (Lauder) 1662**B**
Weill, Janet (Dumbarton) 1628
Weir, Agnes (DU) 1630, 1631**B**
Weir, Bessie (Pollockshaws RE) 1677**A** p137
Weir, Jane, Jean or Grissel, sister of Thomas (Edinburgh) 1670**A** pp134-136
Weir, Janet (LA) 1629**B**
Weir, John (Penston EL) 1649**B**
Weir, Major Thomas (Edinburgh) 1670**A** pp134-136
Welsh, James (Samuelston EL) 1661
Wenham, Jane (Hertford) 1712**E*** pp154, 166
Wentoun, Helen (Newburgh FI) 1662**B**
White, Mrs. (Pittenweem FI) 1704?
Whyt - see under Quheitt
Whyte, Janet (Torryburn FI) 1704
Whyte, Jonet (Largs) 1662**B**
Whyte, Margaret (Peterhead AB) 1630**B**
Whyte, Margaret (Overhartsame) 1649**E**
Whyte, Margaret (Lasswade ML) 1678**B**

Whyte, Margaret (Bo'Ness WL) 1680**B**
Whythill, Jean (Glasgow) 1700**E**
Widdrow, Helen (Barphillan) 1632**D**
Widdrow or Wodrow, Janet (Inchinan RE) 1696
Wight, Helen (BE) 1662
Wight, Isobel (Melrose RX)) 1629**B**
Wightman, Katharine (Alloa CL) 1658
Wightman, Margaret (Haddington EL) 1679**D**
Wightman, Nicoles (Crichton ML) 1649**B**
Wilkie, Janet (Wester Wemyss FI) 1630**B**
Wilkieson, Christian (Greenlaw, Jedburgh) 1708
Wilkin, Margaret (Annan DU) 1683
Will,——, wife of Mathow (Peterhead AB) 1630**B**
William, Ann Nin 1680
Williamson, Agnes (EL) c. 1649
Williamson, Agnes (Samuelston EL) 1661, 1662**E** p124
Williamson, Elspeth (Torryburn FI) 1704
Williamson or Williamesoune, Jennet (Eyemouth BE) 1629**E**, 1634**B**
Williamson, Katharine 1662
Wilson, Agnes 1628-29**A**
Wilson, Agnes (Eyemouth BE) 1634**A**
Wilson, Alison 1628-29**A**
Wilson, Alison (Eyemouth BE) 1634**A**
Wilson, Bessie (Inverkeithing FI) 1649
Wilson, Bessie (Dunfermline FI) 1649
Wilson, Bessie, known as Throw-The-Cornyard (Auldearn NA) 1662 p128
Wilson, Catherine (Grangepans FI?) 1649**B**
Wilson, Christian (Kirkcaldy FI) 1638
Wilson,——, daughters of above 1638
Wilson, Christian, known as Lantern (Dalkeith ML) 1661**A** p123
Wilson, Christian (EL) 1662
Wilson, Elizabeth (Pencaitland EL) 1649**B**
Wilson, Elspeth (Eyemouth BE) 1634**B**
Wilson, Helen (Tranent EL) 1659

Appendix 3 p207

Wilson, Helen (Pentland ML) 1661
Wilson, Helen (Ayr) 1683**E**
Wilson, Hendry (Duns) 1669**B**
Wilson, Isobel (Carriden WL) c. 1649**B**
Wilson, Janet 1630
Wilson, John (EL) 1652
Wilson, Katharine (Duns) 1631**E**
    pp193-194
Wilson, Margaret, known as Pickle-
    Nearest-The-Wind (Auldearn NA)
    1662 p128
Wilson, Marjory (Newbattle ML) 1661**A**
    p123
Wilson, Mary (Torryburn FI) 1704
Wilson, Robert (Crook of Devon KN)
    1662**A**
Wilson, Thomas (Galashiels BE) 1649**B**
Wilson, Thomas (Moffat DU) 1661
Wilsone, Bessie, 1660
Wilsone, Bessie (Gilmerton, Edinburgh)
    1661**A** p123
Wilsone, Christiane (Newbattle ML)
    1661**A**
Wilsone, Jonnet (EL) 1661
Wilsone, Jonnet (Samuelston EL) 1661
Wilsone, Margaret (Peebles) 1649**B**
Wilsone, Margret (Auldearn NA) 1662
Wilsoun, Bessie (Jedburgh) 1649**B**
Wilsoun or Neilsoun, Elspet (Dysart FI)
    1626**B**
Wilsoun, Helene (Dysart FI) 1626**B**
Wilsoun, Janet (BE) 1630
Wilsoun, Malie (Ayr) 1618**B**
Wilsoun, Margaret (LA) 1629
Wilsoun, Michael (AY) 1583
Wilsoun, Robert (AY) 1583
Wilsoune, Christian (Eyemouth BE)
    1629**B**
Wilsoune, Jonnet (Ayr) 1658
Wilsoune, Marion (Stenton EL) 1659**A**
Wir,——, wife of Robert (Liberton, Edin-
    burgh) 1661
Wischert, Jonnet (Aberdeen) 1596**A** p20
Wishart, Margret (Collessie FI) 1662**B**

Witch, -----, (Dunross-ness Orkney) 1708
    p163
Witch,-----, (RO) 1726 p166
Witch,-----, (Tarbet RO) 1727 p167
Wmpherstoun or Umpherston, Cristine
    (EL) 1661
Wobster or Vobstcr, Agnes (Aberdeen)
    1597**A**
Wod, Barbara (Lauder BE) 1629**B**
Wod, Margarett (Crail FI) 1621**B**
Wode, Katharine (PE) 1629**B**
Wodrow, James (Torryburn FI) 1704
Wodrow, Janet (Erskine RE) [No Date]
Wodrow, Janet (Paisley) 1696**D**
Wodsyde, Bessie (Ayr) 1658
Wood, Anna (Bo'ness WL) 1704**D** p162
Wood, Elizabeth (Peaston EL) 1678
Wood, Elspeth (Glasgow) 1699**E**
Wood, Elspeth (Ballgillo FI?) 1709
Wood, Geilis (Pencaitland EL) 1649**B**
Wood, Janet (Torine, Stenton EL) 1659
Wood, Jonet (Stenton EL) 1659**E**
Wood, Marion (EL) c.1649**B**
Wood, Marion (EL) 1662
Woodrow, Jean (Glasgow) 1700**E**
Wrath, Agnes (Kilraine RO) 1699**C**
Wright, Bessie (Scone ST) 1626
Wright, Bessie (Perth) 1628**B**
Wright, Janet (Niddrie, Edinburgh)
    1628**B**
Wright, Margaret (Dumbarton) 1677**B**
Wrycht, Bessie (Prestonpans EL) 1590
Wylie, Cristian (Montrose AN) 1662**B**
Wylie, Margret (Montrose AN) 1662
Wyllie, Margaret (Edinburgh) 1661**D**
Wynd, Gilbert or Cuthbert (Gilmerton/
    Liberton, Edinburgh) 1661**B**

Yerkine, Margaret (PE) 1629**B**
Yester, Elspeth (Spott EL) 1661**B**
Yool, Marioun (Tranent EL) 1660
Young, ——, mother of James 1628**B**
Young, Beatrix (Chirnside BE) 1649**B**
Young, Beatrix (Eyemouth BE) 1649
Young, Bessie (Auldearn NA) 1662

Young, Christian (Crook of Devon KN) 1662**B**
Young, Elspeth (Abernethy PR) 1662**B**
Young, Ewphame (Cockburnspath BE) 1613**B**
Young, Grissell (Niddrie, Edinburgh) 1661
Young, Helen (Balmerino FI) 1648**D**
Young, Isobel (Eastbarns EL) 1629**A** pp36-38, 193
Young, Isobel (South Queensferry WL) 1643-44**B**
Young, John (Inverkeithing FI) 1623 p34
Young, John (Mebrstown, Auldearn NA) 1662 pp 128-129

Young, Jonet (Ayr) 1600**A**
Young, Jonet (Jedburgh) 1649B
Young, Jonet (PR) 1662**B**
Young, Jonnet (Niddrie, Edinburgh) 1661
Young, Katherine (PE) 1628, 1629**B**
Young, Margaret (Dysart FI) 1644**E**
Young, Margaret (Prestonpans EL) 1628**B**
Young, Margaret (Queensferry WL) 1644**D**?
Young, Margaret (Crook of Devon KN) 1649**B**
Young, William (AB) 1626**B**

Added to the names above are the following unidentified cases: sources are identified by author where the source has been listed in the bibliography

1563	Seven witches in Fife and Galloway	Works of Knox ed. D Laing
	Four witches	
1569	Four witches	
	A witch in East Lothian	
	Several witches in St Andrews	
	A company of witches in Dundee	
1572	A witch burnt in St Andrews	*Journal of the Transactions in Scotland,* R Bannatyne (ed, 1806)
1586	Unnamed witches	Dalyell, J G
	Unnamed persons in Aberdeen	*Spalding Club Miscellany* (Aberdeen 1841-52)
	Others along with James Findlaw	Black, G
1590	Sundry witches in Edinburgh	*Calendar of State Papers relating to Scotland (CSP)*
	Familiars of Lady Fowlis, Rosshire	Black, G
1592	Several people in Edinburgh	*CSP*
	Morven Witches in Midcalder	Gilmore, J
1595	Witches executed in Edinburgh	*CSP*
	Three witches in Caithness	*CSP*
1597	Many witches in St Andrews	*CSP*
	A witch in Stirling	*Burgh Records of Stirling*
1603	A witch in Aberdeen	Gilmore, J

1608	A witch in Aberdeen	*Burgh Sheriff Court Records,*
	" " "	*Aberdeen*
	Persons in Aberdeen	Gilmore, J
1609	Persons in Peeblesshire	
	Person in Glasgow	
	Persons in Stirlingshire	
1618	A witch in Ayr	
1619	A witch in Aberdeen	
1623	Witches in Perth	
1628	A witch in Stirling	
1629	Three witches in Peeblesshire	Buchan, J
1631	Several witches in Bute	Gilmore, J
1632	A witch in Dysart	*Presbytery Book of Kirkcaldy*
		(Kirkcaldy, 1900)
1640	A number of witches in Peeblesshire	Chambers, R
	Nine women in Leith	Ramsay
1644	Two witches in Bo'ness	Sinclair G.
	Nine witches burnt on Leith Links	
	'Impannelit' witches to be executed in	Buchan J.
	Peebles	
	Some witches in Anstruther Wester at Crail	Larner C.
1645	Certain witches in Midcalder	McCall, H B
1648	Several persons in Carriden	Gilmore, J
	Six witches in Linlithgow	
1649	A witch in Dalgety	
	Five witches executed in Burntisland	Arnot, H
	Three witches in Whittingehame	Waddell, P H
	Certain persons in Renfrewshire	Murray, J
	Unnamed witch in Broughtonshiells	*Records of the Committe of Estates*
	Forty persons in Fife of whom there are	Lyon, C S
	no details	
	Certain people in Brechin	Black, D
	Two women along with Isobel Bairdie in	Arnot, H
	Burntisland	
	Two women along with Janet Brown in	
	Burntisland	
	Several witches in Aberdour	Ross, W
	Certain persons in Tyninghame	Waddell, P H
	Twenty persons executed near Berwick	Whitelock, B
1650	Ten witches executed in Dunbar	Waddell, P H
	Some witches in Kelso	*Register of the Presbytery of Kelso*
	Four witches in Peebles	Buchan, J
	A witch in Whittingehame	Waddell, P H
	Several witches in Eckford, Berwickshire	*Berwickshire Naturalists' Club*
	Sixteen witches executed in Ayr between	Paterson, G

	March and May	
	Five witches executed in Berwick	Whitelock, B
	Five witches executed in Irvine	Paterson, J
	Certain persons in Glasgow	Wodrow, R
	A witch in Greenlaw, Berwickshire	Gilmore, J
	A witch in Lilliesleaf, Roxburghshire	
	Several persons in Dalry, Ayrshire	
	Several persons in Dalkeith	
	Thirty witches executed in Mordington, Berwickshire	Gardiner, S R
1656	Four witches in Redgorton, Perthshire	Nicoll, J
1657	Two women exceuted in Dumfries	McDowell, W
1658	Six witches in Edinburgh	Nicoll, J
1659	Five witches from Dunbar executed in Edinburgh	
1660	Several persons in Rothesay given non-capital punishment	Gilmore, J
1661	Several women in Humbie, East Lothian	Dalyell, J G
	Two women executed in Newburgh, Fife	Lamont, J
	A woman in Elgin	Gilmore, J
	Several persons in Saltpreston (Prestonpans)	East Lothian
	A woman executed in Paisley	Hume Brown, P
1662	Unnamed persons in Dyke (Dice?) Aberdeenshire	Brodie, A
	Unnamed woman in Broxburn, Dunbar, East Lothian	*Records of the High Court of Justiciary*
	More than five unnamed witches	Fraser, J
	Two women executed in Forres, Banff	
	One woman in Elgin	
1663	Several persons in Auchtertool, Fife	Ross, W
1665	A woman executed in Culross, Fife	Mackenzie, Sir G
1667	Witchcraft cases in Dunfermline	Henderson, E
1670	A witch in Bo'Ness	Salmon, T
1671	Eight witches in Dumfries	McDowall, W
1672	Two witches in Greenock	Metcalfe, W M
1675	Two witches executed in Shetland	Sinclair, G
1678	Two witches in Fala, Midlothian, one of whom executed	Fountainhall, Lord
	Five witches executed in Edinburgh	
	Nine witches executed in Loanhead, Midlothian	Dalyell, J G
1694	Seven witches executed in Coldingham, Berwickshire	Chambers, R
1695	A witch executed in Old Kirkpatrick, Dumfriesshire	*Old Statistical Account*

1696	Several persons in Kilmacolm	Metcalfe, W M
	Others along with Donald Moir, Kilernan,	Black, G
	Ross-shire	
1697	Several people in Killearn, Stirlingshire	Larner, C
	Several people in Glasgow	*Glasgow Burgh Records*
	Several warlocks in Glasgow	
1698	Several witches in Glasgow	
1699	Several warlocks in Glasgow	
1705	Many witches burnt at Spott Loan,	*Spott Kirk Session Records*
	East Lothian	
	A witch at Penninghame, Wigtonshire	Paterson, G
1706	A witch at Kilmorie, Bute	Gilmore, J
1720	Several persons in Linlithgow, West Lothian	
1723	A witch in Linton, Roxburghshire	
1726	Several persons in Ross-shire	Wodrow, R

Summary:

Cases identified by name	= 2,200?	
Cases unnamed but numbered	= 268	
Cases unnamed and unquantified	= 240	(assuming an average of five people in each entry)
Total identified	= 2,708	
Add cases between 1560-1590	= 1,500	(assuming 50 unrecorded cases a year)
Grand total	= 4,208	

The Index was compiled from the following sources:

Privy Council *Registers* (1560-1689)
A Calendar of Witchcraft in Scotland (1510-1727), G.F. Black (rep in *Articles on Witchcraft, Magic and Demonology (Witchcraft in Scotland* vol. 7)) B. Levack
A Source-Book of Scottish Witchcraft, Dr. Christina Larner
Local authority records e.g. burgh accounts.
Church session minute-books
Local histories listed in the *Bibliography*

Glossary

A'thing	=	everything
Ableeze	=	ablaze
Advisement	=	council, advice
Aff	=	off
Afore	=	before
Aftwhiles	=	often
Ain	=	own
Airts	=	arts
Ane	=	one
Assyse, assize	=	trial, panel of judges
Aught	=	anything
Auld	=	old
Auld Clootie	=	nickname for the Devil
Auld Lichts	=	secessional church of 1743, more conservative than established church
Aye	=	always or more commonly, yes
Bairn	=	child
Bairn-bed	=	childbirth bed
Baith	=	both
Bauld	=	bold
Bamboozle	=	confuse
Bidin	=	staying
Bluesleeves	=	the hen harrier, often known as the blue hawk-nicknmae for Isobel Cunningham, a witch in Paxton, Berwickshire
Boot	=	instrument of torture; a wooden boot fitted to a victim's leg with wedges driven inside it to crush the ankles
Bowel-hive	=	inflammation of the bowels, esp. among children
Breeched	=	skirts tucked up to the thighs
Breid	=	bread
Brocht	=	brought
Brent, brint, brunt	=	burnt
Brose	=	porridge, broth
Cairt	=	cart
Canny-wife	=	midwife
Cantraip	=	witch spell
Carlin	=	witch
Cashielaws	=	instrument of torture; an iron frame applied to a victim's leg and heated over a brazier
Caunle-dowp	=	candle-end
Causey-clash	=	street gossip
Caution	=	security or bail

Chance-bairn	=	illegitemate child
Clamjamfray	=	a mob
Club-taed	=	club-footed
Compear	=	appear before court to answer summons
Contemption	=	contempt, disobedience
Contrabands	=	smugglers
Contumacy	=	disobedience
Coog, coogie	=	wooden vessel or bowl
Coup	=	capsize
Craturs	=	creatures
Cried	=	called, named
Dae	=	do
Deid-chack	=	meal taken after a funeral or execution
Deid	=	died, death, dead
Deil's bird	=	the magpie
Deil's milk	=	the dandelion plant
Deein	=	dying
Delation	=	accusation (delator=accuser)
Dentelion	=	the dandelion
Dempster, or Doomster	=	Court official who pronounces sentence
Ding doon	=	to throw down, demolish
Disponed	=	disposed of
Dirten-gab	=	slut, foul mouthed
Dittay	=	indictment
Doon-sitting	=	sederunt or formal meeting of kirk session
Drave	=	annual herring-fishing which at one time was centred in Dunbar
Drink siller	=	drink money, a tip
Dug's lugs	=	the foxglove-see also witch thimmles
Dunbar-wedder	=	herring caught at the Dunbar Drave in August/September
Earnit	=	earned
Easement	=	evacuation of bowels
Eebroo	=	eyebrow
Efter	=	after
Eldritch	=	weird
Etled	=	intended
Fankle	=	entangle
Fathom	=	to measure with outstretched arms eg a fisherman describing his catch
Feared	=	afraid
Feart	=	afraid
Focht	=	fought

Forbye	=	besides
Foresay	=	deny
Forespoke	=	denied
Frae	=	from
Freend	=	friend
Fricht,-en	=	fright, frighten

Gae	=	go
Gaither	=	gather
Gang	=	go
Gauger	=	customs officer
Gaun	=	going
Gie	=	give
Glimmer-worm	=	glow-worm
Good-wife	=	midwife
Growsin, girnin	=	growling or grumbling

Hae	=	has, have
Hag-wife	=	midwife
Handsel Monday	=	first Monday of Scottish New Year (New Style), when presents were given to children in lieu of Christmas presents
Haugh	=	to clear the throat of phlegm
Hauchlin	=	shuffling walk
Hell words	=	a witch's spell
Heid	=	head
Hive gress	=	wild flower known as ladies' mantle
Hemming	=	throat clearing, sometimes as a rebuke.
Hoo	=	how
Howdie-fee	=	money paid to midwife
Howdie-wife	=	midwife
Howff	=	dwelling place
Humpy-backit	=	hunchbacked

Ill-willed	=	bad-tempered

Jine	=	join
Jougs	=	neck fetter, usually found at the door of a kirk and chained to the building
Jowkin	=	dancing

Keek	=	look furtively at
Ken	=	know
Kist	=	coffin

Lang	=	long
Lichtit	=	lit
Lock	=	handful
Mair	=	more
Maist	=	most
Maun	=	must, may
Mercat Cross	=	market cross, found in the High Street of most Scottish burghs, usually the place for trading
Micht	=	might
Mickle	=	small
Mirk	=	darkness
Mony	=	many
Morn	=	morning, the next day
Muckle	=	large
Nae	=	no
Nobbut	=	nothing but
Nocht	=	nothing
Noo	=	now
O't	=	of it
Ocht	=	ought, also means belonging to
Oppone	=	bring evidence against an accused person
Oxter-deep	=	up to the armpits, colloquial term for being inundated with something
Pairish	=	parish
Panel, pannell	=	prisoner
Puckle	=	small amount
Renunce	=	renounce
Rid	=	red
Roon	=	around
Seik, -ness	=	sick, sickness
Sic	=	such
Sicht	=	sight
Siller	=	silver, normally money
Sleekit	=	sly
Spewed	=	vomited
Spleiter	=	idle talk
Stirk	=	bullock
Syne	=	since

Tak	=	take
Telt	=	told
Thocht	=	thought
Thole	=	bear, as in tolerate
Thraipple	=	throat
Tongue o'butter	=	smooth talker, one who flatters to deceive
Towbeath	=	tolbooth, or burgh jail
Unco	=	weird, odd
Vipariously	=	malignantly
Wame	=	stomach
Wardit	=	imprisoned
Weel kent	=	well known
Wey	=	way, manner of it
Wha, whae	=	who
Whaur	=	where
Wheen	=	small amount
Wheesht	=	order to be silent
Whiles	=	a long time since
Whittrick	=	the weasel, nickname for a sly person
Wise-woman	=	sooth sayer, fortune teller
Witch bridle	=	instrument of torture; an open metal frame which fitted over the head and was padlocked. A sharpened crucifix was mounted on this frame and inserted into the mouth. The crucifix could pierce either side of the mouth, roof or tongue if the victim tried to speak.
Witch-gowan	=	the dandelion
Witch's milk	=	juice from the dandelion
Witch thimmles	=	literally witch thimbles, the foxglove
Wise woman	=	one who could cure illness by spells and charms
Worryit	=	strangled, choked
Yabble	=	speak incoherently
Yersel	=	yourself
Yestreen	=	yesterday evening
Yirb wife	=	woman who makes concoctions from herbs, usually to cure illness

Bibliography

Official Primary Sources

Calendar of State Papers Relating to Scotland (Edinburgh, 1936)
Registers of the Privy Council, ed. D Masson and P H Brown: First Series, vols. VI-XIV,
Second Series, vols. I-VIII, Third Series vols. I-XIV (Edinburgh, 1877-1970)

Other Sources

Adam, Isabel   Witch Hunt: The Great Scottish Witch Trials of 1697 (London,
                        1978)

Arnot, Hugo   A Collection of Celebrated Criminal Trials in Scotland 1536-1784
                        (Edinburgh, 1785)

Baillie, Robert   Letters and Journals of Robert Baillie, vols. i-iii ed. D Laing
                        (Bannatyne Club, Edinburgh, 1841-42)

Balfour, Sir James   Historical Works, vols. i-iv, ed. J Haig (Edinburgh, 1824-25)

Bell, Rev. John   An Ingenious and Scientific Discourse on Witchcraft (1705)

Beveridge, D   Culross and Tulliallan, vols. i-ii (Edinburgh, 1885)

Black, D   History of Brechin (Edinburgh, 1867)

Black, George F   A Calendar of Witchcraft in Scotland 1510-1727 (rep. from the
                        Bulletin of the New York Public Library, New York, 1938)

Brodie, Alexander   The Diary of Alexander Brodie of Brodie ed. D Laing (Spalding
                        Club, Aberdeen, 1863)

Buchan, J   History of Peeblesshire (Glasgow,1925-27)

Burt, Edward   Letters from the North of Scotland ed. R Jamieson (London and
                        Edinburgh, 1974)

Cameron, CW   Scottish Witches (Norwich, 1984)

Chambers, Robert	Domestic Annals of Scotland, vols. i-iii (Edinburgh and London, 1861, 1874)
	Book of Days (London and Edinburgh, 1864)
Chambers, W	History of Peeblesshire (Edinburgh, 1864)
Craig-Brown, T	History of Selkirkshire (Edinburgh, 1866)
Currie History Society	Bulletin, March 2000
Dalyell, J G	The Darker Superstitions of Scotland (Edinburgh, 1834)
Davidson, Thomas	Rowan Tree and Red Thread (Edinburgh, 1949)
Dow, F D	Cromwellian Scotland 1651-60 (Glasgow, 1974)
Dunn, J A	History of Renfrew (Paisley, 1932)
Easton, T	Ritual Marks on Historic Buildings (Weald and Downland Open Air Museum, 1999)
Fountainhall, Lord	Historical Notices (Edinburgh, 1848)
Fraser, J	Chronicle of the Frasers - see under Scottish History Society
Fraser, Sir William	Memoirs of the Maxwells of Pollock (Edinburgh, 1863)
Gilmour, J	Witchcraft and the Church in Scotland Subsequent to the Reformation (unpub. thesis in Glasgow University Library, 1948 quoted in Larner)
Henderson, I E	Annals of Dunfermline (Glasgow, 1879)
Hendrie, W F	Forth to the Sea (Glasgow, 1980)
Holmes, Ronald	Witchcraft in British History (London, 1976)
Hume Brown, P	Scotland before 1700 (Edinburgh, 1893)

James VI of Scotland Daemonologie (Edinburgh, 1597)

Kennaway, Mary   Fast Castle The Early Years (Edinburgh, 1992)

Kirk, Russell   St Andrews (London, 1954)

Laing, A   Lindores Abbey and its Burgh of Newburgh (Edinburgh, 1876)

Lamont, J   Diary (Maitland Club, Edinburgh, 1830)

Larner, Christina   A Source-Book of Scottish Witchcraft (Glasgow, 1977)

                     Enemies of God (Oxford, 1981)

Lawson, J P   The Book of Perth (Edinburgh, 1847)

Legge, F   Witchcraft in Scotland (The Scottish Review, vol. xviii, London
                     and Paisley, October 1891)

Levack, Brian   Articles on Witchcraft, Magic and Demonology (Witchcraft in
                     Scotland, vol. 7) (New York and London, 1992)

Lockhart, S   History of the Lockharts of Lee and Carnwath: Seven Centuries
                     (Carnwath, 1976)

Lockwood, D   Dunfries' Story (Dumfries, 1988)

Mackay, Charles   Memoirs of Extraordinary Popular Delusions (London, 1841)

McCall, H B   History of Mid Calder (Edinburgh, 1894)

McDowell, W   History of the Burgh of Dumfries (Edinburgh, 1867)

Mackenzie, Sir   Laws and Customs of Scotland in Criminal Matters (Edinburgh,
George   1678)

MacKintosh, H B   Elgin Past and Present (Elgin, 1914)

Maxwell, H E   History of Dumfries and Galloway (Edinburgh, 1896)

Metcalfe, W M   History of Renfrew (Paisley, 1905)

259

Murray, J   Kilmalcolm (Paisley, 1907)

Newall, V   The Witch in History (New York, 1996)

Nicoll, G   Transactions 1650-67 (Bannatyne Club, Edinburgh, 1836)

Paterson, G   History of Ayr and Wigton (Edinburgh, 1863-66)

Pitcairn, Robert   Criminal Trials in Scotland 1488-1624 (Edinburgh, 1833)

Ramsay   Elninthologie (London, 1668)

Rogers, Charles   Scotland Social and Domestic (Grampian Club, Aberdeen, 1869)

Ross, W   Aberdour and Inchcolme (Edinburgh, 1885)

Salmon, T   Borrowstouness [Bo'Ness] and District (Edinburgh, 1913)

Scot, Reginald   The Discoverie of Witchcraft (rep. from 1594, Arundel, 1964)

Scott, Sir Walter Letters on Demonology and Witchcraft (London, 1830)

Scottish History Letters and Papers Illustrating the Relations between Charles II
Society   and Scotland in 1650 ed. S R Gardiner (vol. 17, Edinburgh, 1894)

                 Scotland and the Commonwealth: Letters and Papers Relating to
the Military Government of Scotland from August 1651 to December 1653 ed. C H Firth (vol. 18, Edinburgh, 1895)

                 The General Assembly: The Records of the Commissions of the
General Assembly of the Church of Scotland 1648-49 ed. A F MItchell and L J Christie (vol. 25, Edinburgh, 1896)

                 Scotland and the Protectorate: Letters and Papers Relating to the
Military Government of Scotland from January 1654 to June 1659 ed. C H Firth (vol. 31, Edinburgh, 1899)

                 Chronicles of the Frasers: The Wardlaw Manuscript, 916-1674,
James Fraser ed. W Mackay (vol.47, Edinburgh, 1905)

Sharpe, C K   A Historical Account of the Belief in Witchcraft in Scotland

(London, 1884)

Simpson, E   Dalgety, The Story of a Parish (Dalgety, 1983)

Sinclair, G   Satan's Invisible World Discovered (Edinburgh, 1685)

Spalding, J   The History of the Troubles and Memorable Transactions in Scotland and in England, 1624-45 ed. J Skene (Bannatyne Club, Edinburgh, 1828-29)

Spottiswoode   Spottiswoode Miscellany ed. J Maidment (Spottiswoode Society, Edinburgh,   1844-45)

Spottiswoode   History of the Church of Scotland, 1655 (Spottiswoode Society, Archbishop J   Edinburgh, 1851)

Steele, R   Social England (London, 1903)

Sprenger, J   Malleus Maleficarum [The Hammer of Witches] 1489 trans. M Summers (London, 1948)

Stephen, W   History of Inverkeithing and Rosyth (Edinburgh, 1938)

Thompson, F   The Supernatural Highlands (London, 1976)

Tweedie, John &   Our District: the hisorical background of Currie and Ratho parishes (Currie District Council, 1975)
Jones Cyril

Urquhart J   Dumfries and Galloway, Our Story in Pictures (Dumfries 1972)

Waddell, P H   An Old Kirk Chronicle (Edinburgh, 1873)

Wilkie, J   Bygone Fife (Edinburgh, 1931)

Whitelock, Bulstrode Memorialls of the English Affairs (London, 1682)

Wodrow, R   Analecta Scotica: Collections illustrative of the Civil, Ecclesiastical and Literary History of Scotland vols. i and ii, ed. J Maidment (Edinburgh, 1842-43)

Wood, W   The East Neuk of Fife (Edinburgh, 1887)